MANAGING GL BALIZATION

Lessons from
China and India

Inaugural Conference of the
Lee Kuan Yew School of Public Policy

MANAGING GLOBALIZATION

Lessons from China and India

Inaugural Conference of the Lee Kuan Yew School of Public Policy

Editors

David A. Kelly
East Asian Institute, National University of Singapore, Singapore

Ramkishen S. Rajan
School of Public Policy, George Mason University, USA

Gillian H. L. Goh
*Lee Kuan Yew School of Public Policy,
National University of Singapore, Singapore*

World Scientific

NEW JERSEY · LONDON · SINGAPORE · BEIJING · SHANGHAI · HONG KONG · TAIPEI · CHENNAI

Published by

World Scientific Publishing Co. Pte. Ltd.

5 Toh Tuck Link, Singapore 596224

USA office: 27 Warren Street, Suite 401-402, Hackensack, NJ 07601

UK office: 57 Shelton Street, Covent Garden, London WC2H 9HE

Library of Congress Cataloging-in-Publication Data
Kelly, D. A. (David A.)
    Managing globalization : lessons from China and India / David
Anthony Kelly, Ramkishen S. Rajan & Gillian H. L. Goh
        p. cm.
Challenges, opportunities and responses to globalization -- Social
security and governance -- National security in the age of globalization --
Ethnicity and identity in the New World.
    Includes bibliographical references.
    ISBN 981-256-462-4 -- ISBN 981-256-494-2 (pbk)
    1. Globalization--Congresses. 2. Globalization--China--Congresses.
    3. Globalization--India--Congresses. I. Rajan, Ramkishen S.   II. Goh, Gillian H.L.
    III. Title.

JZ1318 K396 2006
303.48'2--dc22   2006048293

British Library Cataloguing-in-Publication Data
A catalogue record for this book is available from the British Library.

Typeset by Stallion Press
Email: enquiries@stallionpress.com

Printed in Singapore by World Scientific Printers (S) Pte Ltd

Keynote Speech by Minister Mentor Lee Kuan Yew at the Official Opening of the Lee Kuan Yew School of Public Policy on Monday, 4 April 2005 at Shangri-la Hotel, Singapore

"Managing Globalization: Lessons from China and India"

Introduction

Renaissance spreads in Asia

An enormous transformation is underway in Asia. Across the region, countries are reforming their methods of governance and the way they decide public policies. They want to catch up and prosper with the rest of the developed world.

The original four Asian Tigers — Hong Kong, Taiwan, South Korea and Singapore — followed Japan. They led the pack followed by Malaysia, Thailand, and Indonesia. The Japanese called this the "flying geese" pattern of economic development, with each new follower gaining technology from the leader and passing it on eventually to the next group of followers. But this formation of countries is not large enough to move the world.

China and India will shake the world. Together, they are home to 40% of the world's population. Both are among the world's fastest-growing economies: China, 8–10%; India, 6–7%. China is the factory of the world; India the outsourcing service center, first in call centers and now moving to more sophisticated business process operations and clinical research activities of global corporations.

The Chinese and Indians are learning not just from Japan and the Asian NIEs, but from the advanced countries. They are selectively adopting and adapting different models and principles of governance to propel them into the front ranks. In some industries, they have already leapfrogged the rest of Asia. The outcome will be a major rebalancing of the world.

Origins of the Lee Kuan Yew School of Public Policy

The Lee Kuan Yew School of Public Policy started in 1992 as a small Public Policy Programme in the National University of Singapore. Its aim was to study the different systems of governance in our immediate region and to offer public officials from the region a rigorous training on the best practices to implement sound public policies.

With China's and India's rise, the new School will expand its research and teaching to include these two largest countries in the world. They provide a rich field of research and may yield clues on why some are more successful in catching up with the advanced economies. Is it a matter of importing particular systems and policies? Or are there deeper factors that have not been studied?

Evolution of my views on China and India

I have taken a deep interest in both China and India ever since I started my political life in 1950. Like all democratic socialists of the 1950s, I have tried to analyze and forecast which giant would make the grade. I had hoped it would be democratic India, not communist China.

By the 1980s, I had become more realistic and accepted the differences between the two. It is simplistic to believe that democracy and free markets are the formula that must lead to progress and wealth. However, I am convinced the contrary axiom is true that central planning and state-owned or nationalized enterprises lead to inefficiency and poor returns, whether the government is authoritarian or democratic. Moreover, even if China and India were both democratic, or authoritarian or communist, their performance would be different. I now believe that, besides the standard economic yardsticks for productivity and competitiveness, there are intangible factors like culture, religion and other ethnic characteristics and national ethos that affect the outcome.

At the start after World War II, China was behind India. China's infrastructure and population were devastated by the Japanese occupation from 1937 to 1945. Then a civil war followed. After the Communist victory in 1949, China adopted the system of governance and economic policies of the Soviet Union.

At independence in August 1947, India had ample sterling balances, a good system of governance and many top-class institutions. It had functioning institutions for a democracy, the rule of law, a neutral highly trained civil service, defence force, and proficiency in the English language.

The situation deteriorated over time. India adopted central planning with results nearly as damaging as those of China. India's political leaders are determined to reform but the Indian bureaucracy has been slower and resistant to change. Regional jostling and corruption do not help. Furthermore, populist democracy makes Indian policies less consistent, with regular changes in ruling parties. For example, Hangzhou and Bangalore are comparable cities. Hangzhou's new airport opened in 2000; Bangalore's has been on the drawing board for years and only given the go ahead by the state government in December 2004.

China, the economically more backward country in 1950, caught up with India and has now surpassed India in several sectors. How did communist China catch up, and why did democratic India lose its lead?

Comparison of the Chinese and Indian public sector

Did China pull ahead because it had better systems of governance and methods of determining public policies?

Tax system. Ten years ago, China had a complicated tax system. There were provincial and municipal sales taxes, provincial border taxes, excise duties, and levies. By imposing a single Value Added Tax on manufactured goods, China has made tax collection efficient and effective.

India has made several unsuccessful attempts to introduce a national VAT, the last on 1 April 2005, when 20 states switched to VAT but eight are still holding out.

Corruption bedevils both, but bureaucratic red tape has lowered India's efficiency and effectiveness more than China's. It takes 88 days to secure all the permits needed to start a business in India, compared to 46 in China. Insolvency procedures take 11 years, as against 2.6 in China. In spite of the disasters of the Great Leap Forward in 1958 and the Cultural Revolution, 1966–1976, China pulled itself up after its open door policy from 1978.

Comparison of the Chinese and Indian private sector

On the other hand, India's private sector is superior to China's. Indian companies, although not on par with the best American or Japanese companies because of India's semi-closed market, nevertheless has several near world-class companies, like Tata Consultancy Services, Infosys, and Wipro. Indian multinationals are now acquiring western companies in their home markets. Moreover, Indian companies follow international rules of corporate governance and offer higher return-on-equity as against Chinese companies. Also India has transparent and functioning capital markets.

China has not yet created great companies, despite being the third-largest spender in the world on R&D. Also Chinese corporate fraud is on a much larger scale.

Singapore — More economic interaction with China than with India

Singapore has more exposure to China's governance and public policies than India's. For 10 years Singapore trained nearly 1000 officials from Suzhou to plan, manage and develop an integrated township called the Suzhou Industrial Park. We trained them in various disciplines with the emphasis on the planning and management of an integrated city with industry, services, commerce, private and public housing, public utilities, schools, hospitals, parks, golf courses, and recreational areas, sited all to be in 70 sq km. There were many difficult problems in the early years because of our different mindsets, although we share similar, but not identical, language and culture. However, despite the travail, after 10 years, the results are startling.

They have not only learned about the specific areas in which we instructed them, but they have observed how we have cleaned up Singapore and its waterways, greened it, planned, built and managed our public housing, and town planning.

In 1994 Suzhou was dilapidated, canals stagnant and fetid, shorn of its charm as the "Venice of China". Now they have flushed the canals and greened up their banks. Boutique restaurants, hotels, shopping malls, and all the attractiveness of a well-lived modern city that preserved their old buildings, spruced up and refurbished. They studied what we have done in Singapore. What we took 40 years to do they were able to adopt, adapt and implement in 10 years.

Over a thousand Chinese officials, selected by different centers, the Communist Party's Central Organization Department, the Central Party School and the China Association of Mayors, have been studying Singapore's system, its economic and social development, public administration, anti-corruption practices, financial management, human resource development, social security and taxation system, urban planning, management, and social development. Several of them have taken Master's degrees at NUS and NTU in Public Management, Public Policy and Business Administration, and Managerial Economics.

They have selectively incorporated and bud-grafted specific policies they find useful. In several Chinese cities where Singapore's Housing and Development Board has done public housing projects, they have been able to replicate these townships with improved designs for the flats to suit their different climatic conditions. The speed at which they have learned has no parallel anywhere else.

In India, Singapore's EDB and a JTC-led consortium invested in the International Technology Park of Bangalore (ITBP). It is a self-contained oasis, with independent power supply. The Park has become an icon showcasing India's accommodation of MNCs. The Indians have duplicated such "oases" in other cities, including the Hi-tech Park in Hyderabad and Tidel Park in Chennai. But the rate of replication appears slower than in China. Could it be bureaucratic inertia? Or are Indian private enterprises and consumers slower than the Chinese in the diffusion of technology and innovation, from one player to the next and one industry to another? Why are mobile phone penetration rates in China higher than in India? This School should study this phenomenon.

China and India: Studying and Learning From Each Other

Thickening ties

The Chinese and Indians realize they have much to learn from one another. China and India are going to assiduously study each other's experiences, and try to acquire the strong points of the other. They will spur each other to excel.

What both must avoid is to be placed in opposing camps, one with the US and the other against.

What can China and India learn from each other?

The Chinese are learning English with great enthusiasm. They may catch up with India, even though they may never have that layer at the top, like the Indians do, who are steeped in the English language and its literature. But the Chinese will have enough English to network easily with businessmen and scholars in America and Europe. In technical and technological skills, China is following India's lead and has started to supply software engineers to multinational corporations like Cisco.

India has grown quite rapidly over the last decade with far lower investment rates than China. China must learn to be as efficient as India in utilizing its resources.

The Chinese are keen to develop a services sector like India's. For example, they have contracted an Indian company to train 1000 Chinese software project managers from Shenzhen in etiquette, communications, and negotiations skills. Huawei, a leading Chinese technology company, has invested in Bangalore to tap its software skills. The Chinese want to attain international standards for the software outsourcing industry and learn how to deal with US and European clients as India is doing.

India wants to be as successful as China in attracting foreign and domestic investments in manufacturing. India must emulate the effective way in which China has built up its extensive communications and transportation infrastructure, power plants and water resources and implements policies that lead to huge FDIs in manufacturing, high job creation and high growth. India's spectacular growth has been in IT services which do not generate high job creation. But it has now drawn up a massive highway construction programme that is more than half completed.

Challenges facing China and India

China and India have their specific advantages but also face similar challenging social, economic, and political problems. China has to restructure its state-owned enterprises, fix its weak banking sector and ensure its economy continues to grow fast enough to absorb the still huge army of unemployed. India has poor infrastructure, high administrative and regulatory barriers to business, and large fiscal deficits, especially at the state level, that are a drag on investment and job creation.

In 50 years, China and the rest of Northeast Asia (Japan, Korea, and Taiwan) will be at the high-end of the technology ladder, Southeast Asia mainly at the lower and middle-end of the value-added ladder where there will still be large opportunities for efficient competitors. On the other hand, India will have certain regions at the high-end of the technology ladder but it may have vast rural areas lagging behind, like the Russian hinterland during the Soviet era. To avoid this India has to build up its infrastructure of expressways across the sub-continent, faster and more railway connections, more airports, expand telecoms and open up its rural areas.

Why are the Chinese ahead

The Chinese are more homogeneous: 90% Han; one language and culture; one written script, with varying pronunciations. Having shared a common destiny over several millennia, they are more united as a people. And they can swiftly mobilize resources across the continent for their tasks.

China's Deng Xiaoping started his open door policy in 1978. In the 28 years since, China has more than tripled its per capita GDP, and the momentum of its reforms has transformed the lives of its people thus making its market reform policies irreversible.

India's one billion people are of different ethnic groups with different languages, cultures and traditions. It recognizes 18 main languages and 844 dialects and six main religions. India has to make continuous and great efforts to hold together different peoples who were brought together in the last two centuries into one polity by the British Raj that joined parts of the Mogul empire with the princely states in the Hindi-speaking north and the Tamil, Telugu and other linguistic/racial groups in the south.

India began liberalizing in 1990, and then in fits and starts. However India's system of democracy and rule of law gives it a long-term advantage over China, although in the early phases China has the advantage of faster implementation of its reforms. As China develops and becomes a largely urban society, its political system must evolve to accommodate a large, better educated middle-class that will be highly educated, better informed and connected with the outside world, one that expects higher quality of life in a clean environment, and wants to have its views heard by a government that is transparent and free from corruption.

China and India are to launch FTA negotiations that may be completed in a few years. I understand Premier Wen Jiabao will be visiting India soon, followed by President Hu Jintao shortly afterward. Their closer economic relations will have a huge impact on the world. ASEAN and Singapore can only benefit from their closer economic links. Many Indians are in influential positions in Wall Street, in US MNCs, the World Bank, IMF and research institutes and universities. This network will give India an extra edge. More Chinese are joining this American-based international network but they do not yet have the same facility in the English language and culture. And because of Sino-US rivalry, there will be greater reserve when Americans interact with them.

For a modern economy to succeed, a whole population must be educated. The Chinese have developed their human capital more effectively through a nationalized education system. In 1999, 98% of Chinese children have completed 5 years of primary education as against 53% of Indian children. India did not have universal education, and educational standards diverge much more sharply than in China. In some states like Kerala participation in primary schools is 90%. In some states it is less than 30%. Overall in 2001, India's illiteracy rate was 42%, against China's 14%.

India had many first-rate universities at independence. Except for a few top universities such as the Indian Institutes of Technology and Indian Institutes of Management that still rank with the best, it could not maintain the high standards of its many other universities. Political pressures made for quotas for admission based on caste or connections with MPs. China has repaired the damage the Cultural Revolution inflicted on their universities. Admission to Chinese universities is based on the entrance examination.

China has built much better physical infrastructure. China has 30,000 km of expressway, 10 times as much as India, and six times as many mobile and fixed-line telephones per 1000 persons. To catch up, India would have to invest massively in its roads, airports, seaports, telecommunications, and power networks. The current Indian government has recognized this in its budget. It must implement the projects expeditiously.

The Chinese bureaucracy has been methodical in adopting best practices in their system of governance and public policies. They have studied and are replicating what Japan, Korea, Taiwan, Singapore, and Hong Kong have done. China's coastal cities are catching up fast. But China's vast rural interior is lagging behind, exposing serious disparities in wealth and job opportunities. The central government is acutely aware of these dangers and have despatched some of the most energetic and successful mayors and provincial governors to these disadvantaged provinces to narrow the gap.

China's response to these looming problems is proactive and multi-faceted. For example, to meet energy needs, China National Petroleum Corporation and China National Offshore Oil Corporation (CNOOC) have moved into Indonesian oil and gas fields. Chinese companies have even gone to Venezuela, Angola, and Sudan.

India signed a recent agreement with Myanmar to import gas by pipeline via Bangladesh. The Indian government plans to consolidate their state-owned oil companies and act proactively like China's CNOOC. The ASEAN-China Free Trade Agreement is an example of China's pre-emptive moves. China moved faster than Japan by opening up its agricultural sector to ASEAN countries. India is also negotiating a Closer Economic Cooperation Agreement with ASEAN, but China has gotten there first.

Caveat

The Financial Times, 29 March 2005, wrote: "The lack of a robust capital market is likely to have a strong influence on the future shape and development of Chinese capitalism. Cheap manufacturing might be China's current competitive advantage but, in the long run, Beijing planners want the country to move more into lucrative high-technology sectors that provide better-paying jobs. China will need a dynamic private sector, run by entrepreneurs who have the drive to build innovative companies. Yet it is exactly these sorts of companies that are being squeezed out by an equity market that caters mostly to state-controlled groups. Private-sector companies can get bank financing, especially if they have good political connections. Yet the lack of an equity funding route is likely to curtail China's ability to develop a strong private sector. In this area, many argue that India is already ahead, as most of its biggest companies come from the private sector and have grown through raising capital on the equity and bond markets. China needs a robust stock market to stave off a looming pensions crisis. One of the by-products of the one-child policy introduced 25 years ago is that in a decade or so many more people will be retiring than entering the workforce." This is China's big negative, its rapidly aging population as a result of its severe one-child family policy. There is no precedent for a country to grow old before it has grown rich. India — average age, 26, compared to China's 33 and still with much faster population growth — will enjoy a bigger demographic dividend, but it would have to educate its people better, or else the opportunity will turn into a burden.

What Can the Lee Kuan Yew School of Public Policy Offer?

The School as a neutral venue

China and India will compete with one another and with the rest of the developed world. Their systems of governance and the way they arrive at and implement public policies will be major factors in their performance.

The Lee Kuan Yew School of Public Policy, based in Singapore, can offer China, India, the region and the world, a neutral venue for scholars and public officials to gather, discuss and understand why a society succeeds. In this neutral venue, scholars will be free to objectively compare and contrast the different systems that exist and assess what have made for better outcomes.

And they can also determine the extent to which non-measurable factors like culture, religion, and language affect the final outcome.

Although Singapore has had broad interaction with both China and India in the last 20 years, our ties with India go back to the time Singapore was founded by the British Raj. Singapore was governed in 1819 from Calcutta. We also have strong links with the United States, Britain, and Europe. The renaissance of China and India in economic, social and cultural fields will shift the world's center of gravity from the Atlantic to the Pacific and Indian Oceans.

Historically, these two great countries have influenced the economies, religions, and cultures of Southeast Asia. Hence the name Indo-Chinese peninsula and its mix of Indian and Chinese culture. The region also has the largest number of Muslims in the world. The Islamic world is in turbulent flux. The outcome in the region will be influenced by developments in the Middle East, China, and India. Southeast Asia is for the first time simultaneously influenced by the Christian West, Islam, China, and India.

Southeast Asian countries have inherited different systems of government from their colonial powers — Indonesia from the Dutch; Vietnam, Laos and Cambodia from the French; Malaysia, Singapore and Brunei from the British. Myanmar lost its British legacy when the Japanese army occupied the country. Thailand, never a colony, has evolved its own system. I believe the British instituted the best system benefiting Singapore, Malaysia, and Brunei. There is no reason why Indonesia, Vietnam, and the other countries cannot adopt the best practices of the successful nations. Indeed Singapore, Malaysia, and Brunei have updated the system they inherited by incorporating better practices from other countries.

For over a decade, the Public Policy Programme has brought together senior officials from all over the region to study the best practices of governance and policymaking. The diverse student mix has helped the diffusion of ideas and practices. Officials have been able to compare notes and learn from one another. The professors have provided consulting services to governments in the region on how to improve their public policies and systems of governance. The School can provide a blend of theory and practice. One of the School's professors is now acting as a WHO consultant to implement performance-based budgeting in government hospitals in the Philippines. This idea was proposed by a group of Filipinos who had studied Singapore's healthcare financing system while attending the former Public Policy Programme. When the School's focus includes China and India, there will be more such value-added outcomes. This School is the venue for scholars, officials and students from the world over, especially from China and India, to gather, research, and exchange ideas on how societies are best governed in a globalizing world. All participants will benefit from a rigorous study of policies that have succeeded and those that failed.

Beyond China, India and Southeast Asia

To increase our understanding of the systems of governance that work and can improve the lives of people, we must compare European and US patterns of governance and public policy formulation with those of China, India, and Southeast Asia.

Singapore's own experiences with governance and public policies may illuminate some of the key factors that made for its successful development by borrowing and modifying policies and ideas from Europe and America.

All said and done, it is the creativity of leadership, its willingness to learn from experience elsewhere, to implement good ideas quickly and decisively through an efficient public service, and to convince the majority of people that tough reforms are worth taking, that decides a country's development and progress. Whether China or India will prove to be the better model for other developing countries we will know by the middle of this century.

Foreword

It has been about 50 years since India and China were last talked about in the same breath. Now commentators and academics are beginning again to compare the reform programmes of the two nations. More importantly, and encouragingly in evidence at the Lee Kuan Yew's School of Public Policy's pioneering conference on "*Managing Globalization: Lessons from China and India,*" Chinese and Indians are prepared to discuss their common problems in an atmosphere of genuine learning from each other.

To send a clear signal that the new School of Public Policy was ready to tackle larger global challenges as well as extend the geographical footprint of its student community beyond Southeast Asia, the School chose the ambitious topic of discussing both globalization as well as the emerging roles of China and India. Clearly, the simultaneous emergence of both China and India, the two most populous countries, is going to change the course of human history.

The response to this ambitious conference was both positive and encouraging. Minister Mentor Lee Kuan Yew agreed to open both the School and the Conference with a major address (which has been reprinted in this volume). The Asia Society of New York and the Brookings Institution of Washington D.C. agreed to co-sponsor the Conference. Their respective Presidents, Ms Vishakha Desai and Mr Strobe Talbott, flew to Singapore to personally participate in the Conference and chair panel discussions. Another panel was chaired by Professor Mary Jo Bane, who represented the Kennedy School of Government from Harvard at the Inaugural Conference. All of them, as well as the paper presenters and commentators, contributed significantly to the success of the Conference. Both we and the School would like to thank them.

In the 1950s, Westerners had hoped that Indian democracy would prove more effective than Chinese Leninism in the struggle for development. In his keynote speech to the conference, Minister Mentor Lee Kuan Yew stated that "[l]ike all democratic socialists of the 1950s, I have tried to analyze and forecast which giant would make the grade. I had hoped it would be democratic India, not communist China."

Although he too was a democratic socialist, Nehru encouraged Indians to believe in friendship rather than competition between the two nations — *hindi–chini bhai bhai*.[a] But Indian intellectuals envied the efficiency and speed with which the Chinese Communist Party (CCP) seemed able to achieve its social and economic goals. It was of course far easier to run a command economy under the one-party rule of the CCP than to reconcile diverging interests in the preparation of Five-Year Plans in India's messy democracy. As relations between the two nations soured at the end of the 1950s, Chinese officials held up India's frequent demonstrations and freewheeling press as negative examples.

Yet the advantages were not always China's. No Indian leader could have contemplated a Great Leap Forward; there was not the disciplined organizational structure to carry it out. But, as Amartya Sen has argued, the Chinese lacked a free press that could have prevented the subsequent catastrophic famine from taking place. Nor did Nehru at the height of his power enjoy the extravagant personality cult that enabled Mao to launch a Cultural Revolution and plunge the nation into chaos and internecine warfare, even had he wished to do so. Commentators who rightly admire the speed and decisiveness with which Deng Xiaoping launched the Chinese reform program in December 1978, often fail to understand that the trauma of the Cultural Revolution forced the Chinese leadership to think the unthinkable and proceed with capitalist-type reforms. India, by contrast, only had to undergo a foreign exchange crisis to impel its leadership to launch its reform program in 1991.

Of course, political systems still make a difference. Indian national governments are coalitions which can usually proceed only at a pace acceptable to the most intransigent partner. Indian states, whether under the control of the dominant partner in the national coalition or not, often go their own way. In China, as a result of the Cultural Revolution, the CCP no longer has the authority and control it had in the 1950s, and it faces daily demonstrations and riots up and down the country: 74,000 in 2004 according to official figures. But despite having caught what some Chinese had thought of as the

---

[a]To mean "Indians and Chinese are brothers."

"Indian disease," the national leadership can still launch a policy initiative in the confidence that, by-and-large, it will be enforced. Barring accidents, or a change of system, China's economic reform programme will continue to outpace India's.

Moreover, as the Minister Mentor remarked, "even if China and India were both democratic, or authoritarian or communist, their performance would be different. I now believe that, besides the standard economic yardsticks for productivity and competitiveness, there are intangible factors like culture, religion, ethnic characteristics and national ethos that affect the outcome."

Yet, even in their differences, there are commonalities below the surface. Take the issue of identity. One of the Indian conferees, Ashutosh Varshney, described his country's identity as a "salad bowl", with its divergent religions and languages. Many commentators consider this a disadvantage, for the national government has to concern itself continually with keeping this mosaic glued together. No Chinese conferee mentioned identity as an issue, doubtless because of the overwhelming dominance of the Han people and the Chinese languages (even though Cantonese is as different from Mandarin as Spanish from French). Yet, in a very real sense, the Chinese elite does have an identity problem.

Down the ages, educated Chinese have sought state office as the path to prestige, power and wealth. To obtain it, they had to pass through a grueling series of examinations in the state ideology — Confucianism in the imperial era — with which they then self-identified and could claim the right to rule a Confucian nation. When the Confucian exam system was abandoned in the reforms of the early 20th century, that bedrock identity disappeared, and intellectuals ransacked the ideological resources of the West in an effort to find a new one. With the CCP's accession to power in 1949, a new state ideology was introduced, Marxism–Leninism, again a legitimator of its adepts' right to rule. But the extravagant claims made for Mao Thought during the Cultural Revolution led to a backlash, and probably few of the CCP's 70 million members, let alone the rest of the population, have much faith in Marxism–Leninism–Mao Zedong Thought any longer, although, apparently, Mao's name conjures up nostalgia among some for a lost era of greater equality. Of course, nationalism can be used to unite the views of party and people, but the Chinese leaders know it is a two-edged weapon which, as in the past, can be turned against them if they seem insufficiently forceful in the national interest. So there are identity issues for the Chinese too.

The key issue for the future of these two nations which, as the Minister Mentor said, "will shake the world" because of their size and rapid growth rates, is not so much comparative speed, but mutual learning, a willingness to learn from both the achievements and the errors of the other in tackling what are often common problems. Even identity, *sui generis* though it is, may be an area where India's unity in diversity could be a mirror for the Chinese. More obviously, poverty, especially in the countryside, health care, education, urbanization, population, care of the environment, issues covered in the social panel of the conference, must be compared because, as one of us said in summing up the conference, these are "ticking time bombs."

Another ticking time bomb, endemic in both countries but not mentioned by conferees, perhaps out of politeness — or our failure to ask them to address it — is massive corruption at all levels. Chinese leaders worry that corruption could bring the CCP down. Indians know that their democracy is diminished when politicians at both the national and state levels are elected despite indictments for criminal acts. If China is to remain attractive to foreign business in a big way and if India is to attract the FDI it needs, both need to tackle corruption. Singapore, with its well-deserved reputation for financial probity, may be an appropriate setting for examining the political, social and economic breeding grounds of corruption, and how best to eliminate or at least mitigate them. Maybe the LKY School of Public Policy could bring together relevant officials from the two countries to discuss these and other pressing issues in the more private setting of a workshop.

The process of mutual learning which we hope that the conference will have done its small part to promote could be derailed by external factors in this age of "geopolitical fluidity." China as the last powerful Communist bastion has an inbuilt suspicion of the democracies ganging up against her. More particularly, since the European nations show little inclination to follow US–China policy, China will be concerned if the USA attempts to use its developing friendship with India to transform that nation into a balancer against China. India has shown no sign of wishing to sign up for a new anti-communist alliance, but the surest guarantee that New Delhi would not change its mind in the future would be a final resolution of the vexing border problems between the two countries. The visit to India by the Chinese Premier

Wen Jiabao shortly after our conference produced encouraging noises about renewed efforts to thrash out the border issues. But since then, there have been few signs of movement in the negotiations.

If our conference is to be seen as a hopeful augury of future meetings to discuss mutual problems, whether in Singapore, Beijing or New Delhi, then Indian and Chinese leaders will have to go over the heads of their bureaucrats, hung up perhaps on narrow geographical issues, and risk their political capital with their colleagues and citizens in order to achieve a lasting compromise. China and India should aim to "shake the world," not each other.

Kishore Mahbubani
Lee Kuan Yew School of Public Policy
National University of Singapore

Roderick MacFarquhar
Harvard University

Contents

CHAPTER 1

Introduction to *Managing Globalization: Lessons from China and India*

David A. Kelly and Ramkishen S. Rajan

1. Introduction

With the exception of the crisis period in 1997–1999, Asia has been the world's fastest growing region for the last three decades. However, the growth dynamics within Asia has undergone significant alterations. Growth in Asia was initially centered in Japan, followed by the newly industrialized economies (NIEs) Korea, Hong Kong, Singapore, and Taiwan in the 1970s till the mid-1980s. Following the Plaza Accord in 1985, which involved a significant revaluation of the yen, there were large-scale inflows of foreign direct investment (FDI) from Japan as well as the US into some Southeast Asian countries (mainly Indonesia, Malaysia, and Thailand). Thus, from mid-1980s to mid-1990s, Southeast Asia had become the most dynamic subregion in Asia. The financial crisis of 1997–1998 stopped Southeast Asia in its tracks.[1] While Southeast Asia has been undertaking the necessary structural reforms and appears to have returned to a path of robust and sustainable growth, the focus of attention since the mid-1990s has shifted squarely to the two Asian giants of China and India. The economic rise of China and India has begun to alter the regional and global landscapes. Both countries are on steep learning curves, and if they continue on current trajectories, both will inevitably play increasingly larger roles on the world stage.

The rapid economic emergence of China as a global trading and manufacturing powerhouse and the world's leading destination for FDI is by now conventional wisdom and does not need to be detailed here. Between 1985 and 2003, China has consistently been the world's fastest growing economy with an average real annual growth of 9% (Fig. 1). By 2004, China's share

1

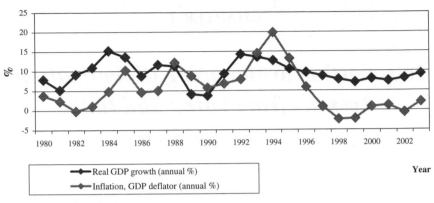

Source: CEIC and World Bank databases.

Fig. 1. China's growth and inflation (%), 1990–2003.

of global trade was about 6%. The recent lifting of the Multifiber Agreement (MFA) that governed world trade in textiles and apparels since 1974 will see China emerge as a much bigger global exporter in these areas than it already is, as will India.[a]

India's rise is of somewhat more recent vintage. While the country has been gradually liberalizing since the mid-1980s, the turning point was the balance of payments crisis in 1991. Since then, the various governments that have been in power have been consistent in their pursuit of economic reforms. While the pace of these reforms has been rather uneven, the medium-term trajectory of liberalization has been sharply positive. India's growth since 1992 has been robust, having averaged slightly over 6% annually (Fig. 2). With favorable monsoons, real output growth in the 2003–2004 fiscal year was 8.5%, the highest over the last decade. India has now firmly emerged on the radar screen of global financial markets and business leaders, and has become the destination of choice for Business Processing Operations (BPOs) and IT operations for many of the world's leading corporations. While services constitute one-half of India's GDP (compared with one-third of China's GDP), the assumption that India's growth story pertains only to trade-able services, or to IT in particular, would be incorrect. The country has

---

[a]This is notwithstanding protectionist measures by the USA and the European Union (EU) to curb Chinese textiles exports in the post MFA era.

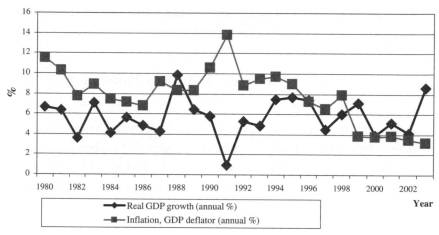

Source: CEIC and World Bank databases.

Fig. 2. India's growth and inflation (%) 1990–2004.

emerging strengths in other areas such as the pharmaceutical and biotechnology sectors, and has also been developing competitiveness and competencies in selected areas in manufacturing like automobiles, auto parts and accessories as well as machine tools. With many important sections of the manufacturing sector joining the growth bandwagon, India's aggregate growth has become far more broad-based and durable.

This volume offers a set of 15 chapters (excluding the introduction) on various dimensions of the economic emergence of China and India and how they have managed globalization. Given the multidimensional nature of globalization and reform, it focuses on four distinct issues. Section 1 (Chapters 2–4) deals with economic growth, reforms, and development strategies in the two countries. Section 2 (Chapters 5–8) focuses on the challenges arising from pension reforms and restructuring of state-owned enterprises (SOEs). Section 3 (Chapters 9–12) tackles issues relating to security and international relations facing and posed by the two Asian giants. Section 4 (Chapters 13–16) focuses on questions of identity and ethnicity among the peoples of China and India. Given the number of chapters as well as the wide-range of themes explored, we make no attempt to systematically summarize the discussions of each chapter. Rather, the remainder of this introductory chapter provides a broad overview of the issues tackled in the various sections as a whole, drawing out some of the wider perspectives while paying particular attention to the economic dimension of China's and India's emergence.

2. Economic Rise of China and India and Differences in Growth Strategies

The three chapters in Section 2 of this volume focus on various aspects of economic reforms and growth in China (Chapter 2 by Zhang Xiaoji) and India (Chapter 3 by Kaushik Basu, and Chapter 4 by Omkar Goswami).

Both China and India have rightly captured regional and global attention, not only because they constitute one-third of the world's population and are already among the world's top four in purchasing power parity (PPP) terms, but also because of their long-term growth potential.[b] In Chapter 2, Zhang Xiaoji notes that China's economy will maintain an annual growth rate of about 8% until 2010 and 7% from 2010 to 2020. In Chapter 3, Omkar Goswami suggests that with sustained reform efforts, India is capable of growing by an average annual rate of 7% till 2015.[c] Some prominent investment houses have offered similar bullish forecasts for even longer periods. For instance, Goldman Sachs[2] has confidently predicted that the 21st century will belong to the "BRICs" — Brazil, Russia, India, and China — if they continue with their respective reform agendas. According to this house, accelerating growth in the BRIC economies and slower growth in the industrial world will imply that China will become the single largest economy even in US$ terms by 2040–2050, and India will be the third largest after China and the US, overtaking Japan. Goldman Sachs predicts that China could grow 30 times (in nominal US$ terms) its current size by 2050, while India could grow by over 50 times.[d]

At the risk of oversimplification, we might say that China's industrialization drive has been fuelled by large-scale FDI in the manufacturing sector, complemented by massive public sector investment which has helped build

---

[b]For a useful discussion on the PPP and international comparisons of economic activity across countries, see Ref. 24.

[c]While Goswami acknowledges that India's growth is still heavily dependent on monsoons, he argues that industry and services, which are relatively monsoon-proof, can be expected to themselves lead to at least 5% growth annually.

[d]See Ref. 25 for a more detailed — and equally bullish — analysis of the Indian economy. Of course, a note of caution is always needed in any such long-term projections — too often they have proven to be far off the mark.

an extremely impressive infrastructure. This growth strategy is not unlike to the experiences of a number of other middle-income Southeast Asian countries, albeit much faster and on a much grander scale. Indeed, this similarity in growth strategies between China and Southeast Asia has raised some concerns among some of our ASEAN neighbors about head-to-head competition from China.[3–5] In contrast, India's industrialization has been more organic in nature, driven largely by domestic companies and entrepreneurs and indigenous funds, with (at least until recently) limited FDI. Private Indian companies such as Infosys, Wipro, Ranbaxy, Reliance, the Tata Group, and others are all world-class firms in knowledge/technology-based industries. There are also many more well-known mid and large-sized Indian companies that have carved unique niches for themselves in the global marketplace; particularly, by capitalizing on their managerial, marketing, and R&D skills.

The differences in growth strategies (top-down in China and bottom-up in India) as well as the speed of economic transformation are partly inevitable in view of their markedly differing political systems. Nevertheless, the differences have fuelled an intellectual debate on which approach is the better and more durable. For instance, Khanna and Huang[6] have argued that while China has consistently outperformed India, it has not done so in all sectors, and more importantly, that India's growth strategy may prove to be more durable than that of China. According to the authors, India, relying mainly on organic growth, is making fuller use of its resources (i.e., better efficiency in resource utilization) and has chosen a path that may well deliver more sustainable progress than China's FDI-driven approach. Indications are that India is utilizing available scarce resources relatively more efficiently than China. For instance, while China has grown over 50% faster than India over the last decade, it invests about 80% more and Indian companies are on average more transparent and efficient than Chinese ones.[6,7] Consequently, questions are increasingly being asked about China's heavy dependence on FDI and the low value-added of its exports.

As against this, others have argued that until India manages to attract massive amounts of foreign or domestic investments in labor-intensive areas in the manufacturing sector at anywhere close to the scale achieved by China, it cannot hope to make any significant progress in poverty alleviation, and India will always lag far behind China in this regard. Indeed, most if not all human and social indicators place China well ahead of India despite both starting out on a somewhat even footing since 1980 when the two countries had a similar per capita income (Table 1).[e] Both Basu in Chapter 3 and Goswami in Chapter 4 concur with the need for India to take urgent steps to boost its literacy rate as well as take steps to develop a more enabling environment to facilitate domestic and foreign direct investments.

There is another viewpoint on China's and India's differing growth strategies, epitomized by the following observation by Stephen Roach of Morgan Stanley:

> It's tempting to make the China–India comparison... I see no reason to frame this in such black and white terms... I am inclined to argue that it's not China or India but, in fact, China and India. Each of these two nations has a distinctly different recipe for economic development — recipes that are complements rather than substitutes as they fit into the broad mosaic of globalization... China has an outward-looking development model... India has much more of a home-grown development model that is now gaining global reach... I have long been a big fan of China's remarkable accomplishments. India's awakening is equally impressive.[8]

China and India appear to be consciously learning from each other, and as they do, so there will be a gradual convergence of development strategies over time in several areas. For instance, while Indian policymakers are keen on emulating China's global manufacturing prowess, China has appreciated India's rapid emergence as a global human resource and outsourcing hub and is looking to learn from the success of its South Asian neighbor. It is instructive that the South Indian city of Bangalore (often dubbed India's, if not Asia's Silicon Valley) has become a "must stop" destination for dignitaries from China when they visit India. For instance, when Chinese Premier Wen Jiabao visited India in April 2005 he made it a point to first stop over in Bangalore before heading to India's capital New Delhi.

Taking another leaf out of India's book, China is consciously building up more of its own domestic enterprises that will have the ability to compete

---

[e]One has to admit, however, that certain social policies implemented in China to raise its socio-economic performance (e.g., one child policy) are simply not feasible in the case of a far more heterogeneous, decentralized and democratic country like India.

Table 1. Selected economic and social indicators for China and India.

	Definition	PRC	India
Economic indicators			
GDP	2003, US$ billion	1409.8	598.9
GDP growth (%)	Annual average, 1980–2003	9.5	5.7
GDP per capita	1980 (US$)	264.0	192.0
GDP per capita	2003 (US$)	563.0	1094.0
GDP per capita growth (%)	Annual average, 1980–2003	4.0	7.0
GDP per capita growth (%)	2002–2003	8.4	6.4
GNI (PPP)	2003, US$ billion	6435.0	3068.0
GNI per capita (PPP)	2003 (US$)	4990.0	2880.0
Agricultural growth	Annual average, 1980–2003 (%)	3.2	2.7
Industrial growth	Annual average, 1980–2003 (%)	11.4	5.9
Manufacturing growth	Annual average, 1980–2003 (%)	10.9	6.4
Services sector growth	Annual average, 1980–2003 (%)	8.4	7.4
Share of agriculture	2003 (% of GDP)	14.8	23.0
Share of industry	2003 (% of GDP)	52.9	26.0
Share of manufacturing	2003 (% of GDP)	35.4	16.3
Share of services	2003 (% of GDP)	32.3	52.0
Average tariff rate	2003 (%)	12.0	30.0
Global merchandise trade share	1980 (%)	0.9	0.4
	2003 (%)	5.7	0.8
Foreign direct investment	2003, US$ billion	53.5	4.3
Gross capital formation (% of GDP)	2003	42.0	24.0
Social Indicators			
Population (million)	2003	1288.0	1064.0
Population growth (%)	Annual average, 1990–2003	1.0	1.7
Life expectancy at birth	2002	71.0	63.0
Under-5 mortality rate Per 1000	2002	38.0	90.0
Adult literacy rate (% of people 15 and above)	2002	91.0	61.0
No. of people living below $1 a day	1981 (million)	789.1	434.3
No. of people living below $1 a day	2002 (million)	203.2	356.8
Population living below the PPP 1$ a day	2002 (% of population)	15.9	34.0
Population below $1 a day (%)	2001	16.6	
Population below $1 a day (%)	1999–2000		34.7
Gini index	2001	44.7	
Gini index	1999–2000		32.5
Percentage share of income or consumption			
Lowest 20%	2001	4.7	
Highest 20%	2001	50.0	

(Continued)

Table 1.   (*Continued*)

	Definition	PRC	India
Percentage share of income or consumption			
Lowest 20%	1999–2000		8.9
Highest 20%	1999–2001		41.6

Source: Ref. 23.

globally.[f] In fact, for all the suggestions of a stronger private corporate sector in India than in China, it is useful to keep in mind that there are a large number of home-grown Chinese companies that are significant global exporters, such as Legend Computers, Haier and others. Focussed "Made by China" as well as "Made in China," Chinese companies like these have realized the importance of developing globally recognized brand names that can capture higher margins and consolidate market niches. Accordingly, many Chinese companies have started to make big-ticket acquisitions so as to acquire rather than build brand name. The Lenovo takeover of IBM's personal computer division is one of the better known cases in point, followed by Haier's bid for Maytag, and most dramatically the much publicized offer by China National Ocean Oil Company (CNOOC) for Unocal, the ninth largest oil company in the USA. There are others which go relatively unnoticed.[9,10] Of course, apart from buying reputations and brand names, another goal of China Inc.'s overseas recent acquisitions has been to ensure the availability of sufficient raw materials and natural resources such as oil, gas, minerals, and timber to sustain future rapid growth.

As noted, India is just as eager and willing to learn from China. The former Indian Minister for disinvestments, information technology, and communications, Arun Shourie made the following important observation:

> India has to learn four crucial lessons from China… First, to formulate policies that focus on higher growth… Second, we need to learn how to implement the policies with impeccable execution. Third, we must learn to pay due importance to the scale of operations… Fourth is to learn how to attract greater foreign investment by facilitating the

---

[f]The acceptance of entrepreneurs as members of the Chinese Communist Party should spur private enterprise to greater heights in China.

relocation of industries from around the world in India (quoted in Ref. 11).

India has belatedly realized the important role that could be played by the members of its overseas diaspora (estimated at over 25 million), and is consciously attracting them back home — or at least soliciting their active re-engagement. This is something that China has been doing very aggressively in the last decade, with much success. India is also trying to attract increasing amounts of FDI, particularly as its infrastructural and supporting policies continue to develop. According to the 2004 Foreign Direct Investment Confidence Index by a global management consulting company AT Kearney, Global Executives "are more likely to invest in China and India than at any time since 1998." While China has been the most attractive FDI destination in the world (ahead of the USA), India has steadily risen from the sixth to the third most likely FDI location globally. Interestingly, the AT Kearney index suggests that, China and India were the top two countries favored by investors in *manufacturing* in particular. This is the first time India has displaced the USA. This implies two things: (1) it emphasizes the significant change in attitudes that global investors and corporate leaders have toward India and (2) appreciation is growing of the fact that the Indian growth story is not limited to services; investors increasingly recognize its potential in manufacturing as well. Similarly, in the areas of Telecom & Utility, China moved from fourth to first and India from fifth to second. Clearly, India has arrived on the global scene in the sense that global investors and corporate leaders appear to have developed the mentality that "we cannot afford not to be in India" — a view that they have held for well over a decade about China.[12,g]

Holding India back from becoming a significant manufacturing hub like China is, in part, its poor infrastructure (in absolute terms and certainly in comparison with China). As Goswami notes in Chapter 4, much is being done in the telecoms area as well as roads, but the pace of infrastructural development still remains too slow; particularly, with regard to development and upgrading of ports, airports, and power supplies. Given India's already burgeoning deficit, this in turn underscores the need for greater private sector

---

[g]While China has undoubtedly received far more FDI inflows than India, there are a number of reasons to believe the official statistics exaggerate FDI inflows into China and understate inflows to India (see Ref. 26).

investments in infrastructural projects. This remains a huge challenge for India.

3. Social Security Reforms and Restructuring of State-owned Enterprises

Despite rapid growth in and general bullishness about the two Asian giants, both China and India still have relatively low per capita incomes and millions of their citizens remain mired in absolute poverty (loosely defined as living below the poverty line of US$1 or US$2 per day). It is critical, therefore, that both countries continue to embrace the forces of globalization as a means of bettering the lives of their respective populace. At the same time, they need to undertake internal economic reforms to ensure that they are able to fully capitalize on the benefits of an open economy and meet the rising expectations of their people.

Some of the key economic challenges specific to China include its weak banking system, including cleaning up the overhang of substantial non-performing loans (NPLs); strengthening the balance sheet of the corporate sector; improving its "institutional infrastructure" such as the legal and judicial systems; ensuring greater protection for intellectual property rights (IPRs); and minimizing susceptibility to sharp booms and busts due to an inherent tendency to over-invest and build-up excess capacity. Apart from creaking infrastructure, many of India's problems can be traced to rather poor public governance (corporate governance in India is relatively robust) and somewhat ineffective public service delivery mechanisms; persistence of administrative and regulatory barriers in some areas that raise the costs of doing business; low-agricultural productivity; and relatively large fiscal deficits (especially at the state level) which may be acting as a drag on investments and growth.[h] All these areas have been identified by the Manmohan Singh government as areas where urgent action is needed.

The foregoing problems apart, as with other countries, both China and India potentially face daunting problems associated with ageing populations. To be sure, India does not yet have an ageing population, and in fact, stands to

---

[h]This point is also emphasized by Kaushik Basu in Chapter 3 and particularly by Omkar Goswami in Chapter 4.

benefit from the growth dividend of a young society in the near and medium terms.[i] The same cannot be said of China, however, which indeed is in the non-enviable position of having become old before becoming rich. If nothing is done in India, it too will be faced with significant challenges in the future. According to some projections, by 2050, the two countries will have about 800 million people above the age of 60 years. Accordingly, Section 3 is devoted to the demographic challenges facing China and India and, in particular, the important and related issue of pension reforms. Indeed, poverty among the aged will be a dominant policy issue in these two countries and much of the industrial world.

Chapter 5 describes and critically evaluates the reforms to China's social security system since 1997. The author, Minxin Pei, stresses that the rebuilding of China's social safety net is imperative in view of the loss of job security with the declining role of the state and specifically the restructuring of the state-owned enterprises. Chapter 6 examines the issue of corporate restructuring of state-owned enterprises in China. As the author Jean Oi, notes, China still does not have an adequate welfare system after "breaking the iron rice bowl." The aim of the Chinese policymakers is to ensure that the state owned enterprises are restructured in such a way so as to keep worker dislocation and discontent at a minimum. Oi describes innovative approaches China has adopted in restructuring its state-owned enterprises As she observes, while the number of these enterprises has sharp decreased, especially since the late 1990s, genuine privatization has been limited. The focus has rather been on minimizing privatization and bankruptcy, in favor of expanding shareholding to include managers and workers. As Oi notes, "China's experience suggests that selected forms of restructuring may be the next best solution while the country is developing a social security system" (p. 5).[j] Going forward, India, which has faced many political obstacles in reducing the role of the state in the corporate sector might learn from China's innovative forms of corporate restructuring.

---

[i]The growing working population in turn brings with it other challenges, including a need to ensure that the population has the appropriate education and skill sets so they are employable.

[j]While there is a high degree of complementarity between Chapters 6 and 7, there is one significant area of disagreement. While Minxin Pei argues that the Chinese state is showing itself to be somewhat weak, and that in turn has hindered progress on social security reform, Jean Oi seems to allude to the relative strength and decisiveness in the Chinese state in its approach to corporate restructuring. This is clearly an area in need of more research.

Chapters 7 and 8 describe aspects of India's pensions system, analyzing the reforms underway, as well as outlining the challenges faced going forward. In a nutshell, a pension scheme must, at the minimum be affordable and fiscally sustainable (i.e., not induce fiscal stress) with non-perverse supply-side effects (i.e., labor incentives). As noted, while China is rapidly aging, making social security reforms imperative, Indian policymakers have begun tackling the issue at an early stage, well before their society starts aging and the problem balloons. The real challenge in both countries is to ensure "scalability", i.e., designing a pension scheme that covers a large proportion of the country's wide population, including those in the unorganized sectors, and is well targeted. As the chapters recognize — particularly, Chapter 8 — the reason why pension reform is highly complex is that it requires interrelated reforms in the financial, capital and labor markets, as well as organizational and administrative reform. India has relatively stronger financial and capital markets and appears to have shown far more commitment thus far to undertake pension reforms than has China.

4. National Security and International Relations

Turning to the international framework in which the accelerating transformation of economies and their supporting social systems is taking place, can we make a point similar to that just cited by Stephen Roach — it is not "China vs India" but "China *and* India?" Hopes for some win–win outcomes have in fact been expressed and underscored in high level state visits. But if economics was once called the dismal science, the study of international relations can be equally grim, quoting as it often does the statement that "there are no permanent friends, only permanent interests."

While structured very differently, China and India have both occupied major regions since ancient times, where they were arguably "superpowers" and certainly dominant norm-setters for extended periods. While over the millennia they had cultural and economic contacts of world-historic significance,[13] one would have to describe their political relations as marked at best by mutually benign indifference. Contact, friction and war belong almost exclusively to living memory, as do close cooperation and even alliance. Both countries suffered in the age of colonialism and imperialism, again in different ways, achieving "liberation" in the immediate post-war years under not too dissimilar banners of anti-Westernism, socialism, and dependence, to differing extents, on the former Soviet bloc. For both, emergence in the global arena has been a matter of stop-start emancipation from all these background conditions. Along the way, the operating development goals have, in both cases, been transformed from utopian cosmopolitanism — the socialist International or Third World-ism — to national interest, more realistically conceived. Higher principles are inevitably still invoked, but both India and China are now emerging powers with points to prove in their own name.

Chapter 9 shows how utopian themes of multipolarity and multilateralism have exerted a deep appeal in Beijing, not least after September 11, 2001. This event enabled the People's Republic to become, as it were, a stakeholder in "US-led hegemonic stability." For all the advantages this yielded, China was not able to switch over to cruise control. The intractable Taiwan problem intervened, drawing the US and Japan closer together and forcing China "to adopt multi-pronged proactive responses." Accepting the reality that this is still an age of "one superpower with many powers," China is committed to a balancing act, for which the language of multipolarity and multilateralism are well suited. In line with official views, Xu concludes that China can sustain its development only through further reforms.

Chapter 10 is focussed on unravelling the logic of the official formulation of "China's peaceful rise," which, for a young slogan, has had quite a chequered career. Announced with a great deal of fanfare by the top leaders in late 2003, by mid-2004 it had been revised to read "peaceful development," apparently for both international and domestic reasons. Internationally, it proved diffi-cult to market. Juxtaposing "peaceful" and "rise" had a tendency to raise more questions than it settled, while domestically the slogan was open to hijacking by the right, the left, and fundamentalist nationalists.[k] Subjecting "peaceful rise" to some close reading, Jia in first place disputes the nation's capacity to be anything other than peaceful. Despite alarms bells constantly rung in Washington and elsewhere, he argues that defence spending has been barely adequate to keep pace with changes in the surrounding world, not least the "revolution in military affairs" signalled by the Gulf War of 1991, and subse-quent developments. As to strategic intentions, China has done much to sound

---

[k] See "Marketing Social Harmony," special issue of the *East Asian Institute Bulletin*, Singapore National University, 2005.

the themes of peace, development, harmony, cultural and political diversity, common development, and the rule of law. Above all, Jia argues that China's fundamental view of international relations has undergone three major shifts, viz. from viewing them in ideological terms to more conventionally; from a zero-sum to a positive-sum game paradigm; and "from suspicion and hostility toward the international system to identifying with it."

In an interesting parallel, Chapter 11 argues that India is moving quietly to habilitate itself in Asia and the world. In line with developing realism in official thinking on international relations, the "Indira Doctrine" — an Indian sphere of influence on the lines of the US Monroe Doctrine[1] — has been advanced (note the similar "Gujral Doctrine" as mentioned in Raja Mohan's paper described below). Here India is a challenger, according to Kanti Bajpai, though not an inordinately successful one, as its claims are not accepted by the powers and are rejected by Pakistan. Beyond the subcontinent, however, India has made progress as a "collaborator," joining the ASEAN Regional Forum (ARF) and taking an active interest in East Asian affairs using the considerable capital deriving from it democratic polity and liberalizing economy.[14,15]

Weighing large in the new strategy are its reformed relations with the USA and with China. In the former case, India like China has benefited from the US's post-September 11 need to link up with potential allies in the war against terrorism. Tensions, however, left over from the border wars of the 1960s clearly remain in their relationship. A rising China is perceived as a threat in some official circles, despite the great progress announced during the visit of Wen Jiabao to New Delhi in April 2005. Nonetheless, "with its strong desire for strategic autonomy, India is unlikely to overtly ally with the USA to contain a rising China."[16] Given that tension must be reduced to avoid a two-front threat from China and Pakistan, Bajpai's account of India's "discrete balancing strategy" will be of continuing relevance.

Where Bajpai sees cautious discretion, Chapter 12 is more inclined to see bold revisionism, paying due attention to the historical framework. After the general collapse of the socialist bloc in 1991, "returning to the West" became a dominant motif of Indian thought. Mohan sums this up as a threefold

---

[1]"The Monroe Doctrine, expressed in 1823, proclaimed that the Americas should be closed to future European colonization and free from European interference in sovereign countries' affairs." See http://en.wikipedia.org/wiki/Monroe_doctrine.

transition: from socialist to capitalist construction, from politics to economics, and from "Third Worldism" to a robust stress on the national interest. Yet another watershed came in 1998, when India's nuclear tests created shock-waves, which even before September 11 ushered in a closer accord with the Bush administration. Both Bajpai and Mohan see continuing economic growth and internal stability as crucial for India's image and continued "peaceful rise." Economically, the former non-aligned champion of the Third World stands up better than many neighbors to neoliberal scrutiny, and in the near future is unlikely to receive a poor score card from Washington as a bastion of freedom and democracy and economic success. Indeed, the USA is increasingly viewing India as a strategic partner in the evolving regional economic, political and security arrangements in Asia, and is keen on working with India to turn it into "a major global power in the 21st century" (see Ref. 17). As this book went to press in March 2006, a major agreement on nuclear energy cooperation was announced on the heels of President Bush's visit to New Delhi. India insists that this was in no way directed at China, but the implication that the USA had moved to curb Chinese influence over the subcontinent was widely drawn. The papers in this section provide excellent background for analysis of these events.

5. Ethnicity and Identity in a New World

The last section of the volume focuses on issues of ethnicity and identity that have proved to be an irreducible dimension of socio-economic development and world affairs alike. Chapters 13 and 14 concentrate more specifically on the issue of Indian identity politics rather than identity *per se*. Both chapters seem to agree that identity politics here is largely influenced by domestic factors: the influence of globalization has been limited. The chapters also emphasize that India's identity politics has been shaped by the principles of Indian democracy. Indeed, as Vibha Pingle and Ashutosh Varshney note, the belief of India's national founders that democracy is an effective way to resolve conflicts allowed them in turn to take a "salad bowl" view of national identity — one which recognizes diversity and pluralism as cornerstones of nation-building. A better known term for the salad bowl view is, of course, "secular nationalism." Despite intermittent attempts to usurp them, democracy and secular nationalism by and large remain firm pillars holding India together.

Democracy, nationalism and similarly abstract ideological constructs, however, rest on broader dimensions of political culture that are somewhat more difficult to bring into analytical and comparative focus than issues of adaptation to a globalizing economy and the creation of social safety nets, complex as the latter are. To make the conceptual transition we need links, intermediary conceptual structures. The notion of the citizen is a candidate, as it receives major inputs from political and cultural history, and has equally major outputs in social and economic policy. What the chapters on identity politics offer us is a series of vantage points on the role of citizenship in India and China. Indeed, national building has been a goal shared by both China and India in the post war era. A cornerstone of such national building in both cases was what may be termed "citizenship projects."

China, while coming to modernity with a rich mix of ethnicities, languages, and traditions, has an overriding theme of Han domination and assimilation. In Chapter 15, David Kelly describes the lingering ideal of a unitary "Zhonghua" Chinese (including non-Han) state in which Han identity is notionally subsumed. Differences of religion, ethnicity and language are not lacking and have played major roles in history. Compared to India, however, these sectors of the population are not under routine circumstances the divisions of most concern to the political elite. Other divisions in society are recurrent sources of tensions — notably between urban and rural residents, between the advantaged and the disadvantaged, between powerful and powerless. Citizenship, as a complex and contentious measure of recognition in society, is a relevant dimension of comparison here.

Lacking an absolutely dominant majority analogous to the Han, there is no default identity in India as stressed in Chapters 13 and 14. Citizenship projects have been arguably more successful in India, and in many ways this is a more useful an index of comparison than the brute presence or absence of a democratic constitution. Like China's, India's "citizenship curve" may be described as smoothly continuous, with tribal people and scheduled castes less likely to realize the full set of "rights to hold rights" which is comprised in the citizenship concept. Despite the tensions that may have surfaced from time to time, India has not seen the disenfranchisement of a social sector as has occurred in China.[18]

The citizenship construct is also useful in appreciating the contributions of "diaspora" or overseas migrant populations. In Chapter 16, Wang Ling-chi shows how, in the American case, Chinese identity carries with it a paradoxical blend of advantages and disadvantages, the latter involving a considerable heritage of antipathy and tension. Despite this, China has shown the way in successfully building notions of deferred or detached citizenship among its emigrant populations, whose subsequent economic contribution to their country of origin is a source of widespread envy and latterly of emulation by countries like India. But again, the useful fiction of China's relative homogeneity, while helpful in building overseas communities, is not seen by all observers — including some in China — as an unalloyed advantage. The deep-seated drive to impose a unitary political and cultural structure (reflected in the current absence of a constitutionally guaranteed voice for regional interests of the kind intrinsic to a federal polity) casts a long shadow. India, by the same token, derives great resilience and, potentially, long-term stability from the experience of its citizens with federal diversity, with multiple jurisdictions and identities that cannot be assumed by default.

6. Concluding Remarks

Asia has undergone an unprecedented transformation in the latter half of the 20th century with the rapid growth and development of a number of Northeast and Southeast Asian economies. Admittedly the century ended on a rather sour note with the regional financial and economic crisis in 1997–1998. However, the ushering in of the 21st century offers much room for optimism, with the rapid economic emergence of China on the world's stage and the more gradual and recent but no less noteworthy (though at times less appreciated) deregulation of the Indian economy since 1991–1992.

Sino-India bilateral relations have also undergone a transformation in the last few years, and especially so in the past 2–3 years. Both countries have shown a refreshing willingness to put aside hostilities, psychological wounds and tensions — which emerged from the 1962 border war (the two countries share a 3500-kilometer-long border) and was aggravated by the Cold War — and are taking earnest steps to engage with one another in a pragmatic and productive manner. Bilateral trade and investment exhibitions as well as visits by high-level visits by political and business leaders and technocrats between the two countries have become much more frequent in recent times. All of these help to build good will, trust and understanding between the two countries, and is making both sides keenly aware of the potential for mutual gains to be reaped through cooperation and collaboration.

There are clear indications of intensified relations on the commercial front. For instance, Sino-India merchandise trade rose from about US$250 million in 1991 to US$5 billion in 2002 and reached US$13.6 billion in 2004–2005.[m] However, while these growth rates are spectacular in themselves, given the size and potential of the two giants, bilateral trade remains paltry. For instance, trade with China constitutes only 5% of India's merchandise global trade, and trade with India constitutes only 1% of China's global merchandise trade. So both countries are clearly underweighted in one another's trade relations despite the rapid acceleration in recent years. The potential for sustained bilateral trade growth is massive. It is important to keep in mind that the foregoing data are only for merchandise trade. While data on bilateral services are not available, there is sufficient anecdotal evidence to suggest that there has been rapid growth in that area as well. Both countries are actively discussing the possibility of a China–India Free Trade Area, having established a joint study group in 2003 to explore its feasibility. The business lobby in India, which once viewed China's "hyper-competitiveness" with suspicion and demanded protection against "Chinese dumping" (as they saw it), is now strongly in favor of such a "mother of all FTAs."[19] This highlights the degree of confidence and change of mindsets in India and among the Indian corporate sector in particular *vis-à-vis* China. Bilateral investments have also been on the rise, as companies from both countries seem to have understood that if they want to be cost competitive on a global basis they need to venture abroad, including getting a market presence in each other's countries. Such investments will also facilitate two-way trade between the countries.

The rest of Asia, including ASEAN should welcome the closer engagement between these two Asian giants. This is a key element of ensuring peace, stability and prosperity in Asia. The ASEAN-China Free Trade Agreement (ACFTA) and ASEAN-India Trade and Investment Agreement should facilitate closer interactions between Southeast Asia and its two neighboring Asian giants.[20] Both China and India have acceded to the 1976 Treaty of Amity and Cooperation in Southeast Asia (TAC) as a means of furthering peace and stability with ASEAN, and both are engaging ASEAN constructively in all spheres (including terrorism, drug and human trafficking, and proliferation

---

[m]The foregoing excludes India's trade with Hong Kong, SAR.

of weapons of mass destruction).[n] There is, more generally, a high degree of policy convergence between China, India and ASEAN. In view of this, serious consideration should be given to establishing a "Zone of Co-prosperity" which could also include Japan and Korea. Others have talked about a growing alliance of like-minded Asian countries or "JACIK" (i.e., Japan, ASEAN-10, China, India, and Korea).[o] Admittedly, this proposal is not path breaking; it appears to be the most pragmatic way forward. It can be made reality by turning the current ASEAN plus Three (China, Japan, and Korea) and ASEAN plus One (India) initiatives into an ASEAN plus Four alliance. It goes without saying that such an alliance or zone will remain open and non-threatening to the rest of the world. There are positive signs in this regard with the proposed East Asian Summit (Asian plus Three) having been extended to include India.

In conclusion, while talk of a "China–India axis complete with 2.4 billion people"[21] is no doubt fanciful, the progress in relations over the 7 years following the nuclear crisis of 1998 is claiming the close attention of observers of world politics. Above and beyond their potential economic synergies, the growth of mutual interests culminated in the announcement of a "China–India Strategic and Cooperative Partnership for Peace and Prosperity" during the visit of Premier Wen Jiabao to India in April 2005.[22] We are likely to see collaboration on many levels, from agriculture, military affairs, regional crises like the tsunami of December 2004, to the Asia regional forums and networks, and in the United Nations. Boundary issues and energy security are potential minefields that will require strategic vision, diplomatic skill and mutual accommodation. Lack of conflict, as many have noted, went hand-in-hand with lack of contact; as contact grows, the avoidance of conflict will require skill and vision on all sides. Both parties speak the language of win–win, and both have specific, real interests in rational multipolarism: in balancing the world's sole superpower while taking a share in the benefits its friendship brings.

Acknowledgments

The authors gratefully acknowledge the research assistance by Jose Kiran, Rahul Sen and Sadhana Srivastava.

---

[n]See Ref. 5 for a brief discussion of how Singapore has been actively engaging China and India in recent times.
[o]See Ref. 27 for an elaboration of JACIK.

References

1. Rajan, R.S. (1999). "Economic Collapse in Southeast Asia." *Policy Study*, Lowe Institute, Claremont McKenna College, March.
2. Goldman Sachs (2003). "Dreaming with BRICs: The Path to 2050." *Global Economics Paper No. 99.*
3. Rajan, R.S. (2003). "Emergence of China as an Economic Power: What Does it Imply for Southeast Asia?" *Economic and Political Weekly*, June 28, pp. 2639–2644.
4. Srivastava, S. and Rajan, R.S. (2004). "What Does the Economic Rise of China Imply for ASEAN and India: Focus on Trade and Investment Flows." In Kehal, H. (ed.) *Foreign Investment in Developing Countries.* Palgrave: McMillan, pp. 171–204.
5. Rajan, R.S. and Sen, R. (2005). "The New Wave of Free Trade Agreements in Asia: With Particular Reference to ASEAN." China and India, forthcoming in ADB volume on *Asian Economic Cooperation and Integration.*
6. Khanna, T. and Huang, Y. (2003). "Can Indian Overtake China?" *Foreign Policy*, July/August, pp. 74–81.
7. *The Economist* (2003). "Survey: India and China — The Insidious Charms of Foreign Investment." March 3.
8. Roach, S. (2004). "India's Awakening." *Global Economic Forum*, Morgan Stanley, April 2, from http://www.morganstanley.com/GEFdata/digests/20040402-fri.html#anchor0
9. Kurtenbach, E. (2004). "China's Buying Spree Spreads Global Impact." *The Detroit News*, October 22.
10. Rajan, R.S. (2005). "Juggernaut China." *Business Times*, September 23.
11. Sahay, T.S. (2003). "Four Lessons to Learn from China: Shourie." *Rediff,* February 4, from http://www.rediff.com/money/2003/feb/04shourie.htm
12. A.T. Kearney (2004). *AT Kearney FDI Confidence Index*, October 15, from http://www.ibef.org/artdisplay.aspx?cat_id=135&art_id=3893
13. Sen, A. (2004). "Passage to China." *New York Review of Books* 51, December 2.
14. Asher, M.G. and Sen, R. (2004). "India: An Integral Part of New Asia." *Working Paper No. 63-04*, Lee Kuan Yew School of Public Policy, National University of Singapore, Singapore.
15. Rajan, R.S. and Rongala, S. (2005). "Warmly Welcome India into EAS." *Business Times*, May 11.
16. Pardesi, M.S. (2005). "India and China: Neither Friends nor Foes." *Asia Times Online,* May 25, from http://www.atimes.com/atimes/South_Asia/GE18Df03.html

17. Mulford, D.C. (2005). "U.S.–India Relationship to Reach New Heights." *Times of India*, March 31.
18. Friedman, E. (2004). "Is China a Success while India is a Failure?" *World Affairs*, Fall, from http://www.findarticles.com/p/articles/mi_m2393/is_2_167/ai_n8691667
19. Asia Times (2005). "The Mother of All FTAs." *Asia Times Online*, March 31, from http://www.atimes.com/atimes/South_Asia/GC31Df06.html
20. Rajan, R.S. and Sen, R. (2005). "Dancing with the Dragon and the Elephant." *Business Times*, August 05.
21. Sisci, F. (2005). "China and India Fall into Step." *Asia Times Online*, June 2, from http://www.atimes.com/atimes/South_Asia/GF02Df03.html
22. *Xinhua* (2005). "China, India Agree on Strategic Partnership." *Xinhuanet*, April 12 from http://www.chinaembassy.org.in/eng/ssygd/zygx/t191496.htm
23. World Bank. (2005). *World Development Report*, New York, Oxford University Press.
24. Pant, B.D. (2004). "Purchasing Power Parities and the International Comparison Program in a Globalized World." *ERD Policy Brief No. 25*, Asian Development Bank, March.
25. Deutsche Bank (2005). "India Rising: A Medium-Term Perspective." Deutsche Bank Research, May 19.
26. Srivastava, S. (2003). "What is the True Level of FDI Flows to India?" *Economic and Political Weekly*, February 15, pp. 608–611.
27. Kumar, N. (2002). "Towards an Asian Economic Community: Vision of a New Asia." Mimeo, Research and Information System for the Non-Aligned and other Developing Countries, New Delhi.

SECTION 1

Challenges, Opportunities and Responses to Globalization

CHAPTER 2

China in the Global Economy

Zhang Xiaoji

1. Introduction

China is the world's largest developing country. Since it adopted the policy of reform and opening up, its economy has maintained an average annual growth rate of 9.4%. In 2004, GDP per capita income exceeded US$1200. On the whole, the 1.3 billion people have made a leap from having only adequate food and clothing to leading a well-off life, and the rural population in poverty has decreased from 250 million to less than 30 million. To adapt to the trend of economic globalization, China has adopted the strategy of promoting reform and development through wider opening. Within a quarter of a century, it has integrated into the global economy from a closed developing economy. Since 1993, it has ranked first in attracting foreign direct investment (FDI) among developing countries. China boasts of a stable political situation, high quality and cheap labor force, good infrastructure and wide domestic market, all of which are attractive to international investors. Through investment in the country, transnational companies have expanded their sales there, or have established export-processing bases for labor-intensive products. FDI has greatly facilitated the development of China's foreign trade. Total amount of its imports and exports rose from US$20.6 billion in 1978 to US$1150 billion in 2004, ranking third in the world, of which over a half was by foreign-invested enterprises.

China is a country with huge potential for economic development. Although its economy has maintained rapid development for more than 20 years, its per capita income has remained low, is ranked after 110th in the world. Although the country's urbanization increases by nearly 1% point annually, at present the ratio of urbanization stands only at 43%, which means that more than half of the population has no opportunity to directly share urban civilization brought by industrialization. The 1.3 billion people's strong desire to raise living standards and the huge development space for urbanization and industrialization will place great demands on China's economic development in the future.

The international environment will have even more influence on China's future economic development. China is a country with unbalanced resource endowment, which is abundant in labor force but short of natural resources like cultivated land, water, and minerals. With the continuous increase of its economy, it will inevitably depend more on overseas resources. China is still at the low end of the international industry chain. While it must make efforts to upgrade its ability of innovation, introducing advanced technologies is still an important source for China's technical advancement in the future. This basic situation determines that only in the way of wider opening, can China propel its development through actively participating in economic globalization.

The increasingly growing economy of China will have a huge influence on the world. China has contributed more and more[a] to the growth of world trade and economy in recent years. The rise of exports to the country vigorously drives the economic growth of some countries. After its entry into the WTO, China has actively participated in new rounds of trade negotiations and is dedicated in constructing a more open, free and stable global trade system. What development strategy will China adopt? What opportunities can China's development bring to the international community? How can it effectively interact with the international community so as to achieve a win-win outcome? All these are important issues that will be deeply considered by people with vision and insight. The paper comprises the following sections: After the Introduction, Section 2 will examine the prospects and development strategy of China's economy; Section 3 will analyze and forecast China's role in and influence on the global trade structure; Section 4 will focus on and forecast China's influence on global direct investment; Section 5 will analyze China's regional economic cooperation strategy and its influence.

---

[a] According to the forecast by associations of large enterprises in the US, the world economy will grow at 4.5% both in 2004 and 2005, to which the economic growth of the US and China is expected to jointly contribute one half. The contribution of China's economic growth will exceed that of the US.

2. Prospects and Strategy of China's Economic Growth

2.1. *Prospects of China's economic development*

China will play an increasingly important role in the world economy. Research institutions at home and abroad have made forecasts and analyzes on the prospects of its economic development. The Chinese government has established a target, that is, GDP per capita by 2020 will be four times of that of 2000; recently the research team of the DRC has completed the latest analysis and forecast on the prospects of China's economic growth to 2020. The team forecasts the levels of China's future economic development based on three scenarios. According to the basic scenario, its economy is to maintain an annual growth rate of about 8% in the period of the Eleventh Five-Year Plan. Calculated according to the constant price and exchange rate of the year of 2000, China's GDP is forecast to reach US$2.3 trillion in 2010, with GDP per capita at about US$1700. Its economy is expected to slow down in its growth from 2010 to 2020, with its annual growth is expected to be maintained at 7%. China's GDP is forecast to reach US$4.7 trillion in 2020, with GDP per capita about US$3200 (Table 1).

Rapid capital formation will still play the major role in driving high economic growth in the period from 2005 to 2020 is expected to contribute 63% (in the harmony scenario), 66.7% (in the basic scenario), and 71.7% (in the risk scenario) respectively to economic growth.

Meanwhile the increase of total factor productivity (TFP), which is brought by urbanization, human capital investment, the reform of economic system, and technical innovation, will contribute more and more to economic

Table 1. Prospects of China's economic growth (2005–2010).

	2000–2005	2005–2010	2010–2015	2015–2020	2000–2020	2005–2020
Basic scenario	8.5	8.1	7.5	6.8	7.7	7.5
Harmony scenario	8.5	8.5	8.2	7.7	8.2	8.1
Risk scenario	8.5	7.5	5.8	4.8	6.6	6.0

Source: Research team of the DRC (written by Li Shantong *et al.*), Economic growth potential and the prospects of economic growth in the period of the Eleventh Five-Year Plan by 2020 (Research report, to be published).

growth. The contribution by TFP in the period from 2015 to 2020 is forecast to rise by 10–15% more than its contribution in the period of the Tenth Five-Year Plan. Its increase is the key to sustainable and rapid economic growth in the future.

2.2. *Supporting factors for China's economic development*

China has a strong capital and technical basis. After dozens of years of rapid economic development, China's GDP now ranks sixth in the world, its investment rate has maintained about 40% for many years and it possesses the second largest foreign exchange reserve in the world. Meanwhile, with the continuous improvement of the investment climate, the country has become one of the most attractive countries to investors. Therefore, China has basically removed the capital bottleneck for future development.

China has utilized its comparative advantage in low-cost manufacturing, and has attracted a large amount of export-oriented FDI. With the development of its economy, China's labor costs will go up gradually, and its comparative advantage will shift from simple assembly to high value added manufacturing activities. However, the increase in productivity can offset the impact of the rise of labor costs on China's competitiveness to a certain degree.

China also has a wide domestic market and huge growth potential. Accelerated urbanization will propel investment and consumption demands. At present China's urbanization ratio stands at 43%, and the country is expected to maintain the strong momentum of urbanization in the future. Its urbanization ratio is forecasted to reach 60% by 2020. The massive immigration of farmers to cities promotes the development of the secondary and tertiary industries, and creates huge demands on the urban infrastructure, driving the rapid expansion of investment. On the other hand, the increase of urban population will promote an increase in urban consumption. This rapid increase of urban investment and consumption demands will gradually spread to rural regions, so that the growth of total demand of whole society will be brought into.

After entry into the WTO, fulfilling its commitment has accelerated the transformation of government functions and the innovation of economic system, domestic investment climate have been improved ceaselessly. The more important contribution to the improvement of the investment climate is in the active private investment in China, which guarantees that China's investment rate maintains at above 35%. Such a high investment rate effectively supports rapid economic growth. With deepening integration into the global economy, China will broaden the formal channel to introduce capital, advanced technology and management expertise from developed countries, and make use of the advantage of underdevelopment to expand its economy.

2.3. *Major restrictive factors for China's future economic development*

Good prospects do not mean a royal road. Actually China will face quite a few restrictive factors in its economic development. To ensure the realization of its economic development goals, China must properly overcome these implicit or explicit problems.

The future 15 years will witness the rapid development of China's industrialization, which means a resource consumption peak. In 2003, China's consumption of petroleum, aluminum, copper, nickel, steel, coal, and cement, respectively, accounted for 7%, 19%, 20%, 21%, 25%, 30%, and 50% of global consumption. The country's per capita possession of resources is far below the world average level.

With its expanding economic scale, it will face more pressure from resources and the environment, although China's demand on resources will fall with the end of the stage of rapid industrialization according to the experience of other industrialized counties. The accelerated development of the heavy industry and urbanization will further increase demand for minerals, land and water resource, resulting in a gap between supply and demand. China will increasingly depend on the international market (see Table 2). If we fail to further transform the intensive way of economic growth, environment quality as a whole may be further aggravated.

The market economy is also far from perfect, resulting in China's poor economic growth quality. First, the investment system reform lags far behind, not adapting to the demands of the market economic development. The investment scope of the government is not clearly defined. The government makes too many administrative interventions in a wide range of competitive fields, ignoring economic returns of investment. Private investment still suffers from excessive access barriers and examination and approval procedures. Second, the reform of the financial system also lags behind, the financial market is

Table 2.   China increasingly depends on the international market for major minerals.

	Dependency on imports (%)		
	2000	2010 (forecast)	2020 (forecast)
Petroleum	31	41	58
Iron	33	34	52
Manganese	16	31	38
Copper	48	72	82
Lead	0	45	52
Zinc	0	53	69

Source: Eleventh Five-Year Plan Research Team of the DRC, written by Lu Zhongyuan, Outstanding contradictions, basic tasks, prospects and policy orientation of China's economic and social development in the period of the Eleventh Five-Year Plan by 2020; internal research report, to be published.

underdeveloped, and the financial market's efficiency of resources allocation is very low, all of which are unfavorable for optimization and upgrade of the domestic industrial structure. Third, the fiscal and taxation system is irregular. Governments at all levels spend too much on economic activities, leaving insufficient fiscal inputs to public services. Fourth, irregular management on resources like land, the environment, etc results in distorted prices. The lack of an incentive and constraint mechanism, where resources can be substituted and saved, causes resources waste and high environmental cost.

Furthermore, China's economic development is characterized by imbalance. The gaps between regions, between urban and rural areas, and the gap of personal income among individuals are expanding continuously. During the rapid development period of industrialization and urbanization, complicated social contradictions will certainly interfere with the stable and harmonious development of the society, especially if the resources allocation of public services cannot be adjusted rationally, the social security system is imperfect, social public communication channel is obstructed, and all coordination mechanisms of social communities unsound.

Also, with a more open economy, China will increasingly depend on international market and resources. The fluctuation of international market prices of energy sources, foodstuffs and minerals will place more stress on domestic market prices, enterprise costs and the relationship between supply and demand, resulting in the fluctuation of domestic economy. Participating in globalization will bring a series of new economic risks, while at the same time China does not have sound macroregulation measures and risk precaution mechanisms to cope with the requirements of an open economy.

2.4. *China's economic development strategy: open and sustainable development*

Just like many other countries in the world, China's development also faces the increasingly severe problem of resources and environment. According to a research by DRC in 2004, China's energy consumption per unit GDP calculated based on constant prices, dropped from 14.34 tons of coal equivalents in 1980 to 4.76 tons in 2002, down 66.8%, while electricity consumption per unit GDP dropped from 7200 to 5200 kWh, down 22.7%. Calculated based on the purchasing power parity, China's energy consumption per unit of added value dropped 68% from 1971 to 1999, while the same indicator of the world, European countries and Asian countries dropped 27.7, 11.2, and 32.3%, respectively, on average. China has made evident progress viewing from the point of international community, but at present its consumption of energy and resources is still higher than in developed countries. In the year of 2000, the gaps of the consumption on physical goods per unit of products between the domestic advanced level and the world advanced level are as follows: 24.1% for coal consumed in thermal power generation, 20.9% for coal consumed in steel manufacturing, 44% for cement's comprehensive energy consumption and 69.7% for energy sources consumed in ethylene manufacturing. China's overall recovery of mineral resources stands at 30%, 20% lower than the world advanced level. The low efficiency of resource utilization and heavy waste are widespread in the fields of production, circulation, and consumption, which means that it is necessary to transform the way of economic growth, and there is huge potential to save resources.

The only way for China to propel modernization under the severe restriction of resources is to change the pattern of economic growth, construct a resources-saving society and achieve sustainable development through relying on scientific and technological progress and adopting a modified road to industrialization. China's government has put forward the strategy of taking a new road to industrialization, which is featured by high scientific and technological content, good economic returns, low resources consumption, little environmental pollution and a full display of advantages in human resources. On this basis, China's new cabinet put forward the new view of development two years ago, which focus on "five-coordinations", namely coordinating urban and rural development, coordinating development among regions, coordinating economic and social development, coordinating development of man and nature, and coordinating domestic development and opening-up to the outside world.

In the next 15 years, China is to vigorously adjust its industrial structure, product structure, technical structure and enterprise organization structure; it is to foster the way of production and consumption favorable for resource conservation through relying on technical, institutional and management innovation, and it is to develop a saving-oriented economy and a conservation-minded society. Therefore, the government is to take the following effective measures. First, the PRC will take conserving resources as a basic state policy. "Control population, save resources and protect the environment" will act as its basic state policies in the new era, so as to form a policy environment and social atmosphere favorable for developing a conservation-minded society. China is also to establish an indicator system reflecting economic development, social progress, resources utilization, environment protection, etc., and the scientific view of development. Second, it will change the intensive way of economic growth characterized by high consumption and pollution, and gradually develop a resources-saving national economic system. Third, China will adjust the key points of its strategy. While continuously advancing industrial energy conservation, it is to strengthen energy saving in the fields of construction, transportation, etc., and advocate a conservation life style.

To achieve a sustainable development under economic globalization, China will continue to practice the policy of opening-up, and to solve the problem of resource scarcity through international exchange. While expanding resource imports, it will pay attention to introduce foreign capital, advanced technology and equipment, especially those in favor of further enhancing the efficiency of resources utilization, so as to ease pressure brought by industrialization upon resources and the ecological environment. In addition, it will actively make international cooperation in the fields of energy, resources and the environment, and find a new path for sustainable development.

3. China's Trade Development and its Implications on Global Trade

3.1. *China's foreign trade has kept on growing, and made significant contributions to the development of world trade*

The last 20 years have witnessed the rapid growth of China's foreign trade, especially since the mid-1990s. From 1983 to 2004, China's foreign trade increased by US$1.1 trillion. Particularly from 1993 to 2004, the increase in foreign trade reached US$950 billion. In 2004, China's foreign trade reached US$1.1548 trillion. The share of China's foreign trade in world trade has kept on increasing. Its share of exports and imports in world trade increased from 1.2 and 1.1% in 1983, to 2.5 and 2.8% in 1993, and further to 5.8 and 5.3% in 2003. According to a forecast by WTO, total world exports actually rose 8.5% in 2004, and China's share in world trade would increase further, ranking third in the world for the first time.

The rapid growth of China's foreign trade has made significant contributions to the development of world trade. In 2000, 2002 and 2003, its exports contributed 7.3, 19.8 and 10.7% to the world exports, respectively, and its imports contributed 7.5, 20.5 and 10.9% to the world imports, respectively. In 2001, both world imports and exports decreased by more than US$200 billion, but its exports and imports increased by US$17 billion and US$18.5 billion, respectively, slowing down the decline in world trade. According to an analysis by the Ministry of Commerce, China would contribute 12% of the growth in global merchandize trade in 2004. According to IMF, at least 20% of the increase of the world trade in 2004 should be ascribed to China (Table 3).

China's domestic demand has also had a significant influence on foreign trade balance. In the second half of the 1990s, the pace of China's economic growth decelerated and its trade surplus increased due to the Asian Financial Crisis and other factors. China's foreign trade surplus rose from US$5.39 billion in 1994 to US$43.47 billion in 1998, with the proportion of the surplus in foreign trade increasing from 2.28% in 1994 to 13.42% in 1998. As a result of proactive macroeconomic policies, China's economic growth accelerated, domestic demand expanded, and imports began rising rapidly after 1998. From 1998 to 2004, China's exports rose by 2.23-fold and its imports rose by 3-fold, with growth rate of imports exceeding that of exports.

Table 3.   China's foreign trade from 1992 to 2004 (Unit: US$100 million).

	Total trade	Exports	Imports	Balance
1992	1655.3	849.4	805.9	43.5
1993	1957	917.4	1039.6	−122.2
1994	2366.2	1210.1	1156.2	53.9
1995	2808.6	1487.8	1320.8	167
1996	2898.8	1510.5	1388.3	122.2
1997	3251.6	1827.9	1423.7	404.2
1998	3239.5	1837.1	1402.4	434.7
1999	3606.3	1949.3	1657	292.3
2000	4743	2492	2250.9	241.1
2001	5096.5	2661	2435.5	225.5
2002	6207.7	3255.7	2952	303.7
2003	8512.1	4383.7	4128.4	255.3
2004	11547.9	5933.7	5614.2	319.5

Source: Statistics from Customs General Administration of the PRC.

China's foreign trade surplus has dropped evidently, with the proportion of foreign trade surplus in foreign trade aggregate decreasing to 2.77% (see Fig. 1).

With economic globalization and the new development of international industrial shift, a new trade structure has taken shape in the Asia–Pacific region since the late 1980s. As an important processing and production base in the new trade structure, China has witnessed the rapid growth of its imports and exports. Not only has it increased the supply in the world product market, but also created huge demand and played an important role in promoting inter-regional trade development. In 2004, China's imports from Asia accounted for 65.8% of China's total imports, while Asian market absorbed 49.8%

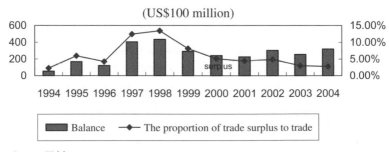

Source: Table 3.

Fig. 1.   China's trade balance from 1994 to 2004.

of China's exports. North America accounted for 9.3% of its imports and 22.5% of its exports, while the European Union accounted 12.5% of China's imports and 18.1% of its exports. Subtracting transit trade via Hong Kong, its trade deficit with Asia stood at US$163.1 billion in 2004, its trade surplus with North America and the EU reached US$81.19 billion and US$37.04 billion, respectively. This indicates that its exports to the European and American market drive its imports from Asia. China has made contributions to inter-regional trade development, and created opportunities for the development of neighboring countries and regions.

3.2. *The development of China's export processing industry results from the international industrial transfer*

In the process that the new trade structure in Asia–Pacific region is taking shape, China, with its abundant labor force resources, good production supporting facilities, and stable social environment, has attracted a large number of enterprises engaged in machinery, household appliance, and information technologies products processing and assembling from Japan, the NIEs in Asia, the EU and the US, which directly drives China's rapid growth of manufactured goods export and its structural upgrade.

In 1980, manufactured goods accounted for 49.7% of China's exports, while textiles and other light industrial goods dominated the exports of manufactured goods, accounting for 44.41%. After more than 20 years' development, China has rapidly expanded its export capacity and improved the product structure of its exports. In 2004, manufactured goods accounted for 93% of China's exports, while machinery and electrical products accounted for 54.5% of total exports and high-tech products accounted for 27.90% of total exports, all of which are significant sources of China's trade surplus. Today, many manufactured goods in industries ranked first in the world both in terms of output and exports. Some products made in China are serving the global market.

According to the statistics from Customs General Administration of the PRC, FIEs exported US$338.61 billion worth of goods in 2004, accounting for 57.1% of China's total exports, among which the processing trade accounted for 78.7% of total exports from FIEs and 44.9% of China's total exports. Most of processing trade is trade inside multinational companies, and if inside trade in other forms is added, the intra-company trade ought to account for more than 50% of China's total exports. Multinational companies have shared the benefits of China's exports and improved performance through the intra-company trade.

Furthermore, FIEs import tariff bonded components and raw materials from their home countries (or parent companies' enterprises in other countries), and export finished goods to places all over the world after processing and manufacturing in China. In recent years, China's trade surplus with the US from machinery and electrical products has kept increasing, while its trade deficits from the same category with Japan and other countries and regions in East Asia soared, which indicates that most of the exported machinery and electrical products, including high-tech products, are manufactured in the way of Original Equipment Manufacturer (OEM). At present, there is a point of view that the growth of China's exports benefited from the undervaluation of RMB. As a matter of fact, the adjustment of the exchange rate has little impact on processing trade, which accounts for more than half of China's exports.

3.3. *China's imports expansion is conducive to global economic growth*

China's imports from developing countries (non-OECD countries) maintained high growth from 2000 to 2004, rising by 29.0% annually and exceeding the average growth rate of China's annual imports in the same period, and their share in China's total imports increased to 46.7% in 2004. China applied zero tariffs on some imports from least developed countries. China imports large amounts of primary goods, raw materials of textiles, and manufactured goods like electronic components from developing countries, which helps them to share the benefits of the growth of the international trade.

China has contributed to the acceleration in the import of primary goods, which had risen by 47.7 and 61.2% in 2003 and 2004, respectively, far above the corresponding growth rates of industrial manufactured goods: 38.3 and 30.6%. The proportion of primary goods in imports increased from 16.7% in 2002 to 17.6% in 2003 and 20.9% in 2004. The rapid growth of China's imports of primary goods becomes the driving force to the exports and economic growth of developing countries.

Table 4. China's imports of crude oil, iron ore, and copper (Unit: 1000 barrels per day, 1000 tons, %).

	Crude oil		Iron ore		Copper	
	China	Proportion in the world	China	Proportion in the world	China	Proportion in the world
2000	8932	4.2	69971	13.8	668	9.8
2001	9145	3.6	92393	18.7	835	12.5
2002	9047	4.2	111423	21.0	1181	17.2
2003	9646	5.2	148128	25.4	1357	20.6

Source: Bloomberg; BP Statistical Review of World Energy June 2004; *Steel Statistical Yearbook 2004*, International Iron and Steel Institute, World Metal Statistics.

Also, the continued growth of China's economy and the expansion of its domestic demand have driven the sharp increase of resources imports like petroleum, iron ore, copper, etc. as indicated in Table 4. In 2004, it imported 200 million tons of iron ore and 120 million tons of crude oil (Fig. 2).

3.4. *China's development needs an open, fair, and stable trade order*

However, China had been the number one target of anti-dumping charges for 9 years from 1995 to 2003. China's exports accounted for 5.9% of the global exports in 2003, but there were 356 anti-dumping investigations against China during those 9 years, accounting for 14.7% of the global total. Meanwhile, 254 cases resulted in anti-dumping measures against it, accounting for 18%

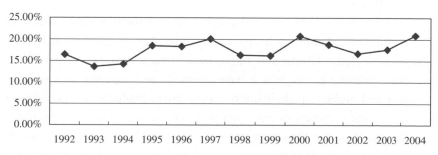

Source: Statistics from Customs General Administration of the PRC.

Fig. 2. The proportion of primary goods in China's imports from 1992 to 2004.

of the global total, of which Chinese enterprises won less than 30%. There were 59 registered anti-dumping and safeguard measures against China in 2003, involving about US$2.2 billion in value. According to a report released by the Ministry of Commerce, 71% of its exporters and 39% of China's exported products were subject to technical barriers to trade in 2002, causing a loss of US$17 billion. The proportion of exported products subject to technical barriers has increased by 56% from 2000, while losses rose by 54%.

China is striving for the smooth transition of textile trade to free trade. To this end, quotas on textiles will be removed completely in 2005, which is a significant result achieved by developing counties in the Uruguay Round and should be shared by textile and clothing supplying countries. Some forecast that China, with its strong international competitiveness in textiles and clothing, may grab 50% of the market share of the world textiles trade, resulting in unemployment of 30 million people elsewhere. The forecast lacks foundation. In the short-term, after the quotas are completely removed, the price decline and quantity increase of textile exports from China and other exporters may mostly result from the fact that the quota rents will be transferred from exporting countries to importing countries. It is an inevitable interest adjustment caused by the transition from distorted market to free trade. Consumers of importing countries benefit most from the adjustment. For example, according to an estimate by the US International Trade Commission, the US consumers pay a price of US$13 billion annually for its trade protection measures of textiles and clothing. China's government authorities has decided to impose export duties on 31 varieties of textiles in six categories by way of unit tax, which is a responsible measure aiming at achieving smooth transition to free trade of textiles.

For now, joint efforts are needed for stabilizing the relationship between supply and demand of the global primary goods. Major importers (such as the US, the EU, Japan, China, and India) have increased imports of petroleum and other primary goods, which have reversed the long-term slide of these products and pushed up their international prices gradually. It is conducive to not only the exporters of resources products but also removing the threat of deflation. However, the rise of resources prices adds additional costs to the economic development of importers including China, especially those underdeveloped. In the long run, the global supply of major resources is able to meet its demand, in the short run, however, factors like the war in Iraq, the devaluation of the US dollar and OPEC's output restriction, etc., which pushed up the prices of resources like petroleum, cannot be ignored. Therefore, for the long-term interests of stabilizing global economic growth, producing and consuming countries should coordinate with each other, and jointly establish a price stabilization mechanism. During the process of its high-speed industrialization, China will still be a major importer of primary goods and resource-intensive products. China will be responsibly committed to establishing a conservation-minded society, actively seeking international cooperation in the fields of energy sources, resources and environment, and contributing to the sustainable development of the global economy.

4. China's Development Brings More Opportunities for Global Direct Investment

An important factor in promoting economic globalization is international capital flow. In particular, FDI brings along opportunities for optimizing resource allocation worldwide, accompanied by international industries transfer. Thus, more and more countries expect to attract more FDI. Even the developed countries making large volumes of outward investment adopt investment promotion policies to upgrade the structure of their domestic industries. Some developing economies have become the source countries of FDI. Cross-border investment is also an important avenue by which China can participate in economic globalization. After entering the 21st century, China began to practice the strategy of "Attracting Foreign Investment" and that of "Going Global" simultaneously. And the expanded FDI inflow and outflow will promote the mutual development of China and other countries.

4.1. *China's position in global cross-border investment*

In recent years, China ranked among the top countries in terms of FDI inflow. However, a large scale of FDI inflow to it has only been a recent phenomenon, its stock of FDI is less than 4% of the world's total.

After reaching the peak of US$1.3 trillion in 2000, due to economic recession and a sharp reduction in the amount of cross-border M & A transactions between developed economies, the inflow of global FDI witnessed a drastic decline for three consecutive years and reached a low of US$580 billion in 2003, the lowest level since 1994. According to the latest information released by UNCTAD, in 2004, the FDI inflow in the world is forecasted preliminarily to increase 6% year-on-year, rising to US$612 billion, hence ending the downward trend and regaining the momentum of growth.

FDI inflow to the developing economies in 2004 is predicted to increase proportionally and to account for 42% of FDI worldwide. In 2001–2003, however, this proportion only stood at 27% on average. In contrast, FDI inflow to the developed economies amounted to US$321 billion, down 16% from the previous year and also the fourth annual fall in a row.

In 2004, FDI actually absorbed by China stood at US$60.6 billion, a 13.3% rise over the previous year, and also the fourth consecutive increase since 2000. But the US registered a drastic increase in the inflow of FDI to US$121 billion, exceeding China and ranking first in the globe.

However, since 1993, China has ranked first, among developing economies at least, in terms of FDI inflow. Some people argued that the large capital inflow to China has deprived many countries of opportunities for development. Although China, like most other countries, has been carrying out foreign investment promotion policies, competition with other developing nations in the field of cross-border investment has obviously been exaggerated. So far China has not published its stock of FDI, while the accumulated amount of foreign fund actually utilized has been used by international organizations to calculate the stock of FDI. By the end of 2004, the accumulated amount of FDI actually utilized by China amounted to US$562.1 billion. If, with respect to FIEs, the suspension/termination of business, assets depreciation, investment withdrawal and other factors are considered, the stock of FDI in China reached US$260 billion as of the end of 2003, equivalent to some 18% of GDP for that year, which is lower than the world's average level of 27%. Another panel of statistics also indicates that China's FDI stock was overestimated. The number of FIEs approved for establishment since 1978 totals 509,000, but only 230,000 of them have registered as operating.

Furthermore, as of the end of 2003, FDI in China only accounted for 0.7% of the US overseas investment stock, lower than 3.4% of Mexico, 1.2% of Brazil, and 3.2% of Singapore. Major EU members, such as the UK, Germany, France, and Italy, only had 0.2–1.5% of their outward investment inject into China. Japan's outward investment in China between 1991 and

2003 accounted for 3.1% of its total outward fund, calculated on an aggregate basis. Therefore, the share of FDI stock in China's economy remains low, and so does the proportion of investment in China to total foreign investment by developed countries.

4.2. *Source, mode, and geographical distribution of FDI*

Over 170 economies have set up businesses in China, of which 70% of the investment came from East Asian economies and some 15% from the developed countries in the EU and North America. Most of the capital from tax heavens has been round-trip investment from Hong Kong, Taiwan province of China and North America.

About 90% of foreign investment in China took the form of setting up new enterprises or the Greenfield Investment. Some M & A cases were completed through buying business assets or acquiring the Chinese party's equities in a joint venture. Since China has no limitations on the proportion of equity held by foreign investors in most of the manufacturing sectors, over 60% of new investment projects took the form of wholly owned businesses.

So far 86% of the investment has flown into the eastern coastal regions. Although this is obviously the result of market forces, the economic gap between the eastern region and the central and western regions has widened. Since the late 1990s, the Chinese government has been implementing the policy of encouraging foreign investors to invest in the central and western regions. However, there has not been any marked effect so far. Notwithstanding this, the Chinese government has not given up the regional policy of guiding foreign investment. Revitalizing the Old Industrial Base in Northeast China has been another initiative in this respect. Since the infrastructure and industrial foundation of the three provinces in Northeast China have institutional reforms which are proceeding smoothly, investors are likely to have new opportunities and space for development.

At the same time, multinationals have been agglomerating in big coastal cities in China and establishing industrial clusters connecting with global production chains. Domestic and international resources and production factors have been moving to the Pearl River Delta, Yangtze River Delta and Bohai Economic Rim at an increasingly fast pace. In these regions, the positive interaction among market size, production chain, business cluster and city clusters has become more and more obvious.

4.3. *The manufacturing industry remains the most attractive sector to investors*

Since the mid-1990s, China has accelerated the process of trade liberalization. Because tariff reduction is likely to result in substitution between trade and investment, some people are concerned that the WTO entry could lead to an increase in trade deficit and a reduction in FDI. However, as the current situation shows that, because of the fierce competition in the global manufacturing sector, multinationals continue to increase their investment in China to gain market shares, and 70% of the investment has flown into the manufacturing industry. Although after China's WTO entry, the openness of the country's service sector obviously increased, foreign investment in the sector did not rise substantially.

In China, FDI increasingly concentrates in IT industry. It is estimated that telecommunications equipment, computer and other electronic equipment account for 15% of foreign investment in the whole manufacturing sector. This trend is gathering momentum. According to statistics of the Ministry of Information Industry, the number of FIEs in the electronic and IT industry stood at 4026 at the end of 2003, representing 23% of the industry's total enterprises. But they contributed 67.5 and 82.7%, respectively, to the industry's total sales and exports. Now China has become one of the world's most important IT processing bases. In 2003, the country's IT sector recorded exports of about US$142.1 billion, with an export dependency ratio of 62.5%.

The automobile sector also enjoys a higher profitability than the manufacturing industry's average level. According to analysis by McKinsey & Company, the production of General Motors in China was equivalent to 3% of its global volume in 2003, but the Mainland business generated 25% of the company's total profits. General Motor's business registered pre-tax profits of over 20%, much higher than the average level of 5% of the global automobile industry. Goldman Sachs also estimated that Volkswagen, the leading automobile company in China, saw 70–80% of its EPS from China in 2003. As tariff rates are gradually reduced, the competition among automakers will become increasingly intense, leading to declining profitability. But having said that, the ever-expanding market is still attractive to new investment.

However, since the labor-intensive manufacturing sector has comparative advantages, foreign investment is still highly concentrated in this sector, and the sector's capital stock is much higher than the manufacturing industry's average level. Most of these labor-intensive FIEs are particularly cost-oriented and show a visible tendency to export. In 2003, the value of exports accounted for nearly 46% of the industrial output (present value) of FIEs in China, and this ratio was even higher in the labor-intensive segment.

4.4. *FDI's contribution to China's economic development*

The contribution of FDI to China's economic growth to the development of newly emerging sectors, to import and export, as well as employment and taxation is obvious. Statistics for 2003 indicates that FIEs accounted for approximately 8% of the total fixed assets investment; they represented 57% of the country's total amount of import and export; constituted 27% of the total industry value-added; contributed 20% to China's total tax revenue; and provided some 25 million jobs, equivalent to 10% of urban employment.

There are debates in the economics circle on how to evaluate the spillover effect of FDI and it role in promoting the upgrade of Chinese industries. One argument is that FDI brings only processing and assembly technologies and creates little technical spillover effect, and excessive dependence on foreign technologies and marketing channels can hardly change the Chinese industry's position in the international division of labor. Another viewpoint is that the processing platforms of newly emerging industries established with FDI, through "learning by doing," have improved the competence of Chinese labor force, and narrowed the technological gap between the manufacturing industry of China and those of developed countries, thus laying a solid foundation for mass production of products developed by China on its own merits. In fact, with economic globalization, even a country like China that boasts a huge domestic market, cannot rely on market protections to develop its national industries. It can seek development opportunities only through competing in the international market and having a share in the international division of labor.

When multinationals come to China and set up businesses, they in fact bring in new business models at the same time, which have been gradually followed and adopted by local enterprises. In the manufacturing and service industries, the market accession and participation of foreign investors have caused a revolutionary change in the business model of local enterprises, which is manifested by the diversification of products and services, the marked improvement of quality, and an increase of operating profits. For example, supermarkets, chain stores, franchised shops and dealerships have been widely used by Chinese enterprises, promoting the development of new distribution businesses.

4.5. *China's industrialization and urbanization will generate huge business opportunities*

Findings of a survey by UNCTAD indicate that China is still probably the most attractive developing country for FDI, at least for the next 2 or 3 years. It is estimated that 15 million jobs will be created directly in China if annual inward foreign investment of US$60 billion remains in the future 10 years.

Given China's vast territory, the advantage of market size is becoming more and more prominent. There are nearly 100 cities each with a population of over 1 million in the country. Each of them could provide huge business opportunities after their GDP per capita exceeds US$1000. Many areas have the preliminary conditions for forming economic growth belts. Therefore, foreign investors have many good choices of regions for investment. As China's urbanization speeds up and the urban middle class increases, more and more domestic and foreign capital will flow into these big cities.

China is also a key link in the global supply chain. Subsidiaries of multinationals in China import equipment, parts and technologies from their parent companies or other subsidiaries or through intra-firm trade, and supply processed and assembled products to the global marketing network of their parent companies. This not only generates profits for themselves, but also promotes import from their own countries to China, creating huge economic benefits for the home countries of FDI. For example, investment from China's neighboring countries has brought along rapid growth of their exports to China and leads to a continued increase in their trade surplus.

Furthermore, the service industry in China and other developing countries are on the way to become a new investment field of multinationals. And rapid development of China's manufacturing industry will create a huge demand in the modern service industry. For example, outsourcing is a new form of cross-border transfer in the service industry. In 2001 alone, Business Process Outsourcing (BPO) in the global market has reached US$127 billion and is estimated to increase to US$310 billion in 2008. China will become another investment destination of outsourcing by multinationals, following India.

Also, with a continuously expanding market and increasing foreign investment in the manufacturing industry, China has been gradually unfolding its advantage of high-calibre low-cost R&D staff. In 2003, 0.7 million Chinese science and engineering students graduated with bachelor's degree, but the figure in USA in the same year was only 60,000. Multinationals have speed up their steps to set up more R&D centers in China, and there have been 700 R&D centers established in the country so far. Establishment of R&D centers by multinationals in China will become a new trend.

4.6. *China will maintain the FDI attraction policy*

Compared with the investment environment of China 10 years ago, laws and regulations, market access, infrastructure, educational levels of work force, etc. have improved substantially, which is largely due to China's fulfilment of its WTO commitments. For example, according to the survey of the Chamber of American Businesses in China, most enterprises praised the country's improved investment environment. Now China is actively deepening reform in establishing the market economy, and further improvement of the investment environment is an essential part of the economic system reform.

Attracting more multinationals to invest in China is in line with the fundamental interest of China's economic development and also an established guideline of Chinese government. The *Interim Measures for the Administration of Examining and Approving Foreign Investment Projects* issued in 2004 proposed changing the examination and approval system to a verification system, further simplifing the contents for approval and enlarging the approving authorities of local governments; the revised *Catalogue for the Guidance of Foreign Investment Industries*, which took effect in 2005 also aims to ease access restrictions on FIEs and speed up the opening of the service industry. These measures fully reflect the active attitude of the Chinese government in improving the investment environment and attracting more multinationals to invest in China.

Creating a fair competition environment is also on the agenda. At present, China applies preferential policies to foreign-invested businesses, such as reduction and exemption of income tax and exemption of import duty on investment goods. With the expansion of areas for market access and the intensification of competition in the domestic market, there have been increasing calls for equal treatment and fair competition with local enterprises. The Chinese government's policy orientation is that preferential treatment should be applied to any enterprises investing in industries and regions which the country encourages to develop, whether they are local or foreign invested enterprises, in order to gradually achieve fair competition among these enterprises.

The government will also implement investment incentives according to specific requirements for investment environment of different foreign investors, and attract more foreign investment to fields such as the modern service industry, equipment industry and R&D activities.

4.7. *China begins to enlarge outward investment*

Currently, some enterprises in China have been prepared for internationalization and have met the requirements for cross-border operation. Now foreign exchange reserves of China have exceeded US$600 billion, and shortage of foreign exchange is no longer a constraint for outward investment by Chinese enterprises. Besides attracting FDI, China also encourages competent enterprises to invest abroad.

According to statistics of the Ministry of Commerce (MOC) of China, the number of Chinese overseas enterprises approved and registered totals 829 in 2004; and non-financial outward FDI was US$3.62 billion, an increase of 27% over the previous year. As of the end of 2004, accumulated FDI outflow of China's enterprises is seen to be growing rapidly and has currently reached approximately US$37 billion.

Also, of the overseas investment stock in 2003, information transmission, computer service and the software industry together accounted for 32.8%, import and export 19.7%, the mining industry, primarily oil and natural gas exploitation, ferrous metal and non-ferrous metal mining, 18%, and the manufacturing industry 6.2%. In 2004, overseas investment mainly flowed into the mining (52.8%) and business service industries (26.5%).

In terms of Asia and Latin America, in 2003, the stock of China's outward investment to the former was US$26.56 billion, accounting for 80% of total stock of outward FDI, and to Latin America, it was US$4.62 billion, accounting for 14%. In addition, the proportion of investment in developed countries such as the US, Japan, and Germany has increased in recent years, and totaled over 20% in 2004.

While the size of China's outward investment has been small relatively, equivalent to 0.45 and 0.48% of the global FDI flow and stock respectively in 2003. But China has been one of the major home countries of FDI in developing countries FDI in 2003, and Chinese investors contributed to strengthening bilateral economic and trade relations as well as economic development and job creation of host countries.

Among the Chinese investors examined and approved in 2003, state-owned enterprises accounted for 43% of overseas investment. But it is estimated that many SMEs, however, were not included in the survey. The proportion of limited liability companies, share-holding corporations and private businesses has increased with the type of investors diversified.

For further integrating China's economy with global economic development, strengthening the capability of its enterprises in participating international competition and coping with challenges from economic globalization, the government has nailed down and issued a number of laws and regulations and policies on overseas investment since 2002, to encourage domestic enterprises to "go global". Besides gradually easing restrictions on foreign exchange management, project examination and approval, etc., the government has also taken many active measures to strengthen information service, credit support, risk assessment and investment guidance. Thus, a comparatively effective preliminary support system of foreign investment has been established and a favorable policy environment has been created for overseas investment by enterprises.

There has been a huge demand for investment in the domestic market. Since Chinese enterprises have no marked "ownership advantage" compared with multinationals of developed countries, many of them invested abroad just for offsetting this disadvantage through different means, such as M&A, and acquisition of technology, brand, marketing channel and human resources.

Thus, Chinese enterprises will gradually realize their potential of expanding investment abroad, since they invest in a wide range of areas, industries and fields.

Encouraging domestic enterprises to "go global" is a long-term policy of the Chinese government. With further improvement of the relevant institution and policy environment, we can predict that China's outward investment will continue rapid development over a long period, and become a new driving force for global cross-border investment activities, making contributions to the economic development of China and the world.

5. China Takes Substantial Steps Toward Regional Economic Cooperation

Under the influence of the expansion of two large trade blocs — European Union and NAFTA, economic globalization is speeding up and all kinds of regional trade arrangements are continuously emerging. As of September 2004, the number of Regional Trade Arrangements (RTAs) that are reported to the WTO reached 305. The intra-regional trade of regional economic groups accounts for 50% of that of the world.

China is also an advocate for regional cooperation in East Asia. With rapid increasing of RTAs in the world, the Asian countries reformulate the regional economic cooperation strategies and actively participate in regional free trade arrangement. Since China's entry into the WTO in 2001, in order to clear the suspicion of China's competitive threat to neighboring countries, Chinese leaders took the initiative in proposing the establishment of a China-ASEAN FTA, which indicated that China began to promote bilateral and regional free trade relationship through institutional arrangements like free trade areas.

The year of 2000 witnessed China's participation in the Bangkok Agreement. In 2002, China signed the Framework Agreement on China-ASEAN Free Trade Area and launched the negotiation on a comprehensive economic partnership with ASEAN. In 2004, China-ASEAN FTA negotiation made breakthrough, with the completion of negotiations on the Agreement of Trade in Goods and the Agreement of Dispute Settlement Mechanism. Also, during the "10 + 3" summit meeting in 2003, Chinese Premier Wen Jiabao proposed to conduct further research on "possibilities of regional economic

Table 5. Institutional regional trade arrangements China participates in.

Pattern	Progress	Members
Preferential Trade Arrangement (PTA)	Entry into or entered into	Bangkok Agreement
Closer Economic Partnership Arrangement (CEPA)	Signed and implemented	Mainland, China–Hong Kong, China Mainland, China–Macao, China
Free Trade Area (FTA)	Partly completed	China–ASEAN (trade in goods, dispute settlement mechanism)
	Started negotiation	China–GCC China–SACU China–Chile, China–New Zealand
	In research	China–Australia East Asia China–Japan–Korea (non-governmental research)
	Proposed	China–India China–Pakistan Shanghai Cooperation Organization (SCO) China–Singapore

Source: Briefings from China's Ministry of Commerce and *China's regional economic cooperation policies*, Long Guoqiang.

cooperation in East Asia," which was appreciated by leaders from other East Asian countries.

At the same time, there are more negotiations taking place on bilateral FTAs. Now China is undertaking negotiation with South African Customs Union (SACU), Gulf Cooperation Council (GCC), Chile and New Zealand, respectively, on establishing bilateral FTA. And the institutional regional cooperation that China participates in is continuously making progress (Table 5).

With China's active promotion, the scope of cooperation in SCO has extended from politics and security to economic cooperation; China, Japan, and Korea are important trade partners with each other, the trilateral cooperation commission set up in 2003 is actively promoting dialogue and cooperation in various fields such as economics, trade, science and technology, energy, and environment protection, etc.; China is conducting joint research respectively with India and Korea on bilateral economic and trade cooperation and making medium-term development plans.

5.1. *China's stance toward regional economic cooperation*

Actively participating in regional economic integration is a long-term strategy for China in developing foreign economic relationship. Article Five of the newly revised Foreign Trade Law of the People's Republic of China has made an additional clause stating that, in accordance with the principle of equality and reciprocity, the People's Republic of China shall boost and develop trade relationships with the other countries and regions, conclude or participate in regional trade and economic pacts such as customs union agreements and FTA agreements, and join regional economic organizations.

The Chinese leaders have also clarified the long-term strategy of developing partnership relation with the neighboring countries repeatedly. That is, stick to the Principle of "Doing Good to the Neighbors and Building a Good-neighborly Relationship and Partnership with them," to strengthen regional cooperation, and maintain peace and stability in the region.

Some people regard China's active attitude toward the regional cooperation in East Asia as "struggling for leadership or dominating status in East Asia with Japan," but this is quite a misunderstanding. The Chinese leaders have repeatedly clarify that China will not seek a special position in regional cooperation. Furthermore, China will get along with each party and welcome a more important role played by Japan in East Asian regional economic integration.

In promoting the regional cooperation and establishing FTA in East Asia, China should not only harmonize the relations with large countries, but also pay attention to the benefits of small countries and less-developed countries so as to form common political willing among East Asian countries.

The levels of economic development in Asian countries are quite different, which, together with the great diversity of politics, culture and religion, are often deemed barriers to the establishment of a regional free trade institution.

However, the regional integration does not aim at eliminating diversity. The ever-closer economic links and complementarities in East Asia will promote sharing the benefits of economic integration benefits and narrow up the development gap. Meanwhile, China is willing to wholly participate in all kinds of regional cooperation mechanisms, hoping to discuss with other Asian countries about establishing diverse FTAs, and finally establishing Asian free trade cooperation network.

Moreover, China advocates that trade liberalization should be based on non-discrimination principle. That is to say, in addition to furthering regional economic cooperation, China will actively extend the exchanges and cooperation with the countries outside the region.

5.2. *Positive implications of China's participating in regional economic integration*

China, as the advocate of the regional economic cooperation in East Asia, is willing to share the benefits and opportunities of the integration with East Asian countries and other regions and pursue a win–win result.

Regional integration will promote economic and trade cooperation between China and its neighboring countries and expand intra-regional trade. In China's foreign trade, the position of East Asian economies was obviously rising.[b] Among the top 10 trade partners of China in 2004, seven are the neighboring countries and regions. The regional trade arrangements will facilitate the elimination of the discriminating terms toward China and improve external market environment.

Also, the "China-ASEAN FTA" framework agreement greatly stimulates some East Asian countries like Japan to expedite the progress of regional economic integration. The "Domino Effect" leads to substantial progress in regional trade arrangements. Currently, East Asia and South Asia have signed 14 FTA agreements and more are initiated or in the process of negotiation. Additionally, financial cooperation is widely carried out.[c]

---

[b] According to statistics, the import and export proportion from Japan, Korea, Chinese Taipei and ASEAN to China increased from 38 and 26% respectively in 1992 to 55 and 44% in 2004.

[c] The financial support mechanism, surveillance mechanism on short-term capital flow and early warning mechanism are established. The year of 2003 witnessed the establishment of Asian Bond Fund.

China and other East Asian economies enjoy more complementarities than competition, so that economic development of East Asia can benefit from regional integration. China's significant role in the global production chain and large market demand make China the important export destination of East Asian economies and they enjoy large-scale of balance surplus to China.[d] Through a great deal of investments in China,[e] Japan, Korea and ASEAN drive the export of the products of upstream industry to China, and after processing in China the products can be re-export to a third country or sell back to home country. Thus the proportion of intra-industry trade rise continuously and bilateral trade increase greatly.[f]

The reality shows that, China's active participation in regional cooperation has brought down-to-earth benefit to the neighboring countries. Now the countries have changed their perspective from "China threat" to "China opportunity."

China's active participation in regional cooperation may also be favorable to the balance of world trade. The global trade is basically balance at present, but the trade between regions and between main countries is highly unbalanced. The economies of East Asia are highly depending on external market and the economic integration is mainly undertaken through industrial division and cooperation, so the trade creation effect is more remarkable. As the largest potential market, China's rapid import growth has become a new drive in global economic development. And the "East Asia FTA" with China's participation will form a regional market with a population of 2 billion people and foreign exchange reserves about US$2000 billion. The large regional market and ever-increasing intra-regional trade and investment in East Asia will enlarge intra-regional consumption demand and help to relieve the severe inter-regional trade unbalance.

---

[d] In 2004, the trade surpluses of Korea, Japan, ASEAN and Russia to China are US$34.4 billion, US$20.9, US$20.1 billion and US$3 billion, respectively.

[e] In 2004, of the total FDI to China, investments from Japan, Korea, ASEAN as well as Hong Kong, Macao and Chinese Taipei account for about 70%.

[f] In 2003 and 2004, China's export to ASEAN increased by 31.2 and 38.7%, while import increased by 51.8 and 33.1%.

6. Conclusion

The rapid growth of China's economy is one of the most significant events of global economic development in 21st century. It means one-fifth of the world total population will share development opportunities brought by globalization and greatly improve their living standard.

The future 15 years are a crucial period for China to build a well-off society in an all-round way. Economic development is standing at a new point, and the capital bottleneck impeding development will ease gradually. Huge demands arising from urbanization, industrialization and upgrade of consumption structure will be an enormous driving force to the growth of the Chinese economy, even to the world economy. However, environment and resource constraints may turn out to be more serious, the pushing forward of reforms will still face many difficulties and there is a long way to go to solving various social contradictions and building a harmonious society. Under these circumstances, the Chinese government has put forward a new concept of development, centering on taking a new road to industrialization and the "five syntheses and coordinations," in order to ensure an all-round, coordinated and sustainable development of China's economy.

With further economic development, China will strengthen cooperation with international society, so as to make a full use of its comparative advantages, improve efficiency of resource allocation based on the world market, and import more natural resources, techniques and equipment to meet its domestic demand.

China's development will bring about new opportunities to investors around the world. China will further open its market to foreign capital with a continuous implementation of incentive policies, and create a fair competitive environment for foreign investors. Foreign investors can benefit from China's development through sharing opportunities from a larger domestic market in China or by bringing the advantages of low production cost into full play. With improved level of economic development, China will gradually become a new source of outflow investment generation. The Chinese government has made adjustments concerning the strategies and policies on outflow investments and encouraged competent enterprises to accelerate investment in the outside world, which will boost up host countries' economic development and enhance China's economy and trade ties with the hosts.

As a big country, China's development will be based on its domestic demands. This means that import scale will also increase correspondingly with export expansion, all of which will make enormous contributions continuously to the growth of world trade and provide foreign enterprises with more and more business opportunities.

At the same time, China's development requires a more open, freer and fairer environment for trade and investment. As the country is suffering most from trade protectionism, China has been striving for equal treatment. This is being recognized by more and more trade partners. Based on the concept of "win–win cooperation," China will continue to promote the process of regional economic cooperation actively in order to create a more liberalized environment for intra-regional trade and investment activities among members. China will enhance cooperation with the international society to establish a more open, free and fair trade and investment system in the interest of all the people in the world.

CHAPTER 3

India Globalizing*

Kaushik Basu

1. Introduction

Writing in the *Financial Times* of February 23, 2005, about China and India, Martin Wolf observed, "The economic rise of Asia's giants is, therefore, the most important story of our age. It heralds the end, in the not too distant a future, of as much as five centuries of domination by the Europeans and their colonial offshoots." Optimistic predictions about China and, more recently, India, have begun appearing with a certain regularity in the media. Ted Fishman wrote in the *New York Times Magazine* (July 4, 2004, p. 27), "If any country is going to supplant the US in the world marketplace, China is it." In an interview to the *IMF Survey* (February 21, 2005, p. 40), Wanda Tseng, mission chief for India in the IMF, said, "India is one of the fastest growing economies in the world and is certainly looking to continue growing strongly." Stephen Cohen in his influential book, *India: Emerging Power* (2001),[18] writes, "India has long been counted among the have-nots. The situation is rapidly changing, which is what will make India such an interesting "great power" for the next dozen years." In Standard and Poor's *CreditWeek* (January 5, 2005, p. 12), Joydeep Mukherji credits China and India as "global success stories in reducing poverty and moving toward a prosperous market economy" and notes that "since China initiated economic reform in 1978, its national income has more than quadrupled; since India began liberalizing its economy in 1991, its per capita income has almost

*This is a revised version of a lecture given at the conference on "Managing Globalization: Lessons from China and India," which was held in Singapore, 4–6 April, 2005, to celebrate the founding of the Lee Kuan Yew School of Public Policy, at the National University of Singapore. I would like to thank Omkar Goswami and Jairam Ramesh for comments and conversation.

doubled." In the inaugural address to this conference, Singapore's Minister Mentor Mr. Lee Kuan Yew, in a speech crammed with statistics and deft analysis, predicted that India will be propelled into the "front ranks" of the global economy, and went on to say that "China and India will shake the world. ... In some industries, [these countries] have already leapfrogged the rest of Asia."

Several Asian economies have grown at record-breaking speeds for the last four decades, but there was no talk of a gestalt change in the world economic order, in the manner suggested by Martin Wolf or MM Lee Kuan Yew, as long as the two largest nations of Asia remained stagnant. But, starting with China in the early 1980s and India in the early 1990s this seems to have changed, certainly in the perceptions of the media. There is an increasing chorus of assertions that the global order is going to alter course, with a cluster of eight or nine Asian countries taking the lead. But before we take this "most important story of our age" as reality, we must check how well it is grounded in facts. Is it really true or one of those "truths" created by repetition?

Irked by the tedious habit of double and treble checking facts in US journalism, the British magazine, *Private Eye*, had once asserted that it relied, instead, on the "legendary British journalistic staple" that some facts are simply "too good to check".[a] It is important for us not to fall into this staple of treating some 'facts' as too newsworthy to check. My first objective in this lecture will be to critically scrutinize this "big story" of our times. China is by now more firmly on the path of rapid growth and militaristic expansion, and so the more interesting question is about India. With India's population comprising some one-sixth of the world, this is important in itself, but it acquires an even greater significance because, if the Indian (or the Chinese) economy stagnates, this will in itself vastly diminish the overall prospect of Asia and, indeed, the world.

I will begin by taking a close look at India's recent performance. It will be argued — to take away any unnecessary suspense from the matter — that the optimism is justified, though in ways that may not always be right. Moreover, it needs to be tempered by an awareness of the pitfalls. Much of the talk of

---

[a]Quoted from Sarah Lyall's "Recipe for Roasting the Sacred Cow, Tastelessly," New York Times, 12 November, 2001.

the rise of India refers to its geo-strategic position, its defence capability and its recent *economic* good performance. The data that has emerged over the last few years show that it is the economy that is the dominant feature of the rise of India. This — though still precarious — has happened more rapidly and in more ways than generally appreciated.

A large part of this paper will dwell on the policy options ahead of India and how these choices have to be made with care if the apple cart is not to be toppled. A sustained GDP growth rate of 8% is feasible for India. And, given that China has already been growing by approximately 10% per annum over the last two decades and shows no sign of slowing, the global economic landscape is indeed likely to change over the next three or four decades like never before.

There are of course lots of possible missteps. A war can put an end not just to growth but people. Political instability can cause any of these countries to spiral downward. And in economic life, as in life, there is always the unforeseen. A century ago most observers were sure that Argentina would be a great economic power and many were skeptical about the US. In the early years, after World War II, the Asian economies, with the exception of Japan, were presumed to be basket cases. Korea, Singapore, Hong Kong, Taiwan, and Malaysia turned these predictions on their head. The risk cannot be discounted that the current optimistic predictions about China and India will once again be turned on their head.

We must therefore tread with caution, trying to evaluate the policy options with as much objectivity as possible. In a globalized world many of the policy choices involve intricate inter-country coordination and so we must discuss these as well. The rapid growth of such large countries bring with it responsibilities not just within the boundary of each nation but for the global economy and polity. And lots of open questions remain about how these responsibilities will be shouldered.

Globalization can cut two ways with countries. It will be argued here that, in the case of India, globalization has been a boon. India has made critical use of it — maybe more so even than China — to restructure its economy and leverage growth. But globalization can also cause large segments of the population to be marginalized. This is not only politically destabilizing but is morally unacceptable. So in crafting the next generation of reforms one has to keep in mind the importance of policies for better distribution of income and for countering some of the negative fallouts of globalization.

2. The Triggers

In his book on Singapore's trajectory from poverty to a developed state MM Lee Kuan Yew spoke of India's unfulfilled potential. "India is a nation of unfulfilled greatness," he wrote[1]; but he also noted that changes were afoot that could launch the economy. He wrote about when Manmohan Singh, the then Finance Minister and P. Chidambaram, the then Commerce Minister, visited Singapore in the early 1990s. "Both ministers were clear on how to improve India's economic growth and knew what had to be done" (p. 409) and that "the impetus to the Indian economy came from Manmohan Singh [Prime Minister Rao's] Finance Minister."

This kind of mixed feeling about the Indian economy was pervasive in the 1990s. What happened over the last 10 or 12 years was beyond what anybody had expected and led to the dramatic optimistic turn in global opinion that I discussed in the last section. Actually, India's growth performance had improved from the late 1970s but there was no indication that this would be sustainable, let alone rise to the point where it raised hopes of India lifting itself out of poverty. But the growth continued and picked up steam; and from 1994 the GDP growth rate broke the 7% mark for three consecutive years and over the last decade averaged over 6% per annum. India's foreign exchange balance, which hovered at a precariously low level for decades began to rise from the early 1990s. India's savings rate that had hovered around 12% in the late 1960s had risen to 23% by the end 1970s. But none of these much-repeated facts is reason enough to merit the optimism of India becoming a major economic power. The reasons for optimism lie in facts that exist beyond these broad aggregates.

First, not only has India's growth been very high over the last decade but, more importantly, this has been the best decade in terms of two *social* indicators. It has been the decade of faster growth in literacy than witnessed in any previous decade since India's independence more than half a century ago. And this last decade is also the one in which poverty seems finally to be on the wane. This is not to gloss over the undisputed fact of worsening inequality, but I will return to this topic later.

Second, for the first time — and this has happened only in the last 2 or 3 years, and could not have been predicted even 5 or 6 years ago, Indian firms have made a small but sure-footed appearance in the global scene and are getting to be known for their good corporate governance (see Ref. 2). The impetus for this came from many sources. Initially, there were the software companies, Infosys, Wipro, and others, which burst onto the global scene as major success stories and had a large advertisement effect for India Inc., in general.[b] These companies were known for their quality products and also for "clean business" — two particularly scarce resources in Indian business. India's large foreign exchange reserves played a role in the internationalization of Indian companies. In the Forbes list of best under-$1 billion companies there were 10 Indian companies in 2001, 13 in 2002, and 18 in 2003.

Third, there has been a windfall in India's outsourcing business, related, somewhat surprisingly, to the US presidential race. Early in his election campaign, candidate John Kerry had criticized US companies that outsourced back-office work to developing countries. He later back-tracked on this, realizing that it was neither good economics nor commendable ethics to propagate protectionism against poor nations. But once this subject made its appearance in the media, it refused to go away. A host of writers and commentators on US television, such as Lou Dobbs on CNN, went out of their way to vilify American companies that outsourced jobs for greed of profit.

This was a clarion call for a host of small American companies that had the greed of profit but did not know of this great opportunity. Company managers employing as few as five or six secretaries realized that, barring the two or three persons they needed on call, they could have the rest of their secretarial staff located in poor English-speaking countries and make huge profits. For the Third World the advertisement effect of the repeat attacks on outsourcing was an unexpected boon. Since advertising on US television is so expensive, they would never have done it on their own. Several countries have gained and India, which already had an organizational structure in place and a ready-supply of English-speaking workers, has done exceedingly well. All statistical indicators show that India has had a sharp rise in outsourcing work over the last year; and, more interestingly, there is now a sudden rise in cubby-hole operations, with three or four persons sitting in a room, glued to computers, and working for American and European companies.

---

[b]For accounts of what spurred this sector see Refs. 3–5.

Fourth, and this has been barely noticed. There is new synergy between India and China. This has no doubt been aided by China's joining of the WTO and the removal of quantity restrictions on imports; but also by the greater maturity of the Indian economy. Trade between India and China has been growing very rapidly over the last three years, the Himalayas not being as big a hindrance to modern trade as they were historically.[c] In 2003 the total trade between China and India was of the value of $7.6 billion; this year it is expected to cross $17 billion. It has been felt in India that this whopping increase is of some strategic value, since it is in the interest of the US to maintain better economic and political balance by bolstering its trade and concomitant political ties with India and China individually, and since the ties with China are already at a high, the main focus will be on India.

Finally, these strong economic developments come with a fortuitous political change. No matter what moral position one takes on this, the fact is that, with the rise of global terror, US political interests have come into alignment with India's. As Thomas Simons, ex-US Ambassador to Pakistan, had noted, the Soviets left Afghanistan in February 1989 and insurgency in Kashmir rose from the summer of that year. This was no coincidence. Some of the same fundamentalist forces that were engaging the Soviets were clearly settling into a new job.

This is today a common problem for the US and India. And, combined with the fact that India and the US share similar political systems, this makes India a natural strategic partner for the US. Moreover, especially with Condoleezza Rice as Secretary of State, the US is likely to embark on a policy of trying to use India as a balancing force against China's inevitable rise to world power, a source of considerable apprehension for the US

The Straits of Malacca, through which more than 60,000 ships pass each year, is a vital artery for Western trade with Asia and, for that very reason, is a potential flash-point in a future US–China conflict. The Indian navy has been a growing presence in the straits. This is clearly happening with US approval, since the Indian flotilla keeps an eye on terrorist activity and at the same time allays the risk of the region coming under exclusive Chinese control. Even for China, it is better to have a third-country presence in the South China seas, than a face off with the US, one on one.

---

[c]Although, even historically, Indo-Chinese interaction was greater than is popularly supposed.[5]

For India to nurture these economic and political advantages will involve a pragmatic assessment of its self-interest but also, I like to believe, a commitment to certain values. It will entail cooperation with China and the US, but also the strength to retain moral independence in matters of global politics and internal economic policy. This may entail giving up some short-term gains, but would command greater respect in the long-run.

Unless India makes a major blunder or gets inadvertently drawn into some costly war or generates so much inequality as to cause political instability, the growth should continue. And to aim for a sustained growth rate of 8% and a rapid decline in poverty is entirely within the realm of the feasible.

3. The Foundations

However, I have moved on too quick. To understand what the major factors were behind the quickening growth rate of India and the recent changing structure of the Indian economy, it is necessary to go back a few decades. It is important also to keep in mind that the cause of as large a phenomenon as a country's overall growth will invariably be diverse. Geography, culture, leadership and the global situation, all play their roles and the absence of one critical factor can stall an otherwise booming economy. Even so, one can try to locate what were the salient factors behind an economy's buoyancy. In trying to answer this, it is however important to determine when the growth spurt first began. In the case of India, there are two possible candidates — the late 1970s and the early 1990s.

A cursory look at the growth rates data and graphs (see Table 1 and Fig. 1) does not reveal very much. The reason is that India's growth rate *peaks* have remained more or less unchanged. Careful examination of the data reveals, however, that the downturns of the economy have become less severe over the years — and that is really the crux of India's recent better performance. In fact, since 1980 independent India has not had any year with a negative growth rate, while, before that, there were four such episodes.

A clever way of seeing this is to construct a moving average. If in each year we plot the average growth rate of the previous 10 years we get the graph shown in the *Economic Survey 2003–2004* of the Ministry of Finance, reproduced in Fig. 2. Once one does this averaging of the growth rates, the changes begin to show quite clearly. The graph begins to move up in the early 1980s.

Table 1.   Growth rate and gross domestic savings rate in India, 1950–2001.

	Rate of gross domestic saving	Annual growth rate of GDP at factor cost		Rate of gross domestic saving	Annual growth rate of GDP at factor cost
50–51	8.9	—	76–77	19.4	1.2
51–52	9.3	2.3	77–78	19.8	7.5
52–53	8.3	2.8	78–79	21.5	5.5
53–54	7.9	6.1	79–80	20.1	−5.2
54–55	9.4	4.2	80–81	18.9	7.2
55–56	12.6	2.6	81–82	18.6	6
56–57	12.2	5.7	82–83	18.3	3.1
57–58	10.4	−1.2	83–84	17.6	7.7
58–59	9.5	7.6	84–85	18.8	4.3
59–60	11.2	2.2	85–86	19.5	4.5
60–61	11.6	7.1	86–87	18.9	4.3
61–62	11.7	3.1	87–88	20.6	3.8
62–63	12.7	2.1	88–89	20.9	10.5
63–64	12.3	5.1	89–90	22	6.7
64–65	11.9	7.6	90–91	23.1	5.6
65–66	14	−3.7	91–92	22	1.3
66–67	14	1	92–93	21.8	5.1
67–68	11.9	8.1	93–94	22.5	5.9
68–69	12.2	2.6	94–95	24.8	7.3
69–70	14.3	6.5	95–96	25.1	7.3
70–71	14.6	5	96–97	23.2	7.8
71–72	15.1	1	97–98	23.5	4.8
72–73	14.6	−0.3	98–99	22	6.6
73–74	16.8	4.6	99–00	22.3	6.4
74–75	16	1.2	00–01	—	5.2
75–76	17.2	9			

Source: Handbook of Statistics on Indian Economy, Reserve Bank of India, 2001.

Another way of looking at this is to examine the average growth rate for each plan period — typically 5 years. This is shown in Table 2. It is immediately clear that there is a break from the late 1970s. Indian economists find it uncomfortable to talk of the emergency years, 1975–1977, when Indira Gandhi took dictatorial control of the country. But there is no denying that, despite the trauma, or maybe because of that, the emergency years mark a break in India's performance. The economy grew by an astonishing 9% in 1975–1976 and the Fifth Plan, 1974–1979, was the first five-year plan period during which the per capita income of the economy grew by over 5% and it would never fall below that again. Hence, the late 1970s break is undeniable.

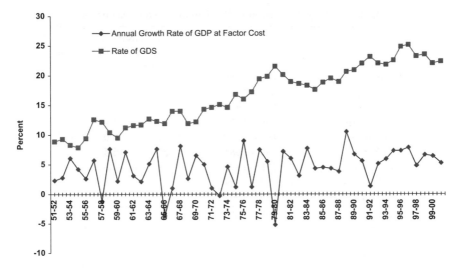

Source: Table 1.

Fig. 1. Gross domestic saving (GDS) and growth rate in India, 1950–2001.

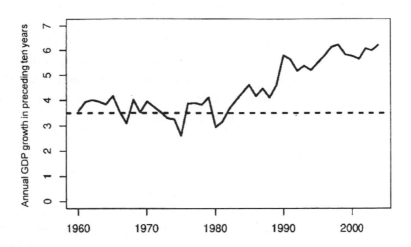

Source: Economic Survey, 2003–2004, Ministry of Finance, Government of India.

Fig. 2. Moving average of growth rate.

Table 2.   Annual average growth rate in India across plan periods.

		GNP at factor cost, 1993–1994 prices
First plan	1951–1956	3.7
Second plan	1956–1961	4.2
Third plan	1961–1966	2.8
Fourth plan	1969–1974	3.4
Fifth plan	1974–1979	5.0
Sixth plan	1980–1985	5.5
Seventh plan	1985–1990	5.8
Eighth plan	1992–1997	6.8
Ninth plan	1997–2002	5.6
Average	**1951–2000**	4.4

Source: National Accounts Statistics 2001, Ministry of Statistics, Government of India; and Economic Survey, 2003–2004, Ministry of Finance, Government of India.

The next break occurs in the early 1990s, as is evident from Fig. 2 and Table 2; and there has been much discussion about which of these two was the serious break from the past, representing some underlying change rather than a temporary and superficial shift.[5,7,8] I believe that there was *some* genuine change in the late 1970s and early 1980s, but the serious take off of the Indian economy occurred in the early 1990s.[d] A part of the higher growth in the 1980s was made possible by heavy government borrowing, large fiscal deficit and also a substantial international debt. The crisis in the early nineties, while triggered by the Gulf War, was inevitable sooner or later.

Moreover, much of what was achieved in the early 1980s was an outcome of a small coterie of entrepreneurs, close to the government, breaking out of the bureaucratic stranglehold that was India. This did give a boost to growth but could be detrimental for the economy and polity in the long run with the risk of sliding into crony capitalism, a risk that is by no means zero even now. The only fundamental change in the late 1970s and the early 1980s was that India's savings and investment rates had risen over the previous decade like in no decade before that (and, for that matter, since) (see Table 1; also Ref. 9).

The sustainable change occurred — I would argue — with the reforms of the early 1990s. These were reforms that, with the removal of industrial

---

[d]This was outperformed only once in independent India's history, in 1988–1989.

licensing, lowering of tariff rates and greater freedom to the state governments to pursue global investment, for the first time attempted allowing freer competition and greater play of anonymous market incentives. For a newly growing economy there is always the risk of anonymity breaking down and a few industrial houses gaining control of the market, thereby causing long-run harm to the economy. And India is in no way immune to this. But from the 1990s, there was hope of genuine competitive markets to come into play. And indeed the 1990s have seen faster growth than any previous period.

The growth would have been even faster but for the slowdown after 1997. But this slowdown, it is arguable, was beyond the country's control. From July 1997 Thailand went into its biggest crisis and this spread from one country to another with alacrity, engulfing most Asian economies and subsequently carrying over to other parts of the world. India, which had very little global exposure at that time — its capital account convertibility was minimal and trade as a fraction of GNP was small — did not get hit directly by a flight of capital or collapse of the rupee, but nevertheless had to cope with the cooling down of the global economy. As a consequence its growth rate fell.

With the Asian crisis behind us, India has bounced back once again, marking a (per capita income) growth rate of 8.5% in 2003–2004 and 6.9% in 2004–2005. That the changes in the 1990s are deeper is also suggested by changes in social indicators, like the literacy rate and poverty. As mentioned earlier, Indian literacy rose rapidly, from 52 to 65%, during 1991–2001. Poverty, as measured by the percentage of people living below the poverty line, also declined in the late 1990s. By some estimates, the decline was sufficiently large that not only did the percentage fall but the absolute number of people below the poverty line declined as well.[10,11] Even though there may be some controversy about the absolute numbers,[12,e] the decline in the head-count ratio of poverty now seems certain.

---

[e]The controversy was caused by the decision of the National Sample Survey (NSS) of India to change the reference period of consumption for most items from 30 days to 7 days. To make this transition smooth it was decided that, in the 55th round of the NSS, data would be collected for consumption in both "the last 30 days" and the "last 7 days." The remarkable consistency that emerged between these two sets of data made it clear that one of those questions may have "contaminated" the other, thereby providing an ideal brew for controversy and confusion. However, while on poverty there is controversy, regarding inequality there is almost total consensus that, no matter how one looks at it — across regions or across individuals, there has been a steady increase.

If the early 1990s mark the take-off of the Indian economy, what are the main causes? I would argue that the most important causes are related to India's international sector. It was a crisis in India's international sector that started the reforms and it is the international sector that has been the engine of growth. The aggregate economy of India has benefited enormously from globalization and there is still scope for huge gains in the future.

In June 1991, India came close to defaulting on its international debt commitments, with balance of payments deficit running high, foreign exchange balance precariously low (enough for 13 days of normal imports) and fiscal deficit high. This prompted major reforms in 1991 and, more so, in 1992. Import tariffs, which had climbed sky high, were brought down; convertibility on the current account was increased; industrial licensing removed; and a variety of incentives to attract foreign capital both as foreign direct investment and as portfolio investment were instituted. These changes, coming on top of the higher savings rate (then hovering at around 23%), that had been achieved by the early 1980s, led to a robust boost to the economy.

If one dissects the overall growth, it becomes clear that the biggest affect has been in the international sector. India's foreign exchange balance grew, steadily and is now at a comfortable level of over 130 billion dollars (see Table 3 and Fig. 3). The information technology (IT) sector had its celebrated take off in this decade.[3,4] India has gained enormously from globalization. If one looks at where the output from the IT sector is going, one will find that 60% of it is being exported. Once this sector made a global name for itself, this

Table 3.   Foreign exchange reserves.

Year	Foreign exchange reserves, US$ millions	Aggregate export of goods and services US$ millions	Short-term debt, as % of forex reserves	Debt-service ratio
1977	5824			
1990	5834	18,477	129	35
1994	25,186	26,855	14	26
1998	32,490	34,298	16	18
2002	75,428	52,512	10	14
2005	130,000	68,000		

Source: Economic Survey (various), Ministry of Finance, Government of India; and Press Releases of the Ministry of Commerce.

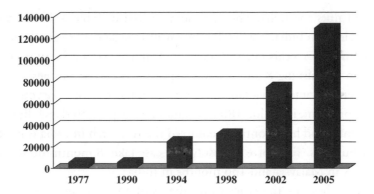

Fig. 3.   Foreign exchange reserves.

had a promotional effect for India as a whole and soon there were other sectors, such as bio-technology and even steel, that began to do well. And now with quotas under the Multifiber Agreement (MFA) having been terminated, textile exports of India are expected to go up from the current annual value of 14 billion dollars to 50 billion dollars by 2010.

4. The Next Round of Reforms

Despite all the good portents, much remains to be done. The country continues to be crushingly poor. Even though poverty has fallen, inequality is on the rise and can reach destabilizing levels. India needs to push on several policy fronts to make a big dent on poverty and for the bottom quintile of the population to feel the prosperity. Turning from this general pronouncement to details, I would emphasize five essential policy thrusts for the next round.

First, governments worry about big things, like money supply, the balance of trade and budgetary deficits. These are of course important but, often, an economy fails not because of these but because of the malfunction of what I have elsewhere[f] called "the nuts and bolts" of the economy. A number of studies have shown that India trails behind other countries when it comes to the enforcement of contracts, the effort spent by citizens on overcoming bureaucratic hurdles, and the time taken to start a business and, more so, to close one. We now have hard statistics to evaluate where India stands on these

---

[f] In BBC News Online column: http://news.bbc.co.uk/1/hi/world/south_asia/3819315.htm.

matters of nuts and bolts. These are summarized in Table 4. If you want to start a business in India, it will take you on average 88 days to get the requisite clearance. In China this takes 46 days, in Malaysia 31 and in Singapore and the US an astonishing 8 and 4 days, respectively. If your business runs into the problem of someone violating a contract, in India it will take you 1 year to solve the problem, in China 180 days and in Singapore 50 days.[g] But even if you can enter and have contracts enforced the real catch in India is in getting out of a business. To resolve an insolvency case takes 8 months in Singapore, 26 months in Malaysia and 136 months in India.

To me, these are the crucial ingredients of an economy's success. If the state can provide these functions efficaciously, the market can take care of much of the rest. To achieve this needs widespread reform of governance. Many mainstream economists believe that all governments have to do is be scarce. It would be nice if life were as simple. In reality governments have to perform certain functions if an economy is to prosper. One can see this somewhat from Table 4. There is little systematic difference in the *number* of government procedures that one has to go through to start a business or to have a contract enforced between more and less successful countries. In fact in India the number of procedures for enforcing a contract is much less than in Singapore, USA or Malaysia. So the problem is not resolved by governments removing the procedures and regulations — a modern economy cannot do without these. There is no getting away from the fact that the government of a modern economy has to have lots of regulations and procedures; it just has to learn to get these jobs done quickly and efficiently.

One specific facility that governments need to provide urgently is that of patenting inventions. Establishing property rights on one's ideas is not a very generous thing to do, but when the industrial world is doing so, one does not have much choice in the matter. According to the latest comparable statistics available,[12] the number of patents filed by Indians in India in 2002 was 220. Of course this will be less than in industrialized nations. What is surprising is how big the gap is. The figure for the US for the same year is 198,339 and for Japan it is 371,495. And it is not as if there is not enough scientific work going on in India. By Third World standards India does fairly well on this.

---

[g]In litigious United States it seems to take as long as in India, though I have some skepticism about this figure.

Table 4. Nuts and bolts of the economy, 2003.

	No. of procedures to start business	Time to start business (days)	Cost to register business (% of per capita income)	No. of procedures to enforce contract	Time to enforce contracts (days)	Time to resolve insolvency of firms (months)	Index of labor regulation most flexible (0) – most rigid (100)
India	10	88	50	11	365	136	51
China	11	46	14	20	180	31	47
Hong Kong	5	11	2	17	180	12	27
Malaysia	8	31	27	22	270	26	25
USA	5	4	1	17	365	36	22
Singapore	7	8	1	23	50	8	20

Source: World Development Indicators, 2004, World Bank, 2004.

In 2001, the number of scientific and technical journal articles published in India was 11,076. The figures for the US and Japan are, respectively, 200,870 and 57,420.

In the US, every university and large institute provides facilities for filing patent protection on ideas. India needs, as do most Third World countries, to move toward this. And this is a task that cannot be left entirely to the market; governments have to shoulder much of the responsibility.

Second, there will have to be important labor market reforms. A legacy of India's Industrial Disputes Act, 1947[h] is that it is exceedingly difficult to layoff or retrench workers. This law was enacted in the belief that this will help employment. But of course a potential employer who knows that he will not be able to retrench his workers may decide not to employ workers in the first place. During a recent visit to some textile factories, outside Delhi, the CEO of Orientcrafts — a major supplier of fashion garments to American department stores — told me that, since in the fashion industry demand has huge seasonalities and in India it is difficult to layoff workers during the lean season, he simply employs, all year round, the number of workers needed during the lean season.

But the problem now goes beyond labor laws. These laws have spawned a *culture* of job guarantee, irrespective of performance, which has — and this is my main concern — hurt labor by keeping labor demand low. While the laws do need reform (see Ref. 14, for discussion), much that happens in the labor market depends on more amorphous factors, like norms and polity. So there will have to be a broad thrust on this front. And it has to begin by educating the trade unions that these changes are needed not for other sectors of the economy but for reasons of the welfare of the workers themselves.

The liberalization of labor laws should be introduced in tandem with the implementation of a basic social security and welfare system. It is possible for India to have a minimal social welfare system which will provide a floor for workers who find themselves temporarily out of work. I return to the topic of direct welfare interventions below.

Third, infrastructure continues to be a bottleneck for further progress. Poor roads, poor ports, uninterrupted electricity and inadequate airport facilities are strangling opportunities in many sectors, especially ones where the

---

[h]Interestingly, this act became effective in April — that is, before India's Independence.

timing of sales is important, such as garments and apparels. From a factory in India to a department store in New York a garment takes on average 32 days. It takes half this time from several East Asian countries. Bureaucracy is a big factor in this but also, the Indian ports being outdated and small, large liners do not come here. So garments have to travel by feeder vessels to be transferred to mother vessels in other ports, before they can set out on their long journey to Europe and the US.

Governments have to spend money on making a big thrust on infrastructure in several dimensions. Investment in infrastructure can boost private sector employment in a big way and this is the best way to create jobs without causing fiscal strain. But, of course, the investment itself will require money. Where will this come from? Governments should use a combination of borrowed money and some of its foreign exchange reserves.

Some analysts, including some IMF economists, have cautioned governments not to do so for reasons of fiscal prudence. The concern — namely, that we must not make the mistake of treating forex reserves of the government as free money — is correct but the conclusion wrong. Suppose Mr. X earns 100 dollars in New York and, on returning to Delhi, changes it to rupees. India's forex reserves would have risen by 100 dollars. If now the government spends this, then, given that X will also be spending his 100-dollars-equivalent in rupees, we will end up spending 200 dollars worth of money as a consequence of having earned 100 dollars. Hence, this will amount to a rise in our fiscal deficit.

But, if this money is spent not on consumption (like paying wages or subsidising products) but on investment, then the pressure on the deficit is not necessarily bad. In fact, *at this juncture of the Indian economy*, that is what I would recommend — the lid has to be firm on the *revenue* deficit, not the entire deficit. It is like a person who has Rs. 1000, but decides to start a new factory by spending Rs. 2000. Of course, he will run up a deficit. Whether this is a good idea or not depends critically on how much faith we have in his ability to run the factory.

With all investments there is what may be called "the risk of Gander." In 1938 the world's largest airport was Gander International. It was an essential refueling stop for planes crossing the Atlantic. The local government calculated that as air traffic grew, the demand for Gander International would inevitably rise and invested heavily in enlarging the airport. But planes became fuel

About this kind of risk — that comes with sudden technology changes or unexpected political shifts — there is nothing we can do. The only mistake would be to allow the fear of this to paralyze us into doing nothing. Since India is on the upswing, it is worth the risk of expanding our infrastructure. Of course this should be done judiciously and with our eyes open. In using some of its dollar reserves India will be exposing itself to the risk of a liquidity crisis. On the other hand, using dollars has the advantage that this will not immediately cause a rise in demand for Indian goods (which could cause inflation). The trick is to use the right combination of borrowed rupees and dollar reserves.

The above policy will also have the desirable byproduct of raising India's investment rate (total investment as a percentage of national income). India may never reach China's investment rate of over 40%, but it is time to break the 30% barrier. India's investment rate has not had any secular rise since the late seventies, when it reached 20%, and in fact had a slight decline in the late 1990s (though it shows signs of an upward movement even as I write this). This is the fourth policy thrust that India needs — to boost its stagnant savings and investment rates. India's savings rate has in fact not had any secular rise since the early 1980s (see Table 1), a slight decline in the late 1990s and a slight upturn in recent months. A part of this stagnation is caused by the large revenue deficit of the government. It is time to think of policy interventions to correct this.

Fifth, the country needs to plan a variety of more imaginative direct interventions to improve the standard of living of the poorer sections. This involves properly targeted government interventions to combat illiteracy, morbidity and inequality. Spending on education, health and social security will cost money. But if we add up the huge subsidies that are given in indirect ways to the rich and the powerful (just consider how well a city is maintained where the rich live), we will find little excuse to skimp on the poor. Moreover, the total revenue (from taxes and other sources) collected by the Indian government is 13% of the national income. This is much below the potential. The figure for most Scandinavian nations is around 40%, for Singapore 25%, and the US 21%. If governments work on correcting this as it raises its spending on the poor, it can keep budgetary pressures under control. It is of course important to design interventions that will not damage market efficiency too much and will result in positive net gain. The scope for action here is immense. It is primarily a matter of resolve on the part of governments.

The problem of inequality is somewhat different from that of poverty. There is more that governments can and should do but, at the same time, there is no getting away from the fact there are severe limits to how much can be done about inequality by a single country in today's globalized world.[15] Inequality needs *global* policy coordination. I have elaborated on this in Ref. 16. The essential idea is this. With globalization, one segment of the labor market that is acquiring greater international mobility is the professional and technically qualified workers. Hence, top-end salaries in Third World nations are being driven up.[i] Unless there is some global coordination in keeping the spread of incomes within limits, a single country's attempt to compress the variance in incomes too much will cause flights of professional labor and capital. This could in turn impede growth and, beyond a point, even increase poverty. When a single country tries to combat inequality, this consequence of unilateral policy action has to be kept in mind.

In Ref. 16 I have tried to develop the principle that inequality should be controlled as long as it does not make poverty worse. My expectation is that this constraint will bind quite quickly in developing countries unless there is coordination of equity policies across nations. The trouble is that, while we currently have international organizations for coordinating trade policies (WTO), labor policies (ILO) and many others, there is no institution or organization for coordinating equity-policies across nations. There is clearly need for some global institution building in this area.

References

1. Lee Kuan Yew (2000). *From Third World to First: The Singapore Story, 1965–2000.* New York: Harper Collins.
2. Goswami, O. (2006). "Corporate Governance." In: Oxford Companion to Economics in India. New Delhi: Oxford University Press. Forthcoming.
3. Narayana Murthy, N. R. (2004). "The Impact of Economic Reforms on Industry in India: A Case Study of the Software Industry." In: Basu, K. (ed.) *India's Emerging Economy: Problems and Prospects in the 1990s and Beyond.* Cambridge, MA: The MIT Press.

---

[i] Some indirect evidence for this is provided in Ref. 17.

4. Singh, N. (2004). "Information Technology and India's Economic Development." In: Basu, K. (ed.) *India's Emerging Economy: Problems and Prospects in the 1990s and Beyond*. Cambridge, MA: The MIT Press.

5. Basu, K. (2004)."The Indian Economy: Up to 1991 and Since." In: Basu K. (ed.) *India's Emerging Economy: Problems and Prospects in the 1990s and Beyond*. Cambridge, MA: The MIT Press.

6. Sen, A. (2004). "Passage to China." *New York Review of Books*. **51**(19).

7. Basu, K. (2000). "Whither India? The Prospect of Prosperity." In: Thapar R. (ed.) *India: Another Millennium?* New Delhi: Penguin Books.

8. Rodrik, D. and Subramanian, A. (2004). "From Hindu Growth to Productivity Surge." NBER working paper: www.nber.org/paper/w10376.

9. Majumdar, M. (1977). "*The East Asian Miracle and India.*" Calcutta: Asiatic Society.

10. Deaton, A. (2001). "*Adjusted Indian Poverty Estimates for 1999–2000.*" Mimeo: Princeton Research Program in Development Studies.

11. Deaton, A. and Dreze, J. (2002). "Poverty and Inequality in India: A Reexamination." *Economic and Political Weekly*, September 7.

12. Sen, A. and Himanshu (2004). "Poverty and Inequality in India, I and II." *Economic and Political Weekly*, **39**.

13. World Bank (2005). *World Development Indicators 2005*. Washington: World Bank.

14. Basu, K. (2005). "Labour Laws and Labour Welfare in the Context of the Indian Economy." to appear in Ravi Kanbur and Alain de Janvry (eds.) *Poverty, Inequality and Development: Essays in Honor of Erik Thorbecke*. Dordrecht: Kluwer.

15. Basu, K. (2004a). "Globalisation and Development: A Re-examination of Development Policy." In: Kohsaka, A. (ed.) *New Development Strategies: Beyond the Washington Consensus*. New York: Palgrave Macmillan.

16. Basu, K. (2005a). "Globalisation, Poverty and Inequality: What is the Relationship? What can be Done?' *World Development*, forthcoming.

17. Banerjee, A. and Picketty, T. (2003). *Top Indian Incomes, 1956–2000*. Mimeo: MIT.

18. Cohen, S. (2001). *India: Emerging Power*. Washington, DC: Brookings Institution.

CHAPTER 4

Elephants can Dance: India's Response to Globalization and the Challenges She Faces

Omkar Goswami

Fourteen years after, the fog of time makes it difficult for many to remember the state of a nation called India in the summer of 1991. The economy was in tatters. Inflation was ruling at over 13%; the combined fiscal deficit of the central and state governments was almost 11% of India's GDP; entrepreneurial growth was totally stultified by a pervasively restrictive environment of industrial licensing, extensive public sector reservations, a dysfunctional anti-monopolies law, severe limitations on the use of foreign exchange, and over 900 products kept reserved for small scale industries; competition was further minimized thanks to a peak tariff of 350%, backed by some of the highest customs duties among industrializing nations and a massive list of quantitative restrictions on imports; decades of poor lending practices and poor recognition and inadequate provisioning of bad debts had led to a seriously weakened banking system; and a severely over-valued fixed exchange rate had contributed to the rapid weakening of balance of payments. It all came to a head when non-resident Indians began to rapidly withdraw their dollar deposits and foreign commercial banks stopped lending to India. Suddenly, the country's foreign exchange reserves were barely enough for two weeks of imports, and there was an acute possibility of a first-time default on international payments.[a]

That is when India was forced to embark on serious economic reforms and greater globalization, which Manmohan Singh as the Finance Minister

---

[a] For details of how bad things were, see Refs. 1–4.

had flagged off with Victor Hugo's famous quote, "Nothing is more powerful than an idea whose time has come".

A decade and four years later, much has changed for the better in the economy, and reforms and globalization have come to stay. To be sure, the path of reforms and the extent of globalization have varied over the years according to real or perceived political expediencies. Moreover, in terms of several indicators of globalization and investment climate — openness of the economy, foreign direct investments and the quality of physical infrastructure, to name three — India still has a long way to go before it can measure up to South-East Asia and China. Nevertheless, India in 2005 is a far cry from what it was in 1991, and much of that is due to the implementation of reforms that embraced the notion of greater globalization.

In this article, I shall attempt to focus on two aspects of reform and globalization: first, the extent to which these have transformed India and, second, the challenges ahead. The first part consists of two sections. In Section 1, I look at various macroeconomic parameters to trace the progress achieved so far, including areas where we have not reformed sufficiently enough. In addition to the macro evidence, I use detailed data from successive rounds of the National Sample Survey and Census of India to highlight the changes that have occurred in rural India to demonstrate that rural is much more than just agriculture and that future policy must focus of rural industries and services at least as much as it might on agriculture. Section 2 looks at infrastructure and investment climate. It evaluates our uneven progress in infrastructure, and examines whether reforms have sufficiently reduced the hassles of doing business. Section 3 covers the second part of the essay, and analyzes three sets of challenges, in increasing order of complexity. The first is the fiscal challenge: how India can get to a system that will rein in state and central government deficits without choking off growth. The second relates to infrastructure and, within it, the FDI, challenge: how can India obtain the huge funds needed for infrastructure over the next decade in an environment where neither the central nor the state governments have enough revenues to finance such projects? The third is demography-education-empowerment challenge: how to ensure that a growing population of youth get the educational inputs needed to be a part of a modern, globally competitive workforce? Section 4 concludes the article by giving a brief idea of the size of the market, and shows that while the Indian elephant will not quickly morph into a sleek jaguar, with adequate reforms it could still dance well enough to seize the opportunities thrown up by globalization. It is unlikely that India will be another China; but, as I shall argue, a more globalized India ought to be an attractive enough destination for all.

Part I: The Journey So Far, 1991–2004

1. India's Performance — An Overview

Hyperbole is an Indian characteristic. Over the last year and a half, with India again being recognized as a growth pole, there seems to be an excessive hype about the nation's economic and corporate performance, especially in the press and television. Conversely, during 1998–2002, when both corporate India and the nation were struggling to achieve better results, the story was often one of excessive gloom. Faced with these mood swings, one rarely gets a balanced, quantitatively driven view of the macroeconomics of India.

The fact is that, despite three downward blips, India's trend rate of real GDP growth between 1993–1994 and 2004–2005 is 6.1% per year. As Fig. 1 shows, during each of these 12 years, India grew faster than the USA, and significantly faster than the Euro zone. Among large, continental sized economies, only China grew faster than India — not only on average but also for each year. This is also highlighted in Table 1, which emphasises that, barring China, no economy in the world with a nominal GDP higher than India's in 2004 grew faster between 1993 and 2004. Thus, since 1993–1994, India has been

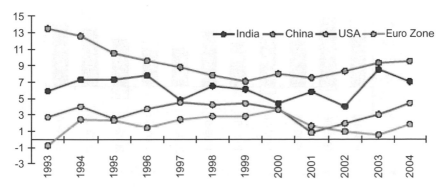

Fig. 1.   Comparative GDP growth rates (%).

Table 1. Only China has grown faster than India during 1993–2004.

	GDP growth (1993–2004) (%)	GDP current, 2004 (US$ bill)	GDP multiple
China	9.5	1662	2.47
Korea, Rep.	5.6	679	1.01
India	6.1	673	1.00
Brazil	2.3	659	0.98
Mexico	2.7	654	0.97
Indonesia	4.0	219	0.33
Thailand	4.5	160	0.24
Malaysia	6.1	111	0.16

the second fastest growing large economy in the world, bested only by China. It is a fact that needs stating.

The second aspect of the growth story is that the economy is becoming less dependent upon the vicissitudes of agriculture. In the 1970s and 1980s, a year of bad monsoons and poor agricultural performance invariably led to significantly lower growth of industry and, in a lesser way, services. As Fig. 2 shows, that does not seem to be the case since the mid-1990s. During 1994–1995 to 2004–2005, agriculture posted negative growth in three years, and negligible growth in another three. Yet, this has hardly affected the fortunes of industry and services — neither the way it did earlier, nor in ways that some economists believe it still does.

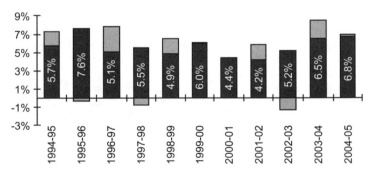

■ Contribution of industry and services to growth ▫ Contribution of agriculture to growth

Fig. 2. Agriculture matters less to growth.

The explanation for this lies in the secular decline in the share of agriculture in GDP. In 1980–1981, agriculture, forestry and fishing accounted for 42% of India's GDP; by 1994–1995, this share had dropped to 30.3%; a decade later, it accounts for 22.1% of GDP. The relative decline in the role of agriculture will be discussed later in this section, where we analyze the changing contours of rural India.

The third aspect of the growth story is the phenomenal increase of the services sector. In 1993–1994, value added from services accounted for less than 43% of India's GDP. Since then, its share has grown steadily, and now constitutes around 52%.[b] Figure 3 plots the annual growth rate of services as well as GDP from 1994–1995 to 2004–2005. It shows that, barring two early years, services have consistently grown faster than GDP. Moreover, for nine out of the 11 years, the sector grew at rates higher than 7% — and for six of them at above 8%.

Such high growth of services has much to do with economic reforms, and goes well beyond the growth of IT, business process outsourcing and IT-enabled services. A simple fact bears this out. India's nominal GDP for 2004–2005 is estimated at US$673 billion, of which services will account for US$350 billion; in comparison, the most optimistic estimate of value added from IT and IT-enabled services will not exceed US$30 billion. In fact,

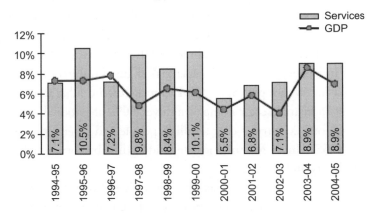

Fig. 3. Growth of services.

[b]To some extent, there may be a bit of overstating of the value added in services due to measurement errors, and also because what cannot be attributed to agriculture and industry goes into services. But, while that can change levels, it is unlikely to seriously overstate growth.

double digit growth rates have occurred in communication services (with over 50 million mobile phones having overtaken 45 million fixed lines), hotels, restaurants, tourism, finance, insurance, and real estate. The growth of each of these sectors is an outcome of economic liberalization, and it would be fair to say that the service sector is by far the most prominent area where reforms have liberated India's entrepreneurial capabilities.

Unfortunately, the growth of industry has fallen well short of that of services.[c] Despite higher growth in industrial production in the last few years, the share of industry has remained more or less constant between 26 and 27% of GDP. There are several explanations for this — all of which have to do with inadequate labor market reforms, paucity of high quality infrastructure and multiplicity of government regulations, especially at the state level. Fourteen years after the advent of reforms, India still does not have flexible labor laws nor an efficient bankruptcy code; the country's roads, ports, and airports are significantly worse than those in most parts of South-East Asia and China; there is still an 8% shortfall between peak power demand and power supply; and despite every state spouting the virtues of "single window clearances" there are still far too many laws, procedures and hurdles to be cleared to set up and run industrial units.

Throughout the 1970s, 1980s and up to the mid-1990s, Asia responded to globalization by rapidly growing their industrial and manufacturing capabilities to cater to the world market. Growth of services came subsequently. Even today, Korea with a per capita GDP that is almost 22 times that of India's has an industrial sector that accounts for over 40% of its national income; with seven times India's per capita GDP, Malaysia's share of industry still stands at 48%; and China, whose per capita GDP is more than double that of India's GDP, has an industrial sector comprising over 50% of national income. As Fig. 4 shows, for a country of over a billion people and a per capita nominal GDP of US$650, India has the most lop-sided distribution of value added between industry and services.

This high relative weight to services vis-à-vis industry has implications for future growth. For India to significantly reduce mass poverty, it will have to transit to a steady state growth rate of around 8% per year over the next

---

[c]Industry comprises four sectors: manufacturing (which accounts for the greatest weight), mining, construction, and public utilities such as electricity.

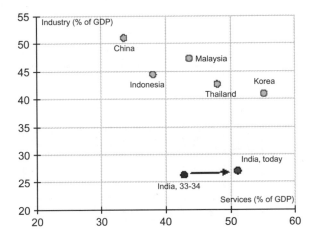

Fig. 4.   Share of industry and services.

10–15 years. This cannot happen without the industrial sector growing at 11% per year, and thus increasing the share of industry to GDP from the present 26% to something like 33%.[d] Today, despite excellent corporate performance, industrial growth is around 7.5%. To grow at 11% will require much greater focus on infrastructure and a more enabling investment climate.

On the trade front, while there has been major reforms compared to the autarkic regime of the 1970s and 1980s, India still has a long way to go before being considered as an open economy. Although the share of exports to GDP has risen from under 7% in 1991–1992 to 10.6% in 2003–2004 — and imports from 7.3 to 12.8% — the country's foreign trade is woefully small compared with South-East Asia and China. For instance, in 2003–2004 India exported US$63.5 billion worth of merchandise; even if one were to add the export of services including IT, the total would not be more then US$78 billion. In the same year, China exported US$438 billion. India's imports in 2003–2004 was US$77 billion; China's was almost US$394 billion. In 2003–2004, trade accounted for 23.4% of India's GDP versus 56.7% of China's. Table 2 gives the comparative data.

---

[d]To average 8% GDP growth over the next 15 years, the share of services will need to rise from 52% to around 55%, and industry from 26 to 33%. Concomitantly, agriculture's share will reduce from 22 to 12% of GDP.

Table 2.   Foreign trade, India versus China (US$ billion).

Years	India				China			
	Export	Import	Export % GDP (%)	Import % GDP (%)	Export	Import	Export % GDP (%)	Import % GDP (%)
1991–1992	17.9	19.4	6.7	7.3	71.9	61.6	18.0	15.4
1992–1993	18.5	21.9	7.2	8.5	84.9	76.7	18.1	16.4
1993–1994	22.2	23.3	8.1	8.5	91.7	98.8	15.3	16.5
1994–1995	26.3	28.7	8.2	8.9	121	108.7	22.3	20.1
1995–1996	31.8	36.7	9.0	10.3	148.8	125.5	21.2	17.9
1996–1997	33.5	39.1	8.7	10.2	151.1	131.5	18.4	16.0
1997–1998	35.0	41.5	8.5	10.1	182.7	136.4	20.2	15.1
1998–1999	33.2	42.4	8.0	10.2	183.5	136.9	19.2	14.4
1999–2000	36.8	49.7	8.2	11.1	194.7	158.7	19.5	15.9
2000–2001	44.6	50.5	9.7	11.0	249.1	214.7	23.1	19.9
2001–2002	43.8	51.4	9.2	10.8	266.1	232.1	22.3	19.5
2002–2003	52.7	61.4	10.4	12.1	325.7	281.5	25.0	21.6
2003–2004	63.5	77.0	10.6	12.8	438.3	393.6	29.9	26.8

Table 3.   India's average customs tariff.

| | US$ billion | | |
	Imports	Customs	Average tariff (%)
1992–1993	634	238	37.5
1993–1994	731	222	30.4
1994–1995	900	268	29.8
1995–1996	1227	358	29.1
1996–1997	1389	429	30.8
1997–1998	1542	402	26.1
1998–1999	1783	407	22.8
1999–2000	2152	484	22.5
2000–2001	2309	475	20.6
2001–2002	2452	403	16.4
2002–2003	2972	449	15.1
2003–2004	3540	486	13.7

Import tariffs, too, have come down from astronomical three-digit rates of the late 1980s. Today, the peak tariff for non-agricultural products is 15% (versus 150% in 1992), and most raw materials and intermediate goods carry a customs duty of 5 or 10%. Table 3 gives the trade-weighted average customs tariff from 1992–1993 to 2003–2004. However, as in foreign trade, while tariff reforms seem impressive compared to where India was in the early 1990s, India's customs duties are still far too high vis-à-vis the ASEAN and China. For instance, in 2002, when India's average customs duty was 15%, China's trade weighted tariff was 6.4%.[e]

The one obvious symptom of the gains from globalization is India's foreign exchange reserves. In June 1991, the country had just US$4.7 billion of reserves and was running a serious risk of defaulting on its international loans. Today, reserves are over US$135 billion, which not only covers 18 months of imports but is also an embarrassment of riches for the Reserve Bank of India. Figure 5 plots the data.

---

[e]While tariff reforms have come to stay — and one can reasonably expect another 5% point cut in the peak in 2006 — there has been, of late, some resistance within industry because of the appreciation of the rupee against the dollar and the euro. Up to 2002, tariff cuts of 5% points per year was easily accepted because of an average 3% depreciation of the rupee. Now it may become more difficult to do — partly because reducing over a low base is politically tricky, and also due to the exchange rate appreciation over the last two years.

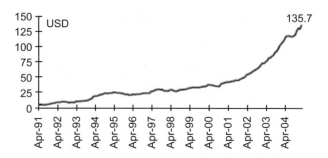

Fig. 5.   Foreign exchange reserves.

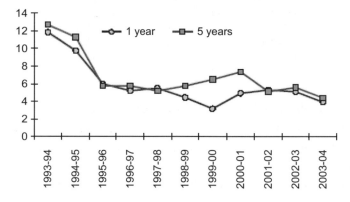

Fig. 6.   Yield on government securities (%).

There are two aspects of the foreign exchange reserves story. The positive is that the increased dollar inflows have allowed interest rates to come down despite high fiscal deficits being run up by the central and state governments. Figure 6 shows the decline in interest rates. However, there is a negative aspect as well. Since the biggest player in the foreign currency market is still the Reserve Bank, and since it wants to limit the extent of exchange rate appreciation, it has had to bear a large cost of sterilization.[f]

For all the progress so far, there has been one serious deficiency in India's reforms process, and that has to do with the government's inability to cut the country's fiscal deficit to manageable levels. Despite the passing of the Fiscal Responsibility and Budget Management (FRBM) Act, the central government has not been able to keep the fiscal and revenue deficit targets and, instead,

---

[f] And as the dollars continue to come in based on the credibility of the India story, it is moot to ask how long the Reserve Bank can keep the rupee appreciating less than most other currencies.

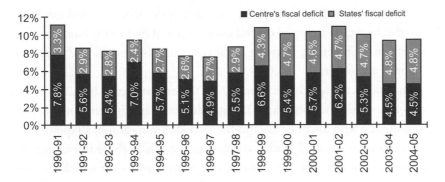

Fig. 7. Fiscal deficit as % of GDP.

has moved the goalpost by two years. Figure 7 gives the combined deficit of central and state governments.

By any canon, a combined fiscal deficit running at 9.4% of GDP leaves much to be desired.[g] And, as Fig. 7 shows, there has been no constancy of purpose at tackling this problem. Up to 1996–1997, barring a year or, there was a slow reduction. However, all attempts at fiscal correction went out of the window between 1998–1999 and 2002–2003. For one, the central government could not keep its expenditures under control; for another, states started having significantly larger deficits which, in tenuous coalitions, had to be tolerated by the central government.[h]

One does not have to be fiscal purist to worry about these persistently high deficits. To me, the most significant concern is that they severely restrict the state and central government's ability to finance infrastructure. It is one thing to advocate the need for greater private–public partnerships (the so-called PPPs) in infrastructure. However, the reality is that for most countries with per capita income under US$1500, the bulk of funds for infrastructure come from public expenditure, and not private investments. I cannot visualize investors immediately lining up in New Delhi and state capitals to participate in rural irrigation, village roads, state highways or the supply of drinking water.

---

[g]In fact, it is actually a percentage point higher because of the deficit on the oil pool account plus contingent liabilities and off-balance sheet deficits of the state governments.

[h]Given the need for the current government to maintain the support of 63 Left MPs and some of the expenditure goals of this coalition government's Common Minimum Programme, there is a genuine concern that neither the fiscal nor the revenue deficit targets of the FRBM Act will be adhered to in the next few years. The reason why such deficits have not yet come home to roost is because of the foreign currency inflows, which have prevented interest rates from hardening.

The investment needs are huge, as we see later in the article — and can hardly be funded by a cash-strapped central exchequer and financially bankrupt state governments. Therefore, a strong fiscal correction is a must, and cannot be postponed any longer.

The one sector which has been forced to perform better because of globalization has been the corporates. Greater domestic and international competition coupled with lower tariffs and the virtual elimination of all quantitative restrictions have required Indian companies, especially those in manufacturing, to focus on efficiency. It shows up in many ways — of which the most telling are the changes in cost structures. Financial data from a common sample of 488 private sector manufacturing companies shows that wages and salaries accounted for 8.1% of net sales for the year ended March 31, 1993.[i] Despite labor law rigidities and a growth in corporate salaries, this share has steadily dropped over the years and, in 2003–2004, accounted for 5.5% of net sales. The same is true for power and fuel costs. Notwithstanding the fact that most manufacturing companies need to operate more expensive captive power plants or diesel generator sets, power and fuel costs have fallen from 7.6% of net sales to 5.6% over the same period. Figure 8 shows the progress on these two fronts.

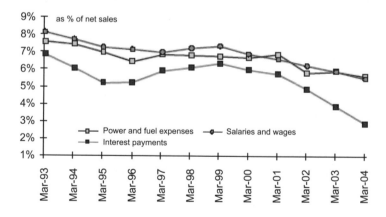

Fig. 8. Improvement in manufacturing costs.

---

[i]In Ref. 5, Prowess. Net sales is sales minus excise payout.

The chart also shows the beneficial effects of softening interest rates. In 1992–1993, the average interest cost for these manufacturing companies was 6.8% of net sales — which was a function of higher gearing as well as harder interest rates. Over the years, and spurred by banking reforms, companies significantly reduced their debt-equity ratios. And as interest rates started moving southward, they swapped higher cost debt for lower interest paying loans and, by 2003–2004, succeeded in reducing average interest cost to 2.9% of net sales.

Reduced costs coupled with growing turnover have led to a significant growth in profitability. Figure 9 gives the data. Not only have the profit rates been impressive, but these have also been maintained over successively higher sales. In fact, Indian profitability now ranks among the best in Asia.

In fact, the story is not about profitability, but about how reforms and globalization have forced competitiveness within Indian industry. This is not just true of IT and allied services, but of many sectors of manufacturing. 1996–2001 saw a large cross-section of manufacturing companies focusing on costs, efficiency, productivity, scale, and good old-fashioned sweating of

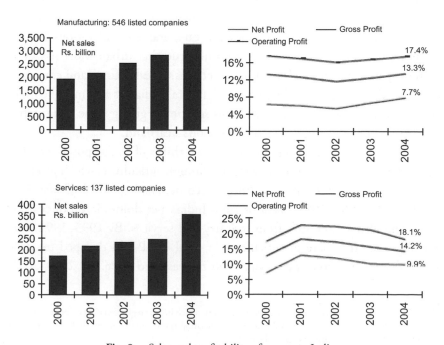

Fig. 9. Sales and profitability of corporate India.

machinery to maximize the return on capital employed. This has now started paying dividends, not only in terms of higher sales and profits but also due to higher Economic Value Added (or EVA®).[j] A common sample of 204 listed manufacturing companies shows that:

- Two-thirds added to corporate value creating by generating positive EVA during 2003–2004, and it occurred despite 64% of the companies having increased average capital employed.
- Over 38% of the companies that generated positive EVA in 2003–2004 have turned around from being negative EVA entities in 2002–2003. Conversely, less than 9% of the companies that generated negative EVA in 2003–2004 were in the positive zone in 2002–2003.
- Although declining interest rates played a role, the improvement in EVA was more due to growth in net operating profits than the fall in cost of capital.[k]

That brings me to a brief description of the changes that have occurred in rural India. Globalization and reforms have created their own symbols, of which the most ubiquitous ones are the images of a talking nation on the move — people driving motorcycles and cars, and shots of various Indians speaking on mobile phones. It is certainly true that urban India has done extremely well during the last 14 years in terms of real income and consumer choices. What is, however, forgotten is that rural India has also morphed very significantly, and it is useful to end this section by giving some quantitative estimates of changing contours of the nation's heartland.

There is an oft-heard statement that two-thirds of India's population live in rural India and eke out their existence through agriculture, which produces only a bit above a fifth of the country's income. *Nothing can be farther from the truth.* In 1980–1981, 64% of rural India's net domestic product came from agriculture, and 36% from industry and services. By 1993–1994, over a rising base, the share of agriculture in rural NDP had dropped to 56%, while that of industry and services had increased to 44%. By 2000–2001,

---

[j]The EVA has been created by Stern, Stewart and Company, which has the registered rights over the acronym. It is essentially the difference between the net of tax operating profits of a company and its opportunity cost of capital, weighted between debt and equity.

[k]In Ref. 6, India: Economic Update, vol. 1, issue 2, forthcoming.

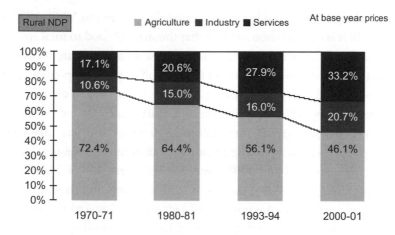

Fig. 10.   Structural shifts in rural India.

the share of agriculture had further fallen to 46%; industry accounted for 21% of rural NDP and services another 33%. In other words, 54% of the net domestic product generated in rural India in 2000–2001 was not directly related to agriculture. That is why, between 1993–1994 and 2000–2001, real rural income has grown at 6.2% per year, while income from agriculture has increased by only 2.4%.[l] Figure 10 shows these trends very clearly.

The second point worth noting is that by 2000–2001, organized factory-sector manufacturing in rural India accounted for 36% of total number of manufacturing units in the country, 38% of total employees, 43% of total output, and 41% of net value added. Moreover, the number of unorganized business enterprises in rural India grew by 14% between 1990 and 1998 — the last year when such a census was carried out — and accounted for almost 14.4 million units.[m] Over the same period, businesses engaged in retail trade grew by 25%. Given that there has been more rapid economic growth between 1998 and 2004, I expect that these percentages would have increased over the last six years.

The third aspect that needs emphasis is that rural India is significantly better off than before. This shows up in the National Sample Survey data

---

[l] In Ref. 7.
[m] *Ibid.*

regarding the growth in real household expenditure between 1987–1988 and 1999–2000. It is evident from the fact that the share of food to total spending has steadily declined across all states and almost all expenditure classes (and non-food has risen), especially among the top half of the rural populace. Even within food categories, more is being spent on luxuries such as milk, meat, fish, fruits, and vegetables than on necessities such as cereals and pulses — an invariably sure sign of greater rural incomes. Moreover, the decennial Census data shows that there has been a significant growth in rural household assets and amenities between 1991 and 2001, especially the ownership of TVs, scooters and motorcycles, phones, and the use of bank accounts and cooking gas.[n] In other words, contrary to the opinion of Left economists and the occasional stories of suicides by indebted farmers, rural India has definitely become better off since 1991 — and at a rate significantly faster than before.[o]

To recapitulate, India has grown at an average rate of around 6% per year for the last 12 years, which makes it the fastest growing large economy after China. There have been significant reforms in industrial and monetary policy and banking, and these have shown up not only in growth of industry and services but also in foreign currency reserves. Although the economy is more open than before, and average tariff rates have fallen over the years, much more needs to be done in the context of ASEAN and China. On the fiscal front, there is still no serious attempt to curtail the large budget deficits of the central and state governments. While this has not yet affected growth, it always carries high risks. The corporate sector has done very well, especially over the last few years. The economy seems to have finally reduced its dependence on monsoons, and over the last decade and half, the rural sector has become much more than just agriculture. All in all, it has been a creditable economic performance. But more needs to be done — for which we now turn to infrastructure and the investment climate.

---

[n] *Ibid.*, and Census of India, 1991 and 2001.
[o] A point made is that inequalities have marginally increased in rural India, especially if one were to compare the Gini coefficient for 1987–1988 with that for 2000–2001. This point is debatable even in terms of numbers. Our estimates show that inequalities have reduced: the Gini has declined from 0.37 in 1987–1988 to 0.26 in 2000–2001 [see Ref. 7]. However, even if the Gini were to marginally increase (greater inequality), it still does not negate the hypothesis that rural real expenditures have risen on average, with the growth across some classes being faster than that of others.

2. Infrastructure and Investment Climate

An impressive aspect of the growth of sales, profitability and value creation of Indian corporates, especially manufacturing companies, is that it has occurred in spite of the country's terrible state of physical infrastructure.

It is well recognized that the country's major airports rank among the worst in Asia.[p] The ports are inefficient, congested, have inadequate linkage facilities and transport corridors, and are a far cry from those in Singapore, Malaysia, Hong Kong or Shanghai. India might technically have the second largest road network in the world with a total length of about 3.3 million kilometers, but it is a network that badly needs serious upgrading.[q] Likewise, the Indian railway is the second largest railway network in the world with 63,122 route kilometers, but it is in severe distress. Excess staffing and operational inefficiencies have eroded the competitiveness of railways; and years of political compulsions have forced the railways to expand networks to commercially unviable areas, highly subsidised passenger fares and raise freight tariffs to a point where traditional long haul traffic in items such as cement, iron and steel and petroleum has shifted to roads or pipelines.

Despite passing of the Electricity Act in 2003, the state of the power sector leaves much to be desired. In 2003–2004, the country faced a shortfall of 7.1% of energy requirements and 11.2% of peak demand, and deficit levels have remained in the vicinity of 7.5% in the last five years.[r] Operationally, India still does not yet have a national, synchronous grid, and inter-regional power transfers are modest because of inadequate transmission line capacity. Moreover, transmission and distribution have been the perennial choke

---

[p]A survey done by the International Air Transport Association (IATA) in 1999 ranked the Mumbai and Delhi airports amongst the three worst airports in the Asia–Pacific region for all 19 service parameters included in the survey. With a rating of 2.3 and 2.6 on a scale of one (very poor) to five (excellent) for Mumbai and Delhi airports, respectively, these airports were adjudged to offer the lowest service levels in terms of overall satisfaction. This reminds me of a droll joke which runs thus: "Q: Why does Mumbai's Sahar airport exist at all? A: Because it makes Delhi's Indira Gandhi Airport look better".

[q]Only 22% of 65,569 km of national highways have been earmarked for 4-lane or 6-lane modernization under the National Highways Development Project. State highways comprise approximately an additional 137,000 km and in most part, are in terrible shape. The remaining road network comprises district and village roads, which constitute more than 90% of the total, but are largely un-surfaced and of very poor quality.

[r]In the first six months of fiscal 2004, the country faced a power shortage of 20,440 million units, representing 6% of the total requirement.

points in power — transmission because of inadequate capacity, and distribution because of obsolescence, poor pricing, over-manning, inefficiencies,
inadequate metering, and outright power theft.

The only area in infrastructure which has shown creditable progress is
telecoms, especially mobile telephony, and is a case study of how the interplay
of competition, good regulations and technology can radically change the
business landscape of infrastructure. Before opening-up in 1994, the sector was
characterized by underinvestment, outdated technology, and limited growth.[s]
The constraint was not demand, but the lack of resources of the public sector
enterprises. Today, thanks to the boom in cellular services, India's teledensity
has reached 8.62% (almost 93 million subscribers) with about 22 million new
customers being added in 2004. The collective revenues of telecom operators
(excluding internet service providers) rose by 30% from Rs. 470 billion in
2003 to Rs. 610 billion in 2004.

As of December 2004, cellular services had a subscriber base of 48 million.
On an average, 1.62 million subscribers were added each month in 2004.
The number of fixed line telephone subscribers stood at around 45 million
as of December 30, 2004. In addition, there are over seven million internet
subscribers, and this number is increasing quite rapidly.

The success of mobile telephony is emphasised in Fig. 11, which shows
the growth in subscribers as well as the sharp fall in effective mobile charges. In
fact, India now happens to have the cheapest mobile tariff rates in the world —
a testimony to the power of competition and an effective, consumer-oriented
regulatory regime.[t]

Barring telecoms, however, India's progress in infrastructure has been
poor. Much has been said in the country about the national highways program and, to be fair, there have been improvements. Financed largely by a
excess of Rs. 1.50 per liter of diesel and petrol, the 4- and 6-laning of 72% of
the Golden Quadrilateral network comprising 5846 km and connecting four
metro cities — Delhi, Mumbai, Chennai, and Kolkata — has been completed;
and the residual 1716 km are under implementation. Another 1452 km of
highways and port connections have been 4-laned. However, even if one were

---

[s]In 1994, the waiting list for telephone connections was as high as 2.2 million or almost 31% of the total
installed base.
[t]Incidentally, despite the lowest rates per minute, the average revenue per subscriber is higher than that of
China's. Clearly, low rates promote lots of talk.

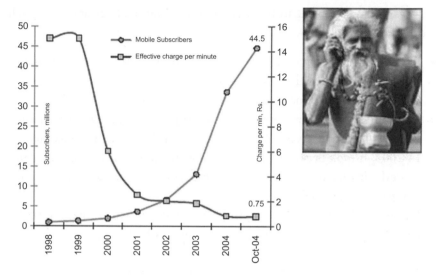

Fig. 11.   The progress of mobile telephony.

to limit oneself to 65,569 km of national highways, it has still left untouched 91% of the network.[u] As in everything in infrastructure, the scope is huge; and for four decades, it has been a road less traveled. Barring ports, where there have been significant reforms and a recent upsurge in private investments, the story is worse for other areas of infrastructure. Except legislating the more enabling Electricity Act in 2003, there has been hardly any movement in electricity generation and transmission. Much has been said about getting better airports, with little to show. And there has been neither reforms nor progress as far as Indian railways is concerned. Simply put, India is way behind the curve in infrastructure compared to South-East Asia and China.

As we saw in Section 1, despite these severe infrastructure handicaps, the corporate sector has performed very well, especially in the last four years. Yet, the overall investment climate — factors that foster domestic and foreign direct investment and better running of productive capacities — is still far from being anywhere close to best-in-class. In 2000 and 2003, the World Bank and the Confederation of Indian Industry (CII) conducted two major

---

[u] In contrast, China has built over 25,000 km of 4/6 lane access controlled expressways over the past 10 years.

surveys of manufacturing firms throughout the country. Here are some results worth reporting[v]:

- As of January 2004, it took an average of 89 days for Indian small companies employing no more than 50 people to obtain the necessary clearances to start business; in China it took 41 days; and in Malaysia, 30 days.
- The average time for completing bankruptcy liquidation formalities in courts is 10 years, versus 2.4 years in China and 2.3 years in Malaysia.
- In 2003, it took between 12 and 14% of Indian senior management time to deal with factory regulatory and inspection issues, excluding taxation, compared to 8% in China.
- Customs delays have reduced in India. In 2000, it took an average of 10 days to clear imports from customs; by 2003 it had fallen to 7 days. Even this, by any canon, is far too long.
- In 2003, it took an average of 48 days for a new manufacturing firm to get connected with the public electricity grid, which increased to 54 days for small firms located in smaller cities. In China it was 25 days, and in Brazil 23 days.
- Because of infrastructure bottlenecks, the average days of inventory of an Indian manufacturer was 33 days in 2003. In China it was 24, and in Brazil 20 days.
- In 2003, 61% of the sample of respondents reported having their own generators to mitigate the problems of power outages, compared to 27% in China, 20% in Malaysia and 17% in Brazil.
- In 2003, India's weighted average real cost of power (public grid plus generators) was 74% higher than Malaysia's and 39% more than China's.
- Despite having generators running at higher costs, Indian respondents claimed that over 8% of their output was lost due to power cuts, versus 2% in Brazil and 1.7% in China.

An interesting aspect of the 2003 study was a careful econometric counterfactual based on the estimates of total factor productivity. The question asked was: what would be the percentage increase in value added per worker if some of the infrastructure and investment climate barriers were to be removed? Not surprisingly, availability of power was the greatest constraint which, if

---

[v]Ref. 8.

removed, would raise the value added per worker by 79–85%. That gives a broad estimate of how much poor infrastructure holds back productivity and reduces India's investment climate vis-à-vis the rest of Asia.[w]

To return to the original question: have reforms reduced the hassles of doing business? A comparison between the investment climate surveys of 2003 and 2000 shows that there have been some improvements. In 2000, there were 11.7 inspections per manufacturing unit per year; this seems to have reduced to 7.4 — which is better than both Brazil (9.6 inspections) and China (36). Also, the number of days to clear imports from customs has fallen from over 10 to around seven, which again seems to be a bit better than both China and Brazil. However, the fact remains that India is still perceived as a country which has many more restrictions and hassles related to business compared to South-East Asia and China; this is not the perception of only foreign investors but is derived from responses of Indian factory managers; and it probably goes a long way to explain why, in its best year, India attracted just a bit over US$6 billion of FDI, while China regularly succeeds in getting well over US$50 million.

Part II: The Way Ahead

3. The Key Challenges

As mentioned in Section 1, India faces several challenges, of which I shall focus on three:

- The fiscal, or being able to control state and central government deficits while at the same time funding public expenditure that will aid growth.
- Infrastructure, or obtain the huge funds, including DFI, needed for infrastructure over the next decade in a milieu where the central and the state governments will not have enough revenue for such projects.
- The demography–education–empowerment challenge, or being able to ensure that a growing population of students and youth get the educational wherewithal and the economic empowerment to be a part of a knowledge-driven workforce.

---

[w] *Ibid.*, 51.

3.1. *The fiscal challenge*

The Union Budget 2005–2006 has been presented, and it is as good a document as any to outline the magnitude of the fiscal challenge. According to the revised estimates for 2004–2005, the central government collected Rs. 3009 billion as revenue receipts. Against this, it spent Rs. 3684 billion only on non-plan expenditure, comprising interest payments on past debt, defence, subsidies, wages and salaries to employees (excluding railways), pensions, and a few other not so significant heads. In other words, during 2004–2005, for every Rs. 100 the government earned by way of taxes, interest income and dividends from its state owned enterprises, it spent Rs. 122 on unproductive heads which would do little to create additional capital stock to enable future growth. Thus, every rupee of the Rs. 1374 billion it will have spent on plan expenditure — including Rs. 477 billion on capital account — will have come from borrowings of one form or another.

This is not an aberration of 2004–2005 brought about by the *tsunami*. Over the last two decades, non-plan expenditures have always mounted and have always been greater than revenue receipts. In fact, it is a vicious cycle: non-plan exceeds revenue, so the government has to borrow to bridge the gap and finance plan spending, which raises internal public debt and thus the future interest burden. Add to this the inability to downsize — wages, salaries and pensions of the central government, excluding the armed forces, accounts for 15% of non-plan expenditure and 18.3% of revenue[x] — and the increasing laundry list of expenditure heads of the more powerful coalition members of the government, and one can see a serious fiscal crisis in the offing.

The consequence has been burgeoning public debt. Today, the central government's public debt amounts to Rs. 19,812 billion (US$461 billion) or 64% of India's nominal GDP at market prices — of which 97% constitutes sovereign rupee debt. By March 31, 2006, it is estimated to grow by another 13%. This, of course, is an underestimate for it does not take into account

---

[x]Contrast this with the data on private sector manufacturing companies, where the wage, salary and superannuation costs have been steadily reduced from 8.1% of net sales in 1992–1993 to 5.5% in 2003–2004.

the borrowings of bankrupt state governments. If state debt is added to that of the center's, then the total public debt of India as a whole exceeds its GDP. In fact, the situation is worse. Since the mid-1990s, many states have circumvented even the limited budget constraints imposed by the centre by creating various corporatized special purpose vehicles (SPVs) for issuing state government guaranteed bonds. At present, these off-balance sheet liabilities are in excess of Rs. 2500 billion; and most such SPVs are in such precarious financial states, that much of these liabilities will eventually devolve to the state governments. So, if we add all these liabilities, the total public debt of India is probably in the region of 110% of its GDP. And the problem is that, unlike the US dollar, the rupee is not a global currency, thus preventing India from exporting its fiscal profligacy.

Clearly, there are only two ways of dealing with the problem: raising revenue without increasing rates, and reducing expenditure. The former is very much on the radar screen of all Finance Ministers, as it should be given that the tax to GDP ratio of the central government is a mere 9.9% — well below the target of at least 12%. A part of the problem is that, thanks to a Constitutional provision, agricultural income comprising 22% of GDP still remains untaxed by the sovereign. Another issue is that over the years there have been a plethora of tax exemptions for companies as well as individual. Thus, for instance, while the corporate tax rate was theoretically 35% up to 2004–2005, multiple exemptions coupled with high depreciation allowances led to an average tax liability of no more than 22% of PBT. Unfortunately, tax exemptions have lives of their own, and it is not easy to either eliminate or grandfather them in one fell swoop. Thus, while exemptions will decrease — more or less in line with what has been suggested by the Vijay Kelkar Committee Report[y] — it will take a while before most them disappear from the statute book.

The biggest lacuna, however, still happens to be tax compliance. While it has improved over the years, the tax administration has not been successful enough to catch the big fish. The IT systems in the revenue department are woefully behind the times; data cannot be tracked to develop tax intelligence and automated flags; and although the number of tax payers have increased

[y] Ref. 9.

substantially, the system is still not geared to catching tax evasion of traders and small and medium businesses.[z]

Another source of revenue for the government is through systematic privatization of its many SOEs. Unfortunately, political alignments of the present coalition government demands the support of 63 MPs belonging to the Left, which effectively eliminates all chances of outright privatization or sale of controlling equity to private players. The government is attempting to circumvent this by selling small lots of SOE shares, especially those of the banks, to the investing public and passing it off as limited divestment. Clearly, it is not the best strategy. Nevertheless, at current stock market values, even this ploy could garner sizeable resources.[aa] Although he has not taken any credit for it in his budget estimates, doubtless, this is what Finance Minister P. Chidambaram proposes to do in the next few years.

Even so, in an environment where finance ministers rightly speak of the importance of moderate tax rates, if tax revenues were not increase faster than normal growth in business and personal income, the government will always fall short of its expenditure needs. This is why the focus has to be on government expenditure. Unfortunately, it is an area which has not received the attention it deserves.

In part, this is because interest payments, the largest head of non-plan expenditure, offer precious little room for manoeuvre. As long as successive budgets run large fiscal and revenue deficits, public debt will increase and so too will interest payments. In a falling interest rate regime, this can be partially mitigated by the government's swapping high cost debt for lower interest bearing paper. But that would depend upon the desire of government security holders to agree to such swaps. Moreover, it can only dampen the growth in interest payouts, not reverse it.

---

[z]To give an example, something like 1% of India's urban population ought to be earning a taxable income of over Rs. 1 million per year. Had it been otherwise, one would not have seen an explosive growth in the market for cars, housing, tourism, and retail loans. Yet, less than 90,000 taxpayers submitted returns with taxable income of Rs. 1 million or more. If one nets out those who earned salaries — whose taxes are deducted at source — the compliance in this category has been woeful. There are, however, some signs of change. Last year, the government introduced a computerized Tax Information Network to be able to track, collate and cross check various tax transactions. Although the jury is out, hopefully the system will be able to plug loopholes and create a more efficient compliance mechanism.

[aa]At current stock valuations, the market capitalization of listed SOEs stands at Rs. 5483 billion. Even if the government were to sell an average of 2% of the shares every year, it could bring in Rs. 110 billion worth of additional resources to finance infrastructure and plan capital expenditure.

However, that kind of helplessness can hardly be said about subsidies — a huge fiscal burden of the government which is so inefficiently managed that they fail to reach most of people for whom they are targeted. In 2004–2005, subsidies accounted for Rs. 465 billion, or over 15% of the center's revenue receipts. Of this, food subsidies, administered via the public distribution system or "ration shops", comprised Rs. 258 billion, or 55% of the total. It is now well established that not even a fifth of this subsidy actually reaches the households below and marginally above the poverty line — for whom these are intended. Indeed, the government could easily halve this subsidy without affecting any outcome. Yet, it has become such a sacred cow, that no government can afford to scale it down without attracting vociferous protests from both the opposition as well as its alliance partners.

Fertilizer subsidies are another source of distortion. In 2004–2005, these accounted for Rs. 106 billion, or 23% of all subsidies. They serve two purposes: first, to give an implicit price support to fertilizer manufacturers; and second, to subsidise the use of urea by richer farmers. The outcome of decades of subsidies coupled with free power to farmers has been the excessive use of urea and ground water in Punjab, Haryana, and western Uttar Pradesh, which has lead to leaching of the soil and depleted water tables — which threaten long term agricultural productivity throughout northern India. However, this is also a political no–no.

The other two areas of non-plan expenditure which are rapidly spiralling out of control are wages and salaries of government employees and pensions. In March 2004 there were 3.3 million central government employees; instead of downsizing or even putting a cap on the number, the staff strength has increased by another 10,000 to 3.4 million employees. Wages and salaries of the central government excluding the armed forces account for over 12% of revenues; and the pension liability, excluding that of railways, has increased by 260% from Rs. 51 billion in 1996–1997 to Rs. 183 billion in 2004–2005.

Given the growth in life expectancy, pensions threaten to be one of the most disruptive influences in government budgets. To be fair, since the last year the government has initiated pensions reform which moves away from pay as you go assured benefits to fully funded assured contribution. This is certainly a step in right direction. However, the new scheme is applicable only to employees who entered the civil service on or after 2004; it does not cover existing government employees. It is, therefore, a partial solution; and unless a sizeable chunk of the pension liabilities of the pre-2004 employees is restructured away from assured benefits, the cost will still remain too high.

In the absence of any concerted political will to trim non-plan expenditure, one sees a peculiar form of fiscal perversion: that of reducing essential plan expenditure, especially on capital account which goes into building public infrastructure. For instance, while the budget estimate of plan capital expenditure for 2004–2005 was Rs. 537 billion, it was actually slashed to Rs. 477 billion. Worse still, the budgeted amount under this head for 2005–2006 is 42% lower at Rs. 275 billion.[bb] This lopsided expenditure structure — where government consumption takes substantial priority over public investments — is one of the most dangerous aspects of India's fiscal situation, and can severely constrain the growth of infrastructure, especially in areas which require major government intervention.

The fiscal challenge, therefore, is serious. In theory, this was explicitly recognized by the government when it notified the FRBM Act in 2004. According to the rules that cover the FRBM Act:

- Fiscal deficit has to be brought down by at least 0.3% of GDP every year, beginning with 2004–2005.
- Revenue deficit has to be reduced by at least 0.5% of GDP each year from 2004 to 2005.
- Progressive reduction of public debt as a share of GDP by at least 1% point per year from 2005 to 2006.
- No government guarantees in excess of 0.5% of GDP per year from 2004 to 2005.

The FRBM Act was notified by the present government in 2004. Yet, its non-plan expenditure compulsions are so strong — thanks to several items in its populist Common Minimum Program — that the Finance Minister has had to push back the goalpost by two years. To my mind this has at least two negative consequences for fiscal correction. First, it tells the world that the government which passed the Act is itself willing to renege on its provisions.

[bb]The government has done this by fobbing off Rs. 290 billion to the states, who are expected to raise this resource from market borrowings. Needless to say, given the bankruptcy of most states, they will not be able to raise the funds — at least at any affordable interest rate.

And second, it effectively signals to the states that they too need not impose any hard budget constraints.

Perhaps the one silver lining is that several, if not all, state governments have agreed to introduce a common state-level VAT from April 1, 2004.[cc] Although, this VAT scheme does not rank among the best in the world and will present many teething troubles in its first couple of years, it is still a step toward having a uniform value added tax structure, and ought to significantly reduce the cascading effects of multiple state-level levies.

There are no soft solutions to the fiscal challenge. At the end of the day, the central government will have to impose hard budget constraints on itself as well as the states. We will have to substantially increase tax compliance; consider a constitutional amendment to introduce agricultural income tax; and seriously curtail non-plan expenditure by gradually downsizing staff strength, cutting subsidies, and reducing defence spending. All of these require political consensus — which would be difficult to obtain within a fractious coalition and in a milieu where the economy is trotting along at 7% or more growth. The impetus to economize rarely comes in times of relative prosperity. Nevertheless, the fiscal challenge will have to be dealt with. After all, an immutable law of economics is that business cycles happen; and when it does, our fiscal profligacy may come home to roost. Logic dictates that corrective actions need to be taken in good times, for it may be too costly in the bad.

3.2. *The infrastructure challenge*

There is a "rough-and-ready" way of estimating the annual infrastructure needs for India. This involves projecting the country's GDP growth, and then attributing a certain "desirable" percentage of the GDP as the infra-structure requirement. The process is far from exact, but serves to give a very broad idea of the investment needs — if only to be a macro guidepost against which one can evaluate more detailed estimates. Assuming that (i) the average annual infrastructure investment needs vary from a low of 5% of GDP to a high of 7% and (ii) a nominal GDP growth rate of 12.5% per year going

---

[cc]Regrettably, the BJP which, while in power, did considerable groundwork on getting state-level consensus on VAT, adopted the worst aspect of opposition politics to publicly state that the five BJP-ruled states will not introduce VAT on April 1, 2005, and would not do so unless all other states agree to the VAT regime.

forward, the first-cut estimate of investments needed during the period 2001–2002 and 2010–2011 is between Rs. 17,967 billion and Rs. 25,154 billion at current prices (or US$418 billion to US$585 billion at an exchange rate of Rs. 43 = US$1).

It so happens that we do have more detailed sector-wise estimates of investment needs. In a study done for the World Bank, we looked at the investment required for roads, power, telecom, railways, ports, and airports.[dd] These are given in Table 4 below.

The total investment in these six sectors up to 2010–2011 amounts to Rs. 19,143 billion. If one were to add investments for the urban sector and the supply and distribution of water, the overall need would be in the region of Rs. 25,000 billion, or what corresponds to the rough estimate based on 7% of nominal GDP. As is evident, mobilizing the necessary funds presents a daunting challenge, especially given the fiscal situation of the land.

Financing can come from only two sources: central and state governments, and the private sector. If we assume for the moment that the provisions for gross budgetary support (GBS) and the internal and extra-budgetary resources (IEBR) of infrastructure SOEs as stated in the 10th and 11th Five-Year Plans are credible, then the difference between the investment requirement and the GBS under each of these infrastructure heads will be the amount that has to

Table 4. Overall investment needs in selected sectors, 2000–2001 to 2010–2011.

	Rs. billion
Roads*	4670
Power**	10,591
Telecommunications***	2143
Railways****	1242
Airports*****	191
Ports	306
Total	19,143

Notes: *: Including village roads and cost of maintenance; **: Up to 2011–2012; ***: Including investment in broadband; ****: The medium-to-high growth scenario of the Rakesh Mohan Expert Group; *****: As given by the Standing Committee of Parliament.

[dd] Ref. 10.

Table 5. Overall financing gap in infrastructure up to 2010–2011 (Rs. billion).

Sectors	Investment needed	Financing gap
Roads	4670	1106
Power	10,591	3500
Telecommunications	2143	478
Railways	1242	151
Airports	191	72
Ports	306	236
Total	19,143	5542

be funded by the private sector, comprising both domestic investments and FDI.[ee] Table 5 outlines the minimum financing gap that must be met by the private sector.

It would be a mistake to rank the challenges to resource mobilization merely in terms of the magnitude of the financing gaps. In some sectors, the gap can be filled by private sector more easily than in others. For instance, though the gap for telecoms is considerably larger than that for railways, under the present scenario it seems much more plausible to mobilize Rs. 478 billion of private investment for telecom than the Rs. 151 billion for railways.[ff]

Clearly, both the investment requirement and the financing gap are enormous. At present, banks and financial institutions tend to hold the view that there are no significant supply side issues for the funding infrastructure; that the real problem lies in the lack of properly appraised bankable projects; and that if such projects were to materialize, the funding could be available. This is perhaps the case today. But it is certainly not so if one were to look at infrastructure needs over a 10-year time horizon. Simply put, obtaining funds will be a major issue — and much of that will depend on India's success in having

---

[ee] In fact, it is a lower-bound private sector funding estimate, because it assumes that all *ex ante* GBS outlined in the 10th and 11th Plans will, in fact, be made available. As we know from the past, this is usually not the case.

[ff] In India, the two key issues which make some infrastructure sectors more attractive than others are the risks of uncertainty in demand and the degree of regulatory barriers. Thus, on one end of the spectrum, private sector investment in roads, greenfield ports and power are impeded by the traffic risks and risks of recovery, while on the other end private investment in sectors like airports and railways has fallen victim to regulatory barriers. The success in telecom has been possible due to a favourable mix of healthy demand and low regulatory barriers.

regimes, systems, and practices in place that consistently encourage PPP in infrastructure.

The extent to which long gestation infrastructure projects can look attractive to private investors depends upon their perceptions of risks. Global experience suggests that there are at least seven different types of risk which characterize most infrastructure projects:

- Public risks, involving political, administrative, legal, regulatory, and dispute resolution and enforcement mechanisms.
- Economic and financial risks, i.e., those dealing with interest rates, currency risks, and macroeconomic factors.
- Market risks, which concern traffic, revenue, and business model forecasts.
- Construction risk, or the problems associated with timely completion and *force majeure*.
- Operating and maintenance risks.
- Environment risks.
- The risk of public unacceptability of project features, such as levels of tariffs, the inability of government entities to levy appropriate user charges and the arbitrary actions of state governments as consumers.

India has been fortunate in the last half a decade to be relative immune to interest rate, currency and macroeconomic risks. Other than that, it has faced all other risks in some measure. Here, we will touch upon a few.

- *Wrong traffic projections*: For the annuity and BOT projects in roads, most traffic projections made by the best of independent consultants are way off the mark, and small revenue perturbations bring about sharp decline to their IRRs.[gg] If traffic projections for roads are difficult, those for ports, especially green-fields, is virtually impossible to estimate. While initial over-estimation tends to get dampened with experience, it still leads to an unintended harmful consequence. Lenders get over-cautious about all traffic projections and almost instinctively evaluate all projects by cutting down the revenue figures.

[gg]For instance, in case of the Delhi–Noida Flyover, traffic was initially overestimated to the tune of 50%. To be fair, overestimating traffic and revenue is a global phenomenon. For instance, the traffic on the toll highway between Mexico City and Acapulco via Cuernavaca was so grossly over estimated that the BOT project incurred severe losses for almost a decade, and needed to be renegotiated twice over.

This immediately increases project risk, reduces IRR and often makes the cost of funding so high as to scuttle the project.

- *Collection risks*: These can, and sometimes do, occur even in instances where the revenue is more or less correctly projected. They relate to cases where, because of political clout, consumers simply refuse to pay the appropriate charges. In India they occur quite frequently in the power sector with both the State Electricity Boards (SEBs) and some final consumers consistently refusing to pay their dues.

- *Arbitrary reneging of contracts*: The power sector in India has been plagued by this problem, with the Maharashtra SEB terminating its power purchase agreement (PPA) with Dabhol, followed by similar terminations in Andhra Pradesh and Karnataka. While Tamil Nadu does not actually terminate PPAs, it frequently threatens to do so with independent power producers whenever the latter try to press for payments. This arbitrary termination risk is extremely severe in India, especially given the precarious financial situation of most SEBs. The problem gets accentuated because most state governments' guarantees are not financially credible.

Almost all infrastructure projects in India suffer from unacceptable delays. Some of these relate to inadequate regulatory frameworks. However, much of it has to do with cascading level of inefficiencies across virtually all approving agencies. Here are some of these barriers:

- *Need for multiple permissions*: Infrastructure projects require multiple clearances at center, state and local levels. This is a time consuming process not only due to the sheer number of approvals but also because clearances are sequential, and not concurrent.[hh] Moreover, in spite of the theoretical concept of a single window clearance, state-level approvals require further clearances from *panchayat*s (village bodies), municipalities, forest departments, environment board, and so on, which cause further delays. According to most developers and financiers, the time taken to obtain all the requisite approvals for an infrastructure project can vary between a low of 18 months to as much as four–five years. Such delays place India very unfavorably compared to China and South-East Asia.

[hh] For example, when a company was setting up internet cafes in different states, it involved over 50 different clearances!

- *Lack of coordination between ministries*: Most infrastructure projects involve multiple ministries. One reason for projects not taking off at the pre-financing stage is that the actions and policies of different ministries are not coordinated and are often at variance with each other. This is particularly true for power, where even if the developer obtains the requisite permission for setting up of a generation facility, he finds it difficult to start operations because of lack of clearance for fuel supply, which involves two other ministries. Similar problems exist regarding the Ministry of Environment.
- *Delays in award of contract*: This is pervasive across all infrastructure sectors. For instance, Kakinada port in Andhra Pradesh took four years to achieve financial closure. Even a well run, relatively efficient organization like the National Highways Authority of India is now causing delays: for example, the bids for the first lot of NHDP III projects were received in March 2004, but have not been awarded till date.

Regulatory impediments vary considerably across sectors. In some, such as telecom, the obstacles and contradictions during the initial phase of the 1990s are things of the past. Through learning-by-doing, the Telecom Regulatory Authority of India has established itself as an efficient, fair, and independent regulator which has created a level playing field and fostered the rapid growth of telecom in India. In contrast, the regulatory environment in power leaves much to be desired; and as yet there is no independent regulatory institution in place for ports or airports. By way of illustration, let me touch upon the regulatory impediments in power.

The power sector probably has the worst regulatory regime, especially at the state government levels. For instance, while the SEBs have been unbundled into three distinct entities (generation, transmission, and distribution) that are supposed to be monitored and regulated by independent State Electricity Regulatory Commissions (SERCs), these are anything but independent. Most SERC members in any state are former employees of the SEBs that they are now expected to regulate. Moreover, the funding of an SERC comes from the state government. In most cases, the SERCs are legally and administratively weakened from inception, which allows large state utilities to remain unresponsive to their regulations.

In addition, while The Electricity Act, 2003 provides for non-discriminatory open access to transmission lines, there are serious regulatory concerns about state-owned transmission companies stifling competition by levying prohibitively high access charges between private sector generating companies and distribution entities. This has often been cited as a major regulatory risk that could prevent an active private sector market for the wheeling of power.

Moreover, as mentioned earlier, every power generation project is based upon fuel supply agreements, be it for coal or gas. Unfortunately, neither source of fuel falls within the domain of the Ministry of Power, and there have been serious delays in power projects because the promised fuel supply agreements have not materialized.

Finally, the financial credibility of almost all state government guarantees — an important condition for private sector involvement — is suspect. By March 2004, outstanding guarantees of all state governments were as high as Rs. 1842 billion or 7.5% of GDP. In addition, the estimated commercial losses of the SEBs in 2002–2003 were approximately Rs. 330 billion. Consequently, there have instances of states reneging on escrows as well as PPAs. Even more serious are cases where SEBs have unilaterally reneged on contractually obligated PPAs. The most widely reported instance is that Maharashtra SEB vis-à-vis the Dabhol project. In addition, there have been PPA reneging and termination in Karnataka and Andhra Pradesh. Tamil Nadu *de facto* reneges very frequently, simply because no independent power producer has the gumption to risk the wrath of the state government by cashing in the guarantees and letters of credit.

The biggest challenge in infrastructure is to create an environment where it is universally treated as one of the nation's most urgent priority. The task is enormous: a huge investment need vis-à-vis inadequate fiscal resources, which requires fostering a policy and procedural environment to actively encourage PPPs. That needs a radically new approach to infrastructure — one that moves away from permissions and delays to regimes that actively woo investments and recognize the opportunity cost of time. To give it the importance that infrastructure deserves, there has to be a clear signal that the ownership lies at the highest level of government. This is not yet the case either in Delhi or most of the state capitals. It would help if, for instance, the Prime Minister's office (PMO) created a dedicated infrastructure secretariat not only to monitor the status of projects in different sectors but also convene quarterly meetings between the Prime Minister and those of his cabinet colleagues in charge of infrastructure ministries. This secretariat could ensure consistency in policy formulation and implementation for various infrastructure sectors, and would liaise with various government agencies to present a single window clearance to the private sector.[ii] This act would certainly demonstrate the government's focused commitment to infrastructure. Finally, however, just having a secretariat in the PMO will not suffice. At the end of it all, it has to be a story of raid implementation — for which both central and state governments need to demonstrate that they follow Nike's maxim: "Just do it".

3.3. *The demography and education challenge*

It has been often said by that one of India's great strength is its young population. The argument goes thus: unlike Europe, Japan and most parts of the developed world, over the next 50 years India will have a much higher percentage of its population comprising young people. Because youth have greater learning potential and constitute the bulk of the job market, India will therefore be the world's greatest source of labor — both for manufacturing as well as services. In fact, proponents of this view argue that since our demographic constellation is even better placed than China's, by the fourth decade of this century we will begin to capture an ever increasing share of the global labor market.

The demographics is correct, as Fig. 12 shows. According the Ref. 11 some 375 million Indians (or 37% of the total) were in the age group of 20–44 — which could classify as the younger working population. By 2050, this group would have increased to 549 million people. In contrast, China's younger

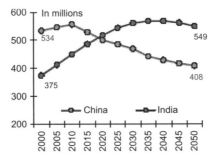

Fig. 12.   Young workforce.

[ii]This should be replicated in some of the key state governments.

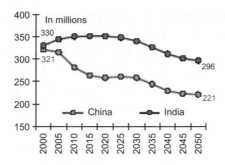

Fig. 13. Student population.

working population would decline from 534 million in 2000 to 408 million in 2050. By 2020, India will have more people belonging to this group than China. The size of this young potential workforce of India will be the largest ever in the world.

While the demography is true enough, the inference need not be. To understand that, let us focus on Fig. 13. In 2000, India's student population (from 5 to 19) accounted for 321 million, or 32% of the total. By 2050, it will have marginally declined to 296 million or almost 19% of the total. Thanks to the "one child policy" China's fall will be much sharper — from 321 million in 2000 to 221 million in 2050. In the knowledge age that we speak of, India's large working young working population requires to be educationally empowered to have a fair chance of being actually employed.

That's where the evidence starts getting worrisome. Consider the latest data on education based on the Seventh All-India School Educational Survey of 2002. Here is some of the evidence:

- Only 53% of rural habitations in India have primary schools, i.e., serving classes 1–5. Orissa, Jammu and Kashmir, Bihar, Assam, Uttar Pradesh, West Bengal, and Himachal Pradesh are below the national average.
- Only 18% of rural India has upper primary schools which are supposed to teach classes 6–8. Jammu and Kashmir, Tamil Nadu, Assam, Uttar Pradesh, Bihar, Himachal Pradesh, and West Bengal are below the average.
- Merely 18% of primary schools in rural India have four or more teachers.
- There are less than 64,000 secondary schools in rural India, which are supposed to teach classes 9 and 10; and there are fewer than 23,000 higher secondary schools, which teach classes 11 and 12.

I could give you more data, but it is not necessary. What becomes apparent is that, at present, India just does not have the basic school and college infrastructure in place throughout vast swathes of the land to educationally empower the over 330 million children of ages 5–19. In such a scenario, it is unlikely that the younger working population will get the jobs to be a part of the younger workforce that is expected to the largest and most competitive in the world.

To me, this is India's greatest developmental challenge. How can we put mechanisms in place that will meaningfully educate over a third of a billion people, so that they can have the basic wherewithal to be a part of tomorrow's workforce? Given the sheer numbers on the one hand, and the pitiful finances as well as governance of most states on the other, it is self-evident that the traditional brick-and-mortar school system will not suffice. States will neither have the resources to open new schools, nor to staff them with competent teachers. India will soon have to adopt an entirely different approach to education.

Such a paradigm will necessarily have to incorporate significantly greater private sector participation and harness the power of IT to supplement inadequate school teaching with more interactive learning. This, in turn, will need major growth in broadband connectivity — initially to the better-off districts and then moving down the line. One has to visualize a system where, to begin with, a fourth of India's 587,250 villages must get stable electricity supply, broadband connectivity, and at least four school computers apiece; where interactive courses prepared by both state and private sector players are piped through these channels; where certification by the interactive, web-based education providers will carry at least as much weight as school and college degrees.

Although the task is enormous, it can be a viable, scalable, volume-based business model. Suppose, by 2010, a distance education company succeeded in locking 5% of the student population into various interactive educational and vocational training modules, at an average price of Rs. 50 per student per month. It would earn Rs. 10.5 billion in revenues (17.5 million students × Rs. 600 per year). It ought to be a profitable business for two reasons: first, creating the various interactive models will constitute a relatively small fixed cost; and second, making these available to students would be based on extremely low marginal costs. The reason why such distance education models have not yet occurred in India has to do with broadband connectivity. Thankfully, this is changing, and broadband is being rolled out at a fairly rapid rate. If the access charges were to be reasonable — as they have been under the regulatory guidance of TRAI — then one could see the growth of large, scalable, nationwide distance education corporations.

At present, all this looks like a distant dream. But it is possible, and has to be done as a key priority. Because the choice is simple: either India's mushrooming youth will be educationally empowered enough to join the global labor force and reap the benefits, or it will revolt at its fate. Political enfranchisement without sufficient economic benefits cannot be a sustainable democratic solution. Less so with youth. For the sake of the polity of India, therefore, we had better focus on newer models of imparting education and training.

4. Even so, Elephants can Dance...

As we have seen, India has progressed significantly since the beginning of reforms in 1991. Equally, the country has miles to go before it can be considered a modern, globalized economy. There are problems with India's fiscal deficits; its infrastructure — physical as well as social — is still considerably below ASEAN and even China's levels; and it has to surmount a major challenge of educationally empowering its youth so as to enable it join the knowledge-driven workforce that is expected of any global major of tomorrow.

And yet, the country presents huge opportunities for investment and growth, which are best summarized by Fig. 14 below.

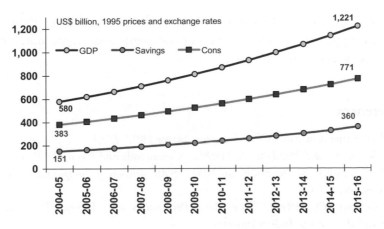

Fig. 14. Market size and savings.

If one were to assume just that much of infrastructure investments to sustain an average growth of 7% per year up to 2015–2016 — something that most economists believe is quite doable for the country — then India's real GDP at 1995 prices and exchange rates will increase from US$580 billion in 2004–2005 to US$1221 billion in 2015–2016. The market — defined as final consumption — will rise from US$383 billion to US$771 billion. And the nation's domestic savings will grow from US$151 billion to $360 billion.

If this process is set in play, the savings rate will gradually increase from 26 to 29% of GDP; and the gross domestic investment rate will have to rise from 28 to 33% of GDP. Hence, there will be widening gap between investment needs and domestic savings, which will need to be met by foreign direct as well as portfolio investments. According to this simulation, foreign investment needs will steadily rise from US$12 billion in the base year to around US$49 billion per year by 2015–2016.

To me, this is a fairly reasonable projection, which can be attained with relatively unspectacular but steady reforms. If it were so, investors would be looking at a market of US$771 billion, and financial institutions will be wanting to leverage the savings of $360 billion. No doubt, China will be way ahead. But given that only China, India, and Brazil can offer such markets, the investment choices will involve all or at least two of three. Which would validate a little known fact of animal behavior — that elephants, too, can dance.

Acknowledgments

I am very grateful to Himanshu Saxena, a colleague at CERG Advisory for research support and critical views. For comments and suggestions, contact omkar.goswami@cergindia.com.

References

1. Government of India GOI, *Economic Survey 1992–1993*.
2. Mohan, R. and Vandana, A. (1990). "Commands and Controls: Planning for Indian Industrial Development, 1951–1990." *Journal of Comparative Economics* 144, 681–713.
3. Goswami, O. (1991). "The Many Perversities of a Licence Raj." Mimeo: Confederation of Indian Industry.

4. Anant, T.C.A. and Goswami, O. (1995). "Getting Everything Wrong: India's Policies Regarding 'Sick' Firms." In: Mookherjee (ed.), *Indian Industry: Policies and Performance*. Oxford: Oxford University Press, pp. 236–288.

5. Centre for Monitoring the Indian Economy CMIE, *Prowess: The Database on Indian Companies*.

6. CERG Advisory (2005). "India: Economic Update," 12, forthcoming.

7. Goswami, O., Bijapurkar, R., More, V. and Narang, S. (2005). "The Changing Character of Rural India." Mimeo: ICICI Bank.

8. The World Bank 2004, *India: Investment Climate Assessment*.

9. Government of India GOI, Ministry of Finance and Company Affairs 2002, *Report of the Task Force on Direct Taxes*.

10. Goswami, O. and Saxena, H. (2005). "India: Addressing Supply Side Constraints to Infrastructure Financing." Mimeo: The World Bank.

11. United Nations Population Division, *Demography Estimates, 2000–2050*.

12. Government of India, GOI, *Census of India, 1991* and *2001*.

13. Government of India GOI, Central Statistical Organisation, *National Income Estimates*.

14. The World Bank, *World Development Indicators*, successive issues.

15. The World Bank, *World Development Report*, successive issues.

SECTION 2

Social Security and Governance

CHAPTER 5

Rebuilding China's Social Safety Net: Why Governance Matters

Minxin Pei

1. Introduction

Among the challenges facing China in its transition from state socialism to a market economy, the reform of its social security system in general, and of its old-age insurance system in particular, must rank as one of the most difficult, both in political and economic terms.[a] The rebuilding of China's social safety net in the era of economic reform has four essential objectives: successfully restructuring state-owned enterprises (SOEs), increasing labor mobility, improving the long-term financial solvency of the country's old-age social security system, and ensuring political stability.[b] Precisely because of the critical importance of reforming the old-age social security system, the Chinese government has attached enormous political importance to this task and, since the late 1990s, has launched a series of major reforms to rebuild a viable old-age social security system. The new Chinese leadership, which assumed power in late 2002, has also demonstrated its commitment to rebuilding China's social safety net. One of the most significant steps taken by China's new leaders was to pass a constitutional amendment in March 2004 which declares that "the state establishes and perfects a social security system that is appropriate to the level of economic development."

---

[a]Three terms — basic retirement system, old-age pension system, and social security system — are used interchangeably in this paper because they refer to the same thing.

[b]See Martin Feldstein, "Social Security Pension Reform in China" (NBER Working Paper 6794, 1998), p. 1; the World Bank, *Old Age Security: Pension Reform in China* (Washington: The World Bank, 1997); the World Bank, *China Pension System Reform* (Beijing: The World Bank Mission, 1996); Chatherine Finer, ed., *Social Policy Reform in China Views from Home and Abroad* (Aldershot: Ashgate, 2003).

Few would dispute the overwhelming need for reforming the social security system that has existed in China since the 1950s. Centered on SOEs, China's old social security system (which provided old-age pensions, health insurance, and other benefits) has grown increasingly unsustainable after the introduction of market-oriented reforms in the late 1970s, as its financial performance deteriorated due to rising competition, poor management, outdated technologies, and escalating pension expenses.[c] More important, the absence of an adequate social safety net also has become a key obstacle to restructuring SOEs because, without such a safety net that could provide a minimal level of social benefits for laid-off workers, reforming SOEs would become socially inequitable and politically destabilizing. Indeed, the state's failure to make pension payments to retirees in shuttered SOEs in the late 1990s caused labor unrest in urban areas, especially in cities hit hard by mass bankruptcies of SOEs.[d] The need to extend the social security system beyond SOEs is further underscored by the rapid expansion of employment in the non-state sector and the relative shrinkage of the state sector. Indeed, in 1989, SOEs employed 101 million workers, while private firms had only 21.4 million workers; but by 2003, the number of workers in SOEs fell to 68.7 million, while that in private and foreign firms reached 89 million, overtaking the employment in the state sector.[e] Unlike workers in SOEs and collective firms, employees in non-state firms (which include Chinese-foreign joint-ventures, wholly owned foreign firms, private firms, township-village enterprises, and businesses owned by self-employed individuals) are not covered by the pre-existing social security system.

Rapid urbanization since the late 1970s has added new urgency to the task of establishing a more encompassing social safety net for the Chinese population. The pre-existing social security system covers only residents in the urban areas, but not the vast rural areas where the majority of the Chinese people reside. Between 1979 and 2003, more than 93 million rural residents have joined the urban labor force, and an additional 40 million peasants have lost their land due to the acquisition of land for commercial development. An

---

[c]Loraine, W. (1999). "Pension Reform in China: Preparing for the Future." *The Journal of Development Studies* 35(3), 153–183; the World Bank, *Old Age Security: Pension Reform in China*, pp. 3–4.

[d]William, H. and Kevin O'Brien (2002). "China's Contentious Pensioners." *The China Quarterly* 170, 345–367.

[e]*Zhongguo tongji nianjian 2004*, pp. 122, 134, 148.

estimated 130 million peasants have also become employees in township and village enterprises. Altogether, 260 million rural peasants have effectively left the land, which provided the ultimate social safety net under the old system. These newly urbanized rural residents, as well as 200–300 million peasants that are expected to become urbanized between 2000 and 2020, are one of the most critical challenges facing the Chinese government in its efforts to sustain economic modernization and social stability.[f]

The ageing of the Chinese population in general, and the rising retiree-to-worker ratio in particular, has put new financial strains on China's under-funded pay-as-you-go (PAYGO) old-age pension system. More than 10% of the Chinese population were 60 years old and above in 2003, making China an ageing society by international standards. In rich Western countries, it took 40 years for the share of those aged 60 years old and above to climb from 5 to 10% of the population. But in China, this process has taken only 18 years. Indeed, China is "getting old before getting rich." At the current rate of ageing, according to the Ministry of Labor and Social Security (MLSS), the dependency ratio will be 0.5 in urban areas by 2030. The ageing of the Chinese population is also reflected in the falling worker-to-retiree ratio. The rapid growth of retirees, currently at 6% a year, is the principal cause of the decline. In 1978, the worker-to-retiree ratio was 30 to 1. It fell to 3.5 to 1 in 2000 and to 3.3 to 1 in 2003. Falling worker-to-retiree ratio is financially costly to the pension system. When the ratio fell from 4 to 1 in 1998 to 3.3 to 1 in 2003, the gap between pension contributions and pension expenditures grew from 10 billion yuan a year to 40 billion yuan a year, a 300% increase.[g] With the increase of the number of retirees from 3 million to close to 39 million in 2000, China's pension expenditures correspondingly grew, especially

---

[f]Zheng Silin (2004). "Laodong he shehui baozhang gaige de xingshi yu renwu" (The situation and tasks of reforming the labor and social security systems). *Zhonggong zhongyang danxiao baogao xuan* (The Communist Central Party School Reports), 6, 23–24.

[g]Zheng Silin, "Laodong he shehui baozhang gaige de xingshi yu renwu," p. 23. It is important to note the regional differences in the dependency ratio. In 1999, the ratio was 11.2 nationally, but some areas, such as Xinjiang and Ningxia, had much lower ratios (about 6.7–6.9) while provinces such as Jiangsu and Zhejiang, had much higher ratios (around 14). Shanghai had the highest dependency ratio (19). The ratio of worker-to-retiree also differed. The national ratio in 1999 was 3.2, but Shanghai's ratio was 1.93, and Liaoning's ratio was 2.7. By comparison, Shandong's ratio was 4.57, and Henan's ratio was 4.61. Peter Whiteford (2003). "From Enterprise Protection to Social Protection: Pension Reform in China." *Global Social Policy* 3, 57.

Table 1. Number of retirees and worker-to-retiree ratio, 1978–2000.

Year	1978	1982	1986	1990	1994	1998	2000
Number of retirees (mill.)	3.1	11.1	18.1	23.0	29.3	35.9	38.8
Worker-to-retiree	30:1	10:1	7:1	6:1	5:1	4:1	3.5:1

Source: Zheng Gongcheng, *Zhongguo shehui baozhang zhidu bianqian yu pinggu* (The evolution of China's social security system: an assessment) (Beijing: Zhongguo renmin daxue chubanshe, 2003), p. 423.

in the 1990s. In 1989, retirement pensions amounted to 0.70% of GDP. By 1999, pensions cost the government 2.35% of GDP (Table 1).[h]

Because the old PAYGO system accumulated no surpluses, rising dependency ratio and falling worker-to-retiree ratio would cause China's long-run pension liabilities or implicit pension debt (IPD) to rise even further, eventually forcing the government to raise pension contribution rates, seek other forms of financing, or reduce benefits. A World Bank study in 1997 estimated that, without reform, China would have to force employers and workers to contribute close to 40% of the total wage bill to fund the PAYGO system in 2033.[i] Even such high contribution rates would not solve the problem of China's ballooning implicit pension debt. Estimates of China's IPD vary. A World Bank study put it in the range of 46–69% of GDP in 1994.[j] Compared with both developing and industrialized countries, China's IPD was actually not excessively large (Table 2). It was half the size of that of Brazil, Hungary and Poland and almost the same as that of Argentina.

However, China has had a wind of opportunity to implement far-reaching reforms to address its looming pension crisis. China's high economic growth has created profitable investment opportunities for pension funds to accrue capital gains. High growth has given the government the chance to allocate more fiscal resources to finance the transition costs. In addition, the massive shift of rural labor into urban areas has brought a younger workforce into the social security system, which could generate new resources to finance pension

---

[h] Whiteford, "From Enterprise Protection to Social Protection," p. 54. Although many retirees did not receive their pension benefits in the late 1990s, official figures showed that pension arrears were relatively small in financial terms, although 10 percent of the retirees were affected. In 1997, unpaid pensions amounted to 3.75 billion yuan (3 percent of total pension outlays) and affected 2.4 million retirees (ten percent of total retirees). Gao Shusheng (2003). "Changhuan yanlaojin zhaiwu de xinshilu" (New ideas on paying off pension debts). *Shehui baoxian yanjiu* (Social Insurance Research) **3**, 3.
[i] The World Bank, *Old Age Security: Pension Reform in China*, pp. 3–4.
[j] The World Bank, *Old Age Security: Pension Reform in China*, p. 32.

Table 2. Implicit pension debt as a percentage of GDP in selected countries (at the time of pension reform).

Country	Mexico (1995)	Argentina (1995)	China (1998)	US (1993)	Japan (1993)	Brazil (1995)	Hungary (1995)	Poland (1995)
IPD as % of GDP	42	86	94	113	162	187	213	220

Source: Yan Wang *et al.*, "Implicit Pension Debt, Transition Cost, Options and Impact of China's Pension Reform" (World Bank Policy Research Working Paper, 2000), pp. 11–12.

expenditures.[k] Apparently aware of both the risks of inaction and the closing window of opportunity for reform, the Chinese government began to adopt a series of major pension reforms in the late 1990s.

In the rest of this paper, I will first detail the measures implemented by the Chinese government since 1997 to reform its old-age social security system. I will then analyze their achievements and limitations. I will conclude with some tentative theoretical observations on why governance — which is broadly defined here as institutional mechanisms designed to allocate political authority, enforce accountability, and minimize opportunism — is a crucial variable in explaining these achievements and limitations.

2. Pension Reform: Process, Achievements, and Limits

Although the Chinese government, under the energetic leadership of then Premier Zhu Rongji, launched a concerted national effort in 1997 to implement a structural pension reform plan based largely on the "three-pillar" model advocated by the World Bank, pension reform in China actually began, albeit with bottom-up experimental approaches and little sustained top-down guidance or pressure, soon after economic reform began in 1979.[l] As early as 1984, several provinces began to experiment with the pooling of retirement funds at the city or county level in order to move away from the enterprise-based old pension system. In 1986, the central government, for the first time, called for the establishment of "a social security system that is appropriate to the

---

[k] The World Bank, *Old Age Security: Pension Reform in China*, pp. 9–10.

[l] The World Bank's three pillar model includes the first pillar (mandatory basic benefit), the second pillar (mandatory fully funded individual accounts) and the third pillar (supplementary individual accounts). See the World Bank, *Old Age Security: Pension Reform in China*, p. 7.

new conditions," but did not follow up with any specific reform measures. In June 1991, the State Council issued *"Guanyu qiye zhigong yanglao baoxian zhidu gaige de jueding"* (decision on reforming the old-age pension system for enterprise workers), an official directive assigning the responsibility of pension management to three ministries. The Ministry of Labor was tasked to administer the pension system of SOEs. The Ministry of Personnel was given the responsibility of managing the pension system for civil servants. The Ministry of Civil Affairs was put in charge of providing social assistance for the poor. However, the State Council took no substantive steps to further pension reform. The first genuine measure of pension reform adopted by the central government was the establishment, authorized by the State Council in late 1993, of pension fund pools for eight industrial sectors, thus initiating the long-delayed reform of the old-age social security system. Soon afterward, with the issuance of the State Council's "Directive on deepening the reform of the old-age pension system for enterprise workers" (*Guanyu shenhua qiye zhigong yanglao baoxian zhidu gaige de tongzhi*) in March 1995, Beijing began to push for the implementation of a new mixed model of social security that combined social pooling with individual accounts. The 1995 directive led to various forms of experimental social security reforms adopted by local governments throughout China.

By all accounts, the most significant and coherent social security reform occurred with the promulgation of the State Council's "Decision on establishing a unified basic old-age pension system for enterprise workers" (*Guanyu jianli tongyi de qiye zhigong jiben yanglao baoxian zhidu de jueding*) in July 1997. This document introduced broad national standards, called for provincial pooling, individual accounts, and restricted investment options for pension funds. As a result, China's "basic retirement system" (*jiben yanglao baoxian tixi*) came into being. Less than a year after this document was issued, the Ministry of Labor and Social Security (MLSS) was established in March 1998 to implement the pension reforms. In July 1998, the State Council announced the decision to establish provincial pension pools and to transfer industrial sectors' pension pools to provincial governments. In an effort to accumulate surpluses to cover pension shortfalls, the government established, in September 2000, the National Social Security Fund, which is charged with managing pension assets for the national social pool (even though China formally does not have national pooling). By the end of 2002, the fund had assets of 124 billion yuan.

Table 3. Number of participants in the basic retirement system, 1989–2003.

Year	1989	1992	1995	1998	2001	2003
No. of participants (mill)	48.2	77.7	87.4	84.8	108.0	116.5

Source: Zhongguo tongji nianjian 2004, p. 896.

Despite the steady rise of participants in the newly reformed pension system (Table 3), the series of reforms adopted after 1997 encountered numerous problems in implementation (such as high contribution rates, low coverage, un-funded individual accounts, and mismanagement of pension assets). In response, in December 2000, the State Council circulated a draft plan on further improving the urban social security system through pilot projects, *"Guanyu yingfa wanshan chengzheng shehui baoxian tixi shidian fangan de tongzhi"* (on circulating a directive on perfecting urban social security system through pilot projects). The proposed reforms included a strict separation of social pooling from individual accounts, and separate management of the social pool and individual accounts. Individual accounts were to be fully funded, and retirement funds could be invested in capital markets. The pilot project was implemented in Liaoning province in July 2001.

Generally speaking, three distinct phases marked China's experience in reforming its old-age pension system. During the first phase (1986–1993), the government treated this reform as part of the restructuring of SOEs and, consequently, did not prioritize it politically or take substantive reform measures. The second phase (1994–1997) may be considered the prelude to the adoption of real reforms. During this period, a new old-age pension system was viewed as one of the key components of a market economy, and experimental reforms were introduced. The third phase, which marked the Chinese government's most systematic and ambitious efforts to tackle the pension challenge, began with the issuance of the milestone decision in July 1997 and continues today.[m] In the following sections, I analyze the specific reform measures adopted during the third phase and evaluate whether the actual implementation of the reform in the subsequent years achieved the primary goals set out in the 1997 reform package. The specific measures include social pooling, unification,

---

[m] Zheng Gongcheng (2003). "Shehui baozhang zhidu gaige bixu queli gongping de jiazhi quxiang" (Reform of the Social Security System must be based on the Orientation of the Values of Equity). *Shehui baoxian yanjiu* 1, 1.

expanded coverage, multi-pillars (basic pension, enterprise supplemental pension, individual savings), and separation of administrative responsibility from asset management.[n]

2.1. *Social pooling and unification*

The 1997 reform package aimed at achieving, among other things, two important goals: the social pooling of pension funds and the unification of standards regarding contribution rates and management of funds. Clearly, social pooling is a defining characteristic of a modern old-age pension system because, through the pooling of pension contributions, governments can ensure the socialization of old-age risks and equity across regions and social strata. To be sure, local governments in China began limited social pooling before 1997. Four provinces established provincial pooling in the 1980s, and nine others set up provincial pooling in the early 1990s. The remaining 18 provinces began to practice provincial pooling after the issuance of the State Council Directive No. 28 in 1998, which ordered provincial pooling. National pooling might be the most desirable way of financing a country's pension system because excess contributions from richer provinces can be used to fund shortfalls in poorer ones. For example, in 1998, 21 provinces reported pension deficits.[o] In 2000, seven provinces — Beijing, Shanghai, Guangdong, Jiangsu, Shandong, Zhejiang, and Fujian — accounted for 62% of the accumulated pension surpluses in China, even though their retirees were only 35% of the national retiree population.[p] In 1998, a few wealthy provinces had accumulated much larger surpluses in their retirement funds than poorer provinces. Two centrally administered municipalities and four coastal provinces (Beijing, Shanghai, Zhejiang, Shandong, Guangdong, and Jiangsu) accounted for one-third of the accumulated 70 billion yuan in pension fund surpluses. In contrast, the other 25 provinces had much smaller surpluses, and many would have run deficits without the

---

[n] Chen Jiagui (2002). *Zhongguo shehui baozhang fazhan baogao 1997–2001* (*Report on the Development of the Social Security System*). Beijing: *Shehui wenxian chubanshe*, pp. 58–59.
[o] Gao Shusheng, "Changhuan yanlaojin zhaiwu de xinshilu," p. 9.
[p] Hu Xiaoyi (2002). "Cong tongfeng hunhe zouxiang tongfeng jiehe" (From a Mixed Model to a Unified Model). *Shehui Baoxian Yanjiu* 3, 4.

central government's fiscal subsidies.[q] But under the current system, China lacks a functioning political mechanism that can transfer substantial financial resources from richer provinces to poorer ones without severe negative political and economic repercussions. In this context, provincial pooling should be considered a significant improvement in strengthening the financing of the pension system, socialising retirement risks, and reducing administrative costs. Given the poor state of public finance and the deficient administrative capacity of China's local governments (mainly counties and cities), provincial pooling represents an important step in the right direction.

The problem is, however, that the progress toward this sub-optimal solution, provincial pooling, has been halting and uneven. Due to the large size of Chinese provinces (each of which can be a medium-to-large-sized country if they were nation-states), economic conditions differ significantly even within the same province, and wealthier local jurisdictions have no incentives to transfer their surpluses to subsidize less wealthy jurisdictions. Thus, intra-provincial pooling has encountered strong resistance. Several years after Beijing managed provincial pooling, only four provinces (Fujian, Shanghai, Beijing, and Tianjin) had set up genuine provincial-level pension pools, while the other 27 provinces established only "redistribution fund" — a system that allows the provincial government to negotiate with cities about the latter's contribution to the provincial pool. Thus, social pooling in most provinces continues to be limited to individual counties or cities. Within provinces, the absence of pooling means cities with deficits cannot expect to get transfers from cities with surpluses. For example, in 1997, Liaoning recorded a pension fund surplus of 3.5 billion yuan, but the province actually had unpaid pensions totaling 800 million yuan (350 million yuan alone in Shenyang, the provincial capital). Meanwhile, the city of Dalian, which is part of Liaoning, had a surplus of 1.6 billion yuan. The provincial government of Liaoning could not touch the surplus. Such evidence indicates that China's efforts to set up provincial pools have largely failed.[r]

---

[q] Jiang Chunze and Li Nanxiong (2002). "Zhongguo yanglao baoxian shengji tongchou yihou de maodung fengxi yu duice yanjiu" (The Contradictions following the Provincial Pooling of Old-Age Pension Insurance: Analysis And Policy Options). *Gaige* (Reform), p. 95.

[r] Mark Frazier, "After Pension Reform: Navigating the 'Third Rail' in China," *Studies in Comparative International Development*, Summer 2004 39(2), pp. 51–54. Gao Shusheng, "Changhuan yanlaojin zhaiwu de xinsilu," p. 3.

The situation has not improved since the central government ordered provincial pooling. In 2002, among China's 31 provinces, four did not have deficits, and 27 provinces reported deficits totaling 41 billion yuan. Only four of the 27 deficit-incurring provinces had implemented provincial pooling. Of the 23 provinces with deficits but that had no real provincial pooling, the size of the pension gap in 2002 was 34.9 billion yuan (about 24% of their pension expenditures that year). But, the same 24 provinces reported that they were carrying accumulated pension surpluses totaling 41.8 billion yuan. This shows that the within the same deficit-incurring provinces, some cities and counties had surpluses while others had deficits, and the provincial governments were unable to pool these funds. Studies show that, on average, provincial governments directly controlled, in 2002, only about 45% of the surplus pension funds and 40% of current-year pension income (contributions and fiscal subsidies) in their jurisdictions.[5]

Another important step taken by the Chinese government toward social pooling has been to merge the so-called "sector pension funds" — pools of retirement savings accumulated by 11 industrial sectors controlled by the state (such as banking, aviation, energy, petroleum, coal, and others) — into provincial pools. Two considerations drove Beijing's decision to force this merger. First, it would simplify administration. Second, it would strengthen provincial pools because these industries, mostly monopolistic sectors, could deliver stronger financial performances and make more contributions. Most important, the Ministry of Finance estimated that the accumulated pension surpluses in these sector funds were as much as 12.8 billion yuan, a sum equivalent to almost one-third of the central government's annual pension subsidies to provincial governments. Transferring this pool of savings to provinces would help shore up their pension balance sheets. Thus, the State Council, in a rare forceful move, succeeded in completing the merger between the 11 sector funds and provincial pools within 8 days in August 1998.

Unfortunately, the State Council was subsequently out-manoeuvred by the bureaucrats managing the sector funds. Instead of transferring all the pension savings in these sector funds to provincial pools, the managers rushed to spend nearly all the savings by offering generous retirement benefits and allowing a

---

[5]Hu Xiaoyi (2004)."Guanyu zhubu tigao yanglao baoxian tongchou cengci" (On Gradually Raising the Level of Pooling in Old-Age Social Security). *Zhongguo shehui baoxian* (Chinese Social Insurance) 1, 19–20.

very large number of workers to retire early. According to provincial data, during the 8 months in early 1998 before the merger, the 11 sectors recorded almost 800,000 new retirees; 438,000 of them (55%) had been given early retirement in violation of government regulations. Of the 12.8 billion yuan in pension surpluses accumulated by the sectors, only 3.4 billion yuan was turned over to the Ministry of Finance, and 600 million yuan was transferred to provincial pools. Altogether, the sectors managed to spend two-thirds of their surpluses within 8 months.[t]

Another crucial task in implementing social pooling is to expand coverage. Because of the emergence of dynamic non-state firms that have become principal sources of employment generation, extending coverage into the non-state sector could tap into the contributions of a younger workforce and strengthen the financing of the social pool. Extending the coverage to the majority of the labor force in urban areas alone could help plug the hole in pension financing. For example, if 90% of the 170 million employees in urban areas in 1999 had been enrolled in the old-age pension system and 90% of the participants actually contributed to the social pool according to the 28% rate, the total social insurance premium contributions would have ranged between 373 and 407 billion yuan. However, in 1999, the total social insurance premium contributions actually collected was 221 billion yuan, which was only 54–59% of the premiums that ought to have been collected.[u] Including the estimated 200 million workers in TVEs and migrant laborers in the pension system would simply produce significant new contributions. If all of them were to be covered by the system, they could contribute at least 144 billion yuan a year and close the yearly pension financing gap.[v]

Many factors have hindered the government's efforts to expand coverage among non-state firms. Private entrepreneurs, self-employed individuals, and workers in these firms view mandatory retirement contributions as another tax. As these firms are relatively young and employ a much younger workforce than SOEs, saving for retirement is not viewed as a top priority, let alone contributing such savings to a social pool controlled by a government that enjoys

---

[t] Jiang and Li, "Zhongguo yanglao baoxian shengji tongchou yihou de maodung fengxi yu duice yanjiu," p. 96. Frazier, "After Pension Reform," pp. 55–56.
[u] Chen Jiagui, Zhongguo shehui baozhang fazhan baogao, 1997–2001, p. 162.
[v] Gao Shusheng, "Changhuan yanlaojin zhaiwu de xinshilu," p. 7.

low policy credibility. Indigenous non-state firms face high labor turnover rates, flexible employment, uncertain policy environment, government discrimination, thin profit margins (especially for small firms and self-employed individuals), and intense competition. A high contribution rate (20% from employers and 8% from employees) would have posed an additional and onerous financial burden on the sector.[w] Although the central government has no official data on the participation by non-state firms, case studies indicate that such participation rates are low. A study of migrant laborers (most of them work for non-state firms) in Jiangsu, Jilin, and Liaoning in 2003 found that the rate was 15% in Jiangsu (a province with a large number of non-state firms) and 10% in Jilin and Liaoning. In the city of Wuxi, Jiangsu province, the rate was 10%, and fewer than one-third of the private firms participated in the retirement system despite the city government's efforts to force them to enrol.[x] In Zhejiang, the province with China's most dynamic private sector, 37% of its labor force were migrant laborers in 2003, but only about one-third of them were enrolled in the old-age pension system. Interviews with these laborers indicate that they gave high priority to health insurance and view old-age pension contributions as unnecessary.[y]

Aggregate national data show that the overall old-age social security coverage rate (of workers in urban areas) was about 45% in 2003. Of the 256 million people employed in urban areas, only 116 million participated in the basic old-age retirement system in 2003.[z] Insufficient social pooling and low coverage together have forced the government to set high contribution rates and, predictably, high contribution rates have further discouraged participation rate and compliance. The nominal contribution rate is 28% of wages, but estimates suggest that due to evasion, the effective rate is only about 9%. From a worker's point of view, social security contribution amounts to another form of income tax because, of the 28%, only 8% (assigned to his personal

---

[w] Qiao Qingmei (2003). "Minying zhongxiao qiye shehui baozhang xianzhuang chengyin yu duice" (The Status of Social Security in Medium and Small Private Firms: Causes and Policy Options). *Shehui baoxian yanjiu* 12, 2–9.

[x] Hua Yingfang (2004). "Jiangsu, Jilin, Liaoning sansheng de nongmingong shehui baozhang" (Social Security for Migrant Labourers in Jiangsu, Jilin, and Liaoning). *Shehui baoxian yanjiu* 5, 23–32.

[y] Shen Changren (2004). "Zhejiangsheng nongmingong shehui baoxian diacha yu jianyi" (Social Insurance for Rural Migrant Laborers in Zhejiang Province: A Study and Recommendations). *Zhongguo shehui baozhang* (Social Security in China) 7, 26–27.

[z] *Zhongguo tongji nianjian 2003*, p. 119, p. 896.

Table 4.   Old-age social insurance premium rates in five cities, 2003.

City	Beijing	Shanghai	Tianjin	Hangzhou	Chengdu
Employer premium rates (percent of payroll)	20	25.5	25	22	20
Employee premium rates (percent of payroll)	8	7	6	7	6
Total	28	32.5	31	29	26

Source: Lin Zhiyuan, "Dangqian jiben shehui baozhang jidai jiejue de wenti" (problems in the current basic social insurance that require urgent solution), Jingji yanjiu cankao, No. 81, 2004, p. 30.

account) is directly beneficial to him. As a result, firms and individual are both motivated to evade it.[aa]

A key objective of the 1997 reform was to unify rates across regions. But judging from the persistence of varying contribution rates across regions, the Chinese government has failed to achieve this goal (Table 4). Despite official regulations limiting the pension premium rate to 20% of the payroll, many local governments raised the rates over that limit to maintain the cash flow in the system.[bb]

2.2. *Individual accounts*

Creating individual accounts fully funded by mandatory contributions (the so-called second pillar in the World Bank's three-pillar model of a robust old-age retirement system) was the second critical objective of the 1997 reform package. According to the State Council regulations issued in 1997, individual accounts were to be funded by a levy of up to 11% of the worker's wage bill (up to 8% would be paid by the worker and the rest by the employer). These contributions would be credited to a worker's individual account. If fully funded, as envisioned by the World Bank's reform proposal, individual accounts would create added incentives for workers to participate in state-sponsored retirement savings and provide an important source of pension income in the future. However, because contributions from the social pool alone cannot meet the on-going pension expenditures, the central government

---

[aa] Martin Feldstein, "Chongjian zhongguo de shehui baozhang tixi" (Rebuilding China's social insurance system), *Caijing* (Finance and Business Review) Sept. 20, 2004, p. 59.
[bb] Frazier, "After Pension Reform," p. 50.

allows local governments to bundle the social pool and the individual accounts, thus effectively diverting the funds in individual accounts to the social pool.

Individual accounts have consequently become "empty accounts" or "notional accounts." At the end of 1999, 72.6 million workers supposedly had set up their individual accounts, with a "notional" value of 191.4 billion yuan. In reality, there was no money in these accounts.[cc] The extent to which the Chinese government depends on the diversion of funds in individual accounts to the social pool can be seen from a study conducted by the MLSS in 2000. After analyzing the data from five cities (Shanghai, Dalian, Chengdu, Beijing, and Xi'an), the MLSS concluded that, if individual accounts were to be fully funded, the social pool would not be able to meet its obligations for the next 25 years, with a total deficit of 1.8 trillion yuan (or 20% of GDP).[dd] In 2002, contributions to individual accounts were 70–75 billion yuan. If this sum was not used to help reduce the deficits in the social pool, the aggregate pension deficit for 2002 would have been 100 billion yuan, not 29 billion yuan.[ee]

If the on-going pension financing constraints have forced the Chinese government to abandon building the second pillar, a host of different factors have impeded the building of the third pillar — voluntary individual supplemental retirement savings. In the Chinese case, the third pillar has taken the form of *qiye nianjin* (enterprise annuities). These are fully funded individual accounts that were modeled after the popular American 401(k) scheme and that sprung up in various localities in the 1990s. Workers can contribute to these accounts, and their employers can contribute up to 4% of the worker's wages to the same account. But unlike the American 401(k) plans, enterprise annuities can be administered by enterprises themselves, financial service firms, or government social security agencies.

The number of participants in enterprise annuities remains relatively small — 6.5 million in 17,000 enterprises as of 2002, or about 5% of total participants in the old-age pension system. The amount of savings in these plans was large relatively to the participation rate. In 2002, enterprise annuities plans had accumulated 30 billion yuan, which equalled 20% of the accumulated national social security surpluses that year. Some Chinese researchers

---

[cc] Gao Shusheng, "Changhuan yanlaojin zhaiwu de xinshilu," p. 5.
[dd] Gao Shusheng, "Changhuan yanlaojin zhaiwu de xinshilu," p. 2
[ee] Ministry of Labor and Social Security, *Zhongguo laodong he shehui baozhang nianjian 2003* (Yearbook of China's Labour and Social Security, 2003) (Beijing, 2003), p. 602. *Zhongguo tongji nianjian 2004*, p. 897.

argue that enterprise annuities have become both a form of tax evasion and an instrument of corruption favored by enterprise managers. Exploiting the enterprise annuities plans allows enterprises to buy insurance policies with tax-deductible contributions and cancel these policies after a period of time so that they can evade the 20% corporate income tax. For individual managers, enterprise annuities represent a lucrative benefit. They can buy expensive life insurance annuities for themselves with pre-tax contributions and then pocket the proceeds after cancelling them.[ff] All of this supports the notion that the enterprise annuities are designed to benefit mostly the managerial staff in SOEs.[gg]

The most serious obstacle to the expansion of enterprise annuities is the lack of explicit legislation or regulations that can signal the support of the central government, clarify their status, unify practices, and provide favorable tax treatment. The State Council did not issue an interim regulation on enterprise annuities until January 2004, and different provinces have different policies on contribution rates and tax treatment. The resulting regulatory void and confusion has been responsible for the questionable practices adopted by SOEs in setting up and administering their enterprise annuities program.

To address the problem of "empty individual accounts," the government launched a new pilot project in Liaoning in June 2001. The most important feature, as well as the central objective, of the new experiment was to fully fund individual accounts and separate the management of the social pool from that of individual accounts. Before the experiment, individual accounts in Liaoning had a deficit of 20 billion yuan (almost 10% of the total accumulated retirement savings in China's "empty individual accounts"). After the pilot project went into effect in July 2001, employers paid 20% of the wage bill into the social pool, while employees paid 8% of their wages into their individual accounts. The social pool were not allowed to tap into the individual accounts; the funds in the social pool and in individual accounts were managed separately; and the shortfalls of the social pool were fully funded with

---

[ff] Zhou and Li, "Woguo qiye nianjin guanli wenti yanjiu," p. 12.
[gg] MLSS, "Zhongguo qiye nianjin fazhan wenti yanjiu" (A study of the Development of Enterprise Annuities), *Shehui baoxian yanjiu*, No. 6, 2004, p. 1; Zhou Yi and Li Gang, "Woguo qiye nianjin guanli wenti yanjiu" (A study of the Problems of Administering China's Company Annuities), *Shehui baoxian yanjiu*, No. 8, 2003, p. 10; Cai Wenwu (2004). "Qiye nianjin banfa jiesha mianshi" (Unveiling the Rules on Enterprise Annuities). *Zhongguo shehui baozhang* 5, 17–19.

fiscal appropriations.[hh] To strengthen the provincial pool, the government set up a provincial "transfer funds" (*tiaojijin*), with each city turning over 5% of its annual basic old-age retirement contributions to a special account in the provincial retirement fund, to be used to fund the shortfalls in deficit-incurring cities. To incentivise employers and employees to contribute to the third-pillar, the pilot plan explicitly allowed enterprises with sufficient funds to establish enterprise annuities, with contributions of up to 4% of the payroll treated as pre-tax labor costs.

By and large, the initial results of the pilot plan were encouraging. From July 2001 to the end of 2002, the individual accounts in Liaoning accumulated 4.8 billion fully funded retirement savings. However, fully funding individual accounts in Liaoning required large infusions of fiscal subsidies from both Beijing and the Liaoning provincial government. During this period, the central government provided Liaoning with a subsidy of 1.5 billion yuan, and Liaoning put up another 500 million yuan to fund individual accounts. If fiscal subsidies are indispensable in keeping individual accounts fully funded, the sustainability of the new model, especially after it is expanded nationally, is highly doubtful.[ii]

2.3. *Enforcement and management*

In implementing its pension reforms, the Chinese government has encountered additional challenges — enforcement of the newly promulgated pension regulations and management of retirement savings. As discussed earlier, the low coverage of China's old-pension retirement system most probably has forced the government to impose high contribution rates. In turn, high contribution rates have discouraged participation, while motivating evasion of pension premiums. To be sure, the evasion of old-age social security premiums was widespread before the implementation of the 1997 reforms. The World Bank found that, in 1995, the effective rate of pension contribution was only 13%, not the nominal rate of 23.5% levied by the government. Typically, employers tried to reduce their pension contributions by understating the wage base.

[hh]Wang Shenshi and Zhang Xiaolong (2004). "Zuoshi geren zhanghu de shijian he sikao" (Pay Attention to the Experiment of Setting Individual Accounts). *Zhongguo shehui baozhang* 2, 21.
[ii]Gao Shusehgn, "Changhuan yanlaojin zhaiwu de xinshilu," p. 5.

This practice continued after the 1997 reforms were implemented. In 1999, the reported wage base in Guangdong was only 70% of the real wage base.[jj] Judging by official press reports, evasion remains a problem today. An audit in 2003 by the MLSS found that firms failed to include 1.68 million employees in the pension program, understated their payroll by 6.4 billion yuan, and underpaid 1.7 billion yuan in pension contributions.[kk] Another sign of trouble for the new reforms is that unpaid old-age pensions, which the central government vowed to eliminate through the 1997 reforms, has persisted. In 1998, enterprises owed 32 billion yuan in unpaid pensions; in 1999, unpaid pensions rose to 39 billion yuan in 1999 and, in 2000, to 40 billion yuan. Most of the pension arrears were owed by SOEs.[ll]

To strengthen its enforcement capacity and combat evasion, the Chinese government decided in July 1998 to assign, on an experimental basis, the responsibility of collecting pension contributions in four regions (Chongqing, Yunnan, Anhui, and Zhejiang) to local tax authorities. The initial results were so encouraging that the experiment was expanded to other regions. By 2003, 19 provinces had adopted this practice. Using local tax authorities to collect social security premiums has two advantages. First, these authorities have more accurate information about the financial conditions of local enterprises and have more legal authority and power, than local social security administrations, in enforcing compliance. The second advantage of this practice is lower administrative costs. In Anhui, the costs incurred by tax agencies in collecting social security premiums were one-fourth of those reported by local social security administrations (which typically charged 2–5% of the assets under administration).[mm] As a result of this practice, compliance rate rose dramatically in the regions where the experiment was introduced. In the case of Anhui, compliance rate rose from an average of 83% during 1995–1997 to above 95% during 1999–2000.[nn] In 2001, the compliance rate in provinces in which local tax authorities collected social security contributions was above

[jj] Wang Wentong and Ai Bin (2002). "Shehui baozhang feigaishui qianjing yuce" (Prognosis on Changing Social Security Fees into Taxes). *Jingji yanjiu cankao* 24, 20.

[kk] MLSS (2004) "2003: laodong he shehui baozhang shiye fazhan zongshu" (A Comprehensive Report on the Development of the Labor and Social Security Sector in 2003), *Zhongguo shehui baozhan* 1, 16.

[ll] Wang and Ai, "Shehui baozhang feigaishui qianjing yuce," pp. 16–23.

[mm] Wang and Ai, "Shehui baozhang feigaishui qianjing yuce," pp. 16–18; Chen Jiagui, *Zhongguo shehui baozhang fazhan baogao 1997–2001*, pp. 52–55.

[nn] Wang and Ai, "Shehui baozhang feigaishui qianjing yuce," pp. 16–18.

95%. In 2002, the premiums collected by local tax authorities in Zhejiang, Guangdong, Jiangsu, Yunnan, and Liaoning increased by more than 20% from the preceding year.[oo] However, new management problems have emerged in recent years. To maximize their own income, local tax collectors have an incentive to delay collection because they can levy extra fines on delayed premium payments made by enterprises. In addition, the computer systems between the tax authorities and social security administrations are not connected, mainly because local social security administrations report to the MLSS, while local tax authorities report to the MOF. Such bureaucratic hurdles have created delays and confusion in managing the new pension system.[pp] Despite these relatively minor glitches, the transfer of the responsibility for collecting old-age social security contributions to local tax authorities should be considered a timely and effective adaptation by the Chinese government.

For a country with under-developed financial markets and weak internal controls inside the state bureaucracies, investing and managing pension savings presents an extremely difficult challenge. In the Chinese case, the mismanagement, if not abuse, of pension funds was such a widespread and serious problem in the 1990s that the central government imposed tight restrictions on the class of assets that pension funds could be invested in. The MOF and the Ministry of Labor issued a joint regulation in 1994 stipulating that 80% of the retirement surpluses must be invested in special treasury retirement savings bonds. In 1997, the State Council mandated that retirement funds can only be invested in treasury bonds and bank deposits; no other investments are allowed. But despite these restrictions, violations have been routine and serious. An audit by the MOF in 10 provinces found that between 1992 and 1995, 6 billion yuan of pension funds were illegally diverted to unauthorized investments.[qq] Examples included a loan of 523 million yuan made by the Hebei provincial government from its retirement savings to invest in "key projects" and technological innovation projects. From 1993 to 1995, Guangdong invested 657 million yuan of its retirement savings in real estate, set up off-the-books

---

[oo] Ma Donglai (2004). "Kaizheng shehui baozhangshui" (Start Collecting Social Security Tax). *The State General Tax Bureau Research Report* **8**, 1–4.

[pp] MOF (2004). "Shehui baozhang zijin couji yu guanli yanjiu" (A Study of the Pooling and Management of Social Security Funds), *Jingji yanjiu cankao*. (Economic Research Reference) **81**, 18–19.

[qq] Chen Jiagui, *Zhongguo shehui baozhang fazhan baogao 1997–2001* (Beijing: Shehui wenxian chubanshe 2002), p. 50.

accounts worth 45 million yuan, and deposited 347 million yuan in non-bank financial institutions.[rr] Altogether, the scale of mismanagement was substantial in aggregate terms. According the report by the Chinese National Auditing Agency, in 1996, 9.2 billion yuan in retirement funds (16% of the total pension surpluses) were illegally diverted, resulting in huge losses. In a four-month audit jointly conducted by the MLSS, the National Auditing Agency, and the MOF, they found that from 1986 to 1997, tens of billions of yuan were illegally diverted or used, with half of the retirement funds lost. Local governments were responsible for diverting or illegally using 32% of the funds; local social security agencies were responsible for illegally diverting or using 29% of the funds.[ss]

In addition to the huge economic losses caused by the mismanagement of pension funds, China has incurred even greater financial losses by investing its pension assets in low-return treasury bonds and bank deposits. Obviously, this policy was adopted by the Chinese government in the face of widespread abuse in the management of pension funds, underdeveloped domestic financial markets, and capital account controls. By restricting the investment options only to low-yield treasury bonds and bank deposits, the Chinese government sought to prevent local authorities from subjecting the bulk of the nation's precious pension savings to unacceptably risky investments (if not abuse and corruption). But it would be wrong not to recognise the enormous opportunity costs China has had to bear due to its flawed internal financial and political institutions. Recognizing the costs of these restrictions on investment options, the central government allowed the newly established National Social Security Fund (but not local social security administrations) to invest in domestic equities in 2001. Although the first investment made by the Fund (shares in the oil giant Sinopec) was a big loser, the policy continued. In June 2003, the Fund signed an agreement with several asset management firms that would manage the retirement assets held by the Fund in domestic equities. As of the end of 2003, less than 5% of the Fund's investments were in domestic equities.[tt] However, some observers doubt whether this new system had the right incentive structure to produce superior performance because the asset

---

[rr] Chen Jiagui, *Zhongguo shehui baozhang fazhan baogao 1997–2001*, pp. 180–182.
[ss] Chen Jiagui, *Zhongguo shehui baozhang fazhan baogao 1997–2001*, p. 169.
[tt] MLSS (2004) "2003: laodong he shehui baozhang shiye fazhan zongshu" (A Comprehensive Report on the Development of the Labor and Social Security Sector in 2003), *Zhongguo shehui baozhan* 1, 15–16.

management firms (all state-owned) picked by the National Social Security Fund are guaranteed a fixed management fee regardless of their performance.[uu]

2.4. *Rural pension reform*

Given the fact that nearly 60% of the Chinese population live in the countryside, the building of a social safety net in the rural areas ought to be a top priority for the Chinese government.[vv] The urgency for doing so is further amplified by key developments: an ageing rural population, the migration of younger residents to urban areas, and the loss of farmland to commercial development. According to official estimates, every three peasants would become landless when two *mu* of farmland is acquired for industrial or commercial use. From 1987 to 2001, such land acquisitions have produced 34 million landless peasants.[ww] Without adequate provisions for their social safety needs, landless peasants can easily become a major source of social instability. But studies also show that local governments have failed to use the proceeds from land sales to build a social safety net for landless peasants. In Zhejiang, for example, nearly 1 million peasants became landless by 2003. However, a survey of landless peasants in five cities found that 82% of them had received only a one-time compensation cash payment; and in 2002, the compensation payment received by peasants could only cover their living expenses for two-and-a-half years.[xx] According to official data, local governments receive the lion share of proceeds from land sales, while peasants receive only a minor share. For example, in Shanghai, which has the highest compensation rate in the country, only 25% of the proceeds from land sales was given as compensation to peasants, and 75% was paid to the municipal government in the form of various taxes.[yy]

In contrast to the full-fledged reforms to which the Chinese government has given top priority, the development of a rural social safety net received

[uu] Lin Zhiyuan (2004) "Danqian jiben shehui baozhang jidai jiejue de wenti" (Problems in the Current Basic Social Insurance that Require Urgent Solution), *Jingji yanjiu cankoa* (Chinese Research Reference) **81**, 34.

[vv] Asian Development Bank, *Old-Age Pensions for the Rural Areas: From Land Reform to Globalization* (Manila: 2002).

[ww] Lu, H. (2003). "Tudi huan baozhang." (Land for Security) *Shehui Baoxian Yanjiu* **5**, 2.

[xx] Yang Yansui (2003) "Daibiao nongmin liyi yao luo zhai shichu" (Peasants' Interests must be Really Represented), *Dangjian yanjiu neican* (Internal Reference of Party-Building) **9**, 2.

[yy] Lu Haiyuan, "Tudi huan baozhang," pp. 3–6.

much less attention or official support. While Premier Zhu Rongji personally championed and pushed urban pension reforms during his tenure, no senior Chinese leader has taken an interest in the issue of rural old-age pensions. In fact, a review of China's efforts in the last two decades in this area shows that the Chinese government has undertaken no systematic reform to establish a viable system of old-age pensions in the countryside.

Ostensibly, China does have a rural pension system funded by voluntary contributions from peasants. However, official data show that participation in such a system has been steadily declining, thus suggesting its lack of success. Indeed, the number of participants alone (an impressive figure of almost 55 million in 2002) can be misleading because this system is severely unfunded and incapable of providing meaningful income support for old rural residents. In the city of Yantai, a wealthy jurisdiction Shandong, its much lauded pilot project on rural pension reform began in 1992. Peasants paid contributions of 48 yuan a year per person in 1991 and 135 yuan per person in 2002 into a local pension fund. However, from 1992 to 2002, the average annual pension payment per participant was less than 90 yuan, a totally inadequate amount for retirees.[zz]

The lack of the state's financial support was the most important reason for the failure of rural pension reform. Although the government has provided hundreds of billions of yuan to subsidise urban pension reform, it has not given any financial support for similar reform in the countryside (with the exception of paying for the start-up costs of administering such a system). The only two incentives offered by the central government for peasants to participate in the rural pension system has been (1) granting permission for villages to use some of its surplus funds to finance the system and (2) providing beneficial pre-tax treatment of the contributions made on behalf of the participants by township-and-village enterprises (TVEs). But because such pension contributions have not been mandatory, only a small number of TVEs have actually made them. More important, as the financial performance of TVEs deteriorated in the late 1990s and as many TVEs were privatized, pension matching funds from TVEs dried up. Public finance in villages fell on hard times in the 1990s as well, due to

---

[zz] Li Xian *et al.* (2004). "Nongchun shehui yanlao baoxian zhidu kunjing de guanca he sikao" (Observations and Thoughts on the Difficulties Facing the Rural Old-Age Social Security System). *Zhongguo shehui baozhang* 9, 20–21.

Table 5.   The number of participants in rural old-age pension schemes.

Year	1996	1997	1998	1999	2000	2002
Rural participants (million)	65.9	70.4	80.2	64.6	61.7	54.6
Change (percent)	n.a.	6.7	14.1	−19.5	−4.5	−28

Sources: Yang Yinan and Li Qiuxiang, "Nongchun shehui yanglao baoxian fazhan huanman de shenchengci yuanyin tanxi" (An exploratory analysis of the deep causes of the slow development of old-age social insurance in rural areas) Shehui baoxian yanjiu, No. 8, 2003, p. 6; Li Xian *et al.*, "Nongchun shehui yanlao baoxian zhidu kunjing de guanca he sikao" (Observations and thoughts on the difficulties facing the rural old-age social security system), Zhongguo shehui baozhang, No. 9, 2004, pp. 20–21.

low prices for agricultural produce and stagnant rural income. Consequently, participation rate fell continuously. The Yantai experience was typical. In 1991, roughly 60,000 residents, or 39% of the participants, received local village or TVE subsidies that amounted to 14% of all paid-in premiums that year. But in 2002, only 12,500 participants received such subsidies. Without sufficient financial incentives to entice them to participate, pension contributions were regarded by peasants as another form of unjustified local taxation.[aaa]

3. Assessment and Reflections

Any assessment of the achievements and limitations of China's pension reform must start with the counterfactual question: what would have happened had China not adopted the reform package? From this perspective, it is impossible to deny the obvious and tremendous economic and political benefits that China has received from the implementation of its pension reform package. For all its design flaws and implementation problems, China has, for the first time, a rudimentary old-age pension system. The functioning of this system has enabled China to maintain relative social peace during some of the most challenging years in its economic reform drive and as it sought to carry out a massive restructuring of its SOEs. It is inconceivable that the pace of economic reform and political stability could have been kept up without the old-age pension reform.

But judging by more stringent standards, China's pension reform has fallen far short of both expectations and achievable results. In its recommendations on reforming China's pension system, the World Bank proposed four general

---

[aaa] Li Xian *et al.*, "Nongchun shehui yanlao baoxian zhidu kunjing de guanca he sikao," pp. 20–21.

principles: unifying the system, reducing the pension burden, introducing funded individual accounts, and ensuring an adequate real rate of return on pension funds.[bbb] Clearly, China's pension reform since 1997 has met none of the four criteria. Its pension system, even at the provincial level, is far from being unified (in terms of contribution and replacement rates); the pension burden has not been reduced; almost all of the individual accounts remain unfunded; and the rate of return on China's pension funds was meagre, if not negative, during this period. In this section, I will advance two arguments. First, China's pension reform has been hampered both by inadequate financial resources and by a lack of political will to introduce painful adjustments that would meaningfully reduce the country's long-run pension liabilities. Second, China's pension reform has been further obstructed by poor governance, the symptoms of which are demonstrated in myriad forms that I will detail below.

3.1. *Inadequate financial resources and lack of political will*

Given the large implicit pension deficits, the rapid increase in the number of retirees (both as a process of ageing and as a result of the restructuring of SOEs), and the limited fiscal capacity of the Chinese state, few would doubt that financing the transition is the most critical hurdle in China's pension reform. The Chinese government has two policy options. It could reduce the pension burden by cutting benefits (through raising the retirement age and reducing the income replacement ratio for retirees); or, it could finance the transition costs by raising additional resources.

By international comparison, China's retirement age is relatively low (60 for men, 55 for women in salaried positions, and 50 for women in blue-collar jobs), while its income replacement ratio, at about 80% nationally, is among the highest in the world.[ccc] Typically, retired government officials have 95–100% replacement rate. Workers with 30 years of employment get 90%.[ddd] This unique characteristic prompted one Western scholar to observe

---

[bbb]The World Bank, *Old-Age Security*, pp. 4–5.
[ccc]China's replacement ratio, at around 80 percent, is the double of the average ratio in OECD countries and the countries in the former Soviet bloc and Latin America. Whiteford, "Social Protection Reform in China," pp. 59–60.
[ddd]Chen Jiagui, *Zhongguo shehui baozhang fazhan baogao 1997–2001*, p. 190; income replacement rate varies across regions – 65 percent in Jiangsu and Hainan to 102 percent in Harbin. The average rate nationwide was 78 percent in 1995. Loraine West, "Pension Reform in China," p. 162.

that China's pension system "mainly benefits a relatively well-off minority, even of the urban population."[eee]

Obviously, raising the retirement age and cutting the replacement ratio could produce substantial pension savings. By one estimate, raising the retirement age by one year, China could save 20 billion yuan in pension spending each year (equivalent to about a third of the government subsidies in 2003).[fff] Similarly, cutting China's income replacement ratio to 60% (which would be almost 50% higher than the international average) could reduce China's pension expenditures by another 25% and eliminated annual deficits. However, the Chinese government, perhaps fearful of the political repercussions from such painful reforms (which would have hurt a sizable segment of the population in the politically important urban areas), has not seriously contemplated them until very recently. In the pilot project introduced in Liaoning since July 2001, the replacement ratio was reduced to 48–58%.[ggg] However, the same political considerations, the fear of increasing the urban unemployment rate if retirement age is raised, have kept the government from even attempting to introduce further experimental reforms.

The same lack of political will appears to have stopped the government from raising additional revenues to finance the transition costs. As the owner of massive state assets, the Chinese government could have liquidated its holdings in listed companies and sold other fixed assets to raise substantial funds to fill the financing gap during pension reform.[hhh] For example, the Chinese state owned 60% of all the shares of the domestically listed companies and controlled other assets valued at 6.7 trillion yuan in 1999.[iii] To its credit, the Chinese government did attempt to reduce its holdings in listed companies to generate revenue for pension reform. In June 2001, the State Council

---

[eee]Whiteford, "Social Protection Reform in China," p. 72.

[fff]Gao Shusheng (2003). "Guanyu dajian zhongguo shehui baozhang xinpingtai de shexiang" (Ideas on Building a New Social Security Platform for China). *Jingji yanjiu cankao* 4, 32.

[ggg]Under the new policy, those who have participated in the system for 15 years can expect the 48% replacement ratio, and those who have participated for 30 years can expect the 58% replacement ratio. Fu Zhihua and Li Chuanfeng (2003). "Dui Liaoning yanglao baoxian gaige shidian moshi de chubu fengxi" (Preliminary Analysis of the Pilot Model in Reforming Liaoning's Old-Age Pension System). *Jingji yanjiu cankao* 60, 36–40.

[hhh]Mark Dorfman and Yvonne Sin (2000). "*China: Social Security Reform, Technical Analysis of Strategic Options*. Washington: The World Bank.

[iii]Wang and Ai, "Shehui baozhang feigaishui qianjing yuce," p. 21.

Table 6. Social retirement funds yearly income and expenditures, 1989–2003.

Year	Pension funds contributions and income (billion yuan)	Central and local government fiscal subsidies (billion yuan)	Pension funds expenditures (billion yuan)	Deficits without fiscal subsidies (billion yuan)	Accumulated surpluses (billion yuan)
1989	14.7 (a)	n.a.	11.9	n.a.	6.8
1992	36.6 (a)	n.a.	32.2	n.a.	22.0
1995	95.0 (a)	n.a.	84.8	n.a.	43.0
1997	133.7 (a)	n.a.	125.1	n.a.	68.3
1998	135.3	13.2	150.1	−14.8	51.8
1999	159.5	25.5	180.8	−21.3	72.7
2000	186.9	40.9	211.6	−24.7	94.7
2001	209.2	39.7	232.1	−22.9	105.4
2002	255.1	62.0	284.2	−29.1	160.8
2003	368.0 (a)	n.a.	312.2	n.a.	220.6

Note: (a) Including central and local government subsidies.
Sources: Ministry of Labor and Social Security, Zhongguo laodong he shehui baozhang nianjian 2003 (Yearbook of China's Labor and Social Security, 2003) (Beijing, 2003), p. 602. Zhongguo tongji nianjian 2004, p. 897.

announced that the government would start gradually selling the state's holdings in listed companies to strengthen the national pension fund. But the stock markets in China reacted so negatively to this decision and share prices plunged so much that, in June 2002, the State Council was forced to indefinitely suspend this program. A plausible political explanation for this retreat was that the government did not want to cause an embarrassing stock market crash on the eve of its important 16th Party Congress scheduled for November 2002. The economic costs of such politically driven decisions can be seen in the rising pension deficits that are putting unsustainable strains on the state's fiscal system (Table 6).

3.2. Governance matters

China's old-age pension reform has also been impeded by two structural factors commonly associated with governance: capacity and incentives. To the extent that strong state capacity contributes positively to government performance, as is believed, weak state capacity in China must bear the responsibility for unfulfilled reform goals. This observation may strike many as wrong, if not ridiculous, because China is thought to possess a strong state, especially relative to other developing countries. Yet, my analysis of the problems associated with the enforcement and implementation of the old-age pension reform shows that political authority is fragmented inside China, both vertically and horizontally. As Kenneth Lieberthal has suggested, decision-making power and enforcement capacity in such a political system as that of China, aptly termed "fragmented authoritarianism," tend to be dispersed, unwieldy, and often ineffective.[jjj] Under such a system, local authorities can, and often do, defy commands from higher authorities with impunity. The most telling evidence in this study is the refusal by local pension administrations to transfer their surpluses to provincial authorities despite the central government's explicit call for provincial pooling. Although China has an authoritarian political system, the ruling Communist Party has shown a lack of political autonomy from powerful constituencies, especially the urban elite (which benefits disproportionately from the flaws in the old-age pension system). It has thus followed a tentative, gradual, and learn-by-doing approach which, despite its advantages, has locked China into an unsustainable path and led to the loss of precious time for more decisive action.

At the level of implementation, the weak bureaucratic capacity of the new social security administration contributed to the ineffective implementation of the reform efforts and eventually forced the government to transfer the function of collecting pension contributions to the local tax authorities.[kkk] The reform process was also undercut by competition among different bureaucracies for oversight over the administration of social security funds. Three ministries, the MOF, the MLSS, and the Ministry of Civil Affairs, all have some jurisdiction over a certain aspect of the new social security system, resulting in overlapping and confusing authorities, bloated personnel, and high administrative costs.[lll] The problem of information asymmetry has further hampered the central government's efforts to ensure compliance with its regulations. Because the local authorities control all the information, it is hard for the

---

[jjj] Kenneth Lieberthal (1992). "Introduction: The 'Fragmented Authoritarianism' Model and Its Limitations." In: Kenneth L. and David L. (eds.), *Bureaucracy, Politics, and Decision Making in Post-Mao China.* Berkeley: University of California Press, pp. 1–30.

[kkk] Frazier, "After Pension Reform," pp. 61–64.

[lll] The MOF (2004). "Shehui baozhang zijin couji yu guanli yanjiu" (A Study of the Pooling and Management of Social Security Funds). *Jingji Yanjiu Cankao* (Economic Research Reference) **81**, 20.

central authorities to know whether local tax and social security authorities collect social security contributions to the fullest extent. The MOF and the National Auditing Agency do not have an effective system or methods to deal with illegal practices such as false reporting, evasion of contributions, and delay in payments of the premiums and disbursements of benefits.[mmm] Poor governance has high economic costs, as seen in both the widespread misuse of pension funds by local authorities and in the incalculable lost investment returns due to the tight restrictions imposed by the central government to prevent or minimize such misuse.

But effective governance is not produced by strong governmental authority alone. In practice, effective governance is likely a combination of strong governmental authority and the right economic incentives to encourage cooperation and minimize opportunism. In this regard, one can see two major contributing causes to ineffective implementation of China's pension reform: opportunism and moral hazard. Even though local governments and state bureaucracies are blamed, often unfairly, for behaving opportunistically to resist reforms demanded by the central government, it is important to recognise that such opportunistic behavior is frequently a self-defensive response to the central government's own opportunistic behavior. In the case of old-age pension reform, there have been two unambiguous instances of opportunistic behavior by the central government. The first was the decision to force the 11 industrial sector pension pools to merge with provincial pools, undertaken by Beijing apparently to seize the surpluses in the industrial sector pools to subsidise the under-funded provincial pools. The second was the State Council's politically driven retreat from liquidating the state's holdings in listed companies to raise new revenues for the national pension fund. In the first instance, opportunism begot opportunism, and Beijing's plan backfired after the managers of the 11 sector funds rushed to spend most the surpluses. In the second case, the central government's action undercut its own commitment to reform. At the local level, the system of evaluating officials on the basis of their ability to deliver high economic growth also encourages opportunistic behavior. Under this system, local officials have the incentive to divert pension funds for local projects because the high economic growth and employment

---

[mmm] *Ibid.*

gains generated by such projects can advance their careers quickly, while the costs of the diversion will be paid by their successors in the distant future.

There also exists a moral hazard problem — provincial and local authorities expect the central government to bail them out and fund pension shortfalls — because political stability is a public good and the national authorities attach far greater value to maintaining social stability than do local governments. Even though the central government has resisted establishing a national pooling and becoming the payer of last resort, Beijing has been forced to provide substantial subsidies to provincial governments to cover their deficits.[nnn] Between 1998 and 2003, the central government spent 180 billion yuan subsidizing local governments' pension expenditures. But local governments have grown dependent on such subsidies. Cities and counties with pension surpluses have refused to transfer surpluses to provinces because they know the central government would bail out provincial governments.[ooo] Some local governments have even excluded the areas with surpluses in reporting the finances of their provincial pools and only report the deficits to Beijing, so that the central government would cover the shortfalls. And once the central government's fiscal subsides arrive, local governments can withdraw their own subsidies.[ppp] Moreover, under the current system of provincial pooling, provincial governments have control over contribution and benefit rates, but the central government is liable for the shortfalls.[qqq]

The root cause of this incentive structure that motivates local authorities to depend on the bail-out of the central government is the different value placed on political stability by local and central government officials. To the extent that political stability is a public good, the value of this public good is much greater for the central government than for local governments. In other words, for fear of undermining their legitimacy and allowing localized instability to spread to the rest of the country, the top leadership of the Communist Party in Beijing is far more motivated to spend money to buy social peace than are local officials. This incentive structure has played a decisive role in shifting an increasing share of the responsibility of paying pension liabilities from local governments to

[nnn] Mark Frazier (2004). "China's Pension Reform and its Discontents." *The China Journal* 51, 97–114.
[ooo] Hu Xiaoyi, "Guanyu zhubu tigao yanlao baoxian tongchou cengci," p. 19.
[ppp] Hu Xiaoyi, "Cong tongfeng hunhe zouxiang tongfeng jiehe" p. 5.
[qqq] Lin Zhiyuan (2004). "Danqian jiben shehui baozhang jidai jiejue de wenti." (Problems in the Current Basic Social Insurance that Require Urgent Solution). *Jingji Yanjiu Cankoa* 81, 32.

Beijing in recent years. In 1996, Beijing paid only 15% of all old-age pension expenditures in the country. But in 2000, the central government paid half of such expenditures.[rrr] Ironically, despite its refusal to become the payer of last resort, Beijing is now finding that it has now, effectively and unwittingly, begun to assume that undesirable role.

[rrr]The MOF, "Shehui baozhang zijin couji yu guanli yanjiu," p. 19.

CHAPTER 6

Corporate Restructuring and Social Security in State Owned Enterprises: Lessons from China

Jean C. Oi

Beginning in the mid to late 1990s, the state no longer wanted to be the sole proprietor of China's publicly owned enterprises, responsible for all profits and losses. This change significantly altered the social contract between the state and the workers and thus their social security. In sharp contrast to the elite status of workers during the Mao period, where the "iron rice bowl" guaranteed all workers stable employment and full benefits,[a] some workers became unemployed, others were laid-off and told to stay home until economic conditions improved; some factories have been sold or closed. The largest and best state owned enterprises had prided themselves on providing workers and their families with the jobs, housing, schools, canteens, and welfare benefits, including pensions and health care.[b] Benefits varied according to a worker's *danwei* (work unit). Nonetheless, regardless of whether it was a big or small state owned enterprise, benefits were underwritten by the state, with funds sent down through the plan. The welfare system was inclusive for workers and payment was guaranteed regardless of firm profits. The end of central planning also meant that enterprises no longer could count on the system to cover all their costs. The social security of workers became dependent on the resources of the factories in which they worked. The iron rice bowl was broken and

[a]I would like to thank Lu Zheng for his assistance with the data and statistical analysis. The research was generously supported by a grant from the Asian Development Bank Institute and a seed grant from the Stanford Institute of International Studies, Stanford University.
[b]See Walder, A. (1986). *Communist Neo-Traditionalism: Work and Authority in Chinese Industry*. CA: University of California Press.

individual enterprises and the local governments that owned them were left to pick up the pieces.

Workers in China were left with a *firm based* welfare system. The state regulated the benefits pensioners should receive, stipulated the creation of worker re-training centers, and mandated subsidies for laid-off workers, but it was up to individual firms to provide the funds for these programs in order to implement the payout policies. The problem was that only the firms that were in relatively good economic conditions had the resources to make the prescribed payments. Firms with lots of pensioners often found themselves in a vicious cycle, finding it almost impossible to become profitable, burdened with many older, less skilled workers, and retirees. Unless local governments could provide adequate support, firms that needed to lay off workers often were also those least likely to have the funds to pay the prescribed subsidies and benefits. Those who were on the brink of closure or those that had stopped production were even less likely to be able to provide workers social security.

Since the late 1990s the state has tried to create a unified welfare system that will take the burden of welfare off firms. But that system is still a work in progress as Minxin Pei's paper details.[c] At best, the current system is centralized only to the provincial level, in many places it is often unified only to the municipal level, and even then some firms are still not fully participating in the social insurance programs. The tremendous variation in the burden and wealth of different localities has created incentive problems to an integrated national system of welfare. Like systems elsewhere, localities are unwilling to pay for the welfare of their poorer neighbors.[d]

The question addressed in this paper is how the Chinese state has been able to proceed with corporate restructuring while the social security system is still being developed. Unlike other Leninist systems that undertook reform, China's economy remained strong and is getting stronger after reform. China has national champions that are not only economically successful domestically but in the international context.[e] Moreover, while there is social dislocation it

---

[c]The guidelines of what the provisions should be can be found in Garnaut, R., Song, L., Tenev, S. and Yao, Y. (2005). *China's Ownership Transformation: Process, Outcomes, Prospects*, Chapter 4. Washington, DC: The International Finance Corporation.

[d]This is not a problem unique to China but common in the process of welfare reform. See Smuthkalin, W. (2005). "The Politics of State-Led Welfare Development: Health Insurance and Pension Institutional Reforms in Thailand, Taiwan, and China." Ph.D. Dissertation, Department of Political Science, Stanford University, 2006.

[e]Also see Nolan, P. (2001). *China and the Global Economy*. Hampshire and New York: Palgrave, for a discussion of China's efforts to build up key national firms.

seems less severe than in Eastern Europe or Russia. How has China handled its lack of an adequate social security system while it undergoes the transition from a centrally planned to a competitive market economy? What lessons can be learned from China's attempts to end the old social contract and create a new social security system? How has China managed to keep its worker dislocation at a minimum?

1. Politically Mediated Corporate Restructuring

Even though China's officials need not worry about being voted out of office, they must worry about the political fallout from restructuring. Breaking the iron rice bowl without an adequate welfare system is a politically dangerous proposition. From the late 1990s onwards, the number of demonstrations has increased as the SOE reforms have taken hold. The plight and discontent of laid-off workers as well as of pensioners who have failed to get their promised benefits have been well documented in the literature.[f] Not all laid-off workers engage in collective action, but enough have done so that officials are now constantly on the alert to safeguard stability (*wending*).[g] Having disgruntled workers take to the streets can negate all other accomplishments (*yipiao foujue*) in annual cadre evaluations.

In the absence of a national social-welfare safety net corporate restructuring in China has been shaped as much by political as economic constraints. Authorities, ever vigilant of worker reaction and constrained by their lack of resources to buy off workers and other "losers from reform" with acceptable severance packages, have had to restructure state owned firms in ways that minimize rather than maximize job loss and worker layoffs. This has caused restructuring and privatization to remain a patchwork of solutions that pushes the limits of reform but then must be reined back to accommodate the political as well

---

[f] Chen, F. (2000). "Subsistence Crises, Managerial Corruption and Labour Protests in China." *The China Journal* (44), 41–63. Dorothy Solinger has also written extensively on the plight of laid-off workers. See, for example, her (2002). "Labour Market Reform and the Plight of the Laid-off Proletariat." *The China Quarterly* (170), 304–326. Also see her (2003). "State and Society in Urban China in the Wake of the 16th Party Congress." *The China Quarterly* (176), 943–959. On pensioners see Hurst, W. and O'Brien, K. J. (2002). "China's Contentious Pensioners." *The China Quarterly* (170), 345–360.

[g] See Cai, Y. (2001). "The Silence of the Dislocated: Chinese Laid-off Employees in the Reform Period." Ph.D. Dissertation, Department of Political Science, Stanford University. Also see his (2002). "The Resistance of Chinese Laid-off Workers in the Reform Period." *The China Quarterly* (170), 327–344; also see Weston, T. (2002). "'Learn from Daqing': More Dark Clouds for Workers in State-Owned Enterprises." *Journal of Contemporary China* 11(33), 721–734.

as economic realities that exist in different localities. Local officials, driven by financial and political pressures, work out *ad hoc* strategies to cut job losses.

The fusion of political and economic agendas in China's enterprise restructuring limits which enterprises can be declared bankrupt or sold and which can be restructured and how. Such constraints explain why some forms of corporate restructuring are preferred over others, why ailing and already dead firms that have stopped production remain open, and why some firms for which there are takers are not privatized. Unlike its once-Communist brethren, political constraints in China have resulted in significant restructuring but relatively little genuine privatization. Restructuring and privatization are distinct and separate processes that do not necessarily lead from one to the other. In the absence of a developed social security system China has used controlled restructuring as an institutional substitute during the transition to ease the changes in the social contract. To achieve these dual goals the state has had to retain control of the process of restructuring and to adopt forms of restructuring that are politically feasible but not necessarily the most economically efficient. The sections that follow will detail the dual strategy that China has adopted as it moves from a centrally planned to a market economy with a still evolving system of social security.

1.1. *State-led restructuring*

Unlike the big bang style of reform practiced in Russia and Eastern Europe, the Chinese state has been proactive and retains control of the reform process to decide whether a firm can restructure, sell, or declare bankruptcy. In China's corporate restructuring the key players are the central state, and particularly its agents at various levels of government who are charged with the task of reform. A firm manager may initiate restructuring, but ultimately the decision must be approved by the local government.

Earlier analysts were correct in stating that local governments have incentives to privatize their state-owned enterprises in the face of the economic costs.[h] But local governments are also subject to political and economic constraints that limit their actions. Economic expediency or efficiency cannot

---

[h]On this see, for example, Cao, Y., Qian, Y. and Weingast, B. R. (1999). "From Federalism, Chinese Style to Privatization, Chinese Style." *Economics of Transition* 7(1), 103–131.

be the sole criterion of action. Local officials must calculate the consequences of changes on their local constituencies and ultimately on their own political survival. It is a path-dependent process shaped by existing institutions and resource endowments. Surplus labor is a key constraint on restructuring.

1.2. *De-link restructuring from unemployment and lay-offs*

Enterprise restructuring need not be synonymous with job loss.[i] In China, restructuring, unemployment and lay offs have followed different logics and often were affected by different factors, especially in the most recent years. Restructuring has been made compatible with minimal layoffs and unemployment. While we lack national data, based on the results of a 2001 survey of over 400 firms in five cities we can see that three-quarters of the firms which restructured retained all their workers.[j] In other cases, the firm took part of the employees, in others the government took responsibility for those adversely affected by restructuring.[k]

This is not to say that there has been no job loss. When we look at the actual unemployment figures, we see that it has been increasing.[l] However, as

---

[i]This conclusion is also supported by findings by Garnaut, R., Song, L., Tenev, S. and Yao, Y. (2005). *China's Ownership Transformation: Process, Outcomes, Prospects.* Washington, DC: The International Finance Corporation, Chapter 4. One of their most important findings is that firms that restructure have few worker layoffs and unemployed than non-restructured firms. As they also point out it is incorrect to simply look at aggregate statistics on the changes in the number of workers in state owned firms. Former state jobs may be reclassified as private sector jobs.

[j]The survey was conducted during late 2000 and early 2001 at 451 firms of different ownership forms in five cities — Wuxi and Yancheng in Jiangsu Province, Hangzhou in Zhejiang Province, Zhengzhou in Henan Province, and Jiangmen in Guangdong Province. The survey focused on four industrial sectors: machinery-building, electronics, textiles, and chemicals.

[k]A more in depth discussion of the patterns of corporate restructuring can be found in my (2005). "Patterns of Corporate Restructuring: Political Constraints on Privatization." *China Journal* (January 2005), pp. 115–136, on which parts of this paper are based.

[l]Actual rates of urban unemployment are unclear. Various estimates exist. For the period 1995–2003, a recent World Bank study cites an increase of urban unemployment increasing from 2.9 to 4.3%. Garnaut, R., Song, L., Tenev, S. and Yao, Y. (2005). *China's Ownership Transformation: Process, Outcomes, Prospects.* Washington, DC: The International Finance Corporation. However, it also cites, p. 90, Giles, J., Park, A. and Zhang, J. (2004). "What is China's True Unemployment Rate?" Unpublished ms., University of Michigan, Ann Arbor, Michigan, who give the "true" rate among "urban permanent residents increased from 6.1% at the end of 1995 to 11.1% at the end of 2002... The unemployment rate of all urban workers, including temporary residents, has increased from over the same period from 4.0% to 7.3%." For an updated, published version of this last cited work, see John Giles, Albert Park, and Fang Cai, "How has Economic Restructuring Affected China's Urban Workers?" *China Quarterly*, 185 (March 2006), 61–95.

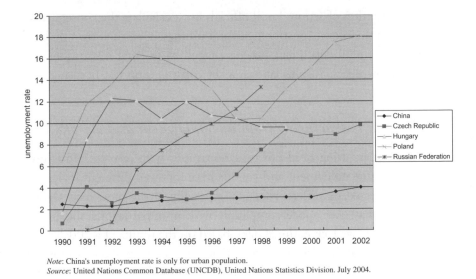

Note: China's unemployment rate is only for urban population.
Source: United Nations Common Database (UNCDB), United Nations Statistics Division. July 2004.

Fig. 1.   Unemployment rate in China, Russia and Eastern European countries over time.

Fig. 1 shows, while there is an upward trend in unemployment in China it is relatively low when compared to trends in Russia and other East European countries.[m]

2. Restructure First, Privatize Second

The decision by the state to retain control of the reform process has meant that forms of restructuring can be phased in and designed to achieve economic or political goals at different stages of the process. The results of restructuring in our five surveyed cities show a distinct pattern. As Fig. 2 below shows, privatization and bankruptcy are limited while shareholding is common.

The often-quoted phrase, "grasp the large and let go of the small," suggests that our aggregate picture might mask a larger number of sales in smaller firms.

---

[m]Garnaut *et al.* assert, p. 90, that "China is close to average unemployment levels in transition economies and has rates of unemployment similar to high-unemployment advanced countries such as Italy, Germany, and France." However, no specific transition countries were listed nor were figures or citations given. It may also be a question of which years are being compared.

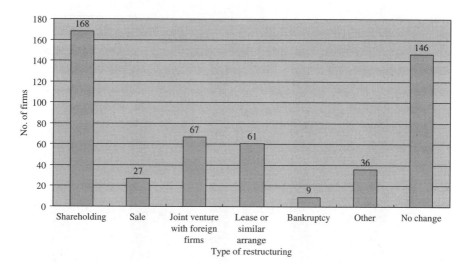

Fig. 2. Patterns of firm restructuring in the 1990s.

However, even when we disaggregate our data, we find that, regardless of firm size, sales totaled no more than 7% of total firms as of 2000.[n]

China also has been very careful to phase its restructuring, adopting the least disruptive first, and then privatizing. Our survey data shows that in each city, privatization came after other forms of restructuring (see Fig. 3).

Interviews suggest that during earlier phases of restructuring it was often difficult to gain official approval for the sale of a SOE even when there was a prospective buyer. Although sales have increased, how the new owner plans to deal with the workers continues to loom large as one of the most important issues in determining whether a firm can be sold. Are workers likely to be laid off with no clear prospects for re-employment? In China, these are not simply economic matters but highly sensitive political issues that stand at the core of what the Party still claims is a socialist system. If an investor is allowed to control the firm and does not agree to retain all the workers, what kind of agreement can be reached that will allow the local authorities to provide laid-off

---

[n]Contrary to what one might expect, in our sample more large firms were sold than small ones. Scale was measured by output as defined by the state statistical bureau. There is some recent evidence to suggest that in some areas, the local authorities have begun to sell their own state shares to outside investors so we may see an increase in privatization. In a Guangdong county near Hong Kong, for example, foreigners who originally held only partial ownership of a local firm have been allowed in recent years to buy out the local government's shares and become full owners.

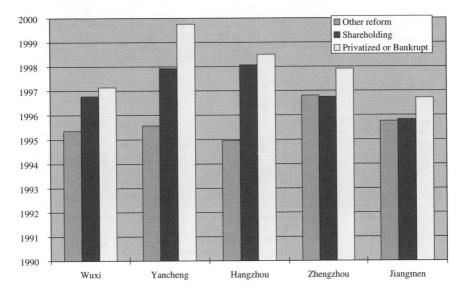

Fig. 3. Timing of various reforms by cities.

workers with an acceptable severance package? Is it likely that the investor will be able to turn the firm around and eventually expand production, and thus increase the number of jobs for the local community and provide increased tax revenues for the government coffers? There is also the problem of how much of the firm's debt the new owner will assume. These are questions that must be addressed before approval is given for a sale.

Similar restrictions apply to bankruptcy. The corporate governance literature points to the difficulties of bankruptcy and how other remedies are often sought to resolve debt issues.[o] Bankruptcy has been a legal option since the 1980s, but even now it is only used in selected cases.[p] In our survey of firms, bankruptcy was never used for any of the large enterprises. In our survey, the largest number of bankruptcies involved medium-sized enterprises.

Because China has maintained a policy of state-led restructuring, an enterprise has no authority to unilaterally undertake a bankruptcy action. In most cases, as with other forms of restructuring, a local government agency initiates

[o]See Schleifer, A. and Vishny, R. W. (1997). "A Survey of Corporate Governance." *The Journal of Finance* **52**(2), 737–783.
[p]On bankruptcy in China's SOEs and related problems, see Holz, C. (2001). "Economic Reforms and State Sector Bankruptcy in China." *The China Quarterly* **166**, 342–367.

the action and it must be approved by the local government as a whole. The assets of the firm are then assessed by the State Asset Management Bureau and are sold to pay off its debts. Even the details of the debt repayment have become political. In one locality in Guangdong, it was only after the bankruptcy rules made clear that workers would receive priority of payment rather than creditors did bankruptcy begin to be more frequently invoked.

Officials and factory managers freely admit in interviews that there are firms that desperately need to be closed and declared bankrupt, but the authorities dare not touch them — there are too many workers involved and no effective way to buy off the workers or find alternative jobs for them.[q] In essence, unless local authorities can come up with sufficient funds to pay off/buy off the workers; an enterprise cannot be declared bankrupt.

It is interesting to note that although some localities have used the bankruptcy option to privatize weak firms; it is not always the worst enterprises that are selected for bankruptcy. In some cases, a failing but salvageable enterprise is declared bankrupt because there is an interest by an investor to restore the enterprise to health, if the price is right.

2.1. *Shareholding: source of jobs, economic turnaround, and capital*

It is not surprising that shareholding emerged as one of the earliest and most widely used form of restructuring in our survey. First, from an ideological perspective, it is most compatible with China's continued allegiance to socialism. Although there are different types of shareholding systems, in most if not all, employees are shareholders. For instance, a shareholding cooperative sells shares in the firm only to its workers and managers.

Second, and perhaps most important, shareholding is less likely to result in unemployment and layoffs.[r] Shareholding was used as a means to minimize layoffs. It was hailed as a strategy that offered workers the opportunity to stop their firm from shutting down. At the same time, at least in theory,

---

[q] For further discussion of the lack on welfare provisions and how this hinders industrial reforms, see Gu, E. (2001). "Beyond the Property Rights Approach: Welfare Policy and the Reform of State-Owned Enterprises in China." *Development and Change* (32), 129–150.

[r] *Op. Cit.* Garnaut, R., Song, L., Tenev, S. and Yao, Y. *China's Ownership Transformation*, Chapter 4, especially pp. 98 and 101, found that employee shareholding reform resulted in significantly less layoffs than sales.

shareholding also held out the hope that if workers and managers became owners they would help turn around their factory, make it profitable, enable it to repay its debts, and thus not need to lay off workers.

Third, shareholding served an economic function — it became a fund-raising scheme for firms to obtain extra capital. The funds from the employee purchase of shares went directly to the enterprise. The sale of shares thus helped fill the void left by decreasing bank loans, which became more difficult to obtain, especially for ailing SOEs, as the state has tried to reform the banks to solve the non-performing loan problem. For SOEs and the state, shareholding became a low-cost way to keep factories open and workers employed without additional support from local government.

Some enterprises had difficulty getting workers to buy shares, especially in the ailing, loss-making ones.[s] As an incentive to lure them, some enterprises allowed workers to enjoy extra dividends from additional shares that they did not need to purchase but were held by the state. However, the property rights over these secondary shares reside with the state. If workers leave their company, they will only receive payment for the shares that they actually purchased, not for all the shares from which they had potentially been earning dividends.

2.2. *Equalize shares first, build big stakeholders second*

One important distinguishing feature of China's shareholding system is that workers and managers were generally allotted equal shares when restructuring began. Unlike in Russia or Poland, where managers have gained large blocks of shares from the state from the start of the process, in China it has been only in recent years, after the initial restructuring, that managers have been allowed and in some cases encouraged to buy a large number of shares (see Fig. 4).

The China case suggests that the speed and time it takes to achieve a market transformation may affect the nature, degree, and consequences of insider privatization.[t] The early forms of restructuring limited the shares that managers

---

[s]This is contrary to some earlier reports of how employee–shareholders have benefited from shareholding arrangements. See Qian, Y. "Reforming Corporate Governance and Finance in China." In: Aoki, M. and Kim, H.-K. (eds.) (1994), *Corporate Governance in Transitional Economies*, pp. 215–252, World Bank. There is evidence to suggest that employees were required to purchase shares.

[t]For a comparative discussion of the different outcomes of privatization according to the speed and constraints, see Walder, A. (2003). "Elite Opportunity in Transitional Economies." *American Sociological Review* 68(6), 899–916.

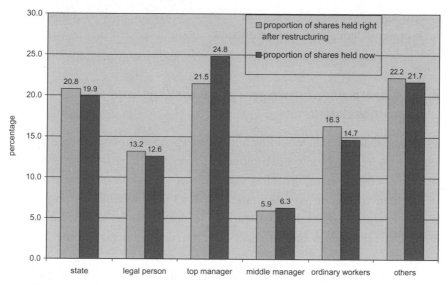

Note: Changes over time for share held by top managers and for share held by ordinary workers are statistically significant.

Fig. 4. Changes of shares held by different parties over time.

were allowed to buy. Only in the latest phases of restructuring is there a trend to promote the concentration of shares in the hands of the management. Research in 2005 suggests that in some parts of the country, manager buyouts are being instituted, skipping the earlier phase of equal shareholding.[u] This change, in part, may be driven by the realization that effective corporate governance requires a major hands-on stakeholder.

Now, when firms are in the second or third phase of restructuring, the political concerns that originally steered the state to favor shareholding systems where workers hold shares are now seen as a problem that may hinder further change. Interviews in 2004 suggest that enterprise managers are frustrated by the power of employee shareholder associations that are blocking opportunities for sales or joint ventures.[v] What may have started out primarily as schemes to raise money through the sale of shares to workers under the shareholding

---

[u] Author China Interviews in Shandong in June–July 2005.
[v] For a different perspective on whether the employee shareholder associations have any influence at all, see Sargeson, S. and Zhang, J. (1999). "Re-assessing the Role of the Local State: A Case Study of Local Government Interventions in Property Rights Reform in a Hangzhou District." *The China Journal* (42), 77–99, especially pp. 91–92.

system may have resulted over time in some power for workers. How potent such power is remains to be investigated.

2.3. *A two-pronged strategy: "grasp the large and let go of the small"*

The above described shareholding and limited privatization schemes may help explain the relatively low unemployment rates, but they fail to explain the success of China's economy. How can some of China's most successful firms still be state owned or partially state owned, all the while minimizing unemployment and layoffs while restructuring? To answer that let us now turn to the larger context in which both the still weak restructured firms and the stronger firms interact in China's complex political economy.

China adopted a differentiated policy for dealing with firms of different size and importance. The large enterprises, in contrast to the medium and small enterprises, are given different options for corporate restructuring. It is in this regard that the phrase "grasp the large and let go of the small" (*zhua da* and *fang xiao*) comes into play. As we indicated above, the term "grasp" (*zhua*) does not necessarily indicate the state's desire to hold on to current forms of ownership. The state's desire to "grasp" (*zhua*) refers to a strategy for its most prized large enterprises — to take back (*zhua*) direct control and provide preferential treatment so that they have the best chance of survival and growth.[w] This involves a two-pronged approach but unlike some of the earlier forms of restructuring discussed above that are designed to the state's political agenda, in this instance it also allows restructured firms to engage in relatively bold economic initiatives. In practice this means that first, it is most important enterprises are allowed to restructure. Second, as part of the restructuring, debt and financial burdens are re-allocated so that the enterprise, or at least a portion of the enterprise, will be in a better position to move forward. The state then can utilize these firms to motivate others to perform better by the formation of enterprise groups. Let us now detail how this process works.

---

[w]Also see Nolan, P. (2001). *China and the Global Economy*. Hampshire and New York: Palgrave for a discussion of China's efforts to build up key national firms.

2.4. *Private spin-offs: unburden the big and best SOEs*

We have long known that Chinese SOEs have been social-service units as well as production units.[x] Under Mao, schools, hospitals, and day-care centers were common in the large SOEs at the core of the state socialist system. These social services have been the source of the high expenditures and thus low profitability of many SOEs, even when the firms were efficient in production. Only recently have SOEs begun to transfer to local government authorities the non-productive social-service sectors of their operations. In some of the largest enterprises, services that cannot be immediately off-loaded have been turned into subsidiary companies that are given a graduated period to become responsible for their own profits and losses.[y] Notably, the state is allowing the largest SOEs to attempt this within a still-socialist state-owned structure. Such a reform is likely to be slow and limited.

However, gradual and radical reforms may take place within the *same* SOE. This has allowed big, important wholly state-owned enterprises to take the best-positioned portion of their state assets to create a new and more efficient private firm. Unlike some forms which earlier analysts have dubbed as spontaneous or informal privatization,[z] these are officially approved at the highest levels, involving key firms in the most important sectors. Rather than something cooked up by the managers, with or without the consent of the workers, these spin-offs have become an officially sanctioned strategy officially sanctioned strategy to allow the largest firms to get ahead without privatizing an entire state-owned enterprise.

In what can be called partial privatization, the enterprises are allowed to hive off the most modern equipment and the most profitable product line from the parent firm. Not surprisingly, these new spun-off firms are in

---

[x]See, e.g., Walder, A. (1986). *Communist Neo-Traditionalism: Work and Authority in Chinese Industry*. Berkeley and LA: University of California Press; and also Henderson, G. and Cohen, M. (1984) *The Chinese Hospital: A Socialist Work Unit*. New Haven, CT: Yale University Press.

[y]For example, one of the largest steel companies in China had little choice but to let portions of the enterprise be reformed at different speeds. It took the subsidiary sectors of the enterprise that were engaged in auxiliary non-productive work such as the service sectors and created separate companies (*buoli chuchu*) within the enterprise. The parent company gave these subsidiaries a schedule (approximately 3 years) to allow them to become increasingly self-sufficient. The parent company realized that it could not do this all at once or they "would die." As of 2000, some of these companies had become profitable. It should be noted that one of the incentives driving these changes was the desire of the parent company to get listed on the stock exchange.

[z]Qian, Y. "*Reforming Corporate Governance*."

good economic shape and free of the socialist institutions from which they were created. The debt, the outdated machines, the retired and less skilled workers and the non-productive aspects of the factory remain the burden of the parent firm. These spin-offs can then become listed as private limited liability companies and can attempt to raise capital on the market. The parent firm remains an SOE, but becomes a shareholder in the new private firm and receives revenue in the form of dividends from its shares. This mix of property rights allows the profitable sectors of otherwise ailing state-owned enterprises to develop rapidly, while providing time for the parent SOE to clear out the socialist institutional residual at a slower pace. Layoffs take place, sometimes in substantial numbers, but these large firms often have the funds to provide their laid-off workers with an acceptable severance package or are able to find them alternative jobs.[aa]

2.5. *Debt-equity swaps: reduce enterprise debt*

Another pivotal piece of the state's strategy for restructuring its large SOEs is the creation of debt-equity swaps (*zhai zhuan gu*). Selected large state-owned enterprises have been allowed to take a portion of their old bank debt and turn it into equity that is then held by newly created asset management companies (AMCs).[bb] The idea is to clear large SOEs of a portion of their debt.[cc] In theory, the AMCs and thus the bank/state will be able to recoup the non-performing loans that are now held as equity when the AMCs sell their shares at a time when the firms finally turn themselves around and become profitable.[dd]

In order to participate in a debt-equity swap, firms first go through the process of corporatization, whereby an SOE is turned into a shareholding company. The asset management company or companies, depending on the number of banks to which the enterprise owed debts, is given a percentage of the shares commensurate with the size of the debt. The other shares of the firm

---

[aa] An excellent example of this phenomenon is described in Weller, R. and Li, J. (2000). "From State-Owned Enterprise to Joint Venture: A Case Study of the Crisis in Urban Social Services." *The China Journal* (43), 83–99.

[bb] These AMCs were formed through the specialized state banks from which the loans were originally borrowed. Each of China's four specialized banks has an AMC created by the State Council and underwritten by the Ministry of Finance.

[cc] The amount of debt that can be off-loaded in this manner is limited and usually restricted to loans accrued before 1997.

[dd] More recently, this debt has been packaged and is being sold to foreign investors.

are held by the state, other enterprises, and sometimes by the employees. The AMC, as a major shareholder, is given a seat on the board of directors of the newly corporatized firm. In theory, the AMCs are supposed to help the firms become profitable, inasmuch as debt-equity swaps eliminate a portion of the SOEs' debt, which then clears the way for the firms to refinance themselves.

2.6. *Enterprise groups: merge resources and management skills*

The state's use of debt equity swaps goes beyond simply reducing enterprise debt. The debt-equity swap is a crucial piece of the state's plans for enterprise restructuring. It allows a once debt-ridden firm to be included in an enterprise group (*jituan*), which is an amalgamation of firms that in most cases had previously operated independently.[ee]

The purpose, particularly among the *jituan* formed in the late 1990s, is for one good core firm to help turn around a number of weaker firms. This core firm may be a newly formed firm derived from a SOE parent or an existing strong SOE, which may or may not have spin-offs. In corporate governance terms, the core enterprise, ideally a listed limited-liability company, intervenes, takes charge and sends in new managers and other leading personnel to the ailing firms until their situation improves. The hope is that eventually all of the enterprises within the group will become internationally competitive after they revamp their technology and management, in part through the pooling of group resources and skills. The formation of a *jituan* is a strategy to keep weak firms alive and thus to salvage the jobs of the workers in these otherwise doomed enterprises.

A striking feature of the recently formed enterprise groups is the mix of ownership forms and the degree of reform that has taken place in different units within the group. The enterprise group is considered an SOE, while the individual firms within the group may be shareholding companies, and thus are non-state or private companies. The enterprise group has shares in the firms that make up the group, and this stake varies depending on the

---

[ee]There are cases where an enterprise group grew from one parent firm. The term is now used rather loosely to refer to various configurations of enterprises. The enterprise group as an institution is not new. Since the 1980s the Chinese state has used it as an alternative form of organization and control, rather than relying on the supervisory role of government bureaus. See Keister, L. (1998). "Engineering Growth: Business Group Structure and Firm Performance in China's Transitional Economy." *American Journal of Sociology* **104**(2), 404–440.

individual firms — it may range from 100% to only minority shareholding. Since the so-called private companies may be largely or entirely owned by the enterprise group, in essence they may still be state owned. The difference is that they are to operate as independent accounting units in a market context. The relationship between the enterprise group and the individual firms is equivalent to that between an owner and a factory manager, not an administrative superior and a subordinate, which was the situation before the reforms. Some of these firms are at the forefront in terms of efficiency and technology, with few older or unskilled workers, whereas others still are burdened with a less skilled workforce, probably with large numbers of pensioners. Thus the social security costs vary tremendously.

Much more research is needed before we can make any judgment about whether this group strategy will work. There are examples where weak firms have begun a turnaround with the help of the stronger core firm. The key is to have a core firm strong enough both to bear the risks and provide the management talent to turn the weaker members around, but this is not always possible and some groups have already started to fall apart. Even when the strategy succeeds, it has a cost. It drains resources away from the few good firms that are currently able to stand on their own. How many of the core enterprises are strong enough to withstand the added management burdens and still move forward with their own development? Would those enterprises that were hived off from less efficient state-owned parents, taking with them the most modern machinery and the most profitable production lines and the ability to generate funds from stock sales, do better if they had been allowed to operate individually, without the *jituan* structure? Is this structure undoing the progress that is made when the profitable sectors of ailing SOEs are allowed to form new firms? These are valid economic questions, but, at least up to now in China, the political goals that drive this type of restructuring outweigh economic concerns.

Interviews with the heads of a number of these successful firms reveal hesitation and sometimes resistance to participating in a *jituan*. Not surprisingly, the major concern was that the poorly performing enterprises in the group would drag down the core firm.[ff] In each of the cases investigated,

---

[ff]This concern extended to the wages of workers in the core firm. However, this leveling does not always happen. For example, in a large steel enterprise group the wages of workers in the core limited-liability company remained significantly higher than those in the other firms within the group.

local authorities had to provide incentives for the core enterprise before it would agree to enter a group. In some cases, the process took several years before agreement was reached. But China is an example of an "agenda-setting government."[gg] The Chinese Party-state still has the ability to implement such restructuring. This is state led restructuring. The national leadership still holds the trump card — leaders of the most important enterprises are directly appointed by an office in the State Council. In at least one case, an enterprise group was established when the former officials of the core enterprise were retired and a new leadership was installed from above.

3. An Intermediate Solution: From Social Contract to Social Security

The creation of a social security system is difficult in any country. In China the process is all the more difficult because of the prior social contract, which provided workers with an iron rice bowl paid for entirely by the state. The state now wants to give workers protection in the form of a new unified, national social security system that will provide adequate yet fiscally sustainable coverage for all of its workers. Unlike the past, however, the central state must convince individual workers, as well as firms and local governments to pay into a new system and share risks, where the rich essentially pay for the benefits of the poor. Like so many other countries, China so far has only made limited headway in its effort to convince richer firms and localities to support their poorer brethren.[hh]

In the interim, China continues to "grasp for stones to cross the river" and "grow out of the plan" by pursuing a policy of phased restructuring, adopting and adjusting shareholding forms as conditions change to mediate worker dislocation and provide for their social security to at least a minimum extent. Aware of the political and social consequences of restructuring where large numbers of workers are displaced without an adequate social security system in place, China restricted privatization and the use of bankruptcy,

---

[gg]On this, see Roland, G. (1995). "Political Economy Issues of Ownership Transformation in Eastern Europe." In: Aoki, M. and Kim, H.-K. (eds.) *Corporate Governance in Transitional Economies: Insider Control and the Role of Banks*. Washington, DC: World Bank, pp. 31–58.

[hh]Smuthkalin, W. "Political Regimes, State Leaders, and Welfare State Development in East Asia: The cases of Taiwan, Thailand, and China." Ph.D. Dissertation, Department of Political Science, Stanford University, 2006.

especially in those large state owned enterprises employing large numbers of workers. In sharp contrast to Russia and Eastern Europe, China's restructuring has been gradual, both in terms of unemployment and change in ownership forms. Instead of following a big bang approach, selling off assets and creating immediate big stake holders through insider privatization by factory managers, China pursued limited shareholding systems were managers only recently have begun to hold large shares.

Certainly, the demonstrations by workers in numerous cities in China suggest that China has not succeeded completely in strategy to placate the losers of reform. However, overall, compared to other former Leninist systems, China has been relatively successful. The China case suggests that the lack of a social security system, while a constraint, need not be an insurmountable barrier to reform. Overall, China's experience suggests that carefully controlled, selective forms of restructuring may be the next best solution while the country is developing a social security system. Lower levels of unemployment can be maintained than would otherwise be the case if a country were to use only economic criteria to determine patterns of restructuring.

Fortunately, China has two conditions in its favor that allow a relatively amicable end to the social contract with workers and buy the system more time. Both stem from its booming economy and revenues. The first, and the one that local and central authorities can directly control, is that the state and its agents can buy an end to the social contract between workers and their firms and thus the state. Firms and local governments can sever their relationship with a worker by providing an acceptable severance package (*maiduan gongling*). As reforms have progressed, this method is being increasingly used in localities such as Shanghai where revenues are plentiful. Second, localities can develop the local private economy and encourage former state workers to take jobs, many of which may be more lucrative than their old SOE jobs, in the growing private sector.[ii] Often these two possibilities are connected and the transition is fairly smooth. In such areas, local governments are on their way to having the funds to underwrite a unified social security system. The problems remain

---

[ii]This is one of the reasons why not all laid off workers are disgruntled. Some have found better paying jobs. See Cai, Y. (2001). "The Silence of the Dislocated: Chinese Laid-off Employees in the Reform Period." Ph.D. Dissertation, Department of Political Science, Stanford University, Also see Cai, Y. (2002). "The Resistance of Chinese Laid-off Workers in the Reform Period." *The China Quarterly* (170), 327–344.

in areas that are both poor fiscally and lack a vibrant private economy that can absorb surplus labor and generate revenues to pay for a social security system.

For China's strategy to work, however, the state has to be in a position to influence, if not directly control, the speed and direction of restructuring. China's restructuring has been state-led with state sponsored privatization.[jj] It has been able to use restructuring to suit its political as well as economic agendas. China's strategy, however, may come at a cost, as I have suggested above. Economic considerations have had to take a back seat to a political agenda. So far, the overall success of China's economic growth has created enough slack and resources to absorb the additional costs. It is unclear whether other systems will be so lucky. The effect on China's economic performance may not yet be evident. How much of a drain are the slowly reforming enterprises on those that China has anointed as the national champions, the new spin offs? Could they be even stronger? How long can they bear the weight of their parent enterprises and weaker siblings? Again, these are all economic concerns. In China's calculus, such economic inefficiencies have been necessary transaction costs to maintain political stability and social cohesion as the system moves from social contract to a system of social security.

[jj]This also holds for the privatization of TVEs. See my (1999). *Rural China Takes Off: Institutional Foundations of Economic Reform*. Berkeley and LA: University of California Press.

CHAPTER 7

Indian Pension Reform: A Sustainable and Scalable Approach

Ajay Shah

1. Introduction: Why Pension Reforms Matter

India is making sound progress on poverty elimination for those who can work. A substantial reduction was seen in the headcount of the poor in the period after 1993. In years to come, it is likely that Indian GDP growth, and hence rising wages, will lead to the elimination of poverty among people in their working years. Poverty amongst the elderly is the next frontier. Poverty amongst the elderly will then become the dominant form of poverty in India, since the elderly do not work and thus do not benefit from higher wages. A parallel development of great importance is the rise in migration flows of labor, and the breakdown of the "joint family," through which the elderly are less likely to cohabit with their children in old age.

Simple dole solutions will not work. A government program that seeks to pay a dole of Rs. 25 per day to 10% of the population would incur a fiscal cost of 4% of GDP, excluding administrative costs. A more useful path is to focus on public programs that target the poor (regardless of whether or not they are elderly). However, the most effective public programs that directly target poverty are the employment guarantee schemes, but these will be ineffective in reaching the elderly poor.

The only solution is a sustainable, scalable pension system. With a formal pension system, individuals would save in their working years, and thus command personal pension wealth, which would ensure they avoid poverty in old age. The two keywords that are of essence in thinking about this pension system are sustainability and scalability. It is possible to design non-scalable subsidy-based programs which work for a few people. It is possible to run unsustainable subsidy programs for a few years. These are incomplete and unsatisfactory solutions. What India needs is a framework which reaches a substantial fraction of the population, reaching into below-median incomes, for the coming 50 years. This would constitute a scalable and sustainable solution.

Pension reforms should be a centerpiece of "second generation reforms." Pension reforms are consistent with present visions of India's strategy for economic growth. Planning for old age is directly material to the empowerment and well being of millions of workers. A pension system where workers are able to manifestly able to see substantial levels of their own personal pension wealth is one where workers will be more comfortable in coping with the ordinary competitive processes of the market economy. By augmenting the flow of savings, and by fostering high quality investment decisions, pension reforms will help India attain higher GDP growth.

Policy issues on pensions are subtle. Sound strategies in pension reforms often diverge from obvious and apparent solutions, for two reasons. First, as compared with many fields of public policy where sectoral knowledge is required for formulating sectoral policies, pension reforms is a particularly complex field involving interlocking considerations spanning the fields of finance, public finance, labor markets, macroeconomics, demographics, IT-intensive administrative procedures, and political economy. The second aspect is that there are long lags between policies and their consequences, and the consequences can be of a macroeconomic scale.

Mistakes in policies on pensions can destabilize the entire economy. As compared with other aspects of economic policy, the pension sector is unusual in that mistakes in policy do not show up for a prolonged period. But when these mistakes do show up, they can easily generate fiscal impacts in tens of percentage points of GDP. Many advanced countries — where economic policy is ordinarily executed competently in areas such as foreign trade or infrastructure — are now laboring under pension-related debt of over 100% of GDP. What are apparently micro issues in the pension sector have a disconcerting way of turning into macroeconomic challenges for the country, two moves ahead. Hence, policies in this area need to be subjected to extremely searching scrutiny, to ensure that difficulties in pensions do not derail India's growth over the next 50 years.

This is the right moment. India is at a remarkable point in its demographic transition. In the period from 2005 to 2030, a substantial decline in the dependency ratio is expected, with a large number of people coming into their working years. This constitutes a historic opportunity to create a pension system in time for these cohorts, who can be empowered to enjoy decades of life in their elderly years using personal control of pension assets. In addition, as of 2005, India now has the required institutional capacity for building sound institutions in the pensions area, which was not available in (say) 1995. Every year lost hurts welfare. The pensions issue is unlike any other part of public policy, in that it is extremely important to execute sound policy decisions, many decades ahead of time. An early effort in pension reforms is essential, so that sound institutions can be in place in time for young people coming into the labor force. The "power of compounding" implies that every additional year matters greatly in building up pension wealth. A person who loses an opportunity to put Rs. 2500 into a pension account at age 20 can lose pension wealth of roughly Rs. 25,000 at age 60. Every year of delay implies that millions of people will be unable to cross the poverty line in old age.

To the extent that pension reforms do not come about today, India will face decades of difficult social and fiscal stress in coping with the consequences.

2. Existing Mechanisms and their Difficulties

Unlike many countries, India does not have a comprehensive population-wide old age income security system. The vast majority continues to rely on support from their children as the main means of obtaining consumption in old age. Two narrow pension mechanisms exist at present.[1,2] They are the civil servants' defined benefit pension — which covers roughly 26 million workers — and the "organized sector" system run by the Employees Provident Fund Organization (EPFO) — which covers roughly 15 million workers.

2.1. *Traditional civil servants pension*

The "traditional civil servants pension" (TCSP) is the pension program that existed for employees of the central government who were recruited prior to 1/1/2004.[a] The TCSP is a pay-as-you-go defined benefit pension. It was an

---

[a]The TCSP for central government employees is administered by the Department of Pensions and Personnel Welfare (DPPW). The TCSP applies (with small variations) to employees of central government, state governments, local governments including municipalities, to "autonomous bodies" such as the Council for Scientific and Industrial Research (CSIR) and to "grant in aid" institutions.

integral part of the employment contract for government employees. There is a minimum requirement of 10 years of service before a worker is entitled to this pension. There is no attempt at having contributions or building up pension assets, i.e. it is unfunded. The benefit promised by the TCSP is a pension which is roughly half of the wage level of the last 10 months of employment.[b] The TCSP is indexed to wages. There is a "one rank, one wage" principle, whereby all retired persons of a certain rank get the same pension. Through this, pension payments are steadily revised to reflect the growth in wages. Hence, the growth in pension benefits in old age is typically higher than inflation.

The standard information released as part of the budgeting process only reveals information for the flow of annual pension payout, for a subset of pensioners, by both centre and states. Estimates of the unfunded liabilities, i.e. the implied pension debt, associated with workers and pensions under the TCSP are not computed nor disseminated by the government. Table 1 shows the growth in the flow of the annual pension outgo of Center and States over the recent 14-year period. The use of a 14-year period over which these growth rates are measured implies that the broad regularities are not driven by special events like the fifth Pay Commission. Over this 14-year period, while nominal

Table 1.   Government pension payments.

| | (Rs. crore) | | | (Percent to GDP) | | |
Year	Center	States	Total	Center	States	Total
1990–1991	3,272	3,131	6,403	0.75	0.7	1.46
2004–2005	27,320	38,370	65,690	0.96	1.35	2.31
Growth rate	6.37	19.6	18.1			

The numbers in this table show the annual flow of pension payments. The central number pertains to employees of central civil ministries, railways, posts, telecom and defence. As of 2004–2005, this is estimated at 4.5 million workers. It excludes pension expenditure of autonomous bodies and grant-in-aid institutions, which are estimated to have 3.4 million employees.

The corresponding number for states covers an estimated 7.4 million direct employees. It does not include employees of local governments, autonomous bodies and grant-in-aid institutions, which are estimated to have 10.4 million employees.

---

[b]The benefit rate is computed as 1/60 for each year of service, subject to a cap of a 50% benefit rate. In case of death after retirement, the spouse gets the full pension for 7 years, after which the benefit rate drops to 30% until the death of the spouse. There is a "commutation provision," under which the pensioner can choose to forgo up to 40% of the pension payout for 15 years, and instead take a lump sum.

GDP grew by a compound rate of 14.3%, the central pension outgo grew at a compound rate of 16.37% and the state pension outgo grew at a compound rate of 19.6%. Through this, the combined outgo went from 1.46% of GDP to 2.31% of GDP over this period.

These magnitudes — with a fast-growing expense which is already at 2.31% of GDP — highlight the fiscal ramifications of pension reforms. As emphasized in Table 1, the situation is more daunting since the publicly available statistics about the pension outgo only pertain to roughly half of the government sector employees.

2.2. *The EPFO*

The EPFO runs two main schemes, the "employee provident fund" (EPF) and the "employee pension scheme" (EPS). Both schemes are mandatory for workers earning below Rs. 6500 a month, in establishments with over 20 workers in 177 defined industries. As of March 31, 2003, there were 344,508 such establishments. EPFO data show the presence of 39.5 million members. However, many of these are dormant accounts, which come about through administrative difficulties in shifting an account from one employer to another. Independent estimates, based on the Indian Retirement Earnings and Savings (IRES) database, database suggest that there are roughly 15 million workers in late 2004.

The EPF is an individual account defined contribution system. It uses a contribution rate of 16%. The flow of contributions in 2002–2003 was Rs. 114 billion, and the stock of assets was Rs. 1.03 trillion. On average, workers tend to retire with very small balances in EPF. In 2002–2003, the mean pension wealth that came into the hands of a newly retired person was merely Rs. 36,000. If this money was used to buy an annuity from LIC, it would yield a pension of Rs. 230 per month, or 9% of per capita GDP.

The EPS is a defined benefit system. It is based on a contribution rate of 8.33%. The government contributes an additional 1.16%. EPS was created in 1995, and it only applies to workers who entered the labor force after 1995. In 2002–2003, the flow of contributions that came into EPS was Rs. 48 billion, and the stock of assets was Rs. 450 billion. The EPS provides a defined benefit at a rate of 1/70 of the salary drawn in the last 12 months preceding the date of exit, for each year of service subject to a maximum of 50%.[c] In the case of both EPF and EPS, EPFO handles all elements of the processes by itself, except for fund management which is outsourced to one external agency (typically the State Bank of India (SBI)). EPFO spent Rs. 4.3 billion in 2002–2003, with roughly Rs. 1.5 trillion of assets under management, giving a mean expense ratio of roughly 0.3%.

Establishments covered under the EPF can seek an exemption from the EPFO for fund management and set up their own self-administered fund. These "exempt funds" are required to use the identical investment regulations as the EPFO's, but at least match the returns of the EPFO.[d]

2.3. *Problems of these pension provisions*

Lack of coverage is the prime difficulty with TCSP and the EPFO. These two systems cover just 11% of the workforce. Hence, the dominant fraction of the workforce — i.e. 89% — lies in the "uncovered sector" and has no formal pension system.

2.3.1. *The civil servants pension*

In the case of the TCSP, the central problem has been that of fiscal stress. The pension payout of the centre and states has risen at a compound average annual growth rate of 18% over the period 1990–2004. The TCSP was designed in a world where most workers who retired at 60 were likely to be dead by 70. The value of the annuity embedded in the TCSP has gone up dramatically owing to the elongation of mortality in recent decades, particularly for the upper echelons of government employees who now have mortality characteristics comparable to those of OECD populations.

While the basic structure of a government-produced defined benefit pension is itself questionable, there are also many opportunities for making progress on parametric reforms to the detailed rules and procedures of the civil service pension[3] so as to reduce distortions, administrative complexity

---

[c]Upon death, the EPS provides for a pension to the spouse for life or till remarriage, and pension to children two at a time up to age 25.
[d]There were a total of 341,944 establishments with exempt funds as of March 2003, covering 3.751 million members.

and fiscal stress. The fiscal stress has been particularly acute at the state level. Some states are reported to have delayed pension payments. In 2003, the state of Tamil Nadu chose to cut pension benefits by reversing recent increases in the pension that followed as a consequence of wage hikes to existing employees. These developments have dented the perception of the TCSP as being one where benefits are defined and predictable.

Some public sector companies have defined benefit pension programs, which are likely to be under-funded, and these liabilities could cause problems at the exchequer at a future date. No data about these are available in the public domain.

The information systems surrounding the TCSP are extremely weak. As highlighted in Table 1, the information in budget documents about the flow of pension payments pertains to roughly half of government employees. No information is available about autonomous bodies, grant-in-aid institutions, and local government. The demographic structure of workers or pensioners is not known, which inhibits computation of India's implied pension debt.

2.3.2. *The EPFO*

The EPFO has several shortcomings which undermine its service provision, financial soundness, and hence its effectiveness as a pension mechanism:

1. While the EPF is an individual account DC system, the existing rules governing the EPF do not cater to steady accumulation of pension wealth over long time spans. If the observed average accumulated EPF balance at retirement were used to buy an annuity, it yields a pension which is 9% of per capita GDP.

   It is difficult to reconcile this failure of the EPF with the high level of the contribution rate into the EPF. As observed earlier, just one year of contribution of Rs. 2500 at age 20 can yield pension wealth of roughly Rs. 25,000 at age 60, in a properly designed pension system. The failure of the EPF to build up meaningful pension wealth may be related to administrative difficulties where accounts get closed or lost across job changes. It may also reflect provisions for premature withdrawal of balances.

2. In the case of the EPS, concerns have been expressed about the funding status. The 10-year interest rate fell dramatically from 13.4% on January 1,

1997 to 5.1% on October 18, 2003, and some modest improvements in mortality took place over this period. However, there was no change in either the contribution rate or the benefit rate for the EPS. This suggests that the EPS was either over-funded in 1998 or under-funded in 2003. While the law mandates that an actuarial report should be produced every year, it appears that one report per year has not been produced, and several recent reports have not been released into the public domain.

3. There are difficulties of implementation and administration with the EPFO's programs. The policies and the processes of the EPFO were established in the 1950s. The transformation in technology and knowledge about pension economics that have come about in the following years have not been reflected in a corresponding transformation in policies and processes. There are many weaknesses in the mechanisms of fund management, operational procedures faced by participants, transparency, and governance.[e] Even if a participant does not exploit windows of opportunity to withdraw assets, the fund management of the EPFO yields low rates of return, and the procedural frictions faced by the participant are acute.

4. The EPFO is burdened with a complex mandate that comprises record-keeping, administration, supervision, and regulation. This is inconsistent with a modern institutional architecture, where unbundling is favored in the interests of transparency and competition, and regulatory functions are sought to be kept distinct from service provision.

5. The accounting systems and policies of EPFO have certain weaknesses. The lack of computerized databases spanning information from the entire country has innately led to difficulties in reconciliation. More importantly, the valuation framework used is one where all bonds are valued at Rs. 100, regardless of market price. The "interest rate" on the EPF that is announced every year is the average coupon rate on the bond portfolio. It is announced at the start of the year, which necessitates a difficult effort in forecasting interest rates during the year. There is an explicit subsidy in the form of assets of roughly Rs. 0.5 trillion which have been deposited in "special deposits" with the government at an above-market rate of return.[4,5,f]

---

[e]For example, account balance statements are only supposed to be sent annually, and as of 2002–2003, there were 13.5 million "pending" accounts where annual statements had not been sent.

[f]The Y. V. Reddy committee has argued that a full scale reform of administrative rates can be undertaken after adequate results are obtained in terms of a modern pension system.

2.4. *Fiscal aspects*

The fiscal subsidies that underlie the EPFO comprise four components:

1. The special deposit of Rs. 0.5 trillion that is maintained by government at an above-market rate of return.
2. The contribution of 1.16% of wage that is paid by the government on behalf of workers for the EPS.
3. The subsidy that is associated with preferential tax treatment.
4. Potential payments from the exchequer in the future owing to funding gaps in either the EPF or the EPS.

Within the membership of the EPF and the TCSP, the fiscal transfers are disproportionately captured by the rich, for two reasons.

1. Among EPF customers, recently released distributional data has shown that only 7% of the accounts have an account balance of above Rs. 50,000. As much as 83% of the EPF assets are controlled by 15% of the accounts. Hence, the bulk of the subsidy that EPF members are enjoying is being captured by the richest among them.
2. The TCSP and the EPS — both defined benefit programs — generate very different payouts for people in different income classes. Poor people are likely to die sooner. Hence, the benefits obtained by the long-lived richer workers in TCSP and EPS are much higher than those obtained by poor people.

In the case of the EPS, even if the EPS is fully funded, the heterogeneity in mortality implies that it constitutes a fiscal transfer from poor people to rich people because poor people die younger and consume a pension for a shorter time-period. The TCSP and the EPFO constitute a regressive subsidy in favor of 11% of relatively affluent workers. As Table 2 shows, the median income of the covered sector — at Rs. 76,000 — is over two times larger than the median income of the uncovered sector — at Rs. 30,000. A striking feature of this data is that the 25th percentile of EPFO customers have a higher income than the median income of the uncovered sector, and the 25th percentile of civil service employees have a higher income than the 75th percentile of the uncovered sector.

Table 2. Income characteristics of sub-groups of labor force (December 2004).

Group	Number (million)	Total annual income (Rs.)		
		25%	Median	75%
Covered	39.2	58,000	76,000	108,000
Central employees	7.9	66,000	92,000	120,000
State employees	17.8	63,600	84,000	116,000
EPFO	14.6	36,000	60,000	90,000
Uncovered	324.8	18,000	30,000	54,000
Total	364.0	19,000	35,000	60,000

Source: Indian Retirement Earnings and Savings (IRES) database, author's calculations.

3. Goals of Reform

The goals of pension reforms in India may be summarized as follows.

1. *Coverage*: It is highly desirable to find ways to reach the vast uncovered sector, going beyond the existing 11% of the labor force covered by the TCSP and the EPFO.
2. *Sustainability*: India has substantial experience with funding difficulties, ranging from the railways pension,[6] the Employee Pension Scheme (EPS) of the EPFO, the "assured returns" products sold by UTI, and failure of banks. Pension reforms must have the discipline of laying a sound foundation using defined contributions, where the wealth of a participant is driven purely by net asset value (NAV), and avoiding assured returns, subsidies, guarantees, or liabilities for the government.

   A pension system which is based on fiscal subsidies will lack sustainability and scalability. It may work for 10 million or 20 million workers for a decade or two. But it will not work for 100 million or 200 million workers for the lifespan of a young person entering the labor market at age 20.

   The modern understanding of pension reforms clearly emphasizes a role for the State as a facilitator, in creating new institutions and in fostering their sound functioning. However, a goal of pension reforms should be to separate government from the process of making monthly pension payments to workers or citizens, over and beyond the monthly contributions paid into the pension accounts of government employees participating in a DC system.

3. *Scalability*: A scalable architecture is desired, which would work not just for the Central government but also for State and Local governments that choose to participate in the new system, and for the larger mass of the population in the uncovered sector.
4. *Outreach*: Institutions and policies need to be designed which cater to the needs of a large mass of participants, who are expected to be financial unsophisticated, who are presently non-customers of the financial sector, engage in small value transactions, and have small corpuses of pension wealth.
5. *Fair play and low cost*: The design should ensure the highest levels of transparency, competition and sound policy making.
6. *Choice*: The design should be highly transparent, and cater to individual choice, giving participants choices between multiple competing pension fund managers, between multiple alternative investment styles, and between multiple competing annuity vendors.
7. *Sound regulation*: The reform effort should create modern investment regulation, which is single-mindedly focused on maximizing the welfare of participants in old age.

4. Unique Features of the Indian Setting

The problems of income security in old age in India are placed in a somewhat unusual setting, when compared with the experiences of the countries which embarked on pension reforms in the recent 20 years. In this section, we take stock of this backdrop, which has major implications for thinking about pension reforms in India.

Demographic transition: India is the last major country in the world to experience the demographic transition; a sharp decline in TFRs only commenced in the late 1980s. In 2016, only 8.9% of the population is expected to be above 60; this fraction is expected to rise to 13.3% in 2026.

Breakdown of traditional support structures: India is experiencing the breakdown of traditional support structures, where the elderly were able to live with their children and derive support from them. One important factor that has affected these traditional relationships is geographical mobility in the labor market. Workers are increasingly likely to find employment at locations which are distant from their parents.

Context of mass poverty: Roughly 20% of India's population is in a state of poverty, and thus has zero savings. Present estimates suggest that roughly 66% of earners have an annual income in excess of Rs. 25,000, and can hence make a pension contribution of Rs. 2500 per year. The remaining 33% must inevitably fall back upon government programs for the elderly poor when they reach old age.

The trend growth rate of real GDP is now around 6.4%. If GDP growth continues at this rate, then within 15 years, wages are likely to grow to a point where individuals in their working years are unlikely to face poverty. In this case, poverty among the elderly may become the central issue in the analysis of poverty in India within 15 years.[7]

Informal labor market: In the 1991 census, 53% of the labor force were self-employed, and 31% were casual labor or contract workers. Only 15% of the labor force had stable, salaried jobs. Similar estimates are visible from the IRES database, e.g. in Table 2. This suggests that the labor market is dominated by informal labor contracting. Fiscal problems of the State from the mid-1980s onward, India has had persistent problems with the fiscal deficit. The aggregate deficit of the center and the states is at around 9% of GDP. This puts constraints in the face of outright transfers from the State to the elderly. Fiscal problems are particularly important in the context of pensions, where modest transfers amount to substantial sums of money.

Administrative capacity: The administrative capacity of the State is limited. For example, there is no universal citizen identification number. This limits our ability to conceive of a complex pension system, which requires large-scale administrative capacity across the country.

Financial sector development: In many countries, an undeveloped financial sector inhibits modern notions of pension fund management. This is less of a problem in India, where the equity market has made major gains in recent years.[8] While the debt market lags the equity market in terms of institutional sophistication, India fares well in this regard also when compared with most developing countries.

There is time-series evidence over 26 years suggesting that there is a robust equity premium.[g] There is a modern stock market index[9] with well-functioning markets for index funds and index derivatives.[10,11]

---

[g]The nominal return on an equity index from 1979 to 2005, a 26 year period, was 19.25% per annum.

The market capitalization of the equity and bond markets are around Rs. 20 trillion and Rs. 10 trillion, respectively, adding up to roughly 100% of GDP. The stock of assets of the pension sector today is just Rs. 1.5 trillion. Hence, for at least a decade, purchases of securities by the pension system will be negligibly small when compared with the size of the securities markets. This is unlike the situation in many other developing countries, which have large pension assets and small asset markets.

Market for annuities: There is a small market for annuities, dominated by LIC. There are a variety of subtle issues in the design of annuity products, and their efficient pricing.[12] These questions will be increasingly important in the future.[13]

A key concern in India concerns the variation of mortality with wealth. There is a tremendous cross-sectional variation in mortality in India, ranging from rich people who have mortality characteristics comparable with those found in OECD countries, all the way to poor people who have an expected lifespan of less than ten years at age 60. At present, insurance companies lump these together in a single pricing schedule for annuities. This generates a subsidy that flows from the poor (who die soon) to the rich (who live and consume annuities). Resolving this problem, and eliminating this cross-subsidy, will be a major area for new work by the insurance companies in the years to come.

The lack of a legacy system: In many countries, the initial conditions faced in pension reforms include a large population-wide pension system, designed some decades ago. These systems generally have extreme infirmities. However, it is extremely difficult to find the political consensus required to obtain major change.

In contrast, India does not have a population-wide pension system today. Old-age security in India, today, is dominated by private transfers. The fraction of the elderly, today, receiving pension is below 10%. Hence, the political complexity encountered when making progress on pension reforms may prove to be smaller.

5. Issues in System Design

With this background, we can evaluate some of the issues in pension system design in India. Our discussion is organized around the following issues:

- Is there a role for a universal, mandatory system?

- Separation of fund management from annuities.
- Role for individual accounts.
- Redistributive aspect in benefits.
- Administrative complexity and cost.
- Policies on premature withdrawals.
- Mandatory annuitization.
- Simplicity when faced with unsophisticated participants.
- Policies on fund management.
- Role for guarantees.
- Tax treatment.

5.1. *Is there a role for a universal, mandatory system?*

Many countries in Europe, Latin America, etc., have adopted population-wide mandatory pension systems. These are often pay-as-you-go systems, where taxes are imposed on the young and used to pay the rich. These systems appear easy to introduce with a young demographic structure, but become extremely difficult to sustain as the population pyramid matures. They have led to enormous political stress and macroeconomic problems in these countries from the 1980s onward.

Should India adopt some kind of universal, mandatory pension system? It appears that there are acute constraints in the face of such a strategy: If the system is a defined benefit system, there is a political risk that at a future date, a government may choose to raise benefit rates, or cut contribution rates, and thus draw upon resources from taxpayers. Given existing demographic projections, for the next 40 years, a solvent population-wide pay-as-you-go defined benefit system for India will require a steady series of policy measures in the nature of raising tax rates and/or cutting benefit rates every few years for the next 40 years. To the extent that such difficult decisions are not taken in time, the system will become insolvent.

If there is an attempt at funding, and the system is not purely pay-as-you-go, there is greater political risk about asset management when it takes place in the framework of a population-wide defined benefit system. This is related to the problem of incentives faced by an individual participant. If an individual participant has a government guarantee of receiving a pension at a future date, there is little incentive to take interest in the governance issues and functioning of the system. Some Indian experience on such problems is described in Ref. 14, where pension programs which did not have individual accounts drifted into poor governance.

Given the enormous size of pension systems, small mistakes in handling assets and liabilities in a population-wide system could result in a fiscal impact of a few percentage points of GDP. Given India's present levels of fiscal stress, this appears to be an imprudent risk for the government to adopt.

- At present, the administrative capacity to collect mandatory contributions from the 364 million earners, spread over 3.3 million km^2, does not exist. For instance, at present, there is no concept of a unique citizen's identity number. As an illustration of the administrative weaknesses, in India today, income tax is only successfully imposed on around 35 million of these 365 million earners. Hence, it would be hard to enforce a population-wide program.

  The EPFO has been fairly successful in enforcing the rule which requires that each establishment with more than 20 workers should be connected up with the EPFO; yet it only covers 5% of the labor force.
- The administrative capacity to correctly pay out benefits does not exist on a population-wide scale. There is a significant risk of fraud in payouts: paying out benefits to dead people, paying benefits multiple times to some individuals, etc.

These arguments suggest that a mandatory, population-wide, pension system is presently not feasible in India.

5.2. *Separation of fund management from annuities*

A defined benefits pension system which is based on holding adequate assets constitutes a vertical integration between two activities: of fund management in the accumulation phase, and paying annuities in the benefits phase. There is a strong consensus that these two activities should be decoupled. In the accumulation phase, contributions go into the pension account, and asset management takes place. At the end of the accumulation phase, i.e. on retirement date, the worker is left with a stock of pension wealth. At this point, annuities can be purchased from life insurance companies. This represents an unbundling of the accumulation phase from the benefits phase.[h]

A key ramification of this unbundling is the removal of guarantees about the pension that will be paid at dates deep in the future. In the unbundled architecture, a worker is not given promises at age 20 about the magnitude of pension payments. The worker embarks on accumulating pension wealth, which evolves as a function of his lifetime wage trajectory, contribution rate, and asset management outcomes. Promises about monthly pension payments are only crystallized at retirement date (roughly age 60), based on the tangible conversion of a visible stock of pension assets into a flow of annuities, based on mortality projections and interest rates that are then prevalent.

For a worker born in 1980, this is the difference between pricing an annuity in 2000 (when he is age 20) and pricing an annuity in 2040 (when he is age 60). In the former case, the insurance company is forced to take a stand in 2000 about mortality and interest rates that will prevail between 2000 and 2040. The large uncertainty faced in these projections will force the insurance company to charge prices that are adverse to the customer.[i] A prudent implementer of the funded defined benefit system will have a bias in favor of (a) investments in government bonds, and (b) pessimistic projections about the decline in mortality in the future (i.e. forecasts which project a very rapid decline in mortality). These biases will make the pension system an expensive source of old age income security. They will hurt the extent to which the pension system can produce income security, at the price of small per-day contributions that are accessible to the poor. In addition, the worker is forced to suffer the credit risk of the insurance company, i.e. the significant risk that over the 40-year horizon, the insurance company might cease to exist.

There are two aspects where the defined benefit system is attractive; both pertain to the extent to which exposure to risk factors is adopted. The first issue is the problem of the investment risk that has to be borne by participants in an

---

[h]This is perhaps analogous to questions in the electricity industry, where there is a choice between vertically integrated electricity companies, as opposed to the unbundling of generation, transmission and distribution. Similarly, the telecom industry has been unbundled into local telephony, long distance, etc., and consumers are able to mix and match multiple vendors operating in each of these markets.

[i]To some extent, mortality projections in India can be made by assuming India will replicate the experiences of other countries in the decrease of death rates. However, there is an innate technological risk about these projections, since improvements in biomedical science and technology could possibly improve longevity considerably in the coming decades.

individual account system.[15] A defined benefit system may offer a mechanism for risk-sharing, thus reducing the risk borne by an individual. The second issue is about decision making in fund management. A defined benefit system is likely to place decisions in the hands of finance professionals, who would be less likely to suffer from poor returns owing to low exposure to systematic risk factors, when compared to the decision-making of many individuals. These are important arguments. However, they presuppose an environment in which a defined benefit system is run with sound policy formulation and governance. It may prove to be difficult to create such an environment in India. The existing evidence on the functioning of defined benefit systems in India reveals problems in governance and policy formulation.[14] It is possible to envision political pressures in favor of generous benefits and low contributions, and policy formulation which imposes liabilities upon the State.

There is another dimension in which simplistic defined benefit systems (such as India's EPS) can yield unsatisfactory outcomes: this is on the question of regressive transfers. The value of an annuity varies strongly with longevity, which is longest for the wealthy and well-educated. Hence, the NPV of a stream of benefits until death is the highest for the wealthy and well-educated.[16,17] This is particularly so in the case in India, where life expectancy for the rich is comparable to that seen in industrialized countries, while overall life expectancy at birth is just 65 years. A promise of a pension of Rs. 1000 per month at age 60 is much more valuable for a rich person, who has high life expectancy, as compared with a poor person, who is likely to die soon. Hence, many defined benefit designs can become a mechanism for transfers from the poor to the rich. For these reasons, a key aspect of a modern pension architecture is the decoupling of the accumulation phase, where the employee is working and requires fund management services, from the benefits phase, where the pensioner requires a life insurance company to sell him an annuity. In the accumulation phase, the pension system is focused on collecting contributions and managing funds. In the benefits phase, the pension system is about paying out annuities. This separation has a considerable impact upon the institutional architecture of the pension system. It involves insurance companies and in the benefits phase, but not in the accumulation phase.

The question of separation between accumulation and benefits is related to the problem of regulatory structure. If pensions were to take place with defined benefits(i.e. assured pension payouts in retirement), then there is a close link to actuarial calculations through the accumulation phase. However, decoupling accumulation from benefits using a defined contribution system has an impact upon the regulatory structure. For four decades, the employee would be purely in the accumulation phase, and here the focus of the pension system is on fund management and not insurance. It is upon retirement, where a lump-sum has to be converted into an annuity, that the employee finds a need for an insurance company.

This suggests a role for a separate regulator for the pension system, which deals with all problems of the pension system, from the date that a person embarks on his labor market career, until the date that the annuity is purchased. At retirement date, there is no "pension system," but the benefits part of the pension business is conducted by plain life insurance companies.

5.3. *Role for individual accounts*

We now turn to the notion of an individual account, defined contribution system without defined benefits, which places significant choices in the hands of participants on questions such as risk exposure or choice of fund manager.

The key appeal of individual accounts is the sense in which individuals interpret their account balances as personal wealth. This reduces the free rider problem, and encourages individuals to take interest in questions of governance and policy formulation in the context of the pension system. As long as individuals do face choices on the questions of risk exposure and the choice of the fund manager, individual accounts appear to require reduced inputs in terms of sound governance, and face lower political risk.

At the same time, an important concern with individual accounts, and the idea of placing critical asset management choices in the hands of individual, is the question of financial literacy. Individuals may face two kinds of choices: between asset classes, and between fund managers.

- *Choosing asset classes.* There is a real risk that individuals may choose to completely avoid portfolio volatility, and thus obtain poor consumption in old age.[j] This issue has a peculiar twist in an environment with mass

---

[j]Several recent papers have looked at this question in the context of industrialized countries.[33,34] These studies find that individuals do seem to often lack the knowledge that is required in consciously exposing themselves to asset pricing factors.

poverty. Given sufficiently small contributions, high investments in equity offer the highest probabilities of avoiding poverty in old age.[18] However, the poorest participants are likely to have the least financial literacy, and are likely to not expose themselves to asset price risk.

- *Choosing between fund managers.* The same question of knowledge in the hands of individuals is also important when it comes to making choices between fund managers. Researchers equipped with econometric models have found it difficult to choose a fund manager who fares well, out of sample. Hence, this selection would be even more difficult for unsophisticated participants of the pension system.

Investors are often seen as not being sensitive to expenses and fees on the part of fund managers. In countries such as Chile and Argentina, there have been concerns about excessively high sales expenses by pension fund managers.

In this situation, there may be a case for the pension system to be designed in a way which helps curtail fees and expenses. The OASIS committee has proposed the selection of pension fund managers using an auction focusing on identifying the fund managers who promise the lowest consolidated pre-committed fees and expenses. It has also proposed the mandatory use of index funds, which assists this goal.

In addition, to the extent that the pension system design reduces the frictions faced by customers in comparing the performance of multiple fund managers, and switching from one fund manager to another, this would improve the pressures upon fund managers to reduce costs and improve performance.

5.4. *Administrative complexity and cost*

A major problem with an individual account system, particularly when contributions or account balances are small, is the question of administrative overhead and transactions costs.[19,20] These questions are particularly important in the Indian setting, where the average contribution and the average account balance would be among the smallest in the world. Hence, in India, large transactions costs could adversely affect pension accumulation.

This aspect has a major impact upon a wide range of policy questions in India. Many systems and institutional designs which work well in OECD countries are not feasible in India, owing to the use of inefficient structures which impose costs that cannot be sustained given the small value transactions and balances in India.[21]

For example, in the securities markets, India's NSE and BSE are ranked 3rd and 5th in the world by the number of trades per year, even though the dollar value of turnover at NSE and BSE is small by world standards. This aspect imposes a constraint upon policy formulation in India, in favor of better thought out institutional structures which impose low transactions costs, and the extensive use of information technology as a way of efficiently engaging in a high volume of small value transactions.

How could transactions become cheaper? James *et al.*[22] suggest that the most important vehicles for keeping costs low are: (a) constrained portfolio choice, using passive management, and (b) reduced sales expenses. The OASIS committee had proposed that centralization of record-keeping, at an agency called the Central Recordkeeping Agency (CRA), could yield significantly lowered transactions costs. This has been the experience of countries like Mexico, Sweden, etc. The simplification of product offerings, which was proposed by the OASIS committee, would help lower transactions costs.

The CRA, as envisioned by Project OASIS, constitutes public infrastructure aimed at reducing transactions costs. It would be a central agency which would have data about the pension accounts of all participants in the system. Contributions would go to the CRA, as would instructions for switching from one investment product to another. The CRA would compute net fund flows in or out of every investment product, and do a single net settlement with respect to each investment product. This would drastically simplify the activities of the asset manager, who would merely to have to deal with one CRA for the purpose of receiving or paying out cash.

Central recordkeeping indirectly impacts upon costs by giving greater competition in pension fund management, by making it easier for employees to switch between fund managers.

This is in contrast with existing mutual fund or insurance products in the country, where there are significant barriers in the way of easily switching between fund managers. Ease of switching obviously tends to be somewhat unpopular with finance companies. However, from a policy perspective, it is a key element of a pro-competitive policy posture.

5.5. *Redistributive aspect in benefits*

The benefits of a pension system can be designed so as to have a redistributive component. For example, Chile has a principle of "topping off" the accumulation upon retirement for the individuals who have assets below a certain threshold.

These schemes rely on a soundly implemented, unique citizen identity number. Otherwise individuals would have incentives to open multiple accounts and receive enhanced benefits. This style of fraudulent behavior is particularly relevant when we think of an individual account system where individuals (as opposed to firms) directly interact with the system. Hence, it appears difficult to have a redistributive aspect in pension system design in India.

From 2004 onwards, a major institutional development has commenced in the form of the SEBI "MAPIN" database, which is managed by NSDL. MAPIN is a database of all individuals involved in the financial sector, required by SEBI in order to engage in market surveillance and enforcement activities. This database uses biometrics (fingerprints and photographs) to ensure that no one individual has more than one account. Once these procedures are proven, and costs come down adequately, they could be scaled up on a population-scale for the pension system. Once this is done, it may be possible to think of a "topping off" concept, where the poorest participants in the pension system are given a State subsidy when they emerge at age 60 with deficient pension assets despite a lifetime of steady accumulation. It may be possible to design such a subsidy to have low fiscal costs and minimal moral hazard. However, such questions lie well into the future, given the nascent stage of implementation of MAPIN, and India's present fiscal crisis.

5.6. *Policies on premature withdrawals*

Many low-income participants in a pension system face extreme credit constraints. When faced with consumption shocks, they find it difficult to obtain credit in order to do consumption smoothing. When faced with such exigencies, it appears reasonable to seek some ways in which pension wealth can play a greater role in such consumption smoothing. Pensions systems are normally focused on building pension wealth on retirement date. This implies a rule set that prohibits premature withdrawals. In other words, it makes the pension wealth illiquid and inaccessible until retirement date. For many individuals who are potential participants in a pension system in India, credit markets are inaccessible when exposed to consumption shocks. If the pension system offers no possibility of premature withdrawals, then it becomes relatively unattractive.[23]

In India, we have one extreme example in the EPF experience, where withdrawals are permitted. EPF uses a tax treatment where contributions, asset returns and premature withdrawals are all tax-free. This has given an outcome with a high rate of withdrawals. This is a polar case which should clearly be avoided.

A rigid prohibition of "premature" withdrawals also faces problems when faced with highly heterogeneous mortality in the country. There are low-income persons in the country who are unable to engage in physical labor at 50, and have an expected lifespan of 15 years more beyond this age. Such individuals would not be well served by a pension system which forces their pension wealth to be illiquid until age 60.

These arguments suggest that the design of a pension system for India should seek to avoid complete illiquidity of pension assets. Certain trade-offs in favor of early withdrawal do need to be designed for.

5.7. *Mandatory annuitization*

In many countries, pension regulations require a certain degree of mandatory annuitization. This is partly motivated by the moral hazard that is implicit in the existence of an extensive safety net.[23] Individuals who run through their pension wealth "too quickly" can count on falling back upon poverty alleviation programs, or minimum pension guarantees, which are offered by the State. This generates private incentives to annuitize too little. In addition, not annuitizing gives workers greater flexibility in terms of bequeathing to children,[k] starting a small business, buying a house, etc.

These concerns are not yet prominent in India. The poverty alleviation programs that presently exist pay subsidies to the elderly of around $5 per

---

[k]There is some evidence which suggests that parents who annuitize more are likely to obtain less care from their children in old age.

month, so they are not very significant. The mandatory annuitization debate is hence primarily about a paternalistic argument, where a worker is not trusted to make prudent decisions about his pension wealth from retirement date till death.

The fledgling market for annuities in India has little experience or sophistication in dealing with the problems of adverse selection. A pension system which requires some kinds of mandatory annuitization would yield diminished problems of adverse selection for annuity providers.

5.8. *Simplicity when faced with unsophisticated participants*

Given a large mass of unsophisticated users of the pension system that we expect in India, simplicity is a key goal. In addition, design choices which favor simplicity tend to be associated with lowered transactions costs. For example, the Thrift Savings Plan, which is used for civil servants in the US, faces a fairly well-educated set of participants. However, it has obtained considerable cost reductions in the implementation of individual accounts by placing restrictions upon flexibility and choice.

A focus on financially unsophisticated users sometimes leads to a design that appears restrictive and paternalistic. Many observers have criticized these kinds of design choices, comparing them unfavorably with the unrestricted product innovation of the mutual fund industry. However, pension system design has to plan for a very different user base, as compared with those that self-select themselves for buying existing mutual fund products. As a first approximation, the pension system is about the non-customers of the mutual funds, since people who are able to use mutual funds and plan for their old age by themselves are less in need of a formal pension system.

The goal of simplicity is assisted by having a small set of choices, with special efforts to make it easy for unsophisticated users to engage in performance comparisons. The OASIS committee has envisioned three standardized product types and a small number of (say) six pension fund managers. This would give a simple 6×3 table of performance that can be easily understood by a relatively unsophisticated person.

5.9. *Policies on fund management*

A core principle in financial economics is the relationship between risk and return, whereby asset classes which experience greater year-to-year volatility are likely (on average) to obtain higher returns. Fairly small differences in average rates of return are magnified by the multi-decade horizons encountered in pension investment. Hence, a key goal of sound asset management for pensions is to have exposure to portfolio volatility over multi-decade horizons.

The empirical evidence in India, from 1979 to 2005, suggests that the long-run average return on the equity index has been around 700 basis points above GOI bonds. This difference in average returns is called "the equity premium." India's experience is broadly consistent in empirical evidence with the performance of the equity index in dozens of other countries over long time periods.[24]

At the same time, no two individuals have the same risk tolerance. Optimal decisions by individuals involve altering risk exposure through the life-cycle. In order to enable these optimal strategies, the pension system should give individuals choices about what level of asset volatility they accept. There are many governance difficulties which flow from a framework where a committee makes choices about the risk that a worker has to bear. Hence, the choice about asset allocation is best placed into the hands of the individual participant in the pension system.

index funds are a particularly convenient investment vehicle through which the equity premium can be harnessed.[11] They focus on capturing the equity premium, without entering into the complexities of choosing an active fund manager, paying the higher fees of active management, and building the regulatory capacity for coping with active fund management.

There are important links between globalization and the pension system. Global diversification of pension assets yields superior diversification; pension fund managers should not have all their eggs in any one basket. International diversification of pension assets is hence in the best interests of employees in the pensions system.

When India embarks upon large-scale pension asset management, with international diversification, this could induce large outward flows of capital. These could induce stress for 22 the balance of payments and the currency regime. India has yet to fully resolve the difficulties of formulating a currency regime[25] and establishing a policy framework required to support substantial capital flows.[26] This may raise difficulties for implementing international diversification for the pension system. Innovative alternatives, such as the "pension swaps" proposal of Zvi Bodie and Robert Merton, could be adopted to overcome these difficulties.[27] In addition, there is considerable knowledge on pension fund management among the best pension fund managers outside India, particularly in the context of internationally diversified asset portfolios. In India, the mutual fund industry has sound skills which are directly applicable to pension fund management in a defined contribution system, with modern investment regulation. It is in the area of internationally diversified portfolio management that there is a lack of knowledge amongst fund managers in India. In order to overcome this problem, and in order to foster the highest possible levels of competition, it is important to bring international experience and expertise to bear upon pension fund management in India. This would help offer better choices to employees, and speed up the institutional development of the pension sector.

5.10. *Role for guarantees*

It is likely that there will be calls for guarantees in connection with India's pension system.[28,29] India's experience with UTI has been a valuable learning ground for the downstream ramifications of promises about future returns. Indeed, this is a central difficulty with defined benefit pension programs. It appears easy to think of "modest" guarantees that are unlikely to be invoked. However, when modest guarantees are carefully priced, they prove to be quite expensive.

The modest and feasible path that can be explored is to create guarantees using financial derivatives. In this framework, individuals in the pension system would have choices about what guarantees are purchased, and would pay for the guarantees that they chose. India has had considerable success with the onset of equity derivatives trading. These instruments can be used for producing guarantees on equity investments (at a price). India has embarked on the creation of an interest rate futures market. This market presently faces many regulatory constraints. When these problems are resolved, and the market attains liquidity, it can be used to produce guarantees on fixed income investments (at a price).

Investments in equity and debt markets outside India are generally likely to go to countries that have strong derivatives markets. Hence, it should be possible to use derivatives markets in those countries for the purpose of producing guarantees also. For this reason, to the extent that the Indian pension system invests in overseas assets, the problem of producing guarantees (if desired) is eased.

5.11. *Tax treatment*

India has had a tradition of "EEE" treatment of "pension" investments, such as the PPF and EPF, whereby contributions, accumulations and benefits are all tax-exempt. This is unsatisfactory from a public finance perspective, since all income should be taxed at least once. In addition, the existing tax treatment of PPF and EPF is particularly unsatisfactory given that these programs do allow early withdrawals, so that they do not effectively constitute pension investment. An EEE treatment, coupled with early withdrawal, effectively constitutes simple tax avoidance.

Two alternatives to EEE which are attractive are the TEE and EET. A TEE treatment is simple and attractive, where income tax is computed without any exemption clauses, but the pension system is free of all tax considerations after that. An EET treatment appears to attract participation in the pension system by back-loading taxation. However, an EET system is more credible in the eyes of households, since a TEE system runs the risk that some decades in the future, when money is leaving the pension account, a future government might choose to tax it.

When thinking about the new pension system, the argument is sometimes made that it has to also use an EEE tax treatment, in order to be competitive in the eyes of consumers who have choices between alternative avenues. At the same time, it is important to design a fiscally responsible pension system, where the rule set would be consistent with sound principles of public finance, and yield stable institutions over many decades. Any new pension system which does not use an EEE tax treatment will be disfavored today, when compared with the EPF and PPF. Yet, if a new pension system used an EEE framework today, it would be hard to bring back taxation at either entry or exit at a future date. Hence, from a long-term perspective, it appears to be useful to put the new pension system on a sound foundation by not using EEE tax treatment, and simultaneously work on improving the policies governing EPF and PPF.

From the viewpoint of the functioning of the CRA, the tax treatment of accumulation is a very important problem. From a recordkeeping perspective, there is considerable cost and complexity in tracking accumulations so that they can be effectively taxed. If accumulation is tax exempt, then this simplifies the problem of creating the CRA. At the same time, once a CRA embarks upon a EET pension system, this assumes that at all future dates, no future government will introduce taxation of accumulation.

6. Pitfalls

Many alternative designs of a new pension system, based on individual accounts and defined contributions, can be articulated, which would roughly achieve the above goals. For example, it is easy to envision systems like the US 401(k) program, which are decentralized systems through which pension fund managers interact with employers. Such decentralized pension systems have run into difficulties in many countries, primarily on the issues of fees and expenses of fund managers, and the extent to which uninformed customers are able to exert competitive pressure on fund managers. By the late 1990s, there was a considerable consensus about the need, in Indian pensions policy thinking, to focus on solving the two major problems which could surface when building an individual account DC system in India:

- *Grand total payments from the pension system participant to finance companies*

  The financial industry imposes a wide variety of fees and expenses upon the participant of the pension system. Under certain assumptions, these payments can amount to numbers as large as 33% of the total pension accumulation.

  These problems are closely related to the difficulty where pension system participants are likely to be financial unsophisticated, and can often be persuaded to part with substantial payments to finance companies in terms of fees and expenses.

  The international experience in pension economics suggests that while the introduction of private pension fund managers in the 1980s worked very well in some respects, the major gap in the design of pension systems of the 1980s was their lack of focus in controlling the total resource flow from the pension system to finance companies. This has motivated fresh efforts, all over the world, in devising new elements of design which would cope with these problems.

- *Transactions costs associated with small value account balances and small value transactions*

India differs from almost all other countries, where pension reforms have been undertaken, in that we expect a large mass of pension system partici- pants to do small transactions and to have small balances. This places new demands on the design of the pension system. If the cost of a money order is Rs. 12, and if a participant contributes Rs. 120 into a pension account, then the transaction involves an overhead of 10%, which is completely unacceptable.

The challenge in Indian pension policy consists of finding innovative design strategies through which these transactions costs can be controlled. The impact of pension reforms in India — measured by the sheer number of households who stand to gain from a modern pension system — will be defined by the extent to which a sound pension system design is able to support small value transactions and small value balances.

6.1. *How many people in the uncovered sector could meaningfully participate?*

As shown in Table 2, earners in the uncovered sector has an income distribution with the following characteristics: 25% are below Rs. 18,000 per year; half are below Rs. 30,000 per year and 75% are below Rs. 54,000 per year.

It is likely that a contribution rate of Rs. 10 per day, or Rs. 2500 per year, can deliver significant pension wealth. In order to estimate the characteristics of the target audience in India, we apply three tests in the IRES database:

1. We focus on the uncovered sector, i.e. those who are not members of the EPFO today and are not in the civil service.
2. We restrict ourselves to earners below age 40.
3. We restrict ourselves to earners with an annual income of above Rs. 25,000.

As of late 2004, there were roughly 95 million people who met these three tests. This group makes up 26% of the earners of India. Of these, 58% are urban and the remainder live in rural areas.

This calculation suggests that there is a substantial mass of potential participants in the country today, for a defined contribution pension system. In addition, the high economic growth rates that India is likely to experience in the coming years will steadily enlarge this set. The international experience with pension reforms suggests that it will take 10–20 years for this group to be fully participating in a formal pension system. Hence, we may envision a ten-year or twenty-year process of a new defined contribution pension system steadily obtaining greater acceptance amidst a steadily growing set of potential participants.

6.2. *How will participants possibly exercise choices?*

Amongst civil servants, or in the uncovered sector, a defined contribution system makes new demands in terms of knowledge since individuals are required to make choices about pension fund managers and investment alternatives. There are concerns that uneducated participants will be unable to exercise these choices. Hence, we obtain some data on the educational status of this set of 95 million people, which is the set of potential participants in a defined contribution pension system.

There are three aspects to this problem. Table 3 shows that only 10.2% of this group are illiterate. The challenge lies in designing a sufficiently simple pension system, and associated educational efforts, so that a substantial subset of this group can learn how to own and operate a pension account in coming years.

The second aspect of this problem lies in the role for the pensions regulator. Knowledge in the minds of households is a public good, and there is a considerable role for the State to engage in knowledge initiatives.

Finally, to a significant extent, individuals today find it difficult to think of exercising choice in the context of pension accounts because India has never had multiple alternatives in a pension system to choose between. Once the choices come about, individuals have an incentive to learn about the alternatives, and choose for themselves. An analogy may be made in the proliferation of two-wheelers which are now ubiquitous in India. More than 10 million two-wheelers are sold every year in India, and many more transactions take place in the used two-wheeler market. Most individuals who buy two-wheelers do not understand subtle issues about ignition and transmission. However, they are able to exercise their choice about what product to purchase. Similarly,

Table 3. Educational status of potential participants in the uncovered sector.

Educational category	Percentage
Illiterate	10.2
Literate (no schooling)	1.6
Below primary	4.4
Primary school	10.6
Middle school	19.3
High school/matric	23.6
Higher secondary/inter	12.1
Tech. education/diploma	2.5
Graduate	11.1
Professional degree	2.3
Post-graduate and above	2.2
Total	100.0

by 2010, there will be 200 million telephones in India. This will imply the existence of 200 million people who have coped with the complexity of multiple competing telephone technologies, vendors, rate plans, etc. It appears reasonable to think that anyone who has a telephone can be a member of a defined contribution pension system.

6.3. *What pension can come out of Rs. 10 per day?*

Outcomes under a defined contribution pension system depend upon future returns on asset classes, which are inherently unpredictable. We show some illustrative calculations here. However, it must be strongly emphasized that the calculations here are not certainties and there are inherent year-to-year fluctuations in all investments. To the extent that these conservative average values are considered plausible, these calculations are illustrative about what might come about for participants of the New Pension System. The PFRDA Bill proposes that the PFRDA will define investment regulations for the pension fund managers (PFMs). For the present purpose, a comprehensive range of six kinds of asset allocations is analysed, ranging from 100% government bonds to 100% equity. In order to simulate future outcomes, it is necessary to make many specific assumptions:

1. All calculations are made in 2005 rupees. This removes inflation from the picture. Hence, we think of asset returns in real terms.

2. It is assumed that a person in the uncovered sector starts contributing Rs. 2500 per year at age 24.[l] The contribution is assumed to grow at 4% per year in real terms till age 60, reflecting 2% for accumulation of experience, and 2% for the growth of the economy.[m] A high level of total fees and expenses of 100 basis points on assets per year is assumed, reflecting the higher costs of delivering services to this class of participants.

3. The present price of an annuity product from LIC is assumed, which is Rs. 4692 of a lump-sum payment for an annuity of Rs. 1 per day. For the purpose of pension calculation, it is assumed that all pension wealth is annuitized.

4. Each of the simulation results shown here focuses on one asset allocation. We assume that a person embarks upon one asset allocation at age 24 and stays in the identical asset allocation until age 60. This is obviously an artificial assumption. The advice given by financial planners to individuals consists of seeking higher returns when young and shifting to safer investments beyond age 50. However, for the purpose of this document, each investment style is analyzed in isolation, assuming a person stays with the investment style for life. This helps us to understand the consequences of a given asset allocation.

Pension outcomes are computed for three sets of assumptions about future asset returns in real terms:

	Set of assumptions		
Asset class	I	II	III
GOI bonds (%)	1.5	2	2.5
Corporate bonds (%)	3	4	4.5
Equity (%)	5	6	6.5

[l]This is a conservative assumption, since most people in the uncovered sector start working before age 24, and would potentially be able to have more years of contribution, magnified by the "power of compounding".
[m]These are conservative assumptions. They imply that holding educational characteristics fixed, a 60-year old worker in 2005 earns twice the income of a 24-year old worker. In addition, given GDP growth of 6.35%, population growth of below 2%, and a wage share of perhaps 70%, the rise in wages owing to the growth of the economy will significantly exceed 2%.

CPI inflation today is at roughly 4%. This implies that an assumption of (say) 2% real returns on government bonds is equivalent to a 6% nominal return on government bonds. These assumptions are highly conservative. As an example, the historical return on an Indian equity index over the 26 year period from 1979 to 2005 works out to 19.25% in nominal terms.

The first investment style that we analyse is pure government bonds. The second style is the "Safe Income" asset allocation recommended by Project OASIS, which has 60% in government bonds, 30% in corporate bonds and 10% in equity. The next style is the "Balanced" asset allocation recommended by Project OASIS, which consists of 40% in government bonds, 35% in corporate bonds and 25% in equities. The "Growth" style recommended by Project OASIS consists of 20% government bonds, 30% corporate bonds and 50% in equity. In the interest of comprehensiveness, we show two more styles, one involving a 50–50 split between corporate bonds and equities, and the last with 100% equities.

The outcomes under these assumptions are summarized in Table 4. These results suggest that even under investment only in government bonds, assuming a real return of only 1.5% and after paying 100 bps for fees and expenses, patient accumulation from age 24 till age 60 is able to deliver a meaningful pension of Rs. 1483 per month in old age. In addition, other asset classes could be of interest to many participants.

Table 4.   Pension outcomes for a 24-year old starting at Rs. 10 per day in the uncovered sector.

Asset allocation	(Monthly pension in rupees) Set of assumptions		
	I	II	III
Pure GOI bonds	1483	1596	1721
OASIS "Safe Income"	1668	1858	2013
OASIS "Balanced"	1829	2079	2259
OASIS "Growth"	2079	2418	2638
50–50 corp. bonds and equities	2187	2595	2836
100% equity	2597	3109	3412

7. The New Pension System

7.1. *The design*

The arguments of this paper favor the following design elements:

- An individual account, defined contribution system.
- Separation between the pension sector (i.e. accumulation) and benefits which are purchased from annuity providers.
- A separate pensions regulator.
- Portability of pension accounts across job changes, and portability of pension assets across multiple fund managers and investment products.
- A menu of investment choices through which asset volatility can be controlled by the individual, where equity investment is available as a choice.
- Reduced pension asset portfolio volatility, using international diversification.
- A simple framework through which individuals face a choice between multiple fund managers and multiple asset classes.
- Central record-keeping infrastructure.
- A focus on IT which will yield low transactions costs despite small value contributions and small value account balances.
- Rules that deter premature withdrawal but do not completely prohibit it.
- Rules that encourage annuitization but do not mandate it.
- Tax treatment using an "EET" system.

In the pensions field, there is a strong distinction between the issues of the "accumulation phase," where a worker is accreting monthly savings through contributions into a pension account, and the "benefits phase," where the worker is retired and drawing down those savings. While the age at retirement in India is presently roughly 60, it is likely to shift to 65 years in coming decades, given improvements in mortality. In this case, from age 20 till age 65, for a period of 45 years, the pensions business consists of building up pension wealth using the services of fund managers. From age 65 till age 85, for a period of 20 years, the pensions business consists of producing pensions using the stock of wealth available at age 65.

Reduction in costs, and transparency on costs, appears to be best achieved through an "unbundled architecture," where the overall pension problem is broken up into four distinct components: front-end services, recordkeeping, fund management and annuity production. Under the New Pension System, each of these is proposed to be handled by specialized agencies, which would excel at performing each role at a low cost.[n] Unbundling has been a powerful tool for obtaining transparency and cost reduction in other areas of public policy, such as electricity or telecom. Unbundling drives down cost through several channels.

- Unbundling fosters specialization, which increases competence and efficiency.
- Scale economies can be harnessed by preventing vertically integrated companies. For example, if a large set of bank branches and post offices constitute a "front-end services industry," which is accessible to all fund managers, this yields lower costs as compared with a design where each fund manager sets about building his own branch network.
- Unbundling fosters transparency about tariffs. Each of the four components of this industry would show transparent prices, and competitive forces can be brought to bear upon three of the four elements, so as to bring down prices. At each of the four stages, services are likely to be purchased from the lowest-cost vendor. In contrast, vertically integrated firms often introduce cross-subsidization schemes.

The proposed design of the new pension system is shown in Fig 1. Front-end services are envisaged to be provided by the large existing network of bank branches, post offices, etc., which would provide an off-the-shelf network of offices. The reuse of existing infrastructure cuts costs. In addition, the sharing of these "points of presence" by multiple different pension fund managers (PFM) eliminates the costs associated with a separate set of front-end offices in the country for each PFM.

Recordkeeping services are envisaged to be centralized in a "Central Recordkeeping Agency." This agency would produce new public goods for the pension sector. There would be a considerable role for the State in the contracting that will lead to the CRA. The CRA would know complete facts about every pension system participant; it would be able to give out comprehensive

---

[n] Such specialization is spontaneously coming about in many aspects of India's financial sector. As an example, many insurance companies and banks now outsource fund management to mutual funds.

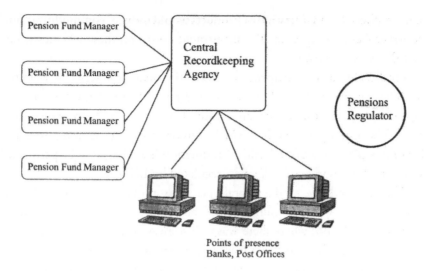

Fig. 1.   Architecture of new pension system.

account balance statements; it would be the single-point at which instructions for switching from one pension fund manager to another would be supplied. The CRA will induce netting efficiencies by aggregating up instructions and contributions across all participants per day, and only executing the net transactions required with respect to fund managers. The CRA has strong increasing returns to scale. The use of such a central facility helps to reduce costs.

Professional fund managers would perform fund management services. It is envisaged through roughly six pension fund managers (PFMs) would be required, each of whom would offer three standardized schemes. The use of standardized schemes would facilitate direct comparison of performance. The six managers would be selected through an auction process, which would focus on fees and expenses. The firms who bid the lowest sum of fees and expenses would get a contract to manage assets for the system. This auction process is expected to result in drastically lower fees and expenses as compared with ordinary market processes that have been observed in (say) the mutual fund industry or the insurance industry.

Through this system, the participant would accumulate pension wealth. In the working years, a regular stream of contributions would go into the pension account. The participant would choose between multiple competing fund managers, each of which would offers a comparable set of standardized three products. Standardization of products would induce "commoditization," and lower fees and expenses. The investment return on these schemes would swell the pension wealth.

Finally, when a participant reaches retirement and seeks to obtain a monthly pension, he would be able to use some or all of the accumulated pension wealth in order to buy an annuity from existing life insurance companies. The annuity is a product which converts a stock of wealth into a flow of monthly payments until death. This function is envisaged to be performed by existing life insurance companies, regulated by IRDA.

This unbundling of the overall pensions problem into four distinct competitive industries is reminiscent of the debates and policy directions in electricity regulation, where there was a shift away from vertically integrated electricity companies to distinct roles of generation, transmission and distribution. Separation into distinct roles produces better information about the tariffs for each unbundled element, and fosters competition between multiple specialized players in each stage.

7.2. *Feasibility of implementation*

This proposed architecture exploits existing institutions available in the country, and does not require new investments on the part of government.

Two of the four components are available off the shelf: these are points of presence and annuity providers. These entities are eager and ready to do business with the new pension system, and merely need to be plugged in.[o]

There is significant competence in India's fund management industry, and amongst international firms with expertize in fund management. These firms are likely to participate in the proposed auction which would select pension fund managers.

The Central Recordkeeping Agency (CRA) is a new element of institutional infrastructure that needs to be created. However, given the successes in the country in the creation of depositories, the Tax Information Network (TIN), etc., it appears that such IT and managerial capacity is readily to be found.

---

[o]Points of presence include banks, post offices, and a range of more recent IT-enabled service centres which can interact with customers in a regulated environment. Annuity providers are the existing life insurance companies, all of whom are ready to sell annuities.

7.3. *Focus on portability*

A key principle of the new pension system is that of portability at all levels. One level of portability pertains to the movement of an individual between government and non-government jobs. The pension account of the person should stay with the person across jobs. There would be no incentive for an employee, under the new pension system, to not leave a government job for a few years so as to ensure that pension payments are not affected.

The other level of portability pertains to shifting between fund managers and investment styles. The new pension system would afford complete flexibility for the participant to shift from one fund manager to another, or from one scheme to another, at any time. Participants would, of course, bear costs associated with the implementation of their decisions. However, apart from this, the system is designed in a way that caters to the contestability of markets.

The use of a central recordkeeping agency fosters high portability. As a contrast, under the existing mutual fund industry, there is a multi-day process of filling forms and interacting with two different fund houses, in moving assets from one fund manager to another. The costs and complexity of this effort serve to deter competitive markets. The existing insurance industry is worse, in that customers are locked in, and substantial fees are imposed on customers which are used to fund the operation of proprietary distribution channels. The proposed pension system architecture is pro-competitive by introducing the central recordkeeping agency (CRA). The participant would merely send one instruction to the CRA. The CRA would sell units of one scheme and invest them in the other, thus making the switch without difficulty.

It is only after retirement, when annuities are purchased, that participants would face the lack of switching that is typically found with insurance products. Until this point, the new pension system would be a pure NAV-based fund management system with full flexibility of switching.

7.4. *How this design addresses the pitfalls*

The proposed use of an auction through which a finite number of pension fund managers is selected would serve to drive down fees and expenses in fund

Table 5.   Cost per debit at NSDL: 2000–2005.

Year	Number of debits (million)	Expenditure (million rupees)	Cost per debit (rupees)
2000–2001	23.772	546.447	22.99
2001–2002	31.039	493.79	15.91
2002–2003	37.375	439.944	11.77
2003–2004	70.071	437.611	6.25
2004–2005	96.097	480.000	4.99

management, which have been known to make up a major part of the costs of a pension sector.

The ease of switching — through the CRA — will induce constant competitive pressures on the pension fund managers. The contestability of this market will foster low costs and higher performance. These built-in pro-competitive elements are a unique strength of this proposed design.

The extensive use of IT from end to end — from the post office interacting with the customer to the CRA to the fund manager — would help drive down costs, as has been seen in numerous other industries in India such as securities, banking, railway reservations, etc. Table 5 shows the time-series of the cost per transaction at the securities depository (NSDL). This evidence suggests that over these 5 years, NSDL was able to grow from 23.8 million transactions to 96 million transactions while enjoying a slight decline in expenditure in nominal terms. This led to a sharp collapse in the cost per debit, which went down from Rs. 23 per transaction to Rs. 5 per transaction in this period.[p] These facts understate the true decline in cost since inflation has been ignored.

The use of existing off-the-shelf firms in the areas of front-end services and annuity production avoids the costs and overheads associated with setting up new companies, building new offices, etc. Banks, post offices, etc. have built up a very large number of offices across the country which can perform front-end services. Life insurance companies are geared up to produce annuities. No new expenditures are required to harness these firms.

---

[p]NSDL's tariff structure differs from this to a certain extent, reflecting the incentive implications of any given tariff structure. For example, NSDL enforces a certain charge upon accounts, and a certain charge upon transactions. However, ultimately these costs are passed on to the end-users of NSDL as user charges.

Hence, the proposed pension system design is likely to fare well in obtaining low payments to finance companies, and in supporting small value transactions and small value balances, thus addressing the pitfalls identified above.

7.5. Regulatory treatment

7.5.1. What are the tasks for the pensions regulator?

In order to operationalize the above design, the tasks required of a government agency are:

1. Contract with an agency for the services of the Central Recordkeeping Agency.
2. Supervision of the existing interim CRA which is presently in operation.
3. Perform key interfacing functions between the government payroll process and the CRA, to ensure smooth transfers of contributions to the CRA.
4. Closely interact with state governments and local governments which may choose to follow the lead of the Central government, and link up to the new pension system.
5. Conduct an auction for the selection of pension fund managers.
6. Regulate fund management.
7. Draft regulations governing the functioning of the front-end services of banks, post offices, etc.
8. Ensure a sound interface to insurance companies when a customer of the pension system chooses to buy an annuity.
9. Opening up the new pension system to the uncovered sector. Numerous NGOs, such as Sewa, have evinced strong interest in bringing in lakhs of participants into the new pension system.
10. These will need to be accompanied by a massive education campaign across the country, in order to educate participants about their rights under the new pension system, while constantly reminding them that this is not an assured government pension or a defined benefit pension.

These tasks appear to require a new regulator, which has been referred to as the Pension Fund Regulatory and Development Agency (PFRDA).[30]

7.5.2. *Evaluating the SEBI option*

SEBI could fit as a regulator for the fund management part, and for the CRA, as the design of the new pension system. This flows from SEBI's experience with mutual funds — India's best experience with a modern regulatory framework covering asset management — and SEBI's experience with depositories, which are similar to the CRA.

However, a distinct PFRDA is important for implementing the new pension system, given the full array of tasks sketched above, which go well beyond fund management and CRA. A new regulator could potentially take over unregulated pension schemes which exist today, which are particularly unfriendly to customers. The PFRDA serves as an ideal agency which would bring together an integrated regulatory treatment of all pensions in the country other than the EPFO.

7.5.3. *Evaluating the IRDA option*

A close examination of these tasks suggest that IRDA would be ill-suited to perform these functions.

1. No actuarial calculations are involved in pension fund management. Actuarial thinking only matters for annuities, not for pension funds. The proposed pension system design envisages using existing life insurance companies for the purpose of obtaining annuities. All aspects of pension system design, in this note, have focused on problems in pension policy other than the problem of producing annuities. IRDA, and insurance companies, lack a focus and professional competence in these problems that go beyond the production of annuities.

At an analytical level, the dominant factor shaping consumption in old age is the rate of return obtained from age 20 to age 65. The power of compounding applies here, and every basis point of higher returns has a magnified impact upon the accumulation of pension wealth. Hence, the dominant problem for policy is creating conditions under which fund management can be done well, so as to maximize the rate of return in these accumulating years.

In contrast, at age 65, once a given stock of pension wealth is in hand, the most that the life insurance industry can do is to reliably deliver actuarially fair prices for annuities. There is little possibility for good knowledge at this second stage in adding to consumption in old age. In contrast, good knowledge about fund management at the first stage can make a major difference to outcomes.

2. A distinct pensions regulator would have a greater focus on the unique implementation problems of pensions. This requires building new IT infrastructure, and a massive focus on education. At present, the new pension system does not exist, and the proposed PFRDA has to proactively set about creating these new institutions. In contrast, SEBI and IRDA have a tradition of sitting back, processing requests for licenses, and regulating existing players.

3. The unbundled architecture proposed here limits the role of insurance companies to the one element where actuarial calculations are required — i.e. production of annuities. The political economy of regulation suggests that IRDA will inherently get lobbied by insurance companies to move in the direction of defined benefits, since insurance companies have a competitive advantage over fund managers when a bundled architecture is used. If even limited movements toward defined benefits take place, this could have grave consequences for Indian macroeconomics in the decades to come.

4. Existing IRDA regulations do not allow an agent — including large distributors like SBI or HDFC — to sell products of more than one life insurance firm.

Hence, under IRDA's framework, a distributor like SBI will only sell products from SBI Life. This implies that the customers of the 10,000 SBI branches would not get the full-fledged benefits of competition and portability. Similar problems would hinder distribution by other life insurance companies.

This focus on proprietary distribution has served to drive up costs in the insurance industry, where each life insurance company tries to build an additional, parallel, proprietary distribution network in the country. This approach is ill-suited to obtain penetration into the vast population of the country.

There is a considerable gap between the existing functioning of the life insurance industry, and the vision of competition and portability that animates the new pension system.

5. Despite the "open competitive market" which prevails in the existing life insurance companies, the problem above (proprietary distribution channels) has led life insurance companies to strongly complain about the rural and social obligations imposed by IRDA. The New Pension System will have to aggressively attack rural and social obligations.

In an examination of the regulatory architecture of 37 large countries, there were only 10 countries where pensions and insurance was handled by the same agency. These 10 were : Belgium, Czech Republic, Finland, Luxembourg, The Netherlands, New Zealand, Poland, Portugal, Spain, and Turkey. The 27 other major countries had either opted for an independent pensions regulator (16 countries)[q] or had placed pensions with an integrated financial regulation agency (11 cases).[r]

It is important to observe that many of these countries have a pension system architecture that fell in place in the 1980s, and are only now in the process of moving toward new concepts and principles similar to those proposed in the new pension system. If these countries had to embark on pension reforms today, their regulatory structure is more likely to have an independent pensions regulator, which focused on issues like the public goods of centralized recordkeeping.

In 2003 and 2004, considerable criticism of the New Pension System emanated from insurance companies. In terms of political economy, this is an unequal battle. The insurance industry in India already exists, and has a sustained capacity for lobbying. In contrast, a comparable pension fund industry does not (at present) exist. The challenge is in ensuring that public policy formulation looks beyond these narrow concerns, and lays the foundations for a vibrant pension sector for the years to come.

8. Work in Pension Reforms Since 1998

A great deal of policy thinking took place on pension reforms in India, starting with Project OASIS which was undertaken by the Ministry of Social Justice and Empowerment in early 1998. Project OASIS was implemented by Invest India Economic Foundation (IIEF), and the expert committee was chaired by Surendra Dave.[31] It was focused on the uncovered sector. In parallel, other arms of government were working on civil service pension reforms.

The first major reform decision came about in the Budget Speech of 2001, by the then finance minister Yashwant Sinha, who said:

> "Pension Reforms
> 83. The Central Government pension liability has reached unsustainable proportions: as a percentage of GDP, it has risen from about

---

[q]Argentina, Chile, Costa Rica, El Salvador, Hong Kong, Ireland, Israel, Kenya, Mexico, Peru, Russia, Slovakia, Tanzania, Japan, United Kingdom, United States of America.
[r]Australia, Austria, Bolivia, Canada, Denmark, Germany, Hungary, Iceland, Korea, Norway, Sweden.

0.5 per cent in 1993–1994 to 1 percent in 2000–2001. As such it is envisaged that those who enter central government services after October 1, 2001 would receive pension through a new pension program based on defined contributions. In order to review the existing pension system and to provide a roadmap for the next steps to be taken by the Government, I propose to constitute a High Level Expert Group, which would give its recommendations within 3 months."

The Bhattacharya Committee was setup to propose this design. The parallel developments on the civil servants pension and the uncovered sector pension came into sharp focus at the Ministry of Finance in late 2002, where a major decision taken was to merge the two parallel strands of work — for the civil service and for the uncovered sector — into a single New Pension System (NPS).

8.1. *New pension system decisions in 2003*

The budget speech of February 2003, by the then finance minister Jaswant Singh, had the following text:

"My predecessor in office had, in 2001, announced a roadmap for a restructured pension scheme for new Central Government employees, and a scheme for the general public. This scheme is now ready. It will apply only to new entrants to government service, except to the armed forces, and upon finalisation, offer a basket of pension choices. It will also be available, on a voluntary basis, to all employers for their employees, as well as to the self-employed.

This new pension system, when introduced, will be based on defined contributions, shared equally in the case of government employees between the government and the employees. There will, of course, be no contribution from the government in respect of individuals who are not government employees. The new pension scheme will be portable, allowing transfer of the benefits in case of change of employment, and will go into 'individual pension accounts' with pension funds. The Ministry of Finance will oversee and supervise the pension funds through a new and independent Pension Fund Regulatory and Development Authority."

On August 23, 2003, the Cabinet approved the proposal to implement the budget announcement of February 2003 relating to introducing a new restructured defined contribution pension system for new entrants to Central Government service, except to Armed Forces, from January 1, 2004 onward.

The new system will also be available, on a voluntary basis, to all persons including self-employed professionals and others in the uncovered sector. However, mandatory programs under the Employee Provident Fund Organization (EPFO) and other special provident funds would continue to operate as per the existing system under the Employee Provident Fund and Miscellaneous Provisions Act, 1952 and other special Acts governing these funds. The Government approved the basic features of the new pension system, and the setting up of an interim pension fund regulatory and development authority (PFRDA). The main features of the new pension system are given below.

- The new pension system will be based on defined contributions, and will use the existing network of bank branches and post offices, etc. to collect contributions and interact with participants, allowing transfer of the benefits in case of change of employment, and offer a basket of pension choices.
- The system will be mandatory for new recruits to the Central Government service except the armed forces and the monthly contribution will be 10% of the salary and DA to be paid by the employee and matched by the Central Government. However, there will be no contribution from the Government in respect of individuals who are not Government employees.

  The contributions and investment returns will be deposited in a non-withdrawable pension tier-I account. The existing provisions of the defined benefit pension and GPF will not be available to the new recruits in the Central Government service.

- In addition to the above pension account, each individual may also have a voluntary tier-II withdrawable account at his option. This option is given since GPF is proposed to be withdrawn for new recruits in Central Government service. Government will make no contribution into this account. These assets will be managed through exactly the above procedures.

However, the individual will be free to withdraw part or all of the "second tier" of his money anytime. This withdrawable account does not constitute pension investment, and will attract no special tax treatment.

- Individuals will be able to normally exit at or after age 60 from Tier-I of the pension system. At exit, the individual will be mandatorily required to invest 40% of pension wealth to purchase an annuity (from an IRDA-regulated life insurance company). In case of Government employees, the annuity will be required to have a survivor clause, through which the spouse will also receive benefits upon death of the pensioner. The individual will receive a lump-sum of the remaining pension wealth, which he will be free to utilize in any manner.

- Individuals will have the flexibility to leave the pension system prior to age 60. However, in this case, 80% of the accumulated pension wealth will have to be mandatorily annuitized. In terms of implementation, the pension system will have the following aspects. It will have centralized record keeping and accounting (CRA) infrastructure, and several competing pension fund managers (PFMs), each of whom will offer three styles of schemes viz. options A–C with different asset class allocations and volatility characteristics. The participating entities (PFMs and CRA) will give out easily understood information about past performance, so that the individual will able to make informed choices about which scheme to choose.

An independent Pension Fund Regulatory and Development Authority (PFRDA) will regulate and develop the pension market. PFRDA will develop its own funding stream based on user charges. Till such time when a statutory PFRDA is established, an interim PFRDA, on the pattern of SEBI and IRDA, should be appointed by an executive order.

There will be different investment choices through the three styles A–C. Style A will have the most fixed income investments and Style C will have the least. Pension fund managers will be free to make investments in international markets subject to regulatory restrictions and oversight in this regard.

It is proposed to evaluate market mechanisms (without any contingent liability upon the exchequer) through which certain investment protection guarantees can be offered for the different schemes.

8.2. *Decisions by the UPA government in 2004*

In May 2004, the United Progressive Alliance (UPA) government won the general elections, and assumed power. The UPA administration chose to continue with the pension reforms effort. It chose to disband the "interim PFRDA," which was intended to setup administrative procedures prior to passage of the legislation.

The budget speech of 8 July 2004, by finance minister P. Chidambaram, had the following text:

> "Pension Reform
>
> 70. A defined contribution pension scheme has been introduced with effect from January 1, 2004 for the Central Government employees recruited on or after that date. A suitable legislation to provide a regulatory framework for the scheme will be introduced in Parliament."

The budget speech of February 28, 2005, by finance minister P. Chidambaram, had the following text:

> "PFRDA
>
> 84. With increasing longevity, the problem of old-age income security can no longer be ignored. Government had announced a defined contribution pension scheme for newly recruited Central Government employees which would also be extended to the unorganized sector. I am happy to inform the House that seven State Governments — Andhra Pradesh, Chhattisgarh, Himachal Pradesh, Jharkhand, Manipur, Rajasthan, and Tamil Nadu — have introduced similar schemes for their employees. Other States have also evinced interest. An Ordinance was promulgated on December 29, 2004 to set up a Pension Fund Regulatory and Development Authority (PFRDA). I propose to introduce a Bill to replace the Ordinance during this session.
>
> 85. Through the new scheme, it is proposed to offer a menu of investment choices to the subscriber and to provide a strong regulatory mechanism to ensure that the interests of subscribers are protected. I appeal to workers all over the country to join the new pension system."

8.3. *Tax treatment*

The new pension system will use an "EET" tax structure, whereby pension contributions and accumulation will be accorded tax preference up to a certain limit, but benefits will be taxed as normal income.

In June 2004, the Task Force on FRBM Implementation (chaired by Vijay Kelkar) proposed a comprehensive reform of the income tax system, away from the existing "savings incentives" through EEE treatment and administered rates of return, to a modern EET framework. An EET framework was introduced into the finance bill in the first budget of July 2004 for the purpose of the New Pension System. The budget speech of February 2005 declared the intention to broaden this into a full EET system. The details of this are expected to be worked out in 2005.

8.4. *Adoption at state governments*

The difficulties of the traditional civil service pension apply equally at the state level as they do at the center.[32] The option of joining the new system is available to the state governments. In the case of state governments, the adoption typically pertains to (a) Employees of state government, (b) Employees of local government, and (c) Employees of "autonomous enterprises" who were entitled to the traditional DB pension.

As of April 2005, states adding up to 38.58% of India's population have adopted the New Pension System (Table 6). Each state has used slightly different cut-off dates, after which new recruits are placed into the New Pension System. Many other states, including Karnataka, Maharashtra, and Goa, are at various stages of implementing similar reforms. These adoptions have substantially increased the size of participants in the early years of the NPS, and have ensured that the NPS will rapidly enjoy economies of scale, in contrast with the difficulties with high fixed costs faced in many fledgling pensions systems in small countries. While exact estimates are hard to obtain in the state of Andhra Pradesh, which has 7.37% of India's population, recruitment is estimated to be leading to 150,000 additional members of the NPS per year. Linear extrapolation suggests that the states listed above might induce roughly 0.8 million members of the NPS per year.

Table 6.   States which have adopted the New Pension System.

State	Fraction of India's population	Cut-off date
Andhra Pradesh	7.37	September 2004
Tamil Nadu	0.05	April 2003
Madhya Pradesh	5.88	n.a.
Rajasthan	5.50	January 2004
Gujarat	4.93	n.a.
Orissa	3.57	n.a.
Kerala	3.10	April 2005
Jharkhand	2.62	December 2004
Assam	2.59	February 2005
Punjab	2.37	n.a.
Chhattisgarh	2.02	November 2004
Himachal Pradesh	0.59	May 2003
Manipur	0.23	January 2005
Total	38.58	

8.5. *Next steps*

As of April 2005, Parliament is engaged in discussing a Bill which will give legislative foundations to the New Pension System. This Bill will create the PFRDA, and empower it to regulate the New Pension System.

In parallel, administrative efforts are underway to setup IT systems for creating accounts, giving out unique identity numbers, handling contributions, and giving out account balance statements.

9. Conclusion

Thrift and self-help can go remarkably far, given the power of compounding.

A contribution rate of Rs. 10 per day for 250 working days is within reach for a substantial swathe of India's labor force. At a real rate of return of 5.9%, the very first year of contribution (Rs. 2500 at age 20) — alone — turns into pension wealth of Rs. 25,000 at age 60. This — alone — yields a monthly pension of Rs. 160 per month. This shows the opportunity for modest contributions to turn to substantial old age social and income security. India faces a threat and an opportunity. India is at a remarkable point in demographic transition, where a substantial mass of young people are coming into the labor force. This constitutes a threat and an opportunity.

The opportunity lies in creating a formal pension system, through which individuals can build up pension wealth in personal accounts. This would empower these individuals in coping with old age. As of 2005, India has the sophisticated institutional capacity that is required to build and operate a modern pension system.

There is a threat of missing this window of opportunity. To the extent that India is unable to engage in such reforms in time, there is a threat of facing severe difficulties when the young cohorts of today approach old age, and have lost the opportunity to build up pension wealth. Every 20 year old who loses a year of contributing Rs. 2500 per year stands to lose roughly Rs. 25,000 of pension wealth at age 60.

The NPS is a sustainable, scalable path. The defining goals of Indian pension reform are sustainability and scalability. The New Pension System has the institutional architecture which can scale across central government employees, state government employees, and millions of individuals in the uncovered sector across the country. The NPS is also a sustainable path for policy, since it does not involve fiscal costs, regardless of whether there are 10 million or 200 million accounts.

The NPS empowers many, but not all, of India's future elderly at a zero fiscal cost. India's problem of ageing is undoubtedly large and complex. Not everyone can meaningfully participate in the NPS. The lifetime poor would be unable to build up significant pension wealth, and earners beyond age 50 have little time to benefit from the power of compounding. There is a certainly a need for designing poverty programs which will be able to effectively target the elderly poor. However, this article has made the case that there is a substantial mass of individuals — roughly 100 million in the uncovered sector as of late 2004 — who can be empowered in old age by the NPS, at no cost to the exchequer.

References

1. Dave, S.A. (1999). "Restructuring pensions for the twenty-first century." In: Hanson, J.A. and Kathuria, S. (eds.) *India: A Financial Sector for the Twenty-First Century.* Oxford: Oxford University Press, pp. 305–334.
2. Patel, U.R. (1997). "Aspects of pension fund reform: Lessons for India." *Economic and Political Weekly* **32**(38), 2395–2402.
3. Asher, M. and Vasudevan, D. (2004). "Civil service pension reform: time to act." *Economic and Political Weekly* **3951**, 5363–5365.

4. Reddy, Y.V. (2001). "Report of the expert committee to review the system of administered rates." Reserve Bank of India.

5. Mohan, R. (2004). "Report of the advisory committee to advise on the administered interest rates and rationalisation of savings instruments." Reserve Bank of India.

6. Mathur, S.N. (1998). "Greying of the indian railways." Technical report, Asian Institute of Transport Development, p. 11.

7. Rajan, S.I. (2001). "Social assistance for poor elderly: How effective?" Technical report. *Economic and Political Weekly* **12**.

8. Shah, A. and Thomas, S. (2003b). "Policy issues in Indian securities markets." In: Krueger, A. and Chinoy, S.Z. (eds.) *Reforming India's External, Financial and Fiscal Policies*. Stanford Studies in International Economics and Development, Stanford University Press, pp. 129–147.

9. Shah, A. and Thomas, S. (1998). "Market microstructure considerations in index construction." In: *CBOT Research Symposium Proceedings*. Chicago Board of Trade, pp. 173–193.

10. Shah, A. and Thomas, S. (2003a). "Equity derivatives in India: The state of the art." In: Thomas, S. (ed.) *Derivatives Markets in India 2003*. Tata McGraw–Hill, Chapter 1, pp. 1–25.

11. Shah, A. and Fernandes, K. (2001). "The relevance of index funds for pension investment in equities." In: Holzmann, R. and Stiglitz, J. (eds.) *New Ideas about Old Age Security: Toward Sustainable Pension Systems in the 21st Century*. World Bank.

12. Valdes-Prieto, S. (1998). "Risk in pensions and annuities: Efficient designs." Technical report, World Bank.

13. James, E. and Sane, R. (2003). "The annuity market in India: Do consumers get their money's worth? What are the key public policy issues?" In: Bordia, A. and Bharadwaj, G. (eds.) *Rethinking Pension Provision for India*. Tata McGraw Hill, pp. 231–262.

14. Srinivas, P.S. and Thomas, S. (2003). "Institutional mechanisms in pension fund management: Lessons from three Indian case studies." *Economic and Political Weekly* **38**(8), 706–719.

15. Alier, M. and Vittas, D. (1999). "Personal pension plans and stock market volatility." In: *New Ideas about Old Age Security: Toward Sustainable Pension Systems in the 21st Century*. World Bank.

16. World Bank (1994). *Averting the Old Age Crisis: Policies to Protect the Old and Promote Growth*. Oxford: Oxford University Press.

17. Lillard, L.A., Brien, M.J. and Panis, C.W.A. (1993). "The value of annuities at age 65: Race, marital status, wealth, health and mortality." Technical report, Rand Corporation.

18. Thomas, S. (1999). "Alternative investment strategies on multi-decade horizons." Technical report, IGIDR.

19. Whitehouse, E. (2000). "Administrative charges for funded pensions: An international comparison and assessment." Technical Report Social Protection Discussion Paper No. 0016, World Bank.

20. Murthi, M., Orszag, J.M. and Orszag, P.R. (1999). "Administrative costs under a decentralised approach to individual accounts: Lessons from the United Kingdom." In: *New Ideas about Old Age Security*.

21. Shah, A. and Thomas, S. (2003c). "Securities market efficiency." In: Hanson, J.A., Honohan, P. and Majnoni, G. (eds.) *Globalisation and National Financial Systems*. The World Bank and Oxford University Press, pp. 145–175.

22. James, E., Smalhout, J. and Vittas, D. (1999). "Administrative costs and the organization of individual account systems: A comparative perspective." In: *New Ideas about Old Age Security*. World Bank.

23. Walliser, J. (1999). "Regulation of withdrawals in individual account systems." In: *New Ideas about Old Age security*. World Bank.

24. Siegel, J. (2002). *Stocks for the Long Run*, 3rd edn. McGraw-Hill.

25. Patnaik, I. (2005). "India's experience with a pegged exchange rate." *India Policy Forum* 1, 189–216.

26. Shah, A. and Patnaik, I. (2006). "Forthcoming, India's experience with capital flows: The elusive quest for a sustainable current account deficit." In: Edwards, S. (ed.) *International Capital Flows*. NBER and University of Chicago Press.

27. Bodie, Z. and Merton, R. (2002). "International pension swaps." *Journal of Pension Economics and Finance* 11, 23.

28. Shah, A. (2003). "Investment risk in the Indian pension sector and the role for pension guarantees." *Economic and Political Weekly* 38(8), 719–728.

29. Pennacchi, G. (1998). "Government guarantees on pension fund returns." Technical report, World Bank.

30. Asher, M. (2001). The case for a regulatory authority for India's pension system, Research report 2-2001, International Center for Pension Research.

31. Dave, S.A. (2000). Project OASIS Report, Committee report, Ministry for Social Justice, Government of India.

32. Bhattacharya, B.K. (2003). "Report of the group to study the pension liabilities of the state governments." Reserve Bank of India.

33. Lillard, L.A. and Willis, R.J. (2000). "Cognition and wealth: The importance of probabilistic thinking." Technical report, University of Michigan.

34. Whitehouse, E. (1999). "Pension reform, financial literacy and public information: A case study of the United Kingdom."

CHAPTER 8

Globalization, Demographic Transition, and Reform of Social Safety Nets in India

Mukul G. Asher and Deepa Vasudevan

1. Introduction

India has been pursuing calibrated globalization for nearly two decades. It has been unilaterally liberalizing its economic environment and deregulating for even longer period, though more progress in these areas is still needed. India has taken several initiatives such as vigorous bilateral dialog with major powers, particularly the United States, Japan, and the EU. Its "Look East" Policy initiative of the early 1990s has succeeded in substantially enhancing relations with rest of Asia.[1,a] India's participation in multilateral fora has also increasingly become more extensive and strategic. India's approach to globalization can be summarized in the words of the Prime Minister, who, when addressing the "India Today" Magazine conclave in early 2005 stated the following:

"We would like to make globalization a win–win game. How we deal with the challenge of globalization and how we make use of its opportunities will shape our relations with the world, and the perception of our capabilities as a nation."

India has achieved a real GDP growth rate of close to 6% for a prolonged period, with reasonable price stability, and sustainable external balance (Table 1). The World Bank estimates India's GDP in 2004 at USD 692 billion, third largest in Asia. India's pluralistic and inclusive political and

---

[a] Invitation by the Association of Southeast Asian Nations (ASEAN) to India to participate in a summit in Kuala Lumpur in December 2005 which will also involve Japan, South Korea, and China, reflects India's deepening engagement in new Asia.

219

Table 1.   India: selected indicators of macroeconomic performance.

Indicator	1991–1992	1995–1996	2001–2002	2002–2003	2003–2004
Income					
Real GDP (Rs. billion)	7018.6	8995.6	12679.5	13183.6QE	14305.5RE
Growth in Real GDP (%)	1.3	7.3	5.8	4.0	8.5
Inflation					
Wholesale Price Index — All commodities (Inflation in %)	13.7	8.1	3.6	3.4	5.4
Consumer Price Index — Industrial Worker (Inflation in %)	13.5	10.2	4.3	4.0	3.9
Domestic investment					
Gross Domestic Capital Formation (% to GDP)	22.6	26.9	22.6	24.8	26.3
Gross Domestic Savings (% to GDP)	22.0	25.1	23.4	26.1	28.1
Foreign investment					
Foreign Exchange Reserves ($ million)	5631	17044	51049	71890	107448
Foreign direct investment ($ million)	129	2144	6131	4660	4675
Portfolio investment ($ million)	4	2748	2021	979	11377
Total Foreign Investment Inflows ($ million)	133	4892	8152	5639	16052
Trade					
Merchandise Exports ($ million)	17865	31797	43827	52719	61718
Merchandise Imports ($ million)	19411	36678	51413	61412	75400
Net Invisibles ($ million)	1620	5449	13485	17047	25425
Current Account Balance ($ million)	−1178	−5910	782	4137	8719
Merchandise Exports/GDP (%)	6.9	9.1	9.3	10.3	10.4
Merchandise Imports/GDP (%)	7.9	12.3	12.0	12.8	13.2
Trade Balance/GDP (%)	−1.0	−3.2	−2.6	−2.5	−2.8
Current Account Balance/GDP (%)	−0.3	−1.7	0.2	0.8	1.4

Notes: QE — Quick estimates; RE — Revised estimates.
Sources: Calculated from Ref. 2, Tables 0.1 and 3, Tables 1, 2, 10, 140, 153, 215, 216, 224 and 225.

economic system requires that pursuit of economic growth be balanced by policies designed to mitigate large inequalities.[4] India's Gini coefficient of consumption has remained around 0.325 for most of the last three decades.[b] Its Gini coefficient for income is at a moderate level of around 0.35, and has also been fairly stable.

India's calibrated globalization is expected to continue regardless of political parties (or coalitions) forming the government. There is sufficient consensus among the key political parties that if India sustains high growth with moderate inequalities, particularly in consumption, and provides wider access to economic opportunities to diverse groups; it can transform the quality of life for its billion-plus people. There is, however, considerable need to strengthen domestic institutions, governance structures and to make government service delivery systems more effective in order to enable India to sustain growth rates of 8% over a prolonged period. India thus needs to focus on how to shift its trend rate of growth from 6 to 8% per annum.

The rest of the paper is organized as follows. The next section briefly enumerates reasons for reform of social safety nets.[c] This is followed by an assessment of the current social security system in India (Section 3). Section 4 focuses on future directions for the social safety nets. The final section provides the concluding remarks.

2. Rationale for Reforming Social Safety Nets

In Refs. 5–7 have argued that globalization makes social safety nets more rather than less necessary, as they cushion the blow for those most severely affected, help maintain the legitimacy of reform, and help avoid a backlash against the social and distributional consequences of globalization. This argument has considerable validity in the case of India.

In addition to globalization, there are other reasons for reforming India's social safety nets. India is experiencing a demographic transition, leading to

---

[b] In Ref. 4, Table 4.1.
[c] In this paper, the term social safety nets is used synonymously with social security system and its components. The term pension reform refers to the NPS which is mandatory for civil servants introduced from January 2004. The NPS is however accessible to individuals in any sector or occupation on a voluntary basis.

lower total fertility rate (the rate was 2.85 children per woman in 2004[d]); increased life expectancy (In 2001, life expectancy at age 60 was 15.7 years for males and 17.1 years for females) and greater proportion of the aged in population. The share of elderly, or persons aged 65 years and above in India's population is expected to rise from 4.6% in 2000 to 9% in 2030. In absolute terms, the number of elderly will rise from 47 million in 2000 to 129 million in 2030 (Table 2).

Table 2.   India: labor force and demographic indicators.

	Indicator	Time period	
1	Life expectancy at birth (Years)	2000–2005	
	Male		63.2
	Female		64.6
2	Life expectancy at age 60 (Years)	2001	
	Male		15.7
	Female		17.1
3	Total fertility rate *(no. of children)	2001	2.85
4	Population (million)	2001	1028
	Females (million)		496
	Males (million)		532
	Sex ratio (Females per thousand males)		933
5	Population above age 65 (million)	2000	46.6
		2030	129.3
	Old age dependency ratio (%)**	2001	11.9
6	Total work force (million)	2001	424.6
	Urban work force (million)		97.7
	Rural work force (million)		326.9
7	Working age population (million)		
		2000	619.7
		2025	921.5
		2050	1048.2

Notes: *Total fertility rate is defined as the average number of live childbirths over a woman's lifetime and **Old age dependency ratio is defined as $\frac{\text{(population above 60 years)}}{\text{(population 15–59 years)}} \times 100$.

Sources: State of World Population, UNFPA, 2004, Adapted from Ref. 9, Liebig and Rajan 2003, p. 20, Table 4, CIA World Fact Book, obtained from http://www.indexmundi.com/g/g.aspx?c=in&v=31; Census of India 2001, www.censusindia.net.

---

[d]There is considerable regional variation in fertility rates. The southern region of the country is experiencing fertility rates at or below replacement rates, while some of the highly populated northern states have high fertility rates, with the western region somewhere in between.[8]

Both the level and the pace of ageing are likely to provide significant challenges as even by 2030, India's per capita income will be relatively low. If the current normal retirement age of 60 is not increased, then the challenge of financing the elderly will be even greater. As women are increasingly living longer than men; greater feminization of the population is taking place.[9] Providing secure and sustainable retirement income therefore ranks high in the social priorities.

The current demographic transition has the potential to provide India with a significant competitive advantage in the form of a "demographic dividend."[e] In absolute numbers, India's working age population is projected to increase from 619.7 million in 2000 to 921.5 million in 2025, and to 1048.2 million in 2050 (Table 2). This is a double-edged advantage as it implies that net jobs creation must get priority over preserving existing jobs if this dividend is to be translated into higher growth and competitive advantage. However, higher working age population provides India with the potential to increase aggregate saving and investment rates, and thereby increase trend rate of growth.[12] As the most important macroeconomic variable in providing economic security for both the young and the old is the trend rate of economic growth, India's demographic advantage phase could potentially permit it to make progress in developing more adequate and equitable social safety nets, while maintaining social cohesion.

To take advantage of the "demographic dividend," modernization of labor market structures and regulations will be required. The balance will need to be shifted to generation of additional jobs which are productive and sustainable rather than on preserving existing jobs. India's labor force in 2001 was 425 million, of which slightly less than a quarter was urban, while the rest was rural (Table 2). Design, structure and capacities concerning social safety nets differ considerably between urban and rural areas.[13] Thus, social assistance type programs, which require fiscal resources and effective public delivery systems, are likely to play a greater role in rural than in urban areas.

The greater prevalence of self-employment in rural areas requires differently designed pension schemes. In the urban sector, the nature of employment

---

[e]A major indicator of this advantage is the rising share of working age population in total population; it is expected that the proportion of the active-workforce in the population (i.e., persons aged 15–59) will rise from 58.2% in 2001 to 64% in 2016.[10] This share will not begin to decline till around 2045.[11]

is also changing, with life-long employment becoming somewhat less prevalent, while labor mobility has become greater. These trends have meant that much greater importance will need to be given to pension benefit mobility across sectors and occupations than has been the case so far, and to more flexible compensation packages incorporating some degree of individual choice among various benefits.[14] The human resource management function is therefore likely to become quite complex.

Reform of social safety nets is also needed to assist in the process of fiscal consolidation (essentially reducing budget deficits) and fiscal flexibility (reallocation of budget toward growth enhancing expenditures). India's combined public sector deficit has been close to 9% for many years, and could act as a major constraint on achieving higher growth.[15] There are also limitations of the existing social security system arising from inappropriate design features, limited professionalism with which they are implemented and inefficient delivery of social assistance benefits.[16]

The confluence of the above factors has resulted in greater importance being given to the reform of the social security system in the public policy agenda in India. The reformed social security system needs to be consistent with India's open economy–open society paradigm. It is also being increasingly recognized that professionalism is essential in design, management and day-to-day administration of social safety nets.

3. An Assessment of the Existing Social Security System

Existing social security arrangement in India may be divided into six components (Fig. 1).

3.1. *Civil service schemes*

The structure of retirement schemes for the 13 million civil servants at the Central, State, and Local Government levels are broadly similar; consisting of three types of retirement benefits. Civil servants receive non-contributory, unfunded, Defined Benefit (DB) pension,[f] which is indexed for prices and

---

[f] In a DB scheme, participants are promised pension benefits, and investment and other risks are borne by the plan sponsor.

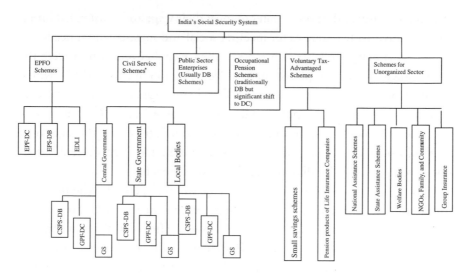

Fig. 1. India's Social Security System: An Overview.

Notes: From January 1, 2004, all newly recruited civil servants at the Centre (except for armed forces)are on a DC scheme. 16 states have also issued notification for a shift to a DC scheme, but their starting dates vary.

Abbreviations used: DB — Defined Benefit; DC — Defined Contribution; EDL — Employees' Deposit Linked Insurance Scheme; EPF — Employees' Provident Fund; EPS — Employees' Pension Scheme; GPF — Government Provident Fund; GS — Gratuity Scheme; CSPS — New Civil service Pension Scheme; NGO — Non-Government Organizations.
Source: Authors.

has fairly generous commutation provisions and survivors' benefits.[g] In addition, each employee is mandated to contribute a percentage of his salary to a Government Provident Fund (GPF) scheme. Finally, civil servants also receive lump sum gratuity benefit based on period of service and the salary level, with a maximum ceiling of Rs. 0.35 million.

In principle, each State has the freedom to design pension plans for its civil servants. In practice, States usually adopt the pension schemes followed by the Center with relatively minor modifications. As a result States with different fiscal capacities end up having similar pension schemes; a practice that severely

---

[g]In India, Pay Commissions are periodically constituted to recommend civil servant's pay and other terms of employment. The upward revision in nominal pay has also been applied to civil service pensioners. Thus, there is also wage indexation which is in addition to price indexation.

affects the ability of the poorer states to meet their wage and pension liabilities, and still leave aside resources for meeting social and infrastructural needs.

From January 2004, new entrants to the Central government (except the armed forces) have been placed under a New Pension System (NPS),[h] which is a portable Defined Contribution (DC) scheme.[i] Under the NPS, no pre-retirement withdrawals are permitted; and at retirement age of 60; purchase of annuities is mandated. Addressing longevity and inflation risks[j] through some form of risk sharing arrangement will be essential. The NPS currently does not have a provision for disability and survivors' benefits.

To realize the objective of establishing suitable pension schemes, it is important that as many States as possible implement the NPS. So far nine States (Rajasthan, Orissa, Manipur, Tamil Nadu, Himachal Pradesh, Andhra Pradesh, Gujarat, Chhattisgarh, and Jharkhand) have notified their intention of introducing a contributory pension scheme on the lines of the NPS. Assam, Orissa, and Punjab are considering implementing the NPS. The absence of two major states with large pension liabilities, namely Maharashtra and West Bengal from the list considering the NPS is striking.

The NPS aims to minimize transactions costs through setting up of Central Recordkeeping Agency (CRA) and limited investment choices to accommodate different risk-preferences of the members.[17] Diversification of pension assets will be permitted, but its extent will depend on choices made by the members.[k] In the initial stages, portfolio diversification is unlikely to be extended to investments internationally. It is envisaged that FDI in pensions sector will be permitted. There is a precedence of permitting such FDI in the insurance sector, and the positive experience in that sector may be helpful in introducing

---

[h] For a detailed analysis of the NPS, Ref. 17.

[i] Under a DC scheme, contributions by the participants are defined. It is the participants individually who bear investment and other risks. So pension benefits are not known in advance.

[j] Longevity risk arises due to the possibility that accumulated balances may be exhausted before a person dies. Inflation risk involves at least preserving the real value of pension (or annuity) at the time of retirement until death.

[k] The NPS is expected to lead to significant accumulation of long-term contractual savings. Some estimates suggest that savings might rise to about 50% of GDP by 2025, from the present level of 25%. With a market capitalization of $440 billion (about 60% of 2004 GDP), Indian capital markets are well placed to channelize contractual savings into productive investments, given enabling policy and regulatory framework (www.ibef.com).

FDI in the pensions sector.[l] The public sector financial institutions are likely to play a prominent role in the NPS. The NPS will be regulated by Pension Fund Regulatory and Development Authority (PFRDA).

3.2. *Employees provident fund organization schemes*

Social security arrangements for private sector employees consist of the three schemes of the Employees Provident Fund Organization (EPFO) set up in 1952. After more than 50 years of operations, the EPFO covers only about 350,000 establishments (not firms); and represents the main instrument through which retirement financing is provided to workers in the organized, non-public sector. It provides a DC scheme, called the Employees Provident Fund (EPF), to 39.5 million members, a DB scheme, called the Employees' Pension Scheme (EPS), to 27.5 million members, and a life insurance scheme called Employees' Deposit Linked Insurance (EDLI).

Combining a DC and a DB Scheme under one organization is unusual, and requires high level of expertise and management skills. Table 3 summarizes the contribution rates for each scheme. The EPF Scheme was established in 1952; EDLI Scheme in 1976; and the EPS in 1995. The EPS scheme is therefore relatively recent. The main challenge of paying promised pension benefits under the EPS, including family pensions to survivors, lies in the future.[m]

The total contributions to three mandatory schemes are 25.66%, subject to a ceiling of Rs. 6500 of wages per month. The wage ceiling has been raised at regular intervals. In addition, EPFO levies administrative charges of 1.11%; and inspection charges on EPFO exempt but regulated funds at 0.185%. These represent benefit provision and administrative costs. From an economy's point of view, cost compliance with EPFO regulations by establishment should also be added.[n]

---

[l] As Insurance companies are the only entities permitted to issue annuities, insurance companies also have a role in the pensions sector, particularly in the pay-out phase.

[m] Estimates suggest that as of 2004 the EPS was under funded by at least Rs. 220 billion.[18]

[n] To our knowledge, no studies estimating such compliance costs have been undertaken. This is a promising area of research.

Table 3.   Contribution rates for the schemes of the EPFO.

Contribution (% of wages)	EPF (1952)	EPS (1995)	EDLI (1976)	Total contribution rate
Employer	3.67	8.33	0.50	12.50
Employee	12.00	nil	nil	12.00
Government	nil	1.16	nil	1.16
Total contribution rate	15.67	9.49	0.5	25.66
Administrative charges paid by employer (unexempted sector only)	1.10	Paid out of EPS fund	0.01	1.11
Inspection charges paid by employer (exempted sector only)	0.18	n.a	0.005	0.185
Benefits	Accumulation plus interest on retirement, resignation, death. Partial withdrawals permitted for specific purposes	Monthly pension on superannuation, retirement, disability, survivor, widow(er), children	Lump sum benefit on death while in service	

Source: Employees Provident Fund and Miscellaneous Provisions Act, 1952.
Notes: As of July 2005, the wage ceiling to which the contribution rates apply was Rs. 6500 per month and the figures in brackets refer to the year in which the scheme was introduced.

On March 31, 2003, cumulative investments under the EPF scheme stood at Rs. 1027.5 billion;[o] and the stock of investments under the EPS 1995 scheme and EDLI scheme were Rs. 450.5 billion and Rs. 34.9 billion, respectively. Thus, collectively, the EPFO held investments worth Rs. 1481.5 billion under its three schemes, equivalent to nearly 6% of India's Gross Domestic Product (GDP) in 2003. The EPFO funds are almost wholly invested in government and public sector fixed investments. The EPFO Board has not permitted any funds to be invested in equities.

---

[o]This includes Rs. 40 billion under EPFO regulated but exempted Trusts.

The key challenge of the EPFO is to ensure that its high contribution rates translate into high benefits to its members and that its relatively large and costly administrative apparatus is commensurate with the quality and quantity of its services.

3.3. *Public sector enterprises*

Public sector enterprises including public sector insurance companies and banks, the Central Bank called the Reserve Bank of India, electricity boards, State oil companies, etc., have their own pension schemes, which are managed by the concerned enterprise with little regulatory oversight or supervision. The schemes are usually contributory in nature, but details about scheme design and their actuarial sustainability are not publicly available. Therefore, the professionalism with which these schemes are designed and administered is also not known.

3.4. *Occupational pension schemes or superannuation schemes*

These refer to employer sponsored schemes that are not statutory, but provide additional post-retirement income to employees on a regular basis.[14] These are governed under the Income Tax Act by the tax authorities. The schemes can be DB or DC in nature; and the liabilities are met by setting up Trust Funds, either self-managed or managed by the Life Insurance Corporation of India (LIC).

Since 1956, LIC has been managing a plan that invests all the monies received from various Employee Retirement Benefit Funds into a pooled fund, of which 95% are invested in government securities and bonds and 5% in equities. Self managed trust funds are governed by the restrictive investment guidelines, which limit the earning potential of these funds.

The investments of insurance company administered superannuation schemes are regulated by the Insurance Regulatory and Development Authority (IRDA), though the overall granting and supervisory authority are the Income Tax authorities. The IRDA has permitted the pension fund component of insurance companies to hold a diversified investment portfolio, including equities. The funds however can only be invested domestically.

Unlike EPFO, the IRDA's guidelines for investment of pension funds managed by the life insurance companies are consistent with modern portfolio management principles and practices.

India's 2005–2006 budget introduced a Fringe Benefits Tax (FBT).[p] The statutory liability for the FBT is on the companies, though economic incidence which involves tax burden sharing among different economic agents once participants adjust their behavior in response to the tax, is unlikely to be solely on the employers (i.e., shareholders). The definition of fringe benefits used is quite broad, and very unusually, includes superannuation benefits.[q] This could negatively impact existing superannuation schemes as well as their growth. Life insurance industry and others have made representations to the government to partially or fully exempt superannuation contributions by the employers from the FBT. The main argument against the FBT is that taxing superannuation contributions is inconsistent with the government's objective that private sector and individuals share greater burden of retirement income security.[r]

3.5. *Voluntary tax advantaged savings schemes*

These comprise small savings schemes (In 2003–2004, outstanding small savings formed 21.1% of the combined domestic liabilities of Center and States, and gross mobilization was at 5.3% of GDP);[19] and individual and group annuity schemes of life insurance companies. Interest rates on small savings instruments have traditionally been set at above market rates, which distorts allocation of savings. In particular, savings intermediated through mutual funds and market-based instruments in financial and capital markets are adversely impacted. Although there has been some rationalization in rates since 2002, more progress is needed.[19]

---

[p]The details of the FBT may be found in Finance Bill 2005.

[q]Countries levying such a tax, such as Australia, specifically exempt superannuation contributions by both the employers and the employees at the time of contribution.

[r]There are other arguments against the FBT. First, it is an *ad hoc* revenue measure which is inconsistent with the government's vision of moving toward low nominal income (and sales) tax rates — a broad base essential for a modern tax system. Second, it will inevitably provide greater discretionary powers to tax administrators and opportunities by industries to engage in lobbying for special exemptions. Both are undesirable. Third, voluntary superannuation funds have the potential to provide long-term funds to the financial and capital markets, and to contribute to financial innovation. These are essential if the government's objective of developing Mumbai into a financial center is to be realized. Given such strong arguments against it, re-thinking on FBT is likely but the changes are unlikely until the 2006–2007 Budget.

3.6. *Schemes for the unorganized sector*

The life time poor are provided assistance through Social Assistance Schemes (SAS), both at the Central and in the State levels. These schemes are usually means-tested and targeted at the destitute and poor and the infirm population over the age of 60 years. The pensions under these welfare schemes are expected to provide between Rs. 55–300 per month, but their coverage is limited to between 10 and 15% of the elderly population.[20] In addition, these schemes are usually under funded, poorly targeted, and suffer from significant leakages.[21] At present, majority of the workers in the unorganized sector (who form more than four-fifths of the country's workforce) are protected only through the efforts of welfare bodies, the community, or NGOs. There is however a recognition that the terms "unorganized" or "informal" and the term "rural" are too heterogeneous to be subjected to broad generalizations, particularly in terms of occupational income and consumption patterns.

Each of the six components of the social security system is in need of urgent reforms. These should address two major limitations of the existing pension system.

First, there is a need to significantly enhance the professionalism with which the core functions are being performed by provident and pension funds. The core functions of any provident or pension fund include the reliable collection of contribution/taxes, and other receipts; payment of benefits for each of the schemes in a correct way; efficient financial management and productive investment of provident and pension assets; maintenance of an effective communication network, including development of accurate data and record keeping mechanisms to support collection, payment and financial activities; and production of financial statements and reports that are tied to providing effective and reliable governance, fiduciary responsibility, transparency, and accountability.[22] The foundation of a sustainable pension system should be built on a judicial system with modern laws and regulations which are consistent with the economic paradigm of the country; enabling regulatory environment; sound scheme design; widespread use of information technology and adoption of good governance principles.

Second, there is no overall systemic perspective of social security, despite over a decade of steady reform in other sectors of the economy. There are four regulatory bodies — IRDA, the EPFO, the Income Tax Authority and the newly set up PFRDA, each with some degree of jurisdiction in specific areas of operation. The presence of multiple regulators reduces the overall accountability of the operators, and does not produce a harmonized legal environment. The tax treatment of various provident and pension fund schemes also varies considerably. This is complicated by high administered interest rates on some of the savings instruments, whose receipts are channeled into government consumption expenditure.

As a result, the current system has many instances where sufficient attention is not being paid to improving professionalism and achieving international standards in management and efficient provision of retirement support. The EPFO, with balances equivalent to about 6% of GDP, may be considered to be among India's largest Non-Banking Financial Institutions. Yet its current governance structure is antithetical to modern norms of corporate governance. It is managed by the Central Board of Trustees, numbering 45 (an unwieldy number), entirely appointed by the Central Government, with no provision for independent experts from outside the government. There are many design provisions (such as permitting members to withdraw balances from the DB pensions scheme and yet retain pension benefits when later contributions are made) which need to be made consistent with modern provident and pension fund practices.

The EPFO itself is both a service provider and the regulator for the sector, which includes over 3000 exempt funds. The EPFO is responsible for granting exemptions and supervising exempt funds. Average balance in the exempt funds is larger than for the EPFO. The EPFO does not have a professional investment or treasury department for managing funds of this dimension, even though it employs close to 20,000 staff. This is possible because it operates under an outmoded investment regime, which does not permit effective asset diversification among asset classes and sectors. Thus EPFO contributors are effectively debarred from earning market-related returns. Excessive political interference allows pension fund providers such as EPFO and post office savings schemes to maintain nominal interest rates which are higher than obtained from investments.[5] This is clearly unsustainable.

---

[5]It has led to the curious practice of the EPFO Board considering interest rate to be credited to members' accounts at the beginning rather than at the end of the financial year.

Civil Service Pensions form only one component of the social security system, covering 3% of the labor force, but outflows on this account make up more than 2% of GDP. The Implicit Pension Debt (IPD), defined as the Net Present Value (NPV) of future payments to existing workers, existing pension pensioners, and family pensioners, is estimated to be about 55% of GDP in 2004 prices.[18,t] In any society, at any given time, only the consumption component of GDP is available for purchasing goods and services by both the young and the old. Since society has many priorities, resources for old age financing compete against other needs. If a small proportion of the elderly (such as civil servants in India) are allotted a disproportionate share of resources that society can set aside for the elderly; there will be severe challenges in addressing the retirement needs of the vast majority, creating marked dualism in social safety net provision. This in turn may negatively impact on political and social cohesion.

The states are also finding that meeting pension liabilities is adversely impacting fiscal consolidation efforts, and expenditure re-allocation toward growth and social cohesion enhancing expenditures. State-wise pension payments as a percentage of states' own revenue receipts have increased from an average of 5.2% during 1980–1990 to 17.2% in 2001–2002.[23] The situation is likely to worsen if no corrective actions are taken.

Little information is available about the actuarial soundness of retirement schemes of public sector enterprises, or on occupational pension schemes. There is obviously a need to regulate them to ensure greater professionalism, transparency, and fiduciary responsibility.

The unorganized sector is quite heterogeneous. In fact, some workers in this sector (for instance, small but prosperous shopkeepers) maybe better equipped financially for retirement as compared to low-wage workers in the formal sector. Thus any social security scheme for the unorganized sector has to be nuanced, with scope for self-selection of participants, and in some cases specifically targeted. This suggests that any government contribution for the so-called unorganized sector will be unwarranted as many in the unorganized sector have the capacity, and perhaps, motivation to save for retirement.

---

[t] While there is a strong case for reforming the civil service pensions, the IPD estimate however should be kept in perspective as while IPD is a stock concept, GDP is a flow concept. Future incomes will also be higher.

However, for a significant proportion that is life-time poor, more effective and generous social assistance programs will be needed. This is an important reason for fiscal consolidation and reform at both the Center and in the States.

4. Reform Directions

It is clear that each element of India's social security system needs to be tackled differently, and improvements made should be consistent with the overall functions of any social security system (namely, smoothing consumption over lifetime, addressing against longevity and inflation risks, income redistribution, and poverty relief achieved in a sustainable manner). While there has been intensive debate on social security reform around the world over the last two decades, predictably no single model suitable for all countries has emerged. The World Bank's most recent position paper on pension reform is structured around a five-tier framework,[u] and it recognizes that local context and capacities are crucial in determining the importance and sequencing of each tier, as well as how each tier is organized. The multi-tier framework is useful as it provides a strong rationale for drawing retirement income from a variety of sources, thus mitigating the risk of over-reliance on one scheme or method. This strongly suggests that each retirement scheme need not provide the requisite retirement resources and risks.

4.1. *Broad directions*

In the case of India, broad directions of reform include expansion of social security coverage; increase in organizational efficiency and professionalism, provision of a systemic perspective and development of the sector in its

---

[u]The tiers are as follows: a basic universal or means-tested social pension financed from budgetary sources forms the tier zero; a mandated socially risk-pooled public pension, DC or notional DC in nature and financed through contributions forms the first tier and mandated occupation or personal pension plans managed publicly or privately form the second tier. Voluntary occupation or personal pension plans form the third tier; and the last includes personal savings, home ownership, family and community support, gold, land and other assets.[24] This version has two new tiers, tier zero and tier four, and it recognizes that individual mandatory savings accounts and solely private management of their investments may not be appropriate when enabling conditions, such as good record-keeping, sufficiently developed financial and capital markets, including requisite human resources.

entirety, including industry professionals such as actuaries and researchers.[v] Reform of social safety nets will require reform in complementary areas including financial and capital markets, fiscal management, labor market, and administrative and civil service reform. Such complementary reforms are a huge challenge in any country, and India is no exception in this regard.

4.2. *Pension regulator*

Establishment of the interim PFRDA[26] in 2004 and the introduction of the PFRDA Bill[27] in the 2005 budget session of the Parliament constitute major milestones. As of July 2005, the Standing Committee on Finance of the Indian Parliament is considering this bill.

As discussed in the previous sections, the case for establishing a pension's regulator in India is overwhelming. Greater professionalism in the pensions industry; lowering of transactions costs in performing tasks noted earlier; greater efficiency in intermediating long term pensions savings to enhance economic growth which is a pre-requisite for economic security for both the young and the old; potential for pensions industry (and complementary reforms) to increased India's competitive edge and diversify export basket for services, all strongly suggest a need for a pensions regulator. It is noteworthy that high-income industrial countries do not leave pensions sector to be solely regulated to the forces of self-regulation or the markets, but have strong state regulators (regulation in this case is a public good which market will significantly under provide), supplemented by transparent rules requiring disclosure and transparency for even the state-run social insurance schemes.[w]

It is essential that while the Parliament is considering the Bill, the interim PFRDA continues its dialogue with the States to ensure smooth integration of State and Central government pension schemes. While some of the parameters

---

[v] Introduction of graduate level degree programs in pension's science, and encouraging rigorous empirical policy relevant research on pensions issues in India merit serious consideration. The aim should be to move away from descriptive, general and ideologically driven work on social security.

[w] Requirements by the Social Security Administration in the US to mandatorily commission actuarial studies spanning 75 years projections, and making them publicly available through the internet are instructive in this regard. Moreover the OECD (Organization for Economic Co-operation and Development) undertakes regular comparative analysis of the impact of social security schemes in the member countries. The contrast with the lack of information about projections of public sector pension schemes in India; and not-easily accessible and often patchy EPFO annual reports is rather striking.

(such as the contribution rates) may differ among various states, and between states and the Centre, the PFRDA must remain the sole regulatory body for the civil service pensions.

The interim PFRDA can also help in ensuring that procedures of collections of pension contributions, record-keeping, member information dissemination, etc., are efficient with low transactions costs. It could also undertake studies of modalities for introducing the Central Record keeping Agency (CRA); Points of Presence (POP) mechanisms; and criteria for selecting pension fund managers.[x]

4.3. *Coverage*

India faces a huge challenge in improving pension coverage (only about a fifth of the labor force is covered), particularly among workers who are not employed in the formal private or government sector. Of the total earning workforce of 425 million, 85%, or 360 million, work in sectors other than the formal private sector and the Government — and are usually classified as belonging to the unorganized sector.

However, the primary occupations of workers in this category are wide-ranging — including self-employed farmers and wage labor (accounting for over 60% of the unorganized sector), self-employed business owners (13.8%), salaried and/or contractual employees in the informal sector (5.4%), self-employed professionals (under 1%), and others (8.9%).[y] There is great diversity in terms of size and regularity of income, savings potential and overall awareness of the need for and ability to save for retirement.[z] This poses serious challenges in achieving pension penetration: schemes have to be structured to enable workers in varying occupations with different income security levels to save for their retirement. The NPS permits any individual to voluntarily join scheme. The PFRDA would therefore need to devise appropriate regulations and schemes to encourage voluntary participation from both the organized and the unorganized sectors.

---

[x] For elaboration on CRA, POP and selection of pension fund managers, Ref. 17.

[y] Source: AC Nielsen and ORG MARG National Data Survey Snapshots on Pension Reform for the Informal Sector in India, 2005, available at http://www.finmin.nic.in/stats_data/pension_data.

[z] In fact, the time may have come to drop the classification of "unorganized" sector for the purpose of pension scheme design and realise that individual sub-categories within this class are too heterogeneous to be combined in this manner.[25] This is also indicated by the AC Neilson — survey noted in footnote w.

A modest increase in coverage may be obtained if the EPFO demonstrates the capacity to efficiently administer, and introduces modern investment management and governance structures. Currently, only establishments employing 20 or more employees are covered by the EPFO. But if it reforms, this can be progressively reduced to 10 employees. This may increase the membership base by perhaps 4–5 million. This is modest in relation to India's labor force, but is significant in terms of absolute numbers. The trade unions therefore have a direct stake in EPFO reforms. Reforms aimed at modernizing EPFO's organizational and governance structures would also end the practice of members withdrawing accumulated balances when changing jobs, and reduce the workload generated by such provision.

4.4. *Longevity and inflation risks*

Adequate retirement provision requires addressing these risks. Traditionally, in the industrial countries, mandatory social insurance schemes covering most of the labor force have addressed these risks fairly satisfactorily, and have also provided disability and survivors' benefits. In a DC scheme such as the NPS, these risks are not addressed in the current design. Thus, high priority must be given to risk sharing arrangements between individual members, insurance companies, and the governments for addressing these risks in an affordable and sustainable manner. This is especially important in view of the mandatory annuity provision of the NPS. This issue is also of major importance in the DC schemes of the developing countries.[28]

The EPFO's pension scheme (EPS) does not have inflation risk sharing mechanism, but its benefits do address longevity risks. However, even the current benefits are unsustainable as EPS is severely under-funded (see endnote r). So before addressing inflation risks, the EPS scheme will need a thorough reform, including substantial reduction in the replacement rate (the promised 50% rate is not sustainable), and modern investment management and administration.

In addition to longevity and inflation risks, the NPS will need to incorporate disability and survivors' benefits. This can be done through a group insurance scheme, with the premiums paid from the contributions to the NPS. Following the international practice, the cost should be borne by the members.

4.5. *Tax arrangements*

The 2005–2006 budget of the Central government has restructured the Income Tax Act (1961) to reflect modern concepts of savings and tax incentives. Tax rebates on life insurance provident fund and pension fund products, that were available under Section 88 of the act, have been abolished. Concurrently, Section 80L of the same act, which provides for deduction up to Rs. 15,000 for interest earned from government securities, National Savings Certificates (NSC) and interest on Public Sector Undertakings (PSU) bonds has been omitted. It is expected that these and other sections pertaining to tax rebates or deductions on savings will be combined together, in order to bring in uniformity in tax treatment for all savings instruments. A simplified income tax slab structure, including much higher initial exempt levels of Rs. 1.25 lakh for women, Rs. 1.5 lakh for senior citizens and Rs. 1 lakh for others has been proposed. However, such differential levels of exemption complicate tax administration and need to be minimized.

It is expected that the investment in pension products purely for tax shelter purposes will be reduced with these measures. Specifically, the attractiveness of EPFO as a tax shelter will be considerably diminished.[aa] Consequently EPFO will be increasingly compared with other PFRDA-regulated schemes in terms of service quality and professionalism, and be pushed to achieve better standards of performance. This implies that greater urgency is needed in modernizing EPFO governance and organizational structures.

This move is also intended to take the tax structure for pensions toward the international best practices of "EET" model — exempt (E) from personal income tax during contribution, exempt (E) for accumulation, and taxed (T) during withdrawal. The budget has proposed the setting up of an Expert committee on operationalization of the EET system for provident and pension funds sector and presumably for other savings as well. The PFRDA schemes

---

[aa] Currently, employees earning up to Rs. 6500 per month contribute between 10 and 12% of their basic pay plus dearness allowance, with a matching contribution by the employer. Those with higher starting salaries need not mandatorily join the EPFO. However, contributions higher than the mandated percentage, and contributions of those beyond the wage ceiling are also entitled to Section 88 tax benefits. As a result all EPF deposits offer a tax-free assured 8.5% nominal rate of return. This does not benefit the poor worker as much as the salaried and savings–surplus strata, which uses the EPFO as a lucrative investment avenue. Data on distribution of EPF supports this premise: As on March 31, 2004, 85% of the contributors had an average balance of Rs. 3133 only, and a mere 3.6% of contributors had total EPF balances exceeding Rs. 100,000.

are already on the EET system, and such treatment needs to be extended to others such as the EPFO schemes, to ensure level and equitable treatment as well as for widening the tax base. Indirectly, tax reforms will encourage the growth of the new civil service and unorganized sector pension scheme set up in January 2004.

4.6. *Competition*

The Budget statement also made it clear that the Government was open to considering Foreign Direct Investment (FDI) in the pensions sector. If the precedence of insurance and banking sectors is any guide, this will assist in introducing greater competition and professionalism in the pensions sector in India. In turn, this will subtly but powerfully impact those components of the social security system which are resistant to reforms. This move will also provide a level playing field in pensions sector with other parts of the financial sector and increase the probability of realizing economies of scale and scope. There is potential for the skills of this sector to become competitive in the export markets, diversifying India's basket of export services.

4.7. *Indirect impact of the 2005–2006 budget*

There are several steps in the 2005–2006 Budget which are expected to have an indirect impact on the provident and pension funds sector. For instance, emphasis on jobs creation, particularly in a labor intensive sector such as textiles, could expand the coverage of the EPFO and increase the pool of long-term savings available for retirement. Other measures such as rationalization of the stamp duty structure; setting up of a high level Expert Committee to examine issues pertaining to corporate bonds and securitization and to suggest reform and encouraging micro-finance organizations to provide micro-insurance and pension products — will also indirectly assist in the development of the sector by improving financial and legal infrastructure.

The budget commits the country to developing Mumbai as a regional financial hub. This will have positive spin-offs for growth, employment and the development of sophisticated financial products, all of which will translate into a subtle but far-reaching impact on the pensions sector. Thus, the dynamics resulting from the NPS and related measures will gradually move the whole social security system in a positive direction.

5. Concluding Remarks

India's open economy — open society paradigm has led to social security reform becoming more prominent on the public policy agenda. There is now political consensus on broad areas of reform as indicated by the current government building on pension reform initiatives of the previous governments. In some details, and for some components, particularly those managed by the Ministry of Labor, there is still significant resistance to reforms. But greater competition and level playing field, recognition for stronger and effective regulation, along with gradual shift away from administered interest rates on retirement-type products are creating dynamics which augurs well for emergence of a multi-tier system of social safety nets. The needs of the life-time poor will have to be met through targeted public assistance programs, requiring enhanced fiscal flexibility and more effective public service delivery system.

The reform process in this sector is creating a knowledge and information base in the country which could be drawn upon by all stakeholders for better policy formulation and evaluation. The importance of evidence-based public policies in this area is being increasingly recognized, though this needs to be nurtured through initiatives in academic and research institutions, and professional bodies.

Challenges in social security reform however are huge, as they require parallel reforms in labor markets, financial, and capital markets, fiscal systems, organizational and administrative reform, and close co-ordination among various regulators. Increasing convergence of different segments of the financial markets suggests that provident and pension funds should be viewed in the overall context of financial capital markets. It is essential that long-term nature of pension promises be recognized, and only those promises which can be fulfilled in a sustainable manner over a long period are made.

India has a good record of making progress in sectors (such as insurance, banking, and telecommunication) which become prominent on the public policy agenda. So in spite of the challenges, cautious optimism is warranted in addressing India's social security challenges. Political commitment, leadership, and vision will however be vital in determining the success India achieves in developing adequate yet sustainable social safety nets.

References

1. Asher, M. and Sen, R. (2004). "India–East Asia Integration: A Win–Win for Asia." RIS Discussion Paper RIS-DP #91/2005, March 2005.
2. Government of India (2005). "Economic Survey 2005–2006." Ministry of Finance, July 2004, New Delhi.
3. Reserve Bank of India (RBI), various years, Handbook of Statistics, Mumbai.
4. Bhalla, S. (2003). "Not as Poor, Nor as Unequal as You Think: Poverty, Inequality and Growth in India: 1950–2001." Final Report of Research Project Undertaken for Planning Commission of India entitled 'The Myth and Reality of Poverty in India'. Retrieved from http://www.oxusresearch.com/downloads/ei041203.pdf.
5. Rodrik, D. (1998). "Globalization, Social Conflict, and Economic Growth (Prebisch Lecture)." *The World Economy* 21(2), 143–158.
6. Katzenstein, P.J. (1983). "The Small European States in the International Economy: Economic Dependence and Corporatist Policies." In: Ruggie, J.G. (ed.) *The Antinomies of Interdependence.* New York: Columbia University Press.
7. Cameron, D.R. (1978). "The Expansion of the Public Economy: A Comparative Analysis." *American Political Science Review* 72(4), 1243–1261.
8. Chakraborti, R.D. (2004). *The Greying of India: Population Ageing in the Context of Asia.* New Delhi: Sage Publications.
9. Liebig, P.S. and Irudaya Rajan, S. (eds.) (2003). *An Aging India: Perspectives, Prospects and Policies.* USA: Haworth Press.
10. Planning Commission (2002). "Tenth Five Year Plan 2002-2007-Volumes I and II." New Delhi, December 2001, from http://planningcommission.nic.in/plans/planrel/fiveyr/10th/.
11. IMF (2004). *World Economic Outlook: The Global Demographic Transition,* September 2004, International Monetary Fund.
12. Sanyal, S. (2005). "Demographics, Savings and Hyper-growth." Deutsche Bank, Global Markets Research, July 5.
13. Dev, M. and Mooij, J. (2005). "Patterns in Social Sector Expenditure: Pre and Post-reform periods." In: Parikh, K.S. and Radhakrishna, R. (eds.) *India Development Report 2004–2005.* New Delhi: Oxford University Press and Indira Gandhi Institute of Development Research.

14. Chatterjee, T.B. (2004). "Retiral Benefits in Existing Regulatory Scenario in India." Paper presented at ICICI Prulife Seminar, Singapore, December 10–11, 2004.

15. IMF (2001). "India: Recent Economic Developments and Selected Issues." IMF Country Report No. 01/181, October 2001, International Monetary Fund.

16. Government of India (2000). *The Project OASIS Report*. New Delhi: Ministry of Social Justice and Empowerment.

17. Shah, A. (2005). "Indian Pension Reform: A Sustainable and Scalable Approach." In this Volume.

18. Bhardwaj, G. and Dave, S.A. (2005). "Towards Estimating India's Implicit Pension Debt on Account of Civil Service Employees." Report, New Delhi, India Invest Economic Foundation. July 2005.

19. Government of India (2004). "Report of the Advisory Committee to Advise on the Administered Interest Rates and Rationalization of Savings Instruments." January 2004, Mumbai.

20. Vaidyanathan, R. (2005). "Country Report: India." In: Noriyuki Takayama (ed.) *Pension in Asia: Incentives, Compliance and their Role in Retirement*. Tokyo: Maruzen Co., pp. 93–120.

21. Irudaya Rajan, S., Mishra, U.S. and Sankara Sarma, P. (1999). *India's Elderly: Burden or Challenge*. New Delhi: Sage Publications.

22. Ross, S.G. (2000). "Rebuilding Pension Institutions: Administrative Issues." Third APEC Regional Forum on Pension Fund Reform, March 30–31, Thailand: Bangkok.

23. Reserve Bank of India (RBI) (2003). "Report of the Group to Study the Pension Liabilities of the State Governments." October 2003, Mumbai.

24. Holzmann, R. and Hinz, R. (2005). *Old-Age Income Support in the 21st Century: An International Perspective on Pension Systems and Reform*. Washington, DC: World Bank.

25. Asher, M. and Vasudevan, D. (2005). "The Role of Pension Regulator." *eSS* (e-Social Sciences) www.eSocialSciences.com.

26. The Pension Fund Regulatory and Development Authority Ordinance (2004). Ord. No. 8 of 2004.

27. The Pension Fund Regulatory and Development Authority Bill (2005). Bill No. 36 of 2005.

28. Impavido, G., Thorbun, C. and Wadsworth, M. (2003). *A Conceptual Framework for Retirement Products, Risk-Sharing Arrangements Between Providers and Retirees*. London: Watson Wyatt, RM-global-01.

SECTION 3

National Security in the
Age of Globalization

CHAPTER 9

A Dialectic of Multipolarity and Multilateralism: China's Regional Security Practice in the Age of Globalization

Xu Xin

1. Introduction

Since the mid 1990s, the "rise of China" has been one of the most dynamic and decisive driving factors in global and regional politics. Against the backdrop of unfolding international structural change and deepening globalization, China's regional security strategy has been undergoing a series of transformations, which are effectively manifest in many aspects of China's regional security practice; that is, despite resilient continuity in its developmental grand strategy, a substantial degree of new thinking and statecrafts have factored in its dealings with important structural, sub-structural, and super-structural issues and challenges, ranging from great power politics and regional security order building, "hot spot" tensions and crises, to regional political economy stability and terrorism. Most significantly, with growing strengths, confidence, and sophistication, China has begun to stake out its own vision of regional and global order for the 21st century under the guiding theme of the *new security concept* (*xin anquan guan*), a broadly defined notion of what constitutes "security" and how to achieve "common security" in the age of globalization.

This paper sets out to examine China's security behavior in East Asia predicated on the threefold proposition: (1) China is not simply an actor in the international system, but more importantly constitutes the most dynamic part of an ongoing structural change at the regional and global level through its robust economic growth and increasingly wider and deeper integration into the international system; (2) the prospect of China's rising confronts China itself with a constant challenge to strike a balance between stability and dynamism, between internal cohesion and external resonance, and between assertiveness and forbearance; and (3) social and strategic interactions between China and the rest of the world will generate dynamism and insights for the construction of a regional and global order in years to come.

This paper argues that China's regional security practice can be seen as a balancing act between seeking a peaceful and stable international environment, preserving its vital interests over the Taiwan question, and facilitating China's peaceful rise against the backdrop of the reinforcement of US-led hegemonic stability, the late development of the ASEAN way of regional multilateralism, and the recurrence of crises on the Korean Peninsula and in the Taiwan Strait. The different degree of congruence between China's security interests and major regional security processes then gives rise to a dialectic of multipolarity and multilateralism in China's regional security behavior, whereby the former emphasizes a more symmetric distribution of power in the international system, and the latter speaks to a fundamental organizing principle for regulating international relations and building a new international order. This dialectic underscores China's differentiated approaches to US-led hegemonic stability and the ASEAN way of regional multilateralism, which manifest in growing divergence between China's preferred regional order and the former on the one hand, and increasing convergence between its preferred regional order and the latter on the other hand. China's approach to these two processes is further complicated by its security interests in the crisis management of the two "hot spots," which in turn reinforces the multipolarity-multilateralism dialectic in China's security behavior and provides a strategic space for China's constructive engagement with the US–Japan alliance and ASEAN Regional Forum. To the extent that China is faced with a continuous challenge to engage with these two processes, it is of necessity for China to present an alternative vision of regional order which serves not only China's own security interests but also greater public good in the eyes of other countries in the region.

Below I will first present an overview of the regional security landscape after the Cold War. Then I will discuss China's regional security interests and objectives in the age of bifurcating world politics driven by power transition and globalization. This will be followed by an analysis of China's security practice in dealing with US hegemonic stability, the ASEAN way of regional multilateralism, and crisis management on the Korean Peninsula and in the Taiwan Strait. Finally, some important points will be revisited in a conclusion.

2. The Regional Security Landscape after the Cold War

The end of the Cold War ushered in a new era of world politics which witnesses the "third grand transformation of the organizing structure and motivating spirit of global politics" since the beginning of the 20th century.[1] From a standpoint of international relations, applying Gilpin's notion of international structural change, this new era of world politics has been unfolding not only primarily as the international *systemic* change in terms of the international distribution of power, identities, and norms, but also possibly as the international *systems* change in terms of "the nature of the principal actors or diverse entities composing the system."[2,a]

Ref. 3 describes the dynamism of this ongoing grand transformation as the "bifurcation of macro global structures into what is called 'the two worlds of world politics'." In other words, the end of the Cold War set the stage for both *international systemic change* in terms of traditional great power politics and *international systems change* in terms of post-traditional politics of globalization all at once.

In this process of grand transformation, regions appear to be assuming a greater importance than ever before. That is, the future shape of a world order will largely depend on political and economic dynamics at the regional level. Against this background, East Asia has entered a new era of the "third transformation of organizing structure of regional politics,"[4] building a new regional order by acting more independently than at any other time in its modern history.[5–9]

In this era of transformative politics, the three most significant structural developments in East Asian regional security landscape have been the consolidation of the US-led alliance system, the emergence of the ASEAN-centered regional multilateralism, and the ascendancy of Chinese power and influence,

---

[a]According to Ref. 2, pp. 41–42, systemic change is "a change within the system" and systems change is "a change of the system itself." Whereas the former "entails changes in the international distribution of power, the hierarchy of prestige, and the rules and rights embodied in the system," the latter involves a major change in the character of the system — "the nature of the principal actors or diverse entities composing the system."

which are concurrently accompanied and complicated by the recurrence of crises on the Korean Peninsula and in the Taiwan Strait, and the evolutionary regionalization. The interaction among these processes has thus constituted the macro-context of structural transformation at the regional level in East Asia.

Of these processes, the redefinition of the US–Japan alliance since the mid-1990s has been a key component of US efforts to reinforce the *hegemonic stability* based on its unchallenged military power and robust alliance network. Despite its bilateral origin, arguably, the US–Japan alliance has been "regionalized" to the effect that its scope has been officially extended from defending the Japanese territory to policing the US-led regional order and stability. Since 9–11, this tendency has gained a new momentum as Japan under the Koizumi cabinet has become more assertive, confident, and determined in moving out of the confines of its "outdated" peace constitution, and playing an international security role in supporting US hegemony.

On the other hand, the late development of *regionalized multilateralism* centered on the ASEAN by the means of the ARF and other mechanisms has been another marked feature of the ongoing "grand transformations" of the organizing structure and motivating spirit of regional politics since the end of the Cold War. Despite distinctive characteristics compared with other major regions, Asia–Pacific regional multilateral institution-building initiatives — as reflected in Asia–Pacific Economic Cooperation (APEC), the ASEAN Regional Forum (ARF), ASEAN Plus Three (APT), the Asia–Europe Meeting (ASEM), Council on Security Cooperation in the Asia–Pacific (CSCAP) and many other "Track I," "Track II" and even "Track III" occasions[b] — have come into being one after another in this very dynamic region since the end of the Cold War, "springing up like bamboo shoots after spring rains."[c] This nascent regional multilateralism has significantly thickened the social nexus of international relations in the region and has evidently provided an alternative

---

[b]Track I refers to government-to-government multilateral activities, while Track II involves semi-governmental think tanks and Track III private institutions. See Ref. 10, p. 161. In the case of China, however, there have been no private institutions involved (although some private institutions in security affairs did come to exist in recent years). By the early 1990s there were about 40 ongoing channels for regional discussions on political and security matters, but by the late 1990s there were about two meetings per week, an increasingly large percentage occurring at a formal governmental level (see Ref. 11, p. 256).
[c]By the early 1990s there were about 40 ongoing channels for regional discussions on political and security matters, but by the late 1990s there were about two meetings per week, an increasingly large percentage occurring at a formal governmental level (see Ref. 11, p. 256).

space for managing ongoing power transition and regulating security politics in the region.

Sharing the same regionalized context of Asia–Pacific political economy and security politics, regional multilateralism, and hegemonic stability nevertheless represent two contrasting — partly competing and partly complementing — logics of regional political transformation. Yet, to the extent that conscious political actions are taken to accommodate the enduring forces of market-driven regionalization, to withstand the growing challenges of globalization, and to deal with the uncertainties of regionalized security politics due to the end of global bipolarity, the Asia–Pacific has begun to emerge steadily as an international subsystem in the post-Cold War era.

Of all regional structural developments, China's spectacular economic growth and steady political advance in regional and global affairs has become one of the most decisive factors in shaping the ongoing international systemic change in the region and beyond. As the "rise of China" explicitly or implicitly underscores the basic rationale of regional security politics represented by the consolidation of US hegemonic stability and the development of ASEAN-centered security multilateralism, it became imperative for China to actively engage with the US–Japan alliance and ASEAN by formulating and articulating its own vision of regional order. Thus, the mutual engagement between a rising China and these two major forces constitutes the core of transformations of Asia–Pacific international relations in the long run.

These changes are basically "structural" in terms of their implications for power configuration in the international system, but some critical "nonstructural" factors — namely, North Korea's nuclear diplomacy and Taiwan's independence movement — have also significantly played into the processes of these structural change, as North Korea has been adventurously defending its threatened security and sovereignty through nuclear diplomacy, and Taiwan has been aggressively seeking a formal status of sovereignty by challenging the status quo premised on the notion of "One China." Whereas North Korea has acted primarily out of fear for its endangered security condition, Taiwan has moved in the expectation that an emerging "new world order" favors a democratic Taiwan over an authoritarian PRC. Yet both seem to find a best chance to achieve "normalcy" in their otherwise problematic status in the regional subsystem of states by staging a challenge to their perceived unjust status quo.

Starting with the Asian financial crisis in 1997–1998 and culminating in the 9–11 events of 2001, East Asian security politics has also seen the acceleration of Asian regionalism in response to deepening globalization, with continued strategic maneuvering and collaboration in interstate relations. It may well be argued that the Asian financial crisis and the 9–11 events in many ways have brought nation-states further together to cope with challenges and threats posed primarily from non-state actors and forces in the age of globalization, thus marking a new era of international relations. In the Gilpinian sense, therefore, while the systemic change continues, the threatening systems change tends to alleviate some formidable interstate problems and compel state actors to cooperate against common problems and challenges posed by globalization and non-state forces.

All these developments are engineered by concerned states in coping with the bifurcating transformations of world politics. The central challenge facing all the countries in the region is whether they can maintain security, stability, and peace by accommodating power transition, managing regional crises, and handling challenges of various global issues while benefiting from growing economic interdependence accelerated by market-driven forces of globalization.

3. China's Regional Security Interests and Objectives

Historically, China's security policy had zigzagged from an alliance-based security policy in the 1950s and 1970s to a non-aligned security policy in the 1960s and 1980s. Being a Soviet ally in the 1950s, a revolutionary and independent power in the 1960s, an American quasi-ally in the 1970s, and a reformist and independent power in the 1980s, China's security practice projected a dynamic pattern of a rising power whose freedom of action was both restrained by and sought to break down barriers of the bipolar system centered on the US–Soviet Union global competition. Acting as a regional power on the grand chessboard of the global bipolar politics, however, China during the Cold War was depicted as "a regional power without a regional policy."[12] When the Cold War came to an end, the loss of a global geostrategic focus thus prodded China to clearly define its security interests in the emerging regionalized world politics.

3.1. *Reinforcing developmental grand strategy*

China's transition away from Maoist socialist "continuous revolution" started with the shift in political leadership, a decade before the end of the Cold War. Two years after Mao's death, Deng Xiaoping came to power in 1978 with three major policy initiatives: revitalizing the "four modernizations" program, installing a policy of peaceful national reunification, and adopting an independent foreign policy of peace, of which economic development as opposed to Maoist political and social revolution was defined as *the* new defining principle of the Dengist grand strategy. Deng defined this strategy as "*changqi jiben guoce*" (a long-term, fundamental state policy), which should be pursued for at least half a century, until when, according to Deng, China reaches the level of secondary developed countries' living standard by 2049, the first centenary of the founding of the PRC.

As early as in September 1989, Deng foresaw the dim prospects of the Soviet Union and worried about how China could avoid the same fate: "The problem now is not whether the banner of the Soviet Union will fall — there is bound to be unrest there — but whether the banner of China will fall."[13] To hold up China's "socialist banner" firmly, Deng's prescription was to reinforce the Communist Party leadership while "continu[ing] to carry on genuine reform and to open wider to the outside."[13] But Deng did feel that doing so would "put the developed countries all the more on guard against us," and that China would have more problematic relations with the West in the post-Cold War world. He thus called for a low-profile approach:

> Notwithstanding, we should maintain friendly exchanges with them. We should keep them as friends but also have a clear understanding of what they are doing. We should not criticize or condemn other countries without good reason or go to extremes in our words and deeds.[13]

In July 1991, Jiang Zemin, the "core" of the third-generation leadership, summarized Deng's insights about how to cope with international turmoil and uncertainties caused by the end of the Cold War as the so-called "28 character directive": "keep cool-headed to observe, be composed to make reactions, stand firmly, hide our capabilities and bide our time, be good at keeping the low profile, never try to take the lead, and be able to accomplish something."[14]

This often-quoted maxim not only suggests a desire to downplay China's ambitions, but also reaffirms a long-term strategy to build up China's comprehensive national power (*zonghe guoli*) with a view to maximizing China's options in the future. Most important, Deng was anxious about the third-generation leadership's commitment to his grand strategy, and took pain to ensure that China would stick to the developmental strategy under the CCP's continued control of political power regardless of drastic changes in the Soviet world. For Deng, the Communist Party's unswerving leadership over the state and society is essential to the effective operation of the developmental grand strategy in a stable domestic and international environment. The Dengist authoritarian-developmental logic eventually prevailed over other contentious alternatives in 1992 when the 14th CCP National Congress officially endorsed it as the "theory of socialist market economy," which revitalized the momentum and dynamism for continuous reform, opening-up, and development. Through the consecutive 15th and 16th CCP National Congresses in 1997 and 2002, the Dengist grand strategy continues to underpin the Party's ideological foundation, remarkably immune from personnel change and power transition within, as well as changing international circumstances without.

As political power transferred from the third generation to the fourth generation in the 16th CCP National Congress in 2002, the Party continued to view "the overriding trend of the present-day world" as moving toward "peace and development." Therefore, "China's development is blessed with a rare period of strategic opportunities (*zhanlue jiyu qi*)." When addressing his audience at Harvard University in 2003, Premier Wen Jiabao talked about the "period of strategic opportunities" plainly:

> And if we do not grasp it, it will slip away. We are determined to secure a peaceful international environment and a stable domestic environment in which to concentrate on our own development, and with it to help promote world peace and development.[15]

3.2. *Securing a stable external environment*

In the early 1990s, when the geostrategic picture became obscured and uncertain due to the collapse of the Soviet Union and the CCP government struggled to maintain domestic stability in the aftermath of the Tiananmen crisis, China's regional security policy was defensively aimed at "gaining a foothold in the Asia–Pacific and stabilizing China's periphery" (*lizhu Ya Tai, wending zhoubian*), which was part of the greater foreign policy effort to break through diplomatic isolation imposed on China by the West as the result of the Tiananmen incident and to absorb the repercussions of the disintegration of the Soviet Union, particularly in Central Asia. Not until China joined the ARF process in 1994 had it begun to explicitly and systematically lay out its regional security policy objectives.

At the first ARF foreign ministers' meeting in 1994, China's Vice Premier and Foreign Minister Qian Qichen put forward three basic objectives for China's regional security policy: (1) maintaining stability and prosperity in China; (2) safeguarding long-term peace and stability in its surrounding; and (3) promoting dialogues and cooperation on the basis of mutual respect and equality.[16] In 1996, China for the first time called for the replacement of the "Cold War thinking" with the new security concept. Again in the third ARF foreign ministers' meeting, Qian Qichen proposed that "countries in the region jointly cultivate a new concept of security, which focuses on enhancing trust through dialog and promoting security through cooperation."[17] Since then, the new security concept has been gradually institutionalized in China's foreign and security policy, as it has been consistently elaborated in the Chinese official discourse — China's biannual white papers on national defence since 1998, keynote speeches by Chinese leaders including President Jiang Zemin on various occasions, some important diplomatic agreements, and most recently, *China's Position Paper on New Security Concept*. As this document concludes: "The new security concept has become an important component of China's foreign policies."[18]

In 2003, Vice Foreign Minister Wang Yi summarized the Chinese conception of security as being composed of three parts: (1) comprehensive security (*zonghe anquan*) as the basic characteristic of the security problematic, whereby the domain of security is no longer confined to traditional military and political security, and national security interests are increasingly intertwined with regional and global security situations; (2) cooperative security (*hezuo anquan*) as a valid approach to international security, which should substitute the old security thinking based on the notion of seeking security superiority through power balancing; and (3) common security (*gongtong anquan*) as the ultimate goal of East Asian security, which requires empathy in security relations among states (*Xinhua*, December 16, 2003).

In fact, China's international identity and behavior have significantly changed with the 1995–1996 Taiwan Strait crisis as a turning point. The place of China in the ongoing international systemic change was rather ambivalent in the early 1990s, but has become more clearly identified since the mid 1990s. Different from being relatively marginalized in the international community in the early 1990s, China has become a central focus of the ongoing systemic change since the crisis. In the early phase of the post-Cold War era, Beijing's diplomatic behavior was colored by two of Deng's 28-character directives — "keep cool-headed to observe, be composed to make reactions" — focused on breaking the diplomatic isolation caused by the Tiananmen crackdown and consolidating its diplomatic influence. The Taiwan Strait crisis provided China an unexpected and uncomfortable opportunity to show off its power in high spotlight. The face-off between Chinese and US military strengths during the height of the crisis symbolized the strategic interaction and tension between China and the United States in the post-Cold War international systemic change. In particular, the emerging Taiwan independence movement began to loom increasingly larger in China's security concerns.

In the aftermath of the crisis, then, Beijing seemed to move forward more with another pair of Deng's tenets: "stand firm and be able to accomplish something." On the one hand, Chinese leaders, most evidently President Jiang himself, took the initiative to build a nested network of great power partnerships, mainly through summit diplomacy, and especially took pains to stabilize and improve China–US relations. They did not hide their intent to create this relationship in order to regain a strategic weight in a positive light. On the other hand, Beijing shifted from its passive and reactive approach to multilateral/institutional security activities in the early and mid 1990s to a positive and proactive approach in the late 1990s. As the leaders became more confident through experience, they even moved beyond the conventional approach to international politics, and initiated their own version of multilateral security cooperation, most notably in the development of Shanghai Cooperation Organization (SCO). Walking on "two legs," Beijing attempted to more actively promote the stable and peaceful external environment conducive to its national interests.

4. Globalization, Multipolarization, and Multilateralism

The Chinese conceptualization of changing world politics rests on the two pairs of overarching notions: multipolarization of the world (*shjie duojihua*) and economic globalization (*jingji quanqiuhua*); with peace and development as the two major themes of the times. Both reflect the Chinese understanding of "objective" external environments, as well as their policy orientation in the changing world. This baseline conceptualization has taken shape as the result of dynamic and contested intellectual discourse and policy debate over the past 15 years. The "Chinese characteristics" in this conceptualization are manifest in three aspects: (1) multipolarization of the world, rather than political multipolarization (*zhengzhi duojihua*) as its critics have argued, highlights the foremost importance China places on changing distribution of power for the future of world order; (2) *economic* globalization, rather than simply globalization, indicates that the Chinese understand and interpret this process primarily in economic terms; (3) peace and development cannot be taken for granted and will not befall and benefit those who do not persistently strive for them.

Beginning with Jiang's keynote speech at the eighth conference of diplomatic envoys in August 1998, Beijing has stressed the importance of economic globalization as a central and enduring feature of the emerging world order in the 21st century. In the Chinese academic discourse references to globalization have since surpassed references to multipolarization.[19]

Most Chinese analysts conceive of globalization primarily as an "objective condition" in the world economy rather than as a manifestation of US hegemony, and see it as positive as reinforcing multipolarity internationally.[20] According to Ref. 21, economic globalization is an inevitable "grand trend" and "objective reality." Yet, it is neither the wholesale integration into a "global village" nor is "Americanization." On the contrary, conflicts of interstate interests continue to exist and even intensify in the age of economic globalization. In a word, economic globalization does not mean political integration and harmonization among states.

In the wake of the Tiananmen crisis, Chinese analysts had already begun to interpret security in a broad sense, containing both military and non-military dimensions.[22] When Deng repeatedly emphasized continued rapid economic growth as the high politics or "the absolute principle" (*ying daoli*), and as the key to the CCP's survival and relevance against ongoing transformation of world politics, he in effect added the economic dimension to the Chinese view on security. The sense of economic security was further reinforced and enriched during the Asian financial crisis of 1997–1998.

As China became more actively involved in regional and global affairs from the mid-1990s, Chinese policy elites have gained a more systematic understanding of security in the era of globalization, and have come up with a more theoretical articulation of the Chinese view on security, as reified in distinguishing between traditional security and non-traditional security and advocating an integrated conception of comprehensive security.

As for multipolarization or multipolarity, a balance-of-power thinking once featured prominently in China's international relations discourse, and in terms of its security behavior, China was depicted as the "high church of realpolitik."[23] The Chinese preference for multipolarity and its skepticism of international institutions, which derive from their historical grievance about power politics of imperialism or its variants, apparently resonates with the neo-realist logic that in the international system of states, power of a state can only be effectively checked and balanced by power of other states. In the Chinese perspective, multipolarity is also a normative good that may better serve interests of weak, less privileged, and less developed countries than unipolarity or bipolarity.

The Chinese discourse on multipolarity started in the 1980s, if not earlier, partly because of changing great power relations and partly because of China's own changed path to modernization and international affairs. Since the end of the Cold War, Chinese analysts have continuously debated whether the world is actually moving toward multipolarity. In the early 1990s, a widely held view suggested that the US-dominated unipolar moment would be of short duration (Interviews 3–94, New York, November 26, 1994).[24] By the late 1990s, however, many had become more realistic or even dubious about multipolarization as it became obvious to them that the power structure in the post-Cold War era continued to be one of *yichao duoqiang* (one super-power and many great powers). "People realized that the leading position of the US would be unshakable and its comprehensive national power would be unparalleled by any single country in the foreseeable future. The US has enough resources and influence to reach its goals abroad. The only uncertainty is the will or the intention of the US."[25] While the world will continue to move toward multipolarity, they tend to believe, it will take quite a long period of time for a multipolar structure to emerge. At least, the pattern of *yichao duoqiang* will not change in the first decade of the 21st century.

For some analysts, the configuration of international economic and political power has virtually experienced the "reverse transformation" — bandwagoning rather than balancing the US hegemony by secondary powers — which has weakened the basis for multipolarization.[26] The nuclear tests conducted by India and Pakistan in 1998 also prodded many Chinese analysts to rethink the merits of a multipolar world. Some openly prefer a predictable US unipolar world to an unpredictable multipolar world (Interviews 2–99, 15–99, 25–99, Beijing and Shanghai, February 10, March 24, April 7, 1999).

On balance, Chinese analysts see a contradiction between multipolarization and unipolarization, whereby the former is slowly deepening and the latter remains robust (*Renmin Ribao* December 14, 2000, p. 7). The Chinese leadership has also embraced the view that multipolarization is a fiercely contested long-term process in which various political forces are interacting.[14] But thanks to globalization and the "democratization of international relations" (*guojiguanxi minzhuhua*), the Chinese are hopeful that a future multipolar world will be different from its historical precedents. Jiang stated at a Central Military Commission enlarged meeting in December 2000:

> In the early 21st century, major world and regional powers as well as groups consisted of countries will enlist each other's strengths, check and balance each other, and compete and coexist throughout the process of interactions. Thanks to the enhancement of world peace and democratic forces, the future multipolar political structure will differ from the political pattern of great powers competing for hegemony in history. This new type of multipolarity combines and interacts with growing economic globalization and progress in science and technology.[14]

Because of these two general trends, peace and development remain the two major themes of world politics. In other words, the mainstream Chinese view holds that China still enjoys relatively the best international environment since 1949 for its continued concentration on the drive for modernization. But most important, only through further reform and opening-up can China sustain its development.

Because it would be unrealistic to expect that the hegemonic status of the United States as a sole superpower be altered in the short run, some Chinese analysts argue, all countries in the world have to live with the reality of power politics.[27] For the sake of improving China's external environment, the mainstream view continues to favor a more dispersed distribution of power in international politics in the long run. But this view also contends that "the effort to foster multipolarization should be balanced with the maintenance of stable China–US relations."[26]

Given the uncertainty of multipolarization as a long and complicated process and the new challenges of globalization, "Chinese leaders have been seeking a new security concept for a new type of security cooperation which is conducive to China's modernization drive in a stable and peaceful external environment."[28] As has been referred earlier, the new security concept, which emphasizes the importance of multilateral institutions and stable bilateral relations based on the five principles of peaceful coexistence, has been posited as an antithesis to the obsolete "Cold War thinking" that continues to undergird traditional military alliances in the post-Cold War world. As the tendency of unilateralism in US foreign policy has become ever stronger since Bush came to office, in Chinese diplomatic statecraft, the notion that multilateralism best represents a general organizing principle of international life as opposed to unilateralism appears to be on the rise relative to the concept of multipolarity.

In the international relations literature, multilateralism, bilateralism, and imperialism are "alternative conceptions of how the world might be organized."[29] Multilateralism, in the view of John Ruggie, is "a deep organizing principle of international affairs,"[29] which "is distinguished from other forms by three properties: indivisibility, generalized principles of conduct, and diffuse reciprocity."[d] The institution of multilateralism, as opposed to merely multilateral organizations or multilateral activities, "is grounded in and appeals to the less formal, less codified habits, practice, ideas, and norms of international society."[29] As such it is a highly demanding mode of international life whose significance cuts more deeply, because it advocates "universal

---

[d] According to James Caporaso's succinct summary, "Indivisibility can be thought of as the scope (both geographic and functional) over which costs and benefits are spread, given an action initiated in or among component units ... Generalized principles of conduct usually come in the form of norms exhorting general if not universal modes of relating to other states, rather than differentiating relations case-by-case on the basis of individual preferences, situational exigencies, or *a priori* particularistic grounds. Diffuse reciprocity adjusts the utilitarian lenses for the long view, emphasizing that actors expect to benefit in the long run and over many issues, rather than every time on every issue" (see Ref. 29, pp. 53–54).

organizing principles" at least for a relevant group of like-minded countries.[29] According to French President Chirac, an ardent advocate of multipolarity and multilateralism, multilateralism is the key to the full participation of all parties in the governance of international affairs; especially with regard to the use of force and the issue of creating universal regimes, multilateralism is the guarantee of legitimacy and democracy (*Renmin Ribao*, September 25, 2003).

In the case of China, evidence shows a growing trend that China has been attaching an increasing importance to multilateralism particularly as opposed to unilateralism. The early reference to multilateralism was made in 1996, when Dai Xianghong, governor of the People's Bank of China, criticized unilateralism in world trade in that a handful of countries caused damages on multilateral rules in trade by resorting to trade sanctions (*Renmin Ribao* October 3, 1996, p. 7). Not until 2001 was multilateralism accorded a more central place in Chinese foreign policy.[e] To be sure, 2001 marked the watershed of China's involvement in world affairs: in June China, along with Russia and four Central Asian countries, turned the "Shanghai Five" process into a multilateral "Shanghai Cooperation Organization"; in July, Beijing was selected as the host to the 2008 Olympic Games; in October China hosted the APEC summit in Shanghai; and in December China finally became a member of the World Trade Organization. In his address to the APEC business leaders meeting, President Jiang stated that the key is the complete enforcement of multilateralism in world economic affairs (*Renmin Ribao* October 19, 2001, p. 1).[f] The emphasis on multilateralism has become more consistent and coherent in Chinese foreign policy since Hu Jintao succeeded Jiang as president. In his letter to Kofi Annan in September 2003, Hu stressed that only by enhancing international cooperation and following the path of multilateralism can the world effectively cope with growing numbers of global challenges (*Renmin Ribao*, September 25, 2003, p. 3).

As a baseline, China has advocated a UN-centric multilateralism with the view that the role of United Nations in global governance needs to be

---

[e]A workshop on "Multilateralism and Multilateral Diplomacy" was held on July 19, 2001 in Beijing. Participants were from universities, think tanks, the media, as well as the government. The papers presented at the workshop later appeared in *World Economics and Politics*, No. 10, 2001.

[f]The official commentary hailed multilateralism embodied in the APEC Shanghai summit as "spirit of cooperation and development and the consensus on civilized principles," as well as the "lighthouse guiding world peace in the new century." *Renmin Ribao*, November 12, 2001, p. 7.

enhanced yet its reform is also necessary and important. In Foreign Minister Li Zhaoxing's words, "multilateralism has become the universal aspiration of the international community. The UN ought to be the common platform for all countries to participate in global governance, promote democratization and legalization of international relations, and preserve common interests (*Renmin Ribao*, September 28, 2003, p. 3)."

Importantly, Beijing came to view multilateralism as an organizing principle compatible with the process of multipolarization and globalization. In particular, "mainstream Chinese strategic thinkers now believe that globalization, as manifested in transnational forces, international institutions, and a greater need for multilateralism, can be used to "democratize" the US hegemonic order to minimize unilateralist power politics."[30] In the view of Li Zhaoxing, the welfare of mankind lies in strengthening international cooperation, adhering to the path of multilateralism, and promoting multipolarization (*Renmin Ribao*, September 26, 2003, p. 3). In the wake of US military campaign in Iraq, China called for a greater role for the UN to play in postwar construction of Iraq, and saw the central role of UN as significant for the practice of multilateralism (*Renmin Ribao*, October 25, 2003, p. 3).

It is tempting to discredit the Chinese discourse on multilateralism simply as the rhetoric or even hypocrisy that contains little substance and that serves as a poor guideline for actual behavior. Skeptics may ask what the actual use is to talk about multilateralism when multilateral institutions, especially the UN, appear so powerless and ineffective in providing security and preserving peace. At best, it is no more than a critique of US unilateralism. Yet skepticism does not do justice to the dynamism and complexity in China's increasing integration into world affairs. As Iain Johnson's survey shows, "China's membership in international institutions and organizations has increased dramatically in the post-Maoist period." "From the mid-1960s to the mid-1990s, China moved from virtual isolation from international organizations to membership numbers approaching about 80% of the comparison states."[19] Moreover, "on a number of international normative questions, China appears to be conforming more with an extant international community, such as it is, than it has in the past."[19] More important, the scope of China's multilateral diplomacy is expanding from economics to politics and security in that China's embrace of multilateralism tends to integrate its overall international activities.

To be sure, the newly found utility of multilateralism largely lies in the growing importance of soft power in international relations, of which the Chinese have become increasingly conscious and appreciative. Instead of confronting the political reality of unipolarity with a hard power approach (power balancing through military build-up and alliance), which may intensify the security dilemma, China has found that it is more realistic and sensible to employ a soft power approach by the way of multilateralism and nested bilateral partnerships to counter the unilateralist tendency of the sole superpower. In so doing China can also dampen other countries' suspicion and apprehension about the "China threat" which has arisen from the ongoing power transition, as China itself as a rising power might easily evoke anti-China balancing if it acted imprudently and unwisely in the arena of power politics.

5. The Dynamism of China's Regional Security Practice

To the extent that the dialectic of multipolarity and multilateralism is driven by a complex set of intertwined security interests and concerns, China's security practice in East Asia can be characterized as a balancing act colored with dynamic stability. That is, China must make a constant effort to secure a stable regional environment while actively participating in the construction of a new regional order. At minimum, it must strive to avoid strategic confrontation with the United States, a new Cold War poising the regional environment for sustained development, and explosion or implosion of "hot spots" — especially curbing Taiwan independence movement; at maximum, it must work toward building a new regional order which accommodates China's domestic modernization, national reunification, and peaceful rise, and best serves common interests of all countries in the region.

In practical terms, China's balancing act has manifested most evidently in its differentiated approaches to the other two major processes of constructing a regional security order, as China becomes increasingly vigilant toward the regionalization of the US–Japan alliance as the anchor of US-led hegemonic stability, and actively participatory in the institutionalization of the "ASEAN Way" of regional security multilateralism centered on the ASEAN Regional Forum — both have apparently changed from China's previous positions when the Cold War ended.

More significantly, a characteristic blend of dynamism and stability has been reflected categorically in China's constant efforts to propose its own vision of a new international order through propagating the new security concept as an alternative to the military alliance-based order and taking the initiative to launch the first-ever China-led multilateral security cooperation — the "Shanghai Five" process since the mid-1990s, as well as the creation of SCO in 2001. This momentum of multilateralism appears to be increasingly robust and coherent as China has made moves on several fronts: its bold initiative in establishing a China–ASEAN FTA in 2001, its strategic concession to ASEAN in accepting a multilateral approach to the South China Sea dispute in 2002 and its accession of Southeast Asian Treaty of Amity and Cooperation in 2003, and its leadership in initiating and facilitating the six-party talks on North Korean nuclear crisis since 2003.

6. Coming to Terms with US-led Hegemonic Stability

In essence, the redefinition of the US–Japan alliance is fundamentally about reinforcing US-led hegemonic stability in the post-Cold War era. This has become clear since the mid-1990s in the aftermath of the 1993–1994 North Korean nuclear crisis and the 1995–1996 Taiwan Strait crisis. The "Nye initiative" of 1995 reaffirmed the US' determination to strengthen its alliance with Japan as a main vehicle for maintaining US hegemonic regional order, and effectively closed up the debate about the future of this alliance in both countries. "The central function of the alliance for regional stability derives from American preparedness to use the alliance for regional contingencies."[31]

The China factor seems to cast a long shadow over post-Cold War regional security politics, but it was only implicit and rather ambiguous in the initial stage of US–Japan negotiations over the redefinition of their alliance in the early 1990s. It became explicit and even salient in the later stage of the redefinition process, decisively due to the Taiwan Strait crisis. Correspondingly, the Taiwan question was not as important as the issue of North Korea for the US–Japan consultation over the redefinition of the alliance in 1994–1995, but became pronounced after the 1995–1996 Taiwan Strait crisis. More significantly, *the Taiwan issue has become important for regional security because of the redefinition of the US–Japan alliance* (Interviews 7–01, Fukuoka, July 20, 2001). The increased salience of the Taiwan issue in regional security politics is well illustrated in China's dispute with the United States and Japan over the notion of "situations in areas surrounding Japan" (SASJ) in the revised US–Japan Defence Guidelines and the development and deployment of the Theater Missile Defence (TMD) system in East Asia. China's specific concern is threefold. First, revitalization of the US–Japan alliance by encouraging Japan to share more of the burden and risk in regional security would release the Japanese military genie from the bottle, thus destabilizing the region; second, a Japanese direct involvement in a Taiwan contingency enabled by the redefinition of the alliance would be more likely than pure US intervention to lead to escalation of tensions or conflicts; and third, even an implicit reference to the Taiwan Strait in a US–Japan joint statement would send a wrong signal to Taiwan secessionists to the extent that they would be emboldened to move toward a formal independence.[32]

As the United States and Japan have intended to jointly engage China through strengthening the US–Japan alliance, China has also attempted to influence how the alliance evolves in the areas that directly or indirectly concern China's vital security interests, especially with regard to Taiwan. Not only has it begun to adopt multi-pronged approaches to protect and pursue its security interests, including enhancing defence modernization, strengthening military cooperation with Russia, launching assertive diplomatic campaigns, and repositioning itself in multilateral diplomacy, but more significantly it has begun to actively seek an alternative regional security order to balance against the US-led, alliance-based "hegemonic stability."

Although Beijing has been annoyed by the continued "Cold War thinking" embodied in the reinforced US–Japan alliance, it has cautiously avoided jeopardising regional stability by confronting the US hegemonic security order head on head; instead, it articulates its own reformist version of security order. In fact, whereas Beijing's rhetoric is indiscriminately critical of power politics and military alliances as outdated Cold War relics, its real concern and policy focus are the implications and impacts of the reinforced US security posture — alliance system, TMD, etc. — to China's vital national interests, particularly the Taiwan question. Instead of attempting to replace the US hegemonic order, China has to tolerate it and create an alternative space to withhold the pressure and live with it peacefully. In essence, China's new security concept represents this reformist approach to a regional security order. It surely aims to "compete with" the predominant conception of security order in international fora of free expression; it does not, however, desire a malignant confrontation between great powers.

An editorial in the April 1, 2002 issue of *Renmin Ribao* calls on China, Japan, and the United States to seek a "common ground" to sustain regional and international stability and preserve prosperity. The editorial is eye-catching, not only because it contains some new ideas (some of which are apparently incorporated from foreign sources), but more importantly because it presents a fresh perspective on China's security relations with the United States and Japan by synthesizing those ideas in a rather coherent and integrated fashion. More significantly, the editorial explicitly links the Taiwan question with the US military presence in the Asia–Pacific region, the US–Japan alliance, and multilateral security cooperation in its proposed scheme.

The following points merit particular attention: (1) In the political and security fields, the US–China–Japan triangle is bilateral, not trilateral, but the formation of a bipolar confrontation will bring instability to the region. (2) Moving from a bilateral military alliance to a multilateral security mechanism, rather than enhancing US-led bilateral alliance, is crucial to regional stability. (3) A unified China would not hurt the interests of the US and Japan — neither in threatening US maritime superiority nor in threatening Japan's maritime lifeline; on the contrary, a divided China serves as an uncertain factor in the region. (4) China will not oppose a US presence in the Asia–Pacific region. What China opposes is US containment of China. (5) To dispel China's concern, the US and Japan should work toward the establishment of a multilateral security mechanism, which should include countries friendly to China (Editorial, *People's Daily*, English Edition, April 1, 2002). That the article was carried in *Renmin Ribao* itself may also indicate a non-trivial change in Chinese strategic thinking.

However, under the Bush and Koizumi administrations, American and Japanese strategic views appeared to have further converged with a rising China in mind. Flirting with the notion that Japan should become Britain in East Asia, the Bush administration has pressed Japan to play a more substantial security role while the Koizumi government has been determined to normalize Japan's status as a fully fledged great power under the framework of its alliance with the United States. The most significant development of US–Japan "joint engagement" with China through strengthening their alliance is best illustrated by the "2 + 2" joint statement made by the US–Japan Security

Consultative Committee in February 2005, which announced that "peaceful resolution of issues concerning the Taiwan Strait" constitutes a "common strategic objective" in the new US–Japan security arrangements.[33] The explicit reference to the Taiwan issue marked a critical shift from previous US–Japan security arrangements, particularly in view of Japan's habitual reluctance to touch upon this sensitive issue in its public dealings with its American ally in the past. While this joint gesture had apparently been pushed by Bush administration officials, some believe that this strategic move was actually initiated by the Japanese side (Interviews 1–05, Singapore, April 5, 2005). Although it is not entirely clear which side took the initiative (Interviews 2–05, Boston, May 9, 2005; 3–05, Boston, May 23, 2005), the mere fact that Japan and the United States for the first time explicitly included the Taiwan Strait in the scope of their alliance is strategically significant in that doing so effectively broke down the strategic ambiguity of the US–Japan alliance in this regard and raised the stakes of all great powers with interests in regional stability. A sharp rebuke from China's foreign ministry and a strong wave of nationalistic reactions in the Chinese society aside, Beijing was not only concerned that this move would embolden the Taiwan independence movement by "sending a wrong signal," but also increasingly wary of the trend of remolding this alliance into an active instrument of containment against China in the long run. Because the review of "common strategic objectives" constitutes only the first part of the ongoing three-stage force structure review between the United States and Japan, the follow-up measures of restructuring US–Japan forces and facilities at the second and third stages will certainly arouse Beijing's greater sense of insecurity.

7. Working Toward Regional Multilateralism

The late development of regional multilateralism in security affairs opened up another process of regional security politics. Unlike the US-led alliance reinforcement, it was ASEAN who as a collective group of middle and small powers took the lead to project the prospect of regional multilateralism — the so-called ASEAN way — as an alternative design and mechanism for regional security. The ARF and CSCAP were set up in 1993 and 1994, respectively, in response to uncertainty about the East Asian security order in the post-Cold War era, and "particularly the rise of China and the regional debate about the appropriate response."[11] As Johnston and Evans note, "both institutions were created with China in mind, either as *a* principal or *the* principal reason for their existence."[11] The architects of the CSCAP and the ARF tended to see these two institutions as "low-cost and non-provocative means for engaging China in regional process."[34]

The China factor indeed figured prominently in the early 1990s, when ASEAN countries began the process of regional institution building. As far as ASEAN was concerned, almost all security issues were related to China. China also appeared to be an economic competitor. "The preponderance of the 'overseas' Chinese, China's compatriots from Hong Kong and Taiwan, and the importance of having Chinese connections (*guanxi*) in doing business in China could also be an area of concern in the ASEAN region."[35]

Singapore's MM Lee Kuan Yew's frequently quoted remarks about the rise of China is representative of ASEAN's vantage point: "It is not possible to pretend that China is another player. This is the biggest player in history of man."[36] In the climate of strategic uncertainty, the rise of China was indeed a key and worrying factor for ASEAN countries.

While many Asian countries harbor deep misgivings about China's role, ASEAN states has not seen wisdom in identifying China as a "threat." Instead, they are keen to ensure that the notion of the "China threat" will not become a self-fulfilling prophecy.[37] In particular, "identifying a country publicly as your adversary goes against the grain of Asian strategic culture."[38] In fact, ASEAN has adopted the so-called "Gulliver Strategy," which aims to enmesh China in regional economic and security institutions so as to persuade China to conform to norms that would support regional stability and order.[39]

To some extent, ASEAN states wanted the United States to be a "balancer" in the region. Many political leaders believed that it would be inevitable and unstoppable for China and Japan to play more prominent roles in the region. Yet by attempting their balancing act, they tended to "play the game of the international community" through multilateralism (Interview with Lee Lai To, 3–98, Beijing, March 25, 1998). "Multilateralism," Acharya argues, "has been viewed as a necessary framework within which to engage China and integrate it into a system of regional order, thereby reducing the need of provocative strategies of 'containment'."[38]

China's initial participation in the ARF, as well as Track II activities, was "skeptical, reluctant, and defensive."[11] Beijing had three major concerns about multilateral regional security cooperation at the time. The first was the Taiwan issue, which was the decisive factor. Beijing would not join any regional security dialog until Taiwan was assuredly excluded. The second concern was the US factor. Beijing always worried that the United States schemed behind the scenes against China or attempted to create a new mechanism to contain it. The third has to do with the lingering sovereignty dispute over the South China Sea. Some observed that three-quarters of Beijing's attitude toward regional security cooperation was related to the first two factors (Interviews 25–98, Beijing, May 21, 1998).

With the period of 1995–1996 as a line of demarcation, "the quality and tone of China's participation in regional security discussions has changed substantially."[11] The signs of change became evident in 1996, when China's approach appeared more positive, enthusiastic, and sophisticated. "In many instances, Chinese participants are better prepared and more attuned to the pattern of the discussion than participants from other countries, including the United States. In CSCAP, the Chinese presence has raised the level of discussion."[11]

Arguably, China has become more active and cooperative in its engagement with ASEAN states in order to influence the ARF process, as well as ASEAN-centered processes, as a significant component of its preferred alternative regional order. The future of China in the 21st century depends on how China establishes a new type of relationship with Asia.[40] China has realized that East Asian multilateralism is in many ways compatible with its basic security interests. First, ASEAN and the ARF are not under the jurisdiction of US hegemony. Second, respect for state sovereignty and non-interference, the two core principles of the ASEAN way, resonate well with Chinese normative tradition based on five principles of peaceful coexistence, which also underscores China's formulation of the new security concept. Third, ASEAN officially regards the Taiwan issue as China's domestic affair and deals with Taiwan normally under the One China framework. Fourth, ASEAN does not resist the rise of China as such; instead, its engagement with China is more genuine and less conditional than that of great powers.

To embrace East Asian multilateralism, however, China has had to reconsider its basic stance and practice with regard to major regional issues that concern the interests of ASEAN states, especially the South China Sea issue, and make adjustments and concessions accordingly. The breakthrough came about in November 2002 when China and ASEAN states signed *Declaration on the Conduct of Parties in the South China SeaDeclaration on the Conduct of Parties in the South China Sea* (DOC), which declared that "The Parties concerned undertake to resolve their territorial and jurisdictional disputes by peaceful means, without resorting to the threat or use of force, through friendly consultations and negotiations by sovereign states directly concerned, in accordance with universally recognized principles of international law, including the 1982 UN Convention on the Law of the Sea."[41]

In December 2004, China and ASEAN states[42] decided to establish the ASEAN–China Joint Working Group on the Implementation of the DOC to study and recommend concrete confidence-building measures. The senior official meeting suggested that "Under the DOC, cooperation activities may include: marine environmental protection, marine scientific research, safety of navigation and communication at sea, search and rescue operation, and combating transnational crime."

In October 2003, China became the first great power to accede to the Treaty of Amity and Cooperation in Southeast Asia, and agreed with ASEAN to establish "a strategic partnership for peace and prosperity," which elevated their rapidly developed relationship to a higher plane of strategic importance to regional security and peace.

China has also entered into a number of agreements with ASEAN in the area of political and security cooperation during the past 4 years, including the Joint Declaration of ASEAN and China on Cooperation in the Field of Non-traditional Security Issues signed in 2002 and an MOU on Cooperation in the Field of Non-traditional Security Issues signed in January 2004. In this regard, ASEAN and China have successfully implemented all activities based on the 2004 Annual Plan to implement the MOU. A new Annual Plan is being developed for 2005.[43] China has also expressed its willingness to work with ASEAN for its early accession to the Protocol to the Treaty on Southeast Asia Nuclear Weapons-Free Zone.

Another context in which China has to calculate its regional security interests is the rise of China's power and influence itself. China, through its proactive foreign policy behavior, has been trying to ensure that it is "one of the rule-makers" for the global and regional environment of the 21st century.[39] Yet the concern about the "China threat" is only natural from the standpoint of international relations and world history. China must address the anxieties of countries in the region about the implications of a new rising power for their interests. To defuse the "China threat," Beijing must nurture its image as a responsible great power and behave in a considerate manner to accommodate other countries' concerns and interests. At the very least, China would want to avoid isolation and regionwide containment against it, making its surrounding areas as friendly as possible. At most, it would like to be received as a good neighbor and a benign great power, making its external environment as friendly as possible. Beijing's self-restraint and acceptance of a multilateral format in its disputes with ASEAN countries over the South China Sea is a case in point.

In terms of the Taiwan question, the case of Germany is instructive in this regard. German unification occurred "not against but within Europe, indeed *for* Europe: The [European] Community channeled the unification process as unification in turn imparted new impulses to integration."[44] Since multilateral regionalism in the Asia–Pacific is rather nascent and China's integration in the region is still shallow, we do not witness explicit efforts to create a linkage between Chinese reunification and regional integration. In particular, Beijing has actually always made sure that the Taiwan issue will not be "internationalized" under any circumstances. The robust persistence of the One China principle in China's foreign policy and ASEAN's embracing of this principle are self-evident of no involvement of the emerging regional community in the Chinese reunification process, at least in terms of Track I activities. However, China's changed behavior in the ARF process and its reformed attitude toward regional multilateralism suggest an implicit and subtle connection between Chinese reunification and regional integration.

Key to this implicit linkage are three factors: (1) China must accept regional/multilateral involvement in the South China Sea issue, which, although concerning territorial sovereignty, is secondary only to the Taiwan issue; it serves as a litmus test, in the eyes of ASEAN states, for China's intention and responsibility in regional affairs. (2) Despite its reluctance, Beijing has to allow for the minimum involvement of the incipient regional community in the Taiwan issue, notably, through CSCAP and other Track-II arrangements.[g] The flourishing Track-II activities involving Taiwan allow participants across the Taiwan Strait and across the region to come to the same table without confronting the sensitive cross-strait sovereignty problem. (3) As long as

---

[g]In the case of APEC, Taiwan's membership (as well as Hong Kong's) is conditionally premised on its status as an "economic entity" so that only economic leaders can represent Taiwan.

China is brought into the regional multilateral process and is responsive to ASEAN's concerns and position about China's behavior in the South China Sea, ASEAN states tend to consider the Taiwan issue categorically as a Chinese problem, not automatically inferring a wider regional implication from Beijing's behavior toward Taiwan. For ASEAN states, there is only the China question, of which the Taiwan question is always a part. Amidst the cross-strait tensions caused by Chen Shui-bian's referendum provocation during Taiwan's 2003–2004 presidential election, ASEAN foreign ministers issued an unusual chairman's statement on the Taiwan issue in March 2004, in which they expressed their concern about any action that may cause deterioration of the situation, namely, Taiwan's upcoming referendum, and reaffirmed their adherence to one China policy (*Xinhua*, March 5, 2004).

8. Crisis Management and Preventive Diplomacy

In the early post-Cold War period, when big powers lost their strategic visions and began to act more out of domestic politically driven impulses, and the geopolitical picture thus became obscure and confusing, small powers found more room on the international stage to maneuver for their previously suppressed autonomy and aspirations.

The paradox of this big power–small power relationship is that the increased freedom of action enjoyed and exercised by small powers helps big powers clarify the blurred geopolitical picture and redefine their shared strategic interests, thus re-imposing restraints on small powers' behavior while somewhat accommodating their preferences and interests. Ironically, it seems that the most effective way for big powers to realize the importance of reinstalling a geopolitical order is for small powers to trigger or create a crisis, intentionally or unintentionally, which might involve big powers in dangerous standoffs. In other words, crises highlight the danger of conflict involving big powers, and thus the shared interest of avoiding such conflict. In East Asia, it was on the Korean Peninsula and in the Taiwan Strait that the two least satisfied actors — North Korea and Taiwan — took the driver's seat and staged unexpected events which challenged big powers privileged positions and interests and called into question the established code of conduct or "norms." To the extent that crises on these "hot spots" threatened to escalate into open hostilities on a larger scale, however, they alarmed and compelled big power to identify shared stake in effectively managing these non-structural or sub-structural challenges.

Since the end of the Cold War, Northeast Asia has witnessed two rounds of crises each on the Korean Peninsula and in the Taiwan Strait: the first round took place in the mid-1990s with the onset of the North Korean nuclear crisis in 1993–1994 and the Taiwan Strait crisis in 1995–1996; and the second round started with another crisis in the Taiwan Strait in 1999–2000 and was followed by a renewed nuclear crisis on the Korean Peninsula from 2001 on.

In the first round of crises, on the one hand, the perceived North Korean nuclear threat provided an explicit rationale for the redefining and reinforcing of the otherwise drifting US–Japan alliance, whereas the Taiwan Strait crisis also served as an implicit concern that prodded the United States and Japan to extend the scope of their bilateral alliance into "situations in surrounding areas." With the Clinton–Hashimoto joint declaration in 1996, the United States reaffirmed its continued commitment to hegemonic stability based on its military presence and alliances, while Japan closed its pro-America versus pro-Asia debate in terms of its post-Cold War foreign policy orientation, and opened a renewed course of an enhanced US–Japan partnership for its security interests.

On the other hand, the Taiwan Strait crisis exposed the remaining sensitivity of the Taiwan question in the post-Cold War era, and the growing vulnerability of malfunctioning US–China strategic cooperation to the maintenance of regional stability. In the aftermath of the crisis, the two countries restored their high-level exchange and strategic dialogue suspended after Tiananmen. Despite all problems, old and new, the United States and China found no choice but to work toward a diplomatic and strategic partnership in dealing with many daunting challenges in the region and the world. The enabling element in stabilizing and redefining US–China strategic relations remains the "One China" framework, as the United States reaffirmed its one China policy while China reiterated its peaceful reunification policy through the Jiang–Clinton summits in 1997 and 1998.

Before long, a new cycle of political elections in Taiwan and the United States set the stage for the second round of crises, this time started in Taiwan. When Taiwan leader Lee Teng-hui attempted to redefine cross-strait relations on a "state to state" basis in 1999, Beijing saw this move as a radical departure from the status quo and reacted swiftly in order to rein in Taipei's further move toward formal independence. The power transition from the pro-unification KMT to the pro-independence DPP in 2000 further intensified Beijing's sense of crisis as the DPP government under Chen Shui-bian was determined to pursue the path of "creeping independence." Most recently, Chen's attempt to set a timetable for formal, *de jure* independence — writing a new constitution in 2006 and then putting it into effect in 2008 — appeared to further close the door to reconciliation across the Taiwan Strait, thus increasing a chance of military conflict. The passage of the Anti-Secession Law by China's National People's Congress on March 14, 2005 is the latest episode of the ongoing drama over the Taiwan question.

On the Korean Peninsula, a new crisis took place when the DPRK announced its decision to withdraw from the Nuclear Non-Proliferation Treaty, and threatened to develop a nuclear weapon program for its security in 2001 after Bush's "axis of evil" speech. Declining the DPRK's request for bilateral negotiations with the US, the Bush administration favored a multi-lateral format involving other regional powers, and in particular pushed China to play an active role.

In the regional context, both the Korean Peninsula and the Taiwan Strait have been regarded as potentially explosive "flash points" that concern the entire region. From China's perspective, the fundamental difference between these two cases is that the Taiwan issue is a matter of sovereignty and ter-ritorial integrity for China, whereas the Korean issue is not. In terms of China's security behavior, therefore, the Taiwan Strait is where multilatera-lism does not apply and bilateralism appeals, while the Korean Peninsula is where the embrace of multilateralism appears to open a window of opportu-nity not only for peaceful resolution of the North Korean nuclear crisis, but also hopefully for reconciliation between different processes of security politics represented by different great powers.

After the Jiang–Bush informal summit at Bush's ranch in October 2002 and then Secretary of State Powell's talks with Jiang in February 2003, China changed its traditional "non-interference" stance regarding the Korean issue and began to play a role of "honest broker" to persuade the DPRK to accept a multilateral format in a search for a peaceful resolution. With China's active involvement, the DPRK came to a multilateral table, starting with a three-way meeting in Beijing in April 2003. It did not take long for Pyongyang to make a further concession, under US tough persistence and China's soft persuasion, by accepting the format of six-party talks. Three rounds of six-party talks had been held up to last June when Pyongyang announced that it suspended participation indefinitely because of the US "hostile policy" against it. The stalemate has continued after Bush won re-election and his inaugural speech. Although Bush did not put North Korea in spotlight in his State of Union address, Pyongyang saw no change in the second Bush administration's hostile approach toward DPRK as Secretary-of-State-to-be Condoleezza Rice in her nomination hearing described North Korea as an "outpost of tyranny." Seeing its role more as a mediator, China has repeatedly called on all parties to show sincerity, flexibility, and patience. While it has made clear its principled position on a nuclear-weapon-free Korean Peninsula, it has also stressed that the DPRK's security concern and energy needs must also be appropriately addressed. The stalemate was lasting until July 9, 2005 when Pyongyang announced that it was to return to the six-party talk in the last week of the month.

China's security concerns and interests on the Korean Peninsula can be discerned in the following aspects. First, China's foremost concern is the abrupt "regime change" caused either by implosion or explosion, which would generate immediate and enormous pressure on its northeast region. The two scenarios — the flood of North Korean refugees and the extended presence of US military forces close to its borders — would mean a serious deterioration of its security environment in Northeast Asia. So China is not only sympathetic to the DPRK's incipient attempt to engineer economic reform, but also sees it to be in China's own security interest to encourage and help its North Korean comrades to carry on reform and make a transition toward market-oriented development. From China's perspective, this is the most basic and effective way to stabilize the situation in North Korea as well as on the entire peninsula.

Second, China's concern about a nuclear DPRK centers on a possible domino effect in Northeast Asia. Although the scenario of a nuclear DPRK may not pose a direct and immediate threat to China, the scenario of a nuclear arms race in Northeast Asia in its aftermath, a nuclear Korean Peninsula and a nuclear arming Japan, would severely destabilize the regional security environment.

And third, the scenario of a new Korean War would be a security nightmare still in relation to the Taiwan issue. One Chinese security scholar put bluntly, from a historical point of view: China has been involved in two wars on the Korean Peninsula in the past and "China lost Taiwan twice because of its forced intervention." So this time around, China will make sure that the same thing would not happen again (Interviews 1–04, Kyoto, March 16, 2004).

Most recently, President Hu Jintao reiterated China's policy in his talks with visiting DPRK Premier Pak Bong Ju: "It is in our common interests to stick to a nuclear-weapon-free Korean Peninsula, resolve DPRK's rational concerns, and maintain peace and stability on the peninsula." Where Hu stressed that dialog is the "only correct choice" for peacefully resolving the nuclear issue on the Korean Peninsula, Premier Wen more specifically referred to the six-party talks as "a realistic choice" to achieve this goal (*Xinhua*, March 22, 2005; March 23, 2005). Despite all uncertainties, China's active yet cautious approach to brokering multilateral talks concerning the North Korean nuclear issue raises a question about the relationship of China's regional role with US-led hegemonic stability, and points to the prospect of a new security order beyond the immediate nuclear problem.[45]

On all counts, to be sure, the key to China's regional security interests remains the handling of the Taiwan issue. In fact, long before 9–11, Chinese analysts had already suggested that China should take advantage of US' One China policy for the purpose of opposing Taiwanese independence as opposed to its traditional preference for US non-intervention. Given that Washington has larger latitude than Beijing to influence the Taiwan authorities and island politics,[46] argues, "it should be one of our strategies toward Taiwan that we make use of US strategic intention to maintain the status quo in the Taiwan Strait to restrain Taiwan leaders' independence orientation."

Since Hu Jintao took office, it appears that Beijing has made considerable adjustments about its Taiwan policy. Drawing lessons from its often frustrating experience in the past 10 years, Beijing tried to regain the initiative in shaping the course of interaction across the Taiwan Strait by acting to curb Taiwan independence and promote reunification rather than reacting to each and every act on the part of Taiwan in its "creeping independence" movement. The new course of action is summarized as three phrases: "strive for negotiations, be prepared to fight, do not fear delaying" (*zhengqu tan, zhunbei da, bupa tuo*).[47] A new emphasis is placed on containing Taiwan independence through legal vehicles and by means of international forces. The use of "soft hand" (carrot) and "hard hand" (stick) must be aimed at achieving real effects. To distinguish between opposing independence and promoting reunification, the central task for now is the maintenance of the status quo (*Ta Kung Pao*, January 22, 2005). On the eve of the passage of the Anti-Secession Law, Hu bluntly stated: the "Taiwan independence" secessionist forces and their activities are increasingly becoming the "biggest obstacle for the development of cross-straits relations" and the "biggest real threat to peace and stability in the region around the Taiwan Strait" (*Xinhua*, March 4, 2005).

The shift of priority from achieving reunification to containing independence has also to do with the growing consciousness about a possible repercussion caused by a drastic change across the Taiwan Strait under current circumstances. According to Chinese analysts, drastic reunification appears to be difficult for all parties concerned; by contrast, a gradualist approach to reunification will benefit both sides of the Taiwan Strait, Asia, and even the whole world.[48]

During the 2003–2004 Taiwan elections, Chen's aggressive referendum initiatives only compelled Bush to tilt further to Beijing in terms of curbing Taiwan's unilateral move toward independence. US informal representative in Taipei Doug Paal expressed a serious concern to Bush about Chen Shui-bian's referendum initiatives.[49] Having learned lessons from 1996 and 2000 Taiwan elections, in public Beijing exercised a maximum self-restraint in response to Taiwan politicians' highly provocative election rhetoric, but behind the scene both decision makers and policy analysts became extremely anxious and worried about Taiwan's unchecked slippery into independence. Before Premier Wen Jiabao's visit to the US in December 2004, Chinese leaders decided to tell Bush that Beijing's patience on Chen was nearly exhausted. On December 9, after meeting with Wen, Bush made a very strong public statement against Taiwan independence: "The United States government's policy is one China, based upon the three communiqués and the Taiwan Relations Act. We oppose any unilateral decision by either China or Taiwan to change the status quo. *And the comments and actions made by the leader of Taiwan indicate that he may be willing to make decisions unilaterally to change the status quo, which we oppose.*"[50]

Beijing's intensified effort to work with Washington to contain Taiwan independence reflects its new emphasis on preventive diplomacy as a main instrument to contain Taiwan independence in the broader international context. Contrasting with its normative position that "the Taiwan issue is China's internal affairs," Beijing's new emphatic position in international diplomacy is: Taiwan secessionist movement is a grave threat to regional security and stability that requires international effort to cope with.

In fact, Beijing has worked very hard to mobilize diplomatic forces to constrain the "international space" for Taiwan independence. In his address to the UN general assembly in September 2004, Foreign Minister Li Zhaoxing called on the international community to fully recognize the grave threat posed by Taiwan's secessionist movement to cross-strait stability and regional peace, and to jointly contain "Taiwan independence" secessionist activities (*Xinhua*, September 28, 2004).

In the same UN session, Singapore cautioned Taiwan against baiting China by pushing for independence, and urged the United Nations to prevent relations between Taipei and Beijing spiralling out of control. Foreign Minister George Yeo stated:

> The push toward independence by certain groups in Taiwan is most dangerous because it will lead to war with mainland China and drag in other countries. The international community should also not allow the deteriorating relationship across the Taiwan Straits to get out of control. At stake is the stability of the entire Asia–Pacific region (*Channel News Asia*, September 25, 2004).

In December 2004, the 10th ASEAN summit issued a chairman's statement in which leaders of ASEAN reaffirm their commitment to a One China policy and expressed their belief that it is in the common interest of all countries in the region to maintain peace and stability in the Taiwan Strait (*China Times*, December 1, 2004).

When President Hu Jintao met with President Bush on the sidelines of the 2004 APEC summit in Santiago, Hu told Bush that "Taiwan independence" would ruin peace, and destroy stability and prosperity in the Asia–Pacific region. So China and the United States should look at the threat of Taiwan independence from this strategic standpoint, and jointly contain "Taiwan independence" forces' secessionist activities (*Xinhua*, November 20, 2004). As the result of Hu's meetings with the leaders of the 14 APEC countries, all his counterparts reaffirmed their commitment to one China policy.

Around this time, Bush appeared to be inclined to defuse the Taiwan problem as an unstable factor in US–China relations during his second term. A series of closed-door discussions involving both officials and experts were held in November, in which three options were put on the table — ambiguity, clarity, and co-managing (with China). Because the last one is more compatible with the Bush administration's interest, it emerged as a widely accepted consensus (*China News Net*, March 22, 2005). As Robert Sutter recently observes, Chinese and American interests appear to converge against the backdrop of Taipei's recent unchecked unilateral movement toward independence.[h] This is well illustrated in Powell's statement, which he made in an interview during his visit to China in October 2004, that "Taiwan is not independent. Taiwan does not enjoy sovereignty as a nation."[51]

In effect, the Beijing–Washington increasing cooperation to rein in Taiwan independence has led to a new expectation by some Chinese and Americans that Washington and Beijing may come to a new strategic understanding about the threat of the Taiwan problem, according which China exercises self-restraint, while the United States practices a policy of containment against Taiwan independence (*Chinese News Net,* July 5, 2004).

9. Conclusion

To be sure, Beijing's primary security concern and interest has been drastically refocused on the Taiwan question since the 1995–1996 Taiwan Strait crisis. As the preceding analysis shows, to the extent that US–Japan alliance politics became intertwined with the complex identity politics embodied in the new Taiwan issue since the mid-1990s, Beijing has shifted from a rather reactive approach to regional security politics in the early post-Cold War period, to a rather proactive approach to regional security order building in the later post-Cold War period. This has been demonstrated in Beijing's gradual shift of emphasis from outright criticism of the redefined US–Japan alliance to constructive participation in multilateral regional security diplomacy; from defensively refuting the "China threat" thesis to constructively nurturing a new image of a cooperative and benign power; and from single-mindedly guarding the One China norm to actively creating a favorable environment for the future reunification of China.

---

[h] Robert Sutter made such remarks at the conference on "US Taiwan Policy and the Dynamics of the Taipei–Beijing–Washington Triangle — Prospects for Democracy and Peace," January 28–29, 2005 at American University in Washington, DC.

In order to debunk the image and theory of the "China threat," China has to present an image of China as a responsible great power by embracing positive trends in the region which reflect the interests of majority countries. Between the US-led hegemonic order and the emerging multilateral order, Beijing has found that the latter is less threatening and more accommodating to China's vital national and security interests.

With the rise of China itself as one of the central components of the ongoing grand transformation of regional politics since the mid-1990s, Beijing has become increasingly positive and confident in participating in the building of the regional order. Through expounding the new security concept, Beijing has made no secret of its intention to strive for an alternative regional order vis-à-vis the hegemonic stability centered on the US alliance system. The basic compatibility between its new security concept and the ASEAN Way of regional order allows for the mutual engagement between China and ASEAN under a socially constructive atmosphere. As the mutual engagement progresses, China and ASEAN have reciprocated with each other on some crucial issue areas that are vital to their interests. This reciprocation has begun to be demonstrated powerfully in two important aspects: first, the two sides have made substantial trade-offs between the Taiwan issue and the South China Sea issue, as ASEAN accommodates Beijing's sovereignty over Taiwan affairs while Beijing embraces ASEAN's multilateral stance on the South China Sea issue; second, the two sides have also reconciled with each other on the role of China in regional affairs, as ASEAN cautiously welcomes China's leadership role in the region while China carefully projects its image as a responsible great power. Across the two phases of the post-Cold War era, these manifestations of reciprocal and constructive engagement have become more potent and productive in the late post-Cold War period.

Furthermore, the emerging cooperative crisis management led by China and the United States over the Korean nuclear crisis and the Taiwan independence movement offers a litmus test on China's balancing act in its security practice, its normative commitment to multipolarity and multilateralism, and most importantly, the chance of reconciliation between China's rise and US hegemony, which will be consequential not only for a regional order but also for the international system as a whole. The hopeful prospect is on the horizon; yet its realization may not come any time soon.

Last but not least, China's regional security practice has reflected Chinese deepening understanding of the dynamism of international relations in the age of globalization, whereby its security interests become more complicated, diverse, and entwined with various traditional and non-traditional issues. In the long and contested process of bifurcating world politics predicated on multipolarization and globalization, China needs a balanced and concerted approach to ensure that it emerges as a winner on both fronts. In this regard, multilateralism appears to have a greater appeal in Chinese diplomatic and security statecrafts than ever before in that it provides counterweight to the "unipolar moment" and traditional power politics in soft, less confrontational fashion while mobilizing sovereign states to cooperate in dealing with challenges of globalization. By articulating its vision of regional and global security order based on the new security concept and working toward to its materialization through multilateral and bilateral diplomacy, China's best hope is that this will not only drive home in the region, but more importantly make the region and the world safer for its peaceful development and ascendancy in the 21st century.

Acknowledgments

I would like to thank Waheguru Pal Singh Sidhu, Strobe Talbott, and Shiping Tang for their excellent comments on the earlier version of this paper, which was presented at an Inaugural Conference on "Managing Globalization: Lessons from China and India," co-sponsored by the Lee Kuan Yew School of Public Policy, the Asia Society, and the Brookings Institution on April 4–6, 2005 at Shangri-La Hotel, Singapore. All remaining errors, however, are author's own.

References

1. Brzezinski, Z. (1991). "Selective Global Commitment." *Foreign Affairs* 70(4), 1–20.
2. Gilpin, R. (1981). *War and Change in World Politics*. Cambridge: Cambridge University Press.
3. Rosenau, J.N. (1990). *Turbulence in World Politics: A Theory of Change and Continuity*. Princeton: Princeton University Press.

4. Pyle, K.B. (1992). *The Japanese Question: Power and Purpose in a New Era*. Washington, DC: The AEI Press.
5. Evans, P.M. (1992). "The Emergence of Eastern Asia and Its Implications for Canada." *International Journal* 47(3), 504–528.
6. Funabashi, Y. (1993). "The Asianization of Asia." *Foreign Affairs* 72(5), 75–85.
7. Mahbubani, K. (1995). "The Pacific Way." *Foreign Affairs* 74(1), 100–111.
8. Alagappa, M. (ed.) (1998). *Asian Security Practice: Material and Ideational Influences*. Stanford: Stanford University Press.
9. Morrison, C.E. (ed.) (2001). *East Asia and the international System*. A Report to the Trilateral Commission: 55, The Trilateral Commission.
10. Katzenstein, P.J. and Okawara, N. (2001). "Japan, Asian–Pacific Security, and the Case for Analytical Eclecticism." *International Security* 26(3), 153–185.
11. Johnston, A.I. and Evans, P. (1999). "China's Engagement with Multilateral Security." In: Johnston, A. and Ross, R.S. (eds.) *Engaging China: The Management of An Emerging Power*. London: Routledge, pp. 235–272.
12. Levine, S.I. (1983). "China in Asia: The PRC as a Regional Power." In: Harry, H. (ed.) *China's Foreign Relations in the 1980s*. New Haven: Yale University Press, pp. 107–145.
13. Deng, X. (1989). "With Stable Policies of Reform and Opening to the Outside World, China Can Have Great Hopes for the Future." *Selected Works of Deng Xiaoping*, vol. 3, Internet version. Retrieved 24 June 2002, from http://english.peopledaily.com.cn/dengxp/vol3/text/d1020.html.
14. Jiang, Z. (2002). *Lun Jianshe You Zhongguo Tese Shehuizhuyi* [*On Socialism with Chinese Characteristics*]. Beijing: Zhongyang Wenxian Chubanshe.
15. Wen, J. (2003). "Turning Your Eyes to China." Remarks at Harvard University, 10 December. Retrieved 22 July 2004, from http://www.hno.harvard.edu/gazette/2003/12.11/10-wenspeech.html.
16. Information Office of the State Council, PRC (1996). *China's Arms Control and Disarmament 1995*, retrieved 21 October 2001, from http://www.fmprc.gov.cn/eng/32222.html.
17. Ministry of Foreign Affairs of the PRC (2002a). *China's Position Paper on Enhanced Cooperation in the Field of Non-Traditional Security Issues*. Retrieved 1 April 2004, from http://www.fmprc.gov.cn/eng/wjb/zzjg/gjs/gjzzyhy/2612/2614/t15318.htm.
18. Ministry of Foreign Affairs of the PRC (2002b). *China's Position Paper on the New Security Concept*. Retrieved 1 April 2004 from http://www.fmprc.gov.cn/eng/wjb/zzjg/gjs/gjzzyhy/2612/2614/t15319.htm
19. Johnson, A.I. (2003). "Is China a Status Quo Power?" *International Security* 27(4), 5–56.

20. Moore, T.G. (2000). "China and Globalization." In: Kim, S.S. (ed.) *East Asia and Globalization*. Lanham, MD: Rowman & Littlefield Publishers, Inc., pp. 105–131.

21. Qian, Q. (2003). *Waijiao Shiji* [*Ten Stories of a Diplomat*]. Beijing: Shijie Zhishi Chubanshe.

22. Xu, X. (1993). *Changing Chinese Security Perceptions*, NPCSD Working Paper, No. 27, Toronto: York University Press.

23. Christensen, T.J. (1996). "Chinese Realpolitik." *Foreign Affairs* 75(5), 37–52.

24. Deng, Y. (2001). "Hegemony on the Offensive: Chinese Perspectives on U.S. Global Strategy." *Political Science Quarterly* 116(3), 343–365.

25. Lampton, D. (ed.) (2001). *The Making of Chinese Foreign and Security Policy in the Era of Reform, 1978–2000*. Stanford: Stanford University Press.

26. Wang, Z. and Fang, H. (2000). Weilai 5–10 Nian Zhongguo de Guoji Zhanlue Huanjing yu Duiwai Zhanlue [China's International Environment and Foreign Strategy in the Next 5–10 Years], in China Institute of Contemporary International Relations (CICIR), *Quanqiu Zhanlue Dageju: Xin Shiji Zhongguo de Guoji Huanjing* [*Global Strategic Structure: China's International Environment in the New Century*]. Beijing: Shishi Publishing House, pp. 130–155.

27. Teng, T., Rong, D., Wang, J. and Lu, A. (eds.) (2001). *Deng Xiaoping Lilun yu Shiji Zhijiao de Zhongguo Guoji Zhanlue* [*Deng Xiaoping Theory and China's International Strategy at the Turn of the Centuries*]. Beijing: Renmin Chubanshe.

28. Yan, X. *et al.* (1999). *Zhongguo yu Ya-Tai Anquan: lengzhan hou Ya-Tai Guojia de Anquan Zhanlue Zouxiang* [*China and Asia-Pacific Security: Security Policy Orientations of Asia-Pacific Countries after the Cold War*]. Beijing: Shishi Chubanshe.

29. Capraso, J.A. (1993). "International Relations Theory and Multilateralism." In: Ruggie, J. (ed.) *Multilateralism Matters: The Theory and Praxis of an International Form*. New York: Colombia University Press, pp. 51–90.

30. Deng, Y. and Moore, T.G. (2004). "China Views Globalization: Toward a New Great-Power Politics?" *Washington Quarterly* 27(3), 117–136.

31. Soeya, Y. (2001). "Taiwan in Japan's Security Considerations." *The China Quarterly* (165), 130–146.

32. Christensen, T.J. (1999). "China, the U.S.-Japan Alliance, and the Security Dilemma in East Asia." *International Security* 23(4), 49–80.

33. "Joint Statement of the US–Japan Security Consultative Committee," 19 February 2005. Retrieved 22 February 2005, from http://www.state.gov/r/pa/prs/ps/2005/42490.htm.

34. Sokolsky, R., Rabasa, A. and Neu, C. (2000). *The Role of Southeast Asia in U.S. Strategy Toward China*. Rand.

35. Lee, L.T. (1993). "ASEAN-PRC Political and Security Cooperation: Problems, Proposals, and Prospects." *Asian Survey* 33(11), 1095–1104.

36. Lee, K.Y. (1993). "Singapore's Proposal." *International Herald Tribute*, April 11, 1993, pp. 1 and 7.
37. Da Cunha, D. (1998). "Southeast Asian Perceptions of China's Future Security Role in Its 'Backyard'." In: Pollack, J. and Yang, R. (eds.) *In China's Shadow: Regional Perspectives on Chinese Foreign Policy and Military Development*. Rand.
38. Acharya, A. (1997). "Multilateralism: Is There an Asia–Pacific Way?" *Analysis* **8**(2), 5–18.
39. Sutter, R. (2002). "China's Recent Approach to Asia: Seeking Long-Term Gains." *NBR Analysis* **13**(1), 13–38.
40. Pang, Z. (2003). "Zaizao Zhongguo yu Yazhou de Guanxi" [Reshape the Relationship between China and Asia], *Renmin Ribao*, December 26. Retrieved 26 December, 2003, from http://www.people.com.cn/GB/guoji/1030/2266989.html.
41. *Declaration on the Conduct of Parties in the South China Sea* (2002). Retreived 24 March 2005, from http://www.aseansec.org/13163.htm.
42. ASEAN Press Release (2004). "ASEAN-China Senior Officials Meeting on the Implementation of the Declaration on the Conduct of Parties in the South China Sea." Kuala Lumpur. Retrieved 7 December 2004, from http://www.aseansec.org/16888.htm.
43. *ASEAN-China Dialogue Relations*. Retrieved 24 June 2005, from http://www.aseansec.org/5874.htm.
44. Anderson, J. (1999). *German Unification and the Union of Europe: The Domestic Politics of Integration Policy*. Cambridge: Cambridge University Press.
45. Snyder, S. and Kim, A.-Y. (2003). "China-ROK-U.S. Relations and Regional Security in Northeast Asia." *Comparative Connections*, Special Annual Issue, Pacific Forum CSIS (July), Honolulu, Hawaii.
46. Huang, R. (1998). "Zhongguo Mianxiang Ershiyi Shiji Baochi Guoji Huanjing Wending de Zhanlue Xuanze" [China's Strategic Choice for Maintaining International Stability toward the 21st Century]. *Shanghai Social Sciences Academic Quarterly* (1), 41–50.
47. Zhong, G. (2004). "Hu Jintao zai Taiwan Wenti shang de Zhengceweitiao" (Hu Jintao's Fine-tuning of the Taiwan Policy), *Chinese News Net*, 24 November. Retrieved 24 November 2004, from http://www2.chinesenewsnet.com/gb/MainNews/Opinion/2004_11_24_15_29_35_823.html.
48. Jiang, Z., Sun, Z. and Wang, D. (2005). "Zhongguo Jianjin Tongyi You Sanda Tese" [Three Major Characteristics of China's Gradualist Reunification]. *Ta Kung Pao* January 24. Retrieved 24 January 2005, from http://www.takungpao.com/inc/print_me.asp?url=/news/2005-1-24/ZM-357213.htm&date=2005-1-24.

49. Christensen, T. (2003). "PRC Security Relations with the United States: Why Things Are Going So Well." *China Leadership Monitor* (8), 1–10.
50. White House Office of the Press Secretary (2003). "President Bush and Premier Wen Jiabao Remarks to the Press." Remarks by President Bush and Premier Wen Jiabao in Photo Opportunity, The Oval Office, 9 December. Retrieved 12 December 2003, from http://www.whitehouse.gov/news/releases/2003/12/20031209-2.html.
51. Powell, C.L. (2004). "Interview with Anthony Yuen of Phoenix TV." Beijing, China. October 25, 2004, from http://www.state.gov/secretary/rm/37361.htm.

CHAPTER 10

Facilitating Peaceful Rise: Principles and Practice of China's Security Policy

Jia Qingguo

The rise of China has not only brought uncertainties to the international community but also fresh challenges to China itself. China has indicated that it wants to have a peaceful rise. Many both in China and in the world, however, remain to be convinced. History, it appears, offers little consolation. More often than not, conflicts and war accompanied the rise of a large country. Some realist theories also predict military confrontation and even war.[a] This has not only provided grounds for international concern for the rise of China but also complicated its efforts to secure a peaceful international environment for development and reforms at home.

However, what happened in history does not necessarily need to happen now. After all, circumstances have changed. To begin with, the world has become interdependent. Interdependence has made it more costly for states to use force to enrich themselves through conquering and annexation. It has also provided fresh opportunities for countries to enhance their welfare through international trade and investment. Furthermore, human beings have invented nuclear weapons. The unacceptable destructiveness of nuclear war has made wars between nuclear powers very unlikely if not impossible. Finally, having experienced the two world wars and being fully aware of the destructiveness of nuclear weapons and other weapons of mass destruction, people in the world are now less inclined to endorse war, especially nuclear war, as a way to settle international disputes than at any time in history. In view of all this, if the possibility of war over the rise of China cannot be completely dismissed, it has become quite unlikely.

---

[a]Mearsheimer, J.J. (2001). *The Tragedy of Great Power Politics*. New York: W. W. Norton & Company.

If, indeed, there is a chance for China to rise peacefully, what should it do to make it happen? It is along this line of thinking that China's security policy has evolved in recent years. This paper will first briefly review the evolution of China's security policy over time. Then it will analyze the major factors shaping its evolution. Finally, it will speculate about the future prospects. It hopes that it will be helpful in our efforts to understand China's security policy in the age of globalization.

1. China's Security Policy

Before getting into the discussion of China's security policy, it may be helpful to define the concept of security used in this paper. Instead of a broader understanding of the concept which covers economy, environment, health, and other issues, it involves a narrow if also more traditional understanding of the concept, that is, military security. Specifically, it refers to China's approach to and efforts at making itself safe from the perceived external military challenges.

With this in mind, one finds that China's security policy has been evolving from one of passive defence which relies on size of the military, strategic depth and independence to a more proactive one which stresses capabilities, assurance, and cooperation.

1.1. *Capabilities*

As in the case of other countries, security begins with one's ability to defend oneself. Ever since the founding of the PRC, the Chinese Government has been trying to build up a modern defence capability. It scored some success in the 1950s and 1960s in transforming the Chinese military into a relatively professional one and in producing some modern military hardware such as nuclear weapons, hydrogen bombs and missiles of various ranges. However, for about two and half decades after the mid-1960s, China's defence capability did not improve very much for various reasons. Between the mid-1960s and late 1970s, the Cultural Revolution did not only disrupted research and production of weapons systems, but also de-professionalized the military. Between the late 1970s and the late 1980s, China's decision to assign high priority to economic development contributed to a 10-year long under-financing of the Chinese defence establishment and also its engagement in commercial

Table 1. China's defence expenditure.[c]

1995	1996	1997	1998	1999	2000	2001	2002	2003	2004	2005
63.7	72	81.3	93.5	103.7	120.8	144.2	170.8	190.8	211.7	244.7

(Unit: RMB billion of Yuan)

activities to supplement its maintenance further damaged the defence establishment's ability to perform its duties effectively.[b] Although the defence budget increased quite significantly after 1989, high inflation wiped out much of the increase during the early 1990s especially between 1992 and 1994.

For the reasons discussed above, by the mid-1990s, despite the emergence of the China threat chorus in international society, China's defence capability was very inadequate. The PLA was under-financed, under-trained, under-equipped and, to some extent, demoralized. However, this situation began to change in 1995. The high inflation finally came down. In the meantime, the double-digit growth of China's defence spending has continued through to this day. As a result of this, China's defence budget is almost quadrupled (unadjusted to inflation) (Table 1).

The quickly expanding budget has given the Chinese military more to spend on upgrading and purchasing weapons, training troops, improving its command, control, communication, computer and intelligence (C^4I) capabilities,[d] restructuring the military to make it smaller, more flexible and more capable of performing its functions, and recruiting better educated and more qualified people. As a result, China's defence capabilities have improved significantly.

While it is true that China's defence spending has increased significantly comparing to the past, it is necessary to put this into a proper perspective. China's defence expenditure is still quite modest compared with that in other major countries. According to China's 2004 defence white paper, "In 2003, China's defence expenditure amounted to only 5.69% of that of the United

---

[b]"From 1979 to 1994 defence spending increased by 6.22% annually in absolute terms, which represented in real terms a negative growth of 1.08% compared to the 7.3% annual increase of the country's general retail price index of commodities in the same period." http://russia.shaps.hawaii.edu/security/3c.

[c]Compiled according China's defence white papers, http://russia.shaps.hawaii.edu/security/3; http://www.fas.org/nuke/guide/china/doctrine/cnd0010/china-001016wp3.htm; http://english.people.com.cn/features/ndpaper2002/nd4.html; http://www.fas.org/nuke/guide/china/doctrine/natdef2004.html#5; http://news.xinhuanet.com/newscenter/2005-03/15/content_2700890_5.htm.

[d]http://www.fas.org/nuke/guide/china/c3i/.

States, 56.78% of that of Japan, 37.07% of that of the United Kingdom, and 75.94% of that of France"[e] (Fig. 1).

In addition, the share of China's defence spending in its GDP has remained low and is still much lower than that in most other major countries (Tables 2 and 3).

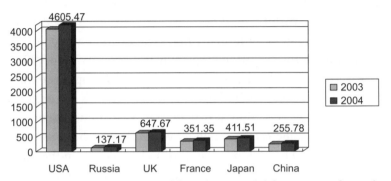

Note 1: Statistics in the charts are sourced from the national defence reports, financial reports and other government reports published by the said countries.
Note 2: The average exchange rate in 2003 was US$ 1.00 = RMB 8.2770. On Nov. 20, 2004, US$ 1.00 = RMB 8.2765.
(Unit: billion US dollars)

Fig. 1. Comparison of the defence expenditures of some countries in 2003 and 2004.[f]

Table 2. Percentage of China's annual defence expenditure in its GDP (1997–2003).

Year	1997	1998	1999	2000	2001	2002	2003
Percentage	1.09	1.19	1.31	1.35	1.48	1.62	1.63

Table 3. The percentages of the defence expenditures in the GDP and financial expenditures of some countries in 2003.[g]

Country	USA	Russia	UK	France	Japan	China
Defence expend. as % of GDP	3.60	2.64	3.11	2.22	0.99	1.63
Defence expend. as % of financial expenditure	16.20	14.69	8.10	11.00	6.06	7.74

[e]http://www.fas.org/nuke/guide/china/doctrine/natdef2004.html#5.
[f]http://www.fas.org/nuke/guide/china/doctrine/natdef2004.html#5.
[g]http://www.fas.org/nuke/guide/china/doctrine/natdef2004.html#5.

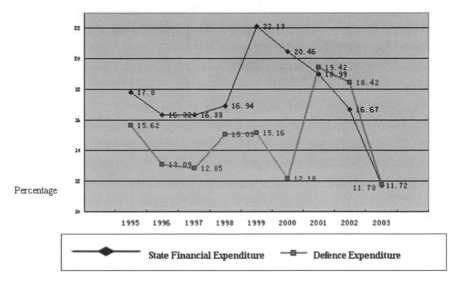

Fig. 2. Comparison between the growth rate of China's defence expenditure and that of its state financial expenditure (1995–2003).[h]

Moreover, the growth of China's defence spending has been in step with the growth of the Chinese economy and state financial expenditure. China has not devoted an amount of resources beyond its economic ability (Fig. 2).

Furthermore, much of China's defence spending has not been used to purchase weapons and training its troops. Instead, it has been spent to enable the military to keep up with the rapidly rising living standards with the rest of the Chinese society and to pick up the cost resulting from the PLA's withdrawal from commercial activities over the past few years. This includes covering the increased spending for carrying out routine duties and operations after the armed forces withdrew from commercial activities, increased spending for the placement of retired officers and their pensions, and increased pay and subsidy for military personnel to keep their living standards in line with the increase of the per capita incomes of urban and rural residents (Fig. 3).

Finally, despite the growth in defence spending, China's defence capabilities are still far short of the level necessary for the defence of a large country like China. While it has acquired some high-tech weapons, PLA's weapon systems are still in general quite backward by the world's standards. That explains why

---

[h]http://www.fas.org/nuke/guide/china/doctrine/natdef2004.html#5.

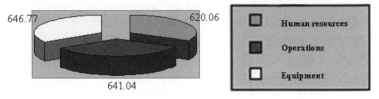

(Unit: RMB billion yuan)

Fig. 3.   China's defence expenditure, 2003 by proportion.[i]

the US is making such a big issue out of the EU decision to lift arms embargo against China at the moment. The PLA needs to develop better C^4I capabilities to keep up with the revolution of military affairs in the world. Given the aggressive posture of the Taiwan separatists and given the recent hardening of the US–Japan military alliance with an increasingly explicit aim to contain China, the current efforts to enhance PLA's capabilities to keep up with the security challenge are even less adequate.

1.2. *Assurance*

In addition to enhancing its defence capabilities, the Chinese Government has also made many efforts to assure the international society that its growing defence capabilities and a stronger China do not pose any serious threat to other countries. For this purpose, it has tried to clarify its goals and objectives and address specific concerns of the international community over China's policies on a whole array of international issues.

1.3. *Clarifying China's goals and objectives*

To begin with, the Chinese Government has repeatedly stressed that the fundamental goal of China's foreign policy is to promote a world favorable for peace and development. In his report at the 16th National Representative Congress of the Chinese Communist Party, Jiang Zemin, the then Secretary General of the CCP Central Committee, stated that the goal of China's foreign policy is

---

[i]http://www.fas.org/nuke/guide/china/doctrine/natdef2004.html#5.

to maintain world peace and promote common development.[j] In his speech at the opening ceremony of Bo'ao Forum for Asia 2004 annual conference, President Hu Jintao stated, "The very purpose of China's foreign policy is to maintain world peace and promote common development."[k] In his address to mark the 50th anniversary of the formulation of the five principles of peaceful coexistence, Premier Wen Jiabao also stressed the high degree of importance China attaches to peace in conducting foreign relations. He promised that China would continue to uphold the five principles of peaceful coexistence in its foreign policy and promote world peace and security through dialog and cooperation.[l]

In addition to peace and development, the Chinese Government has stated that China wants a harmonious world that respects national sovereignty, tolerates diversity, and benefits all countries. The Chinese Government maintains that the international community should respect national sovereignty. According to Premier Wen Jiabao, national sovereignty is the essence of national independence. It constitutes the collective manifestation and reliable protection of national interests. He pointed out that despite growing interdependence between states in the age of globalization, national sovereignty remains important and useful. No state has the right to impose its will on other states. The practice of disrespect for other states' sovereignty in international relations is not going to work.[m]

The Chinese Government has also argued that China wants to have a world of cultural and political diversity. Premier Wen Jiabao said that diversity of world civilizations is a basic feature of human society. It is also an important driving force for world progress. The numerous differences in historical tradition, religion, culture, social system, values, and levels of development are what make the world colorful and fascinating. Countries should recognize and accept such a reality. They should show greater tolerance and respect for

---

[j]Zemin, J. (2002). "*Quanmian jianshe xiaokang shehui: kaichuang zhongguo tese shehuizhuyi shiye xin jumian.*" Beijing: Renmin Publishing House, p. 47.

[k]Hu Jintao, "China's Development Is an Opportunity for Asia." April 27, 2004, http://www.chinataiwan.org/web/webportal/W5023952/A2175.html.

[l]Wen Jiabao, "Hongyang wu xiang yuanze: cujin heping fazhan" (Uphold five principles and promote peace and development), June 28, 2004, http://www.fmprc.gov.cn/chn/wjdt/zyjh/t140781.htm.

[m]Wen Jiabao, "Hongyang wu xiang yuanze: cujin heping fazhan" (Uphold five principles and promote peace and development), June 28, 2004, http://www.fmprc.gov.cn/chn/wjdt/zyjh/t140781.htm.

diversity. They should learn to live in peace despite the differences between and among them.[n]

The Chinese Government has also made clear that China wants to have a world of common prosperity. To the Chinese Government, one of the most important challenges to the international community is to provide a favorable environment for the poorer countries to catch up with the richer ones and arresting the trend of further polarization of the world. To meet the challenge, the international community should respect each state's priority to pursue development according to their own conditions.[o] And the international society should help the developing countries' efforts to do so. As Chinese Foreign Minister Tang Jiaxuan put it, "Assisting the developing countries today is to invest in the common destiny of all human beings." The developing countries sustain greater difficulties in the age of globalization. "The developed countries ought to lend them a helping hand in such areas as finance, trade, technology transfer and development aid and make good on their debt relief promises."[p]

The Chinese Government has also said that China wants to have a world of rule of law and multilateral cooperation. Multilateral cooperation is necessary for the maintenance of peace. As former Vice Premier Qian Qichen put it in 2004, "we should opt for multilateralism and give full play to the important role of the UN. Our world is a one big family. Naturally, family affairs should be handled by all its members through consultations." The United Nations, Qian said, is "the core of the collective security mechanism and the best venue for multilateral interchanges." It therefore "should continue to play its important role in international affairs. Facts have proved that no major international issues can be tackled by just one or two countries or a group of countries laying down the law."[q]

Multilateral cooperation is also required for the promotion of development. As Chinese Foreign Minister Tang Jiaxuan put it in 2002, "It would

---

[n] Wen Jiabao, "Hongyang wu xiang yuanze: cujin heping fazhan" (Uphold five principles and promote peace and development), June 28, 2004, http://www.fmprc.gov.cn/chn/wjdt/zyjh/t140781.htm.

[o] Wen Jiabao, "Hongyang wu xiang yuanze: cujin heping fazhan" (Uphold five principles and promote peace and development), June 28, 2004, http://www.fmprc.gov.cn/chn/wjdt/zyjh/t140781.htm.

[p] "Statement by H.E. Tang Jiaxuan, Minister of Foreign Affairs of the People's Republic of China, and Head of the Chinese Delegation, at the General Debate of the 57th Session of the United Nations Gener." September 13, 2002, http://www.fmprc.gov.cn/eng/wjdt/zyjh/t25092.htm.

[q] "Multilateralism, the Way to Respond to Threats and Challenges: Statement by H.E. Mr. Qian Qichen, Former Vice Premier of China at the New Delhi Conference." July 2, 2004, http://www.fmprc.gov.cn/eng/wjdt/zyjh/t142393.htm.

not be in the interest of a sound world economy if the laws of the marketplace were given a free rein to dominate globalization. The international community needs to reform the current rules in the world economy, strengthen guidance and management of the globalization process, take account of fairness and reduce risks while seeking efficiency, and steer globalization in an "all-win" direction of coexistence."[r]

To the Chinese Government, dialog and cooperation is the preferred way to deal with world problems. As Premier Wen stated, it is time to abandon the old cold war mentality and develop a new way of thinking on the basis of mutual trust, mutual benefit, equality, and cooperation. The international community should seek security through dialog and stability through cooperation. It should work together to fight against terrorism, proliferation of weapons, drug smuggling, and other forms of transnational crimes. It should also join hands in dealing with such global problems as aids and ecological degradation.[s]

Finally, the Chinese Government has reaffirmed its position that it will not seek hegemony even when it becomes strong and powerful. In his speech at the second annual meeting of the Bo'ao Forum, Premier Wen Jiabao announced that one should rest assured that a dynamic, strong and prosperous China will be dedicated to world peace and development and will never seek hegemony.[t]

In sum, peace, development, harmony, cultural and political diversity, common development, and rule of law, these are the goals and objectives the Chinese Government tells the world that it wishes to promote. Dialog and cooperation is its preferred means to attain these objectives. Even when China becomes strong, China would not seek hegemony. Therefore, the rise of China does not pose any danger; instead, it holds much promise for a better world.

2. Addressing Specific Concerns

Aside from clarifying the broad objectives of its foreign policy, the Chinese Government has also sought to address the specific concerns of the outside

---

[r] "Statement by H.E. Tang Jiaxuan, Minister of Foreign Affairs of the People's Republic of China, and Head of the Chinese Delegation, at the General Debate of the 57th Session of the United Nations Gener," September 13, 2002, http://www.fmprc.gov.cn/eng/wjdt/zyjh/t25092.htm.

[s] Wen Jiabao, "Hongyang wu xiang yuanze: cujin heping fazhan" (Uphold five principles and promote peace and development), June 28, 2004, http://www.fmprc.gov.cn/chn/wjdt/zyjh/t140781.htm.

[t] Wen Jiabao, "Yong bu chengba de zhongguo jiang wei yazhou zhenxing zuochu xin gongxian" (the China that never seeks hegemony will make new contributions to the rise of Asia), November 2, 2003, http://finance.sina.com.cn/g/20031102/1129501516.shtml.

world on many issues. On the question of terrorism, the Chinese Government has repeatedly stated that it is opposed to terrorism. Shen Guofang, Assistant Foreign Minister, said at the Opening Session of ASEM Seminar on Anti-Terrorism on September 22, 2003, "As a victim of terrorism, China has firmly supported and actively participated in the international campaign against terrorism while pushing for the leading role of the UN in this regard." He said that China "has earnestly implemented the relevant Security Council resolutions and acceded to most counter-terrorism conventions. China has advocated vigorous regional anti-terrorism cooperation and conducted fruitful bilateral cooperation with countries concerned. China has also stepped up within our competent departments the crackdown on terrorism, including measures in legislation, aviation, finance, customs and other fields with a view to preventing terrorist incidents."[u]

On the question of non-proliferation, the Chinese Government has repeatedly stated it is committed to this. According to Vice Foreign Minister Zhang Yesui, the Chinese Government is firmly opposed to the proliferation of weapons of mass destruction and their means of delivery. He said that China has already set up a complete system of laws and regulations on export control "covering various kinds of sensitive technologies and items in nuclear, biological, chemical and missile fields, employed universally practiced export control measures including the end user/use certificate, licensing system, control list and catch-all, and introduced clear-cut punishment measures against acts in breach of the relevant laws and regulations." As a result of these efforts, China's non-proliferation export control practice is "basically in line with such mechanisms as MTCR and NSG and the practice of the US."[v]

On the question of regional security mechanisms, the Chinese Government has voiced its full support to efforts at institutionalizing regional security cooperation. For example, China has endorsed the 10 + 3 Cooperation Mechanism between ASEAN and China, Japan and the ROK. It commended the mechanism for respecting "the diversity of national conditions and the unevenness in the level of economic development of various countries," following "such principles as mutual benefit, incremental progress and stressing

---

[u] "Speech by H.E. Mr. Shen Guofang, Assistant Foreign Minister of China, at the Opening Session of ASEM Seminar on Anti-Terrorism," September 22, 2003, http://www.fmprc.gov.cn/eng/wjdt/zyjh/t26278.htm.
[v] "Speech by Vice Foreign Minister Zhang Yesui at the Fifth China-US Conference on Arms Control, Disarmament and Non-Proliferation," July 20, 2004, http://www.fmprc.gov.cn/eng/wjdt/zyjh/t143538.htm.

on practical results," and also giving "full consideration to the interests of all parties, the small and medium-sized countries in particular, which makes it unique among regional cooperation mechanisms in the world."[w]

On the question of human rights', the Chinese Government has made clear its intention to improve its human rights situation and engage in international efforts to promote human rights on a basis of equality and mutual respect. According to Vice Foreign Minister Wang Guangya, human beings are "the most precious among all things on earth." "To promote their development and protect all their due rights is not only the common pursuit of mankind, but also the symbol for the evolving progress of human civilization. For hundreds and thousands of years, people of all lands have made unremitting efforts to ensure the fundamental rights and freedoms for themselves."[x] Speaking about China's human rights situation, the Chinese Government acknowledges that it is "not perfect." In the words of Wang Guangya, China still has "a long way to go before human rights and fundamental freedoms are fully realized." However, he said that the Chinese Government and Chinese people will be "firmly and unswervingly committed to such a goal." China stands ready to strengthen dialogues and exchanges, on the basis of equality and mutual respect with all countries, the Office of the UN High Commissioner for Human Rights (UNHCHR) and other international organizations "with a positive and open attitude, with a view to learning from each other and making common progress."[y]

On the question of international economic relations, the Chinese Government has proposed the idea of establishing "a global partnership geared to development." In his speech at the General Debate of the 57th Session of the United Nations General Assembly on September 13, 2002, Chinese Foreign Minister Tang Jiaxuan said, "Governments, international organizations, transnational corporations, and non-governmental groups are all parties to the cause of development and should work together for the implementation

---

[w] "Premier Zhu Rongji Attended the 5th Leaders' Meeting between the Association of Southeast Asian Nations (ASEAN) and China, Japan and the Republic of Korea and Issued A Speech," November 5, 2001, http://www.fmprc.gov.cn/eng/wjdt/zyjh/t25045.htm.

[x] "Make Joint Efforts Towards a Healthy Development of the Cause of Human Rights: Statement by Vice Foreign Minister Wang Guangya at the 58th Session of the United Nations Commission on Human Rights," Geneva, April 2, 2002, http://www.fmprc.gov.cn/eng/wjdt/zyjh/t25072.htm.

[y] "Make Joint Efforts Towards a Healthy Development of the Cause of Human Rights: Statement by Vice Foreign Minister Wang Guangya at the 58th Session of the United Nations Commission on Human Rights," Geneva, April 2, 2002, http://www.fmprc.gov.cn/eng/wjdt/zyjh/t25072.htm.

of the UNs millennium development goals. Between the South and the North, the aid recipient countries and international aid institutions, there should be a partnership characterized by mutual benefit, equality, and cooperation."[z]

Addressing international concerns over China's growing economic competitiveness, the Chinese Government says that the development of China not only poses challenges to the outside world but also offers fresh opportunities. Premier Zhu Rongji said at 5th China-ASEAN Summit on November 6, 2001, China's accession to the WTO would "not only give a new impetus to China's economic development but also provide other countries. . . with better environment for investment and more business opportunities."[aa] According to Wen Jiabao, "China's growth will provide enormous business opportunities for all countries and regions of the world."[bb]

Similarly, Hu Jintao said, "A more prosperous China is destined to offer more business opportunities to the rest of the world." "It will take part in international economic and technological cooperation and competition with still greater depth, in still more areas, and at still higher levels." He pointed out that "China's WTO accession has resulted in further improvement in its investment environment." He promised that China would "keep its market open by reducing access restrictions, improving our laws and regulations on foreign investment and making more services and trade available to foreign investors." It would "create new ways of attracting foreign investment, and push for greater reform in government administrative system by building a predictable and more transparent management system for sectors open to foreign investment." And it would "protect still more effectively the intellectual property rights of overseas investors and their enterprises in China and provide a better environment and more favorable terms to both foreign investment in China and China's foreign trade and economic cooperation with the other countries."[cc]

---

[z] "Statement by H.E. Tang Jiaxuan, Minister of Foreign Affairs of the People's Republic of China, and Head of the Chinese Delegation, at the General Debate of the 57th Session of the United Nations Gener," September 13, 2002, http://www.fmprc.gov.cn/eng/wjdt/zyjh/t25092.htm.

[aa] "Working Together to Create a New Phase of China-ASEAN Cooperation–Address by Premier Zhu Rongji at 5th China-ASEAN Summit," November 6, 2001, http://www.fmprc.gov.cn/eng/wjdt/zyjh/t25046.htm.

[bb] Wen Jiabao, "Strengthening Partnership Through Increased Dialogue and Cooperation: Speech at the Fifth Asia-Europe Meeting," October 9, 2004, http://www.fmprc.gov.cn/eng/wjdt/zyjh/t164329.htm.

[cc] Hu Jintao, "Advancing Win–Win Cooperation for Sustainable Development: Speech by President Hu Jintao of China At the APEC CEO Summit," November 19, 2004, http://www.fmprc.gov.cn/eng/wjdt/zyjh/t172475.htm.

On the question of environmental protection, the Chinese Government states that it attaches great importance to it and expresses its determination to do more in this regard. Premier Zhu Rongji said at the World Summit on Sustainable Development on September 3, 2002, "We in China will, as always, energetically participate in international environment cooperation and work with all other countries in protecting global environment and realizing sustainable development throughout the world."[dd]

On the question of Korean nuclear crisis, the Chinese Government has stated that it is opposed to nuclearization of the Korean peninsula and supports peaceful resolution of the crisis. Premier Wen said that China advocates for a nuclear-free Peninsula and a peaceful solution of the DPRK nuclear issue with diplomatic means, to maintain peace and stability of the Peninsula.[ee]

Finally, on the question of the Taiwan problem, the Chinese Government has made it clear that even though the Taiwan problem is a domestic issue, it will take into account of other countries concerns and interests and make utmost efforts to seek a peaceful resolution. In his visit to the US, Premier Wen told President Bush that China would try its best with utmost sincerity to achieve the peaceful reunification of the motherland.[ff]

3. Cooperation

In part to back up its assurances, the Chinese Government has engaged in international security cooperation in the spirit of its new security concept, that is, "mutual trust, mutual benefit, equality and coordination."[gg] To begin with, it has assumed many legally binding international responsibilities through subscribing to international agreements and covenants. On the question of arms control, for example, it is a party of the Protocol for the Prohibition of the Use in War of Asphyxiating, Poisonous or Other Gases, and of Bacteriological

---

[dd] Zhu Rongji, "Steadfastly Take the Road of Sustainable Development: Speech by H.E. Mr. Zhu Rongji, Premier of the State Council of the People's Republic of China, at the World Summit on Sustainable Development," September 3, 2002, http://www.fmprc.gov.cn/eng/wjdt/zyjh/t25091.htm.

[ee] "Premier Wen Jiabao Holds Talks with the US President Bush," December 10, 2003, http://www.china-un.org/eng/xw/t56088.htm.

[ff] "Premier Wen Jiabao Holds Talks with the US President Bush," December 10, 2003, http://www.china-un.org/eng/xw/t56088.htm.

[gg] http://www.fas.org/nuke/guide/china/doctrine/natdef2004.html#5.

Methods of Warfare, the Convention on Prohibition or Restriction on the Use of Certain Conventional Weapons Which May Be Deemed to Be Excessively Injurious or to Have Indiscriminate Effects, the Antarctic Treaty, the Treaty on Principles Governing the Activities of States in the Exploration and Use of Outer Space, Including the Moon and Other Celestial Bodies, the Convention on the Prohibition of the Development, Production and Stockpiling of Bacteriological (Biological) and Toxin Weapons and on Their Destruction, the Treaty on the Prohibition of the Emplacement of Nuclear Weapons and Other Weapons of Mass Destruction on the Seabed and the Ocean Floor and in the Subsoil Thereof, and the Treaty on the Non-Proliferation of Nuclear Weapons. China has also subscribed to the Convention on the Prohibition of the Development, Production, Stockpiling and Use of Chemical Weapons and on Their Destruction.[hh]

In the second place, China has made significant efforts to improve security relations with its neighbors. It has concluded several border agreements with its neighbors including Russia, Kazakhstan, Tajikistan, Kyrgyzstan, and Vietnam. It has stepped up border negotiations with India. It has also established the Shanghai Cooperation Organization together with Russia and Kazakhstan, Tajikistan, Kyrgyzstan, and Uzbekistan to maintain and promote political, economic, and security cooperation among these countries. It has even refrained from undertaking strong reactions to repeated provocations from the Japanese rightists and Government to take unilateral actions to impose control on the Diaoyu Island, a Chinese territory in China's view.

In the third place, China has increased its support to multilateral cooperation both at the global and regional levels. In recent years, it has sharply increased its financial contribution to the UN.[ii] It has participated in an increasing number of UN peace-keeping operations.[jj] It has taken part

---

[hh] Information Office of the State Council of the People's Republic of China, "China: Arms Control and Disarmament," November 1995, http://www.china.org.cn/e-white/army/a-7.htm.

[ii] China's share of the UN membership fee was increased to 2% of the total UN member fee, making China the 9th largest contributor to the UN in 2003. http://www.un.org/chinese/av/radio/transcript/china031225.htm.

[jj] "China's representative said his country's assessment for 2004–2006 would increase by 35.18 per cent over the last period.... Not only had China fulfilled its financial obligations to the Organisation, but as a permanent member of the Security Council it had also assumed additional financial obligations towards peace-keeping." UN Press Release, GA/AB/3576, http://www.un.org/News/Press/docs/2003/gaab3576.doc.htm.

in international counter-terrorism cooperations. It has promoted military exchanges in various forms. It has worked to establish security dialog mechanisms such as the six-party talks on the Korean nuclear crisis. It has taken part in "bilateral or multilateral joint military exercises in non-traditional security fields."[kk] It has also actively participated in regional security mechanisms such as ASEAN Regional Forum and many second-track security dialogues.

In the fourth place, China made significant concessions to join the WTO and has made many efforts to fulfill its commitments. It has repealed, revised or enacted more than 1000 laws, regulations and other administrative measures in its efforts to comply WTO requirements.[ll] It has lowered its trade tariffs, reduced thresholds for foreign investment in previously restricted sectors, and given greater access to foreign presence in financial, legal and other previously closed sectors in China.[mm] China has concluded agreements on establishing free trade area with ASEAN countries and is engaged in negotiations on establishment of free trade areas with more than a dozen other countries.[nn]

Finally, China has tried to promote peaceful settlement of the Korean nuclear crisis. Ever since tension over the alleged North Korean nuclear program escalated, the Chinese Government has tried to bring the concerned parties together and push for a peaceful settlement of the problem. It conducted shuttle diplomacy between Washington, Pyongyang, Seoul, Moscow, and other capitals. And it has successively hosted several rounds of six party talks.

To sum up, China's security policy has three aspects: capability, assurance, and cooperation. It has become more sophisticated and nuanced both in rhetoric and in implementation over time. Its central objective is to develop a strong and effective military capable of providing sufficient security to China and acceptable to the international community.

[kk] http://www.fas.org/nuke/guide/china/doctrine/natdef2004.html#5.

[ll] US Trade Representative, 2004 Report to Congress on China's WTO Compliance, p.3. http://www.cecc.gov/pages/virtualAcad/commercial/USTR.china.2004.pdf?PHPSESSID=fdbf190484029bff1b8d5fb0881d1c2d; "Zhongguo jiji lvxing jiaru shimao zuzhi youguan falv chengnuo" (China actively live up to its commitments to WTO accession), December 12, 2002, http://news.xinhuanet.com/newscenter/2002 12/02/content_647029.htm.

[mm] "Zhongguo-shimao" (China and WTO), http://www.china.org.cn/chinese/zhuanti/2004zgjk/655334. htm.

[nn] "Zhongguo qidong she 23 guo ziyou maoyiqu tanpan" (China has engaged in talks on fta with 23 countries), January 10, 2005, Qilu Evening News, http://news.sina.com.cn/c/2005-01-10/07324772055s.shtml.

4. Factors Shaping China's Security Policy

Five factors are believed important in shaping China's current security policy: (1) revolution in military affairs; (2) perceived increasing security challenges to China; (3) China's political and economic integration with the outside world; (4) evolution in China's view of its relations with the rest of the world; and (5) the need to assuage the fear about the implications of the rise of China.

4.1. *Revolution in military affairs*

In addition to crushing the Iraqi military forces, the Gulf War in 1991 demonstrated to the world that a revolution was taking place in military affairs. High-tech has fundamentally changed the way war is fought: the effective command, the high degree of coordination of various forces, the precision in the attacks especially air strikes, the smart bombs, the asymmetry of war. As the Chinese military analysts put it, "The forms of war are undergoing changes from mechanization to informationalization. Informationalization has become the key factor in enhancing the warfighting capability of the armed forces. Confrontation between systems has become the principal feature of confrontation on the battlefield. Asymmetrical, non-contiguous and non-linear operations have become important patterns of operations."[oo]

All this left the Chinese Government with a deep impression. If the significant increase of defence spending in 1989 and 1990 represented a reward to the PLA for standing firmly on the side of the Chinese Government during the political crisis in 1989, the continued high rate of growth in defence spending since 1991 reflects the keen awareness of the security vulnerability of China in face of the revolution in military affairs. As China's 2004 Defence White Paper puts it, "The world's major countries are making readjustments in their security and military strategies and stepping up transformation of their armed forces by way of developing high-tech weaponry and military equipment and putting forth new military doctrines. As a result, the generation gap in military technology between informationalization on the one hand and mechanization and semi-mechanization on the other is still widening, and military imbalance

---

[oo] http://www.fas.org/nuke/guide/china/doctrine/natdef2004.html#5.

worldwide has further increased. The role played by military power in safe-guarding national security is assuming greater prominence."[PP] Accordingly, China has no alternative but to keep up with this historical trend in order to maintain its security.

4.2. *Increasing security challenges*

In addition to the revolution in military affairs, the increasing security chal-lenges China has been confronted with has reconfirmed the necessity to make greater efforts to enhance its defence capabilities. In the late 1980s and early 1990s, the collapse of the Soviet Union and abandonment of communism by the former communist camp left China as one of the few remaining coun-tries adhering to the communist system and greatly encouraged the West in its efforts to propagate, and impose when it saw fit, its version of democracy to the rest of the world. As the anti-Soviet strategic logic for US cooperation with China disappeared, the US Government began to focus on the differ-ences between the two countries and to apply increasing pressures on China to make political changes according to US standards. Finally, the outbreak of the Tiananmen Incident in 1989 brought international outrage and furore against China. Under the circumstances, China's international security environment sharply worsened. Against this backdrop that the Chinese Government felt it needed to strengthen its military capabilities to cope with the perceived security challenges.

Before the previously discussed security challenges discussed subsided, another and even more threatening security problem emerged. Having con-solidated his power, Lee Teng-hui, the head of the Taiwan authorities, began to show his true colors as a Taiwan separatist. Among other things, he had been pushing for the so-called pragmatic diplomacy, which called for promotion of Taiwan's ties with foreign countries through an active and flexible approach so as to gain broader international recognition of Taiwan's separate "sovereign statehood." In doing so, the Taiwan authorities had used aid and bribes to lure the potential target countries. In this respect, no other country represented a greater prize than the US. Lee Teng-hui figured that his independence cause would be greatly advanced if he could get the US change its one China policy.

[PP] http://www.fas.org/nuke/guide/china/doctrine/natdef2004.html#5.

Through careful manipulation, he managed to get the Clinton Administration to issue a visa to him to visit the US, a decision that led to the outbreak of the Taiwan Strait crisis in 1995 and 1996. During the crisis, China and the United States found themselves in a military standoff in the Taiwan Strait in the wake of China's military exercises there to deter Taiwan separatism and protest against the perceived American encouragement. For the first time since the Sino-American rapprochement in the early 1970s, the militaries of the two countries confronted each other face to face. To the Chinese Government, the double security threat from the Taiwan separatism and US military intervention highlighted not only the necessity but also the urgency to enhance its defence capabilities.

Then as Chinese economy continued to expand and China's international influence increase, especially despite the Asian financial crisis, China found itself confronted with an even more challenging security problem: the US concern and worry with the rise of China. Quite a few Americans subscribe the view of offensive realism[qq] and believe that conflict between the interests of the established power and those of the rising is irreconcilable. The US is the established power and China the rising one. And given the current trend of development in China, China is bound to threaten US interests and challenge its position in world affairs. Thus writes an offensive realist scholar, "Over time... China could become the most powerful rival the United States has ever faced."[rr] The sentiment also finds expression in the most recent Quadrennial Defence Review Report of the US Defence Department: "Although the United States will not face a peer competitor in the near future, the potential exists for regional powers to develop sufficient capabilities to threaten stability in regions critical to US interests."[ss]

Although this view is not held by the majority of Americans, it is quite popular in Washington and has a significant impact on the Bush Administration's approach to China. Confronted with a US that vowed to do "whatever it takes" to deny Taiwan to China, the Chinese Government knew that the only way it could defend its territorial integrity and sovereignty was to boost its

---

[qq]The term is borrowed from the title of a study group meeting of the Council on Foreign Relations held on December 1998 in New York. http://www.cfr.org/public/resource.cgi?meet!1646#

[rr]Mearsheimer, J.J. (2001). "The Future of the American Pacifier," *Foreign Affairs*, 80(15), September/October. http://www.foreignaffairs.org/20010901faessay5569/john-j-mearsheimer/the-future-of-the-american-pacifier.html.

[ss]Department of DefenceDefence, Quadrennial DefenceDefence Review Report, September 30, 2001, p. 4.

military capabilities. The outbreak of the 9/11 helped reduce the US threat to China for a number of years in part because it diverted the US attention away from China. However, as China's rise continued, the Bush Administration is redirecting its attention to the so-called China threat. Among other things, the Bush Administration has been strengthened its military alliance with Japan with a view to contain China. The reference of most recent statement on the part of the Bush Administration and Japanese Government to Taiwan caused many Chinese concern about a joint US–Japan military intervention in the Taiwan Strait should a crisis occur there. This has given an additional reason for the Chinese Government to enhance its military capabilities.

4.3. *China's political and economic integration with the outside world*

If previously discussed security challenges have encouraged China to enhance its military capabilities, China's political and economic integration with the outside world has given China strong incentives to define its relations with the outside world in a constructive and positive manner. Following China's rapprochement with the United States in the early 1970s, China established diplomatic relations with most countries in the world and joined most important international governmental organizations. Meanwhile, especially after 1979, China's economic relations with the outside world increased rapidly. The increasing political and economic linkages between China and the outside world have given China normal channels to express its views, defend its legitimate interests, and promote reforms of the existing international order. This development has reduced the distrust and hostility China used to harbor toward that order as a result of its bitter experience in the first two decades of the People's Republic and given China a sense of identity with the existing international order. Meanwhile, as time wore on, China also developed the expertise and experience to take advantage of the opportunities offered by the existing international institutions to defend and facilitate China's interests and aspirations. This includes reform of existing rules and formulation of new rules for proper international behavior. Finally, increasing economic relations between China and the outside world have given China an ever larger stake in international stability and prosperity.

The rise of China has attracted much international attention since 1993. Some have made use of it to advocate the China threat thesis. However, the immediate impact of the rise of China is harmonization of interests between China and the rest of the world. To begin with, the rise of China is part and parcel of a process of China's integration with the international order. Such a process has given China an increasing stake in international stability and prosperity. In addition, as China's interests are increasingly brought in line with those of the international community, more and more Chinese have given up the view that the existing international system poses an insurmountable obstacle to China's development and prosperity. Rather they begin to see important opportunities of development the system offers. Consequently they no longer feel necessary to challenge the system as they used to before. Moreover, to increasing number of Chinese, the experience of China's rise has demonstrated that international stability is a precondition for China's further development. Therefore, as China's relations with the rest of the world become closer, China also increasingly sees the maintenance of international stability as essential to its own interests. Under the circumstances, although Chinese still believe that the existing international system can be unequal and unfair and will continue to press for its reforms, they are more and more inclined to make greater efforts to maintain the stability of the system.[tt] All this has encouraged China to be an increasingly active participant in multilateral activities and play an ever supportive role in the existing international arrangements.[uu]

4.4. *Evolution in China's view of its relations with the rest of the world*

China's changing perceptions of its relations with the outside world has also enhanced its resolve to approach to international problems in a constructive way. As China's interactions with the rest of the world increases, China's view of international relations has undergone three successive and broad changes: (1) from viewing international relations in ideological terms[vv] to

---

[tt]After the end of the cold war, the Chinese Government has made many efforts to maintain peace and stability in the world and the Asia-Pacific region such as participation in the Cambodian peacekeeping operations, cooperation with various parties in search of a peaceful solution of the Korean problem, observation and promotion of the international non-proliferation regime, joining the nuclear test ban treaty, and taking various constructive measures to cope with the on-going Asian financial crisis.

[uu]At the moment, China is a strong supporter of the United Nations system. See 1997: Guoji xingshi nianjian (1997: Yearbook on international situations) (Shanghai: Shanghai Jiaoyu Publishing House, 1997), p. 111.

[vv]Here the concept "ideology" is defined narrowly to refer to Marxist or Communist ideology.

viewing it in more conventional terms; (2) from viewing international relations as a zero-sum game to viewing it as a positive-sum game; and (3) from suspicion and hostility toward the international system to identifying with it. These attitudinal changes have in turn influenced China's conceptualization of its relations with the outside world and the definition of the goals and objectives of its security policy.

4.5. *The need to assuage the fear about the implications of the rise of China*

While it is entirely understandable that the rise of China, a very large country, has caused much uncertainty and concern on the part of the international community, China is fully aware of the fact that suspicion and hostility on the part of the international community of China threatens to undermine China's peaceful international environment and China's efforts at modernization. Accordingly, the Chinese Government has spared no efforts to reassure the international community that the rise of China does not only present challenges but more important opportunities. One significant attempt in this regard is the short-term promotion of the peaceful rise argument. Although the term is no longer used in official rhetoric, the Chinese Government has made it clear that it wants its rise or development to be peaceful.

In sum, the perceived revolution in military affairs and growing security challenges have contributed to China's increasing efforts to enhance its defence capabilities. China's international integration and changing perceptions of the nature of its relations with the outside world have helped shape the way China reassure the international community and engage in international cooperation. The rising international concern over the rise of China has made it necessary for China to step up its efforts to reassure the international community of China's benign intentions and of the benefits of the rise of China.

5. Future Prospects

Will the Chinese Government adhere to the security policy outlined in the previous passages? Analysis of the factors shaping this policy appears to show that it will. To begin with, the revolution in military affairs is going on unabated. Major Powers in the world are busy developing newer and more destructive weapons and perfecting C^{4}I systems. The Chinese Government will continue to feel the urgency to keep up with the change so as to maintain an adequate level defence for China.

In the second place, given the still large gap between Chinese military capabilities and those of the more developed countries and the growing security challenges to China's security as outlined in the previous passages, more likely than not, the Chinese Government is going to maintain the current level of growth in defence spending if not to increase it in the foreseeable future.

In the third place, as China's integration with the outside world deepens and its view of its relations with the outside world assuming a non-zero sum nature, China is likely to continue to define its interests and advocate policies basically consistent with the interests of the international community. This will continue to be a defining feature of China's security strategy.

Finally, as China's rise continues, the need for China to reassure the international community is likely to grow. In response, China is likely to make more efforts in the days to come to reassure the international community that its rise presents more opportunities than challenges.

In conclusion, China believes that its current security policy serves both its own interests and those of the international community and is likely to adhere to it in the foreseeable future.

CHAPTER 11

India in the International Order: Challenger and Stabilizer

Kanti Prasad Bajpai

As an emerging power, India will be consequential for the international system. India's conception of its ambitions and security in certain respects challenges global norms supported by the major powers, especially the United States. In particular, India's nuclear program, its desire to be a permanent veto member of the UN Security Council, its need for modern technology, its wish to sit at the high table of Asian security discussions, and its preference for a South Asian order in which it is dominant all challenge norms that have been globalized over the past decade.

At the same time, India is a pluralistic, constitutional, democratic polity, a liberalizing economy of great potential, a country that is a target of terrorism, and a possible counterweight to the emerging superpower-in-the-making, China. India has improved relations with all the major powers and is interested in a greater diffusion of power in the international system as well as greater consultations between the major powers. India is also therefore a force for stability and a potential collaborator.

Which way India develops in the years to come will depend on the extent to which some of India's hopes and ambitions are realized at the international level, its regional ties improve, and its domestic politics remain open and inclusive.

Before we deal with ambivalent India in relation to the international order, we should be clear what is meant by international order in this essay. The term "international order" is used here to describe the set of values, rules, practices, and institutions that are promoted and defended primarily by the US and its allies.

1. India as Challenger

India appears as a challenge to the international order in five ways:

- its determination to maintain a nuclear weapons program;
- its desire to enter the Security Council as a permanent member with all the rights and obligations of that position;
- its need for modern technology, including defence technology;
- its wish to sit at the high table of Asian security;
- its preference for a South Asian regional order in which it is dominant.

2. A Nuclear Weapons Power

India is determined to maintain a nuclear weapons program. It is clear that the international system led by the United States and the other P-5 as well as other major centers of power (such as Japan) are distinctly uncomfortable with India's desire for nuclear arms. At best they could have lived with an Indian capability that was non-weaponized, that is, roughly where India was before the tests of 1998. India with the scientific knowledge to build weapons, with a fissile material stock, with some missiles (preferably of very modest payloads and ranges), and perhaps even some untested nuclear weapons was tolerable. More than that is worrisome for the major powers. The Indian program might be unsafe and therefore prone to accidents and accidental use. It may legitimize the acquisition of nuclear weapons by others, less stable than India, such as Pakistan, Iran, and North Korea. It may be insufficiently protected and could therefore be at risk of pilferage and unauthorized transfers. It might come to challenge the second tier nuclear powers in terms of size and sophistication. And, perhaps most importantly, it might lead to a confrontation with a nuclear Pakistan or even China, with risks for the entire international community as a result.[a]

---

[a]The United States had led the campaign against the Indian nuclear program. While the Bush Administration has said that it does not want to hold the US–India relationship captive to non-proliferation issues, it is clear that Washington still does not altogether endorse New Delhi's nuclear weapons plans. "The India–US Joint Statement," issued in July 2005 during Prime Minister Manmohan Singh's visit to Washington, indicates that India has committed itself to a moratorium on testing and pledged to work with the US on a fissile material cutoff, both of which will certainly play a role in limiting India's nuclear options. At the same time, Washington is pledged to help India with its civilian nuclear program. For an assessment of the agreements, from various Indian perspectives, see *Economic and Political Weekly* (Mumbai), **XL**(32)

India's motives in building and expanding a nuclear weapons program are complex. Officially, nuclear weapons are for deterrence against other nuclear weapons states, principally, Pakistan and China. There are strategic analysts who think that, in the long run, the program must be big and sophisticated enough to deal with all nuclear-armed states including the United States.[b] While New Delhi is silent on the United States as a potential adversary, it should not be forgotten that the decision to test in 1974 was related to the US's show of force in the Bay of Bengal in 1971 during the India–Pakistan war — or at least, this is a widespread perception of the tests, amongst Indian officials and armed forces personnel. Nuclear weapons also bring prestige and the reputation for (if not the substance of) power, and they are therefore regarded in India as a vital resource in a world that continues to be ordered, at some level, by military power.[c] Nuclear weapons are also a bargaining chip. There is a school of thought in India that testing and developing nuclear weapons was necessary in order to gain the attention of a world that increasingly was not paying attention to India. In this view, after the Cold War, India had become a marginal player in spite of its economic liberalization and its greater salience in multilateral efforts and institutions such as peacekeeping and the Conference on Disarmament (CD). Nuclear weapons "crashed" a largely inattentive international system and forced the big powers, once their outrage at the tests had subsided, to consider how India might be made a more satisfied power.[d]

However questionable these views of the utility of nuclear weapons may be for those engaging India, they are a living, existential reality for Indian policy makers and negotiators. Nuclear weapons are still seen as crucial for Indian defence. They continue to vivify India's preoccupation with status. And they

---

(August 6–12, 2005), pp. 3577–3591. Selling the deal to the US Congress has already run into heavy weather. As the pressure on the Bush Administration has grown, it has insisted that India must show progress on separating the civilian and military part of its nuclear program before the US can move to honor its part of the deal more fully. The US has begun to talk to other nuclear powers about the resumption of nuclear trading with India, so Washington has not been altogether idle in terms of working on the deal.

[b] Bharat Karnad (2002). *Nuclear Weapons and Indian Security: The Realist Foundations of Strategy*. New Delhi: Macmillan India, pp. 446–701.

[c] See Amitabh Mattoo (1999). "India's Nuclear Policy in an Anarchic World." In: Amitabh Mattoo (ed.) *India's Nuclear Deterrent: Pokhran II and Beyond*. New Delhi: Har Anand, pp. 12–14.

[d] C. Raja Mohan (2003). *Crossing the Rubicon*. New Delhi: Penguin India, pp. 89–96, in a section titled "Nuclear Defiance and Reconciliation."

are still regarded as bargaining chips in the sense that Indian decisions in the longer term regarding the size and nature of its weapons program could be influenced by the international system's responses on other issues of importance to India.

3. Permanent Seat on the Security Council

India also challenges international order in respect of its desire to be a veto-bearing member of the Security Council. New Delhi's reaction, over the past decade, to UN reforms has varied. In the middle to late 1990s, New Delhi evinced a fair degree of interest in promoting India's case for a place on the Security Council, with full rights and obligations, along side the P-5. That India did not get voted into the Security Council at that time, and was there-after considered a poor second to Japan and others, was a blow to New Delhi's diplomacy and caused it to withdraw from active lobbying. In 2004–2005, New Delhi overcame its hesitations. Its reaction to the UN report on reforms was indicative of its determination to be a serious candidate. It haughtily turned down the idea of anything less than full veto membership in the Security Council and engaged Brazil, Germany, and Japan to evolve a common stand on the issue.[e] It also lined up friends and allies: every visiting statesman who declared his or her country's support for India's position was given a fair degree of publicity.[f]

India's case for full permanent membership in the UN is, like its case for going nuclear, quite complex. International status is certainly a motive. The

---

[e] India, Brazil, Germany, and Japan constitute the so-called G-4 that have argued that there ought to be more veto-bearing members of the UN Security Council and that they are the best candidates in any expansion of permanent membership.

[f] Most recently, the Indian press reported that Singapore had supported India's candidacy. See Raakhee Suryaprakash, "Singapore–India Relations: CECA and Beyond." *South Asia Analysis Group*, Paper No. 1493, 18 August 2005, downloaded from http://www.saag.org/%5Cpaper1493.html. Singapore opposed veto membership for the new entrants. US officials have opposed the veto for new permanent members and openly named Japan as their first choice in any expansion of permanent membership. See Joel Brinkley, "US Rules Out a Veto for New Council Seats." *International Herald Tribune*, Americas, May 16, 2005, downloaded from http://www.iht.com/articles/2005/05/15/news/un-5034135.php. On the veto, see also "US Opposes UN Council Reform Plan." *BBC News*, UK Edition, downloaded from http://news.bbc.co.uk/1/hi/world/americas/4677545.stm.

desire to shape the international order is another. Diplomatic protection is a third reason. During the Cold War, India at various times could count on the UK, US, and, most enduringly, the Soviet Union to use the veto in its favor. After the Cold War, India had no friends in high places. At the same time, India was increasingly under scrutiny after the Cold War. India was pilloried publicly for its handling of the Punjab and then Kashmir militancies and was embarrassed at fairly regular intervals about its human rights record. It was also the object of a newly-charged global non-proliferation drive led by the US but joined in substantial measure by the UK and various other European and non-European powers. Its economy too was criticized for being too protectionist. New Delhi does not like this vulnerability. As a permanent, veto-bearing member of the Security Council, it hopes to be able to exercise the veto in its own defence when required, mindful of the fact that it has no reliable protectors any more.

Does India have the credentials for permanent membership of the Security Council? Its overall size (population plus land area), its military power, its growing economic presence (reputedly the fourth biggest economy in terms of purchasing power parity), and its role as a good global citizen particularly in respect of peacekeeping are the basis for India's membership drive. Given that every fourth or fifth person in the world is Indian, it should be represented at the high table of global decision-making. With a million under arms, and land, sea, and air forces that can increasingly be projected outside of its own region, it could be an asset to the world beyond its present "Blue Helmet" UN role. Indian economic growth rates, at 6%, are amongst the highest in the world, and there is every reason to believe that it will maintain respectable rates. It must therefore be brought into economic decision-making at a global level. As a growing economic power, it should be in a position to increase its contributions to the UN as well. Lastly, India has been an integral part of UN peacekeeping operations at least since the 1960s and therefore the country has a record of good global citizenship that merits reward and encouragement. The size and competence of its military are resources for the international community. The skills of India's diplomats are worth a mention. Many are working in international bureaucracies and many others, as India's representatives, do play a constructive role in multilateral negotiations. It is worth mentioning in passing that India has, in addition, a historical claim on membership: millions of Indian soldiers fought in both the first and second world wars. India, though not independent, was a major part of the allied coalition that then went on to claim permanent membership in the Security Council.[g]

The reluctance of the big powers to give India membership is also based on quite a complex set of considerations. The Indian argument, namely, that the P-5 countries do not wish to allow India into the club because they want to keep India weak and in a position of supplication, is useful enough for domestic and international propaganda purposes, but it is not terribly accurate. P-5 concerns arise from the fact that a bigger veto-bearing club could paralyse the UN and the Security Council in particular.[h] The inclusion of Germany and Japan, which surely have strong claims, has various international and regional implications that are every bit as complicated as India's entry.[i] How far India's inclusion would legitimize the notion that countries can "crash" into the Security Council by testing nuclear weapons and thumbing their noses at the established international order is another concern of the P-5 and other states. India cannot dismiss these concerns, nor can the big powers ignore India's claims.

4. Access to Modern Technology

Over the past two decades, a fairly constant refrain in India has been its desire to access modern technology. Indian decision makers are convinced that the country has been the target of a campaign of denial by the developed economies.[j]

---

[g]The United States publicly listed several of the criteria listed above as governing its choice for a second permanent member of the Security Council after Japan. See *Ambassador Shirin Tahir-Kheli, Senior Advisor to the Secretary of State for UN Reform, on UN Reform, in the General Assembly, July 12, 2005*, USUN Press Release # 130 (05), July 12, 2005, downloaded from http://www.un.int/usa/05_130.htm. The criteria included size of economy and population, military capacity, contribution to peacekeeping operations, commitment to democracy and human rights, financial contribution to the UN, non-proliferation and counter-terrorism record, and geographic balance within the UN.

[h]For a typical statement, see Schaefer, B.D. (1997). "The United States Should Oppose Expansion of the UN Security Council." Backgrounder #1140, *The Heritage Foundation*, September 22, downloaded from http://www.heritage.org/Research/InternationalOrganisations/BG1140.cfm.

[i]The regional opposition alone is pretty formidable. Germany is opposed by various European powers but most stringently by Italy. Japan is opposed by China, Russia, and South Korea. Brazil is opposed principally by Argentina. And India is opposed by Pakistan.

[j]A typical statement of this view traces the roots back to British colonialism and the demands of empire: "The British rulers ensured that not only India missed the industrial revolution but remained technologically backward." See Raj Chengappa (2000). *Weapons of Peace: The Secret Story of India's Quest to be a Nuclear Power*. New Delhi: HarperCollins Publishers India, p. 63.

India's need for technology relates to both security and development. From independence, Indian leaders have held the view that the subjugation of India in the colonial period arose from technological inferiority.[k] India's defeat at the hands of the colonial powers was in the end a military failure based on inferior technology. At a deeper level, it was India's developmental backwardness, also based on its technological backwardness, that led to its undoing at the hands of Europeans. Indian leaders are determined therefore that modern India should never again be left behind technologically. India must be a technological power in its own right, which means government-backed research and development, private sector involvement in technology, and an educational system that produces first-rate scientists and engineers. However, at least this historical juncture and in crucial areas, India must rely on imports from the developed countries as well. Indians feel that the developing countries have a right to technology from the more advanced countries, as restitution for colonialism and as repayment for post-colonial economic exploitation of the developing countries.[l]

Indians are convinced that over the past 50 years the Western countries in particular have been niggardly about technology transfers to India. The West, Indians reason, has a number of reasons for denying India the technology it seeks. At the most general level, the West fears that a technologically sophisticated India may become a major economic power. In relation to dual-use technologies, India could use these to produce modern arms to compete with the West militarily as also commercially (through arms sales). Nuclear and missile related technology is a major concern here, but chemical and biological technologies also have military applications. The West harbors the view

---

[k] See Indiresan, P.V. (1999). "The Role of Science and Technology in India's National Security." In: Brahma Chellaney (ed.) *Securing India's Future in the New* Millennium. New Delhi: Orient Longman and Centre for Policy Research, p. 23 on how India is conquered and plundered repeatedly due to its technological backwardness. See the quote from former Indian National Security Adviser, Brajesh Mishra, in Chengappa, *Weapons of Peace*, p. 45: "If you look at Indian history we were defeated not because our soldiers were not brave enough. But because they lacked superior technology." It is another matter that this judgment is historically inaccurate. Indian military forces were quite sophisticated. On India's efforts at being technologically independent, see Baldev Raj Nayar (1983). *India's Quest for Technological Independence*, 2 vols. New Delhi: Lancer's.

[l] See Seema Gahlaut (1999). "Reenergising the Debate: Indo-US Nuclear Issues." In: Gary K. Bertsch, Seema Gahlaut and Anupam Srivastava (eds.) *Engaging India: US Strategic Relations with the World's Largest Democracy*. New York: Routledge, p. 120 on how technology is the right of the colonized given their exploitation by the Western colonial powers.

that Indians are not "safe" with advanced technology and might not use it "responsibly." A version of this argument is that Indians may transfer technology to others in violation of agreements with supplier countries. The West uses a variety of methods to deny India technology. It emphasizes national security worries and concerns over India's commitment to intellectual property rights. It resorts to global control regimes that cannot admit of "exceptions" (so India is not the explicit target of controls — it is the "bad guys" that are the locus of worry, but controls must apply to everyone, etc.). And it prices technologies out of India's reach.[m]

India is aware that for many years to come it must rely on Western technology for its security and development. Increasingly, it is willing to pay for technology and to reassure the Western states in respect of its use of technology. Its success in accessing technology has however been fairly limited. The nuclear tests of 1998 were a risk in this respect. The Western powers could make India's access to technology even more strenuous; or, in time, they could come round to the view that India could be restrained by a bargain on nuclear weapons in which technological access would be part of the deal. The liberalization of India's economy, New Delhi hopes, will also attract Western technology. Market forces, and the lure of India's market, the government hopes will persuade Western governments to find a way of circumventing technology controls and will cause them to overcome their prejudices or fears about India just as they dealt with a reformist China in the late 1970s.[n] Historically, India has tried to mobilize global opinion on the iniquities of technology controls. New Delhi argues that the West has a moral obligation to share technology. It also points out that the Western powers have double standards. They insist on free markets and unfettered trade as a general principle and then find ways

---

[m] For a summary of the typical concerns and worries of India on technology and technology controls, see for instance Richard T. Cupitt and Seema Gahlaut, "Non-Proliferation Export Controls: US and Indian Perspectives." In: Bertsch, Gahlaut, and Srivastava (eds.) *Engaging India*, pp. 169–190. On the US's unwillingness to deal with India as an exception even as it makes exceptions for Israel, Pakistan, and China, see Gahlaut, "Reenergising the Debate," pp. 120–121.

[n] Chengappa, *Weapons of Peace*, pp. 48–49 on the Indian government's calculations in 1998 on how the US would return to a more pragmatic agenda with India within 6 months of nuclear testing. At least one calculation was that the common worry about China would help reconcile US opinion to the Indian tests. It was this that led Prime Minister Atal Behari Vajpayee to write to President Bill Clinton, in the wake of the tests, claiming that China was a major factor in the decision to test. See Raja Mohan, *Crossing the Rubicon*, p. 90 on the argument in India that nuclear testing and defying the US "was absolutely necessary to transform both India's security condition and the long-term relationship with Washington."

to regulate market forces when it suits their interests. Indian analysts suggest that sharing technology is in the interest of the West itself. Technology will help the development of the rest of the world, which is an investment in global security and will serve the commercial interests of Western suppliers. Finally, India makes the case that if there are to be exceptions to the West's technology control regime, then India qualifies to be one because of its shared values with the West — democracy, pluralism, and the fight against authoritarian and extremist social forces. India is not a competitor for the West but rather a potential strategic ally.[o]

5. An Asian Security Role

In contrast to India's insistence on being a nuclear power and a permanent member of the Security Council, its interest in sitting at the high table of Asian security decision-making is hardly mentioned at all in polite company. Yet, India does increasingly see itself, along with China, Japan, Russia, and the US, as being an integral part of the development of a new Asian order.[p]

In the late 1950s and certainly by the mid-1960s, India's interest in playing a major role in Asian security outside of South Asia had waned. The debacle at Bandung in 1955, where the Chinese made great gains and where India often was criticized, was the beginning of New Delhi's retreat.[q] By the time the US had become involved in the Vietnam War, India was in further retreat. In 1967, when ASEAN was launched, India disdained the invitation to join, signalling that it had more or less abdicated any meaningful role in Southeast Asia. Strains with Japan that had been building since the late 1950s and the conflict with China in this period meant that India was no factor in Northeast Asia either. Of course, New Delhi's rather difficult relationship with Washington on several issues of Asian security helped deal it out of the international politics of Asia.[r]

---

[o] Raja Mohan, *Crossing the Rubicon*, pp. 57–115.
[p] Raja Mohan, *Crossing the Rubicon*, pp. 204–236 on India's Asian role.
[q] For a recent appraisal of the significance of Bandung and of India's positive role, see Amitav Acharya (2003–2004). "Will Asia's Past Be its Future?" *International Security* 28(3), 149–164.
[r] On India's relations with Southeast Asia and the rest of Asia, historically as well as post Cold War, see Christophe Jaffrelot (2003). "India's Look East Polic: An Asianist Strategy in Perspective." *India Review* 2(2), 35–68.

With the end of the Cold War, India has seen an opportunity to return to Asia. Its "look East" policy, active lobbying for ASEAN membership, acceptance of dialog partner status with ASEAN, participating in the ASEAN Regional Forum (ARF), and increasing economic ties with the region over the past decade have partially dealt it back into Asia. India has also developed a number of bilateral relationships — with Burma, Thailand, Laos, Cambodia, Vietnam, and Singapore, in particular. In addition, India has shown an interest in various regional efforts: an Indian Ocean community (this has petered out), a grouping consisting of Bangladesh, Burma, and Thailand, among others, and a free trade arrangements such as with Singapore. These regional involvements have been furthered by the deepening of cultural, economic, and military ties. The Indian Navy has been an arm of India's diplomacy. It has sought to dispel earlier suspicions of its growing reach by inviting regional navies to its naval galas, by making more ports of call (as far away as China), and by conducting joint exercises. Its interception of international pirates that had raided a Japanese ship has enhanced its image as a regional good citizen.[5] Most recently, the navy's role in the region's post-tsunami relief efforts have earned it praise and appreciation.[t] With Australia, discussions are on to collaborate on the high seas in and around the Strait of Malacca. Canberra has publicly acknowledged that it is now more comfortable with the Indian naval presence in the Pacific and Indian Oceans.[u]

India has been moving quietly but fairly steadily therefore to habilitate itself in Asia, to understand the Asian security paradigm as it has evolved with the growth of ASEAN, and to identify areas where it could serve as a good

---

[5]On the Japanese piracy episode, see Vice Admiral Mihir Roy, "Maritime Security in South West Asia," downloaded from http://www.iips.org/Roy-paper.pdf, p. 11.

[t]On the navy's post-tsunami effort, see John Lancaster, "India Takes Major Role in Sri Lanka Tsunami Relief: Aid is Sign of Nation's as a Regional Power," *Washingtonpost.com*, downloaded from http://www.washingtonpost.com/wp-dyn/articles/A22194-2005Jan19.html. On Sri Lanka's appreciation of the Indian Navy after the tsunami, see Sandeep Dikshit, "Navy's Prowess Draws Praise," *The Hindu*, January 14, 2005, downloaded from http://www.hindu.com/2005/01/14/stories/200501140390.1200.htm.

[u]On India-Australia cooperation, see Amit Baruah, "India, Australia Plan Strategic Dialogue," *The Hindu*, June 22, 2001, downloaded from http://www.hinduonnet.com/thehindu/2001/06/22/stories/03220007.htm, Ravi Tomar, "Australia-India Relations: Strategic Convergence?" Research Note 5, 2001-02, Parliamentary Library, Parliament of Australia, downloaded from http://www.alpha.gov.au/library/pubs/rn/2001-02/02RN05.htm, and Penny Wensley, Australian High Commissioner to India, "Charting Cooperation and Challenges: Australia and the Indian Ocean Region," The Inaugural Indian Ocean Lecture, Punjab University, Chandigarh, November 17, 2002, downloaded from http://www.ausgovindia.com/speeches/iclspeech_17nov2002.pdf.

citizen. Its motivations in doing so include a desire for status: it wants to be recognized as a great power in Asia, and it needs the acknowledgment of regional states for this to happen.[v] Beyond the psychological satisfaction of great power status, New Delhi perceives there to be significant security challenges ahead in Asia that require it to sit at the high table. Among these are the rise of China, the role of the United States (will it stay or will it go?), the future of Japan's "normalization" (especially its growing military status), the stability of the Korean peninsula, Southeast Asia, and Central Asia, the rise of Islamic extremism in Asia, the proliferation and transfer of arms (including nuclear weapons and missile technology), and the safety of sea lines of communication (SLOCs) which provide passage to Indian trade and naval contingents. India would like to be part of Asian security discussions on issues such as these. Its membership of the ARF has brought it into a regional security conversation, but it is still seen as a relatively marginal player in the organization.

6. Leadership of South Asia

Over the years, India has made it clear that it regards itself as the leader of South Asia. This implies several things. For one, India wants the international system to acknowledge that India is the leading power of the region and that the major powers do not "equate" India with any of the others. Given India's size, it is futile to equate India with its neighbors in the region in terms of any index of power, but New Delhi is allergic to references or gestures that imply a symbolic equivalence between India and the smaller states, not even in the sense that the interests of others can occupy outsiders as much as India's interests. As a country with four times the population of the rest of the region combined, New Delhi feels that India's interests are legitimately more important than the interests of the others.

Without saying so openly, which would be vulgar diplomatically, Indian leaders want the rest of the world to accept that South Asia is India's sphere of influence and that India has in effect a *droit de regard* in terms of both the

---

[v] Dinshaw Mistry, "A Theoretical and Empirical Assessment of India as an Emerging World Power," *India Review*, vol. 3, no. 1 (January 2004), p. 71 and 73 notes that India's emergence as a world power will require it to improve its relations with Pakistan and other regional countries in which Mistry includes not only India's South Asian neighbors but also its more distant Asian neighbors. See also S.D. Muni, "Neighbours: Win Their Awe and Affection," *The Tribune* (Chandigarh), September 24, 2005, p. 9.

external and internal policies of its neighbors. The so-called Indira Doctrine enunciated the notion that it was India that would be responsible for regional stability and that the smaller states should seek Indian help with internal and external security problems before they turned to non-regional powers.[w]

Regional leadership implies, relatedly, that the great powers or regional powers from nearby regions stay out of South Asian affairs except when New Delhi solicits outside help. Most importantly, outside powers should leave India to manage the security of the region. India's view is that the involvement of outsiders is bound to lead to more trouble. Whether outsiders intend it or not, their efforts to become involved in the region usually encourage the smaller states to be less amenable to negotiations with India. The smaller states expect the bigger powers to intervene on their behalf diplomatically and, at the limit, perhaps even militarily and to help balance India. Their incentive to be pragmatic with India and to seek a workable and just solution is thereby reduced. The Indian claim, implicitly, is that a region led by India in this way would be a contribution to international stability. It would reduce the competition between great powers who could "leave" South Asia to India which would be neutral and would therefore not allow the region to slip strategically into the grasp of one or other great power.

The great powers and the international system more broadly have been loath to confer this recognition on India. The biggest obstacle has been Pakistan. Pakistan has most categorically rejected India's claims to be the rightful big power of the region. While it does from time to time state that India is the biggest power in South Asia and that it is the "big brother," this is usually a way of embarrassing India into making concessions by a drawing a contrast between India's size/power and its niggardliness in terms of accommodating the claims of the smaller powers. India, in this portraiture, appears quite simply as a bully rather than as a caring elder sibling.

The international system and most of the great powers also publicly acknowledge India's power and leading position. At the limit though, when it comes to crucial choices and decisions, outsiders have not deferred to Indian

---

[w]Bhabhani Sengupta was the originator of the phrase, "the Indira Doctrine" in reference to Mrs. Indira Gandhi's view that South Asia was primarily an Indian sphere of influence and responsibility. Since then it has been widely used. On whether this view of the region is sustainable in the new century, see C. Raja Mohan, "Beyond India's Monroe Doctrine," *The Hindu*, 2 June 2003, downloaded from http://meaindia.nic.in/opinion/2003/01/01/02o02.htm.

preferences often enough to satisfy New Delhi, especially in respect of Pakistan's relations to powerful outsiders. Pakistan's strategic credentials have repeatedly trumped India's claims to provide international stability through regional leadership. Pakistan's location, its armed forces, its image as a "moderate" Islamic state, and, ironically, its ability to act as a disrupter and danger have repeatedly brought the great powers round to supporting various Pakistani goals including its rejection of Indian leadership and primacy in South Asia.[x]

7. India as Stabilizer

India challenges the established order, but it is also a force for stability by virtue of the following:

- India is a pluralistic, constitutional, democratic polity and a liberalizing economy of great potential.
- It is a target of terrorism.
- It is a possible counterweight to the superpower-in-the-making, China.
- It has improved relations with all the major powers and is interested in a greater diffusion of power in the international system as well as greater consultations between the major powers.

8. A Democratic and Economic Partner

India is a pluralistic, constitutional, democratic polity, and a liberalizing economy. It is a partner of those who uphold these values and a beacon of hope for those aspiring to them.

India is pluralistic in the sense that there is a diffusion of power, both politically and sociologically, such that it is very difficult for any one person, institution, or group to monopolize government. It is constitutional in that it has an explicit set of codes governed by an overarching document that gives legitimacy to the form of government and rule-making, a document that is regarded as legitimate by a large number of the country's population, and, crucially, that enunciates and protects the rights of citizens and communities. It is democratic to the extent that elections are held regularly, are generally

---

[x] Stephen P. Cohen (2005). *The Idea of Pakistan*. New Delhi: Oxford University Press, pp. 301–306.

free and fair, and rulers at various levels of government, from the municipal to the provincial and national, can be and are replaced from time to time by full-franchise voting. Democracy is more than this, and India's democracy is greater in scope than indicated by this simple metric, but it is minimally at least this.[y]

These are values and practices that the major Western powers, which are the most powerful states in international order, support and encourage. India's polity therefore is convergent with the dominant view of how peoples should be organized collectively and how they should conduct their internal affairs. Among the developing countries, there is no country of any size or importance that can match India's democratic record, although this record is by no means unsullied. While it has not always been seen as a beacon, India's importance should not be underrated. If a country of India's size and diversity, its poverty and inequalities and its conflicts and tensions has opted for, sustained, and celebrated democracy, this is an indication that others too can construct, manage, and enjoy democracy. It is therefore a partner of those who believe that international order is related to the nature of domestic orders and that a democratic domestic order is vital for a peaceful, lawful, and just international order.

India is also a liberalizing economy of great potential. The Indian economy, a mixed economy for 60 years, has been liberalized over the past decade to encourage market forces to generate wealth, reduce poverty, and increase equity. Under liberalization, India has grown at about 5–6% per annum for nearly 15 years and has therefore doubled its national income.[z] It is the world's fourth largest economy and is projected to continue to grow at these rates, or more, for the foreseeable future backed by one of the youngest populations in the world.[aa] Liberalization has widespread support amongst political parties

---

[y] On India's democracy, see Pratap Bhanu Mehta (2003). *The Burden of Democracy*. New Delhi: Penguin India, and Atul Kohli (ed.) (2001). *The Success of India's Democracy*. New York: Cambridge University Press.
[z] On India's economic growth since 1992–1993, see *India.Infoline.com*, Table 2.2, downloaded from http://indiainfoline.com/econ/andb/nia/nia2.html. India grew at an average of 6% during this period.
[aa] In 2015, China will have 1 billion working age people. By mid-century, India will have a population of 1.6 billion and 220 million more workers than China. See "India's Potential More Than China." The *Economic Times*, August 16, 2005, downloaded from http://www.economictimes.indiatimes.com/articleshow/1201533.cms. China has also recognised that India will surpass it in demographic terms. See "China-Japan-India Axis Strategy," *People's Daily Online*, April 30, 2004, downloaded from http://english.people.com.ca/200404/29/eng20040429_141908.shtml. The article notes that by 2020, India will have the largest working age population and largest number of consumers.

and social groups, although there are differences over the pace and direction of reforms. As a country committed to economic liberalization and given its size, India is a vital part of an international order that is dominated by states that believe in the efficacy of market forces.

Market forces are a necessary thought not sufficient condition of a democratic polity. To that extent, India's economic liberalization should help sustain its democracy though it would short-sighted and simplistic to suggest that economic liberalization and political democracy are seamlessly related. On two crucial counts, then, India is in accord with the dominant view of how societies should organize their polities and economies.

9. Victim of Terrorism

India has been the target of terrorist violence for a good part of its post-independence history. The most violent and sophisticated terrorist groups have featured since the late 1970s — in the Punjab, in Kashmir, in the Northeast, and in various states where the "naxalite" or maoist outfits operate. There are a number of definitions of terrorism. I use the term here to refer to deliberate acts of violence against non-combatants (civilian and military) intended to spread fear in the service of an avowedly political purpose. States and non-state actors (these can include actors that aspire to be or see themselves as state-like) can indulge in acts of terror. That is, they can use violence against non-combatants for political purposes. In India, non-state actors that have resorted to terror include ethnic secessionists (or national liberation movements), religious fundamentalists, and maoists. Many if not all of these groups have had outside support, both from states and non-state actors.[bb]

It is only after the events of September 11, 2001 that the international community led by the US has openly acknowledged and been more attentive to India's claims about being a victim of terrorism. Before that, India's terrorism was largely its own problem and was attributed to India's bad policies, internally and externally. Even now, there is a tendency to make a distinction between the terrorism India faces and "global terrorism." India's terrorism is still seen as largely India's problems whereas "global terrorism" (real

---

[bb] Kanti Bajpai (2002). *Roots of Terrorism*. New Delhi: Penguin India, on the role of foreign powers in supporting terrorist groups.

Islamic extremists and fundamentalists) is everyone's problem. The fact that virtually all of India's terrorists receive money, weapons, sanctuary, and training from foreign countries and groups suggests that India's fight is an international one. That terrorist groups all over the world cooperate with each other also suggests that India's terrorists are part of a much larger network of violence.

The terrorist threat to the Western countries from Islamic extremists and India's terrorist problem are not the same, but they are also not completely unrelated. While many of the terrorist threats that India is dealing with are not from Muslim groups, all the major groups operating in Kashmir are avowedly Islamic. In Kashmir, Indian authorities face international Islamic extremists fighting alongside local militants. Osama bin Laden and Al Qaeda have said publicly that India along with the US and Israel will be the target of terrorism from their cells and sympathizers.[cc] In any case, in the fight against terrorism, if it is to have much meaning, there must be a united front against terrorists all over the world, regardless of their stripes. India and the international community are in a common fight.

Since 9/11, India has shared terrorism-related intelligence to an unprecedented degree in intelligence sharing on terrorism with other countries, especially the US. Both sides can learn from each other in a variety of ways. India has information and methods that other governments could benefit from. Others can share information and methods with New Delhi to improve its efficiency in dealing with terrorism. The international community has not appreciated the enormous experience of India's armed forces, police, and intelligence organizations, its officials, its political leaders, and its public in dealing with terrorism. Its use of social and political engineering and its military strategies and tactics are worthy of study.[dd] While India continues to battle terrorism, it has had some outright successes (e.g., Punjab), and it has coped with terrorism over a long period of time. Indians have not become hysterical about terrorism nor have successive Indian governments used indiscriminate

---

[cc] For instance see Rezaul H. Laskar, "Al Qaeda Threat Proof of Involvement in J&K Terror: India." *Rediff.com US Edition*, downloaded from http://www.rediff.com/us/2001/oct/14ny4.htm which refers to Al Qaeda's warning to the US for its ostensive "support" to Jews and Hindus in their persecution of Muslims in Palestine and Jammu and Kashmir.

[dd] On how India has coped with ethnic, i.e., religious, linguistic, regional, and caste diversity and has dealt with the threat of separatist violence see Bajpai, *Roots of Terrorism*.

and massive violence as a counter to terror. As the world gets used to a chronic threat of terrorist violence, a threat that is likely to be around for decades, the Indian experience is one that is worthy of attention. India could be a useful ally in the fight against terror not just because it may have good intelligence on Islamic extremists, but more importantly because it can contribute to the global understanding of terrorism and how to combat it. It is an important fact that India has remained a democracy in spite of 60 years of terrorist violence in one theatre or another of the country. Democracies may be more vulnerable to terrorism, but they are also resilient in coping with terrorist violence.

10. Balancing — and Engaging — China

The rise of China is one of the greatest developments in international relations over the past decade. How to deal with its rise is an issue that will occupy diplomats and soldiers in Asia and other parts of the world for some years to come. At least one way of dealing with China is to fashion a balance of power such that Chinese actions will be constrained. India is regarded as a possible member of a balancing coalition. Balancing power is an age-old instrument in international orders and does not mean unremitting hostility or preparation for conquest and invasion. It does mean watchfulness and vigilance and a determination to dispose of enough military capacity and to ally with others to prevent neighboring and other powers from achieving ascendancy. From this point of view, balance of power is not a dirty word.

Having said that, it has already become politically incorrect to talk about balancing China. This is a measure of Chinese power. China's neighbors are reluctant to resort to a vocabulary that might annoy Beijing too much. The only other country that expects and gets such treatment is the US. Nevertheless, balancing China is a strategic option, one that the other major powers in the international system must contemplate in the service of international order. It might seem strange to argue that balancing China is a contribution to international order. Understandably, China today finds this irksome. However, Beijing itself has practiced balance of power in the interest of China's own security as well as international order and done so rather adeptly. During the Cold War, China astutely allied, first, with the Soviet Union against the US-led capitalist world, and then, after 1971, with the US against Soviet power. China is hardly the only state to resort to balance of power manoeuvring. Balance of power is a classical element of international order.[ee]

Whether it is Russia, Japan, South Korea, the Southeast Asian states, Australia, India, or the US, there is a fear among the major powers that the behemoth that is China cannot be held in check by any single country, especially geographically distant ones. The only hope of balancing China is to build a series of alliance-like relationships around China. China has more neighbors than any other country in the world, and therefore the prospects of regional balancing are good. Also, the states that are contiguous to China include countries of size and power — Russia, Japan, South Korea, Vietnam, Indonesia, Thailand, Burma, and India, principally.

In the long term, the only country from amongst those in the Eurasian landmass that can seriously match China's power is India. By 2050, India's population is estimated to surpass China's. India will also have a younger work population which, if educated and skilled, could make it a very dynamic economy. India's arable land area is larger than that of China, even though its total land area is one-third that of its northern neighbor.[ff] India's military is just under a million strong and is fairly sophisticated and battle hardened. In short, India has the wherewithal to balance, some might even predict, to surpass China in 50 years from now. India's other advantage as a balancer is that it is a democratic state and has political values in common with the US and other Western and Asian countries who are democracies and who fear China.

The challenge before the major powers is how to balance without seeming to balance, how to get regional neighbors to join a balancing coalition against China when Beijing is doing its best to prevent encirclement, and how to maintain a working relationship with China in areas where Chinese cooperation is required even as a balance is sought to be constructed. India has had a complex relationship with China, from the "hindi–chini bhai bhai" days of the 1950s, to the cold war of the 1960s and 1970s, to the détente of the

---

[ee] On the role of balance of power in sustaining international order, see the nuanced statement in Hedley Bull (1977). *The Anarchical Society*. New York: Columbia University Press.

[ff] China's total land area is 933 million hectares while India's is only 297 million hectares. However, China's arable land is only 124 million hectares while India's is 162 million hectares. See Bhanoji Rao, "China and India: Musings on Recent Economic History," *Business Line*, May 3, 2005, downloaded from http://www.thehindubusinessline.com/2005/05/03/stories/2005050300160800.htm.

1980s, and to the growing economic and diplomatic engagement of the 1990s (in spite of India's nuclear tests in 1998). It has struggled at various points to answer questions such as these. It is wary of Chinese power and yet wants to avoid tensions with Beijing so that it is not forced to fight on two fronts simultaneously — Pakistan and China. It does not want to give the Chinese cause to help Pakistan (and some of India's other neighbors) more than they already do. Nor does it want Chinese power to be let loose on its internal politics, especially in the unstable northeastern part of the country.

Out of the glare of publicity, Indian officials are quite willing to talk about the threat of a rising China. Some of this talk is self-serving in that it is intended to give more strategic depth to the discussions with key interlocutors, such as the Americans, than the dialog might otherwise possess. Having said that, there is real unease in India, as elsewhere, over the spectacular growth of Chinese power.[gg] Perhaps the most realistic and practical sense in which India can be a balance to China is in the continued development of the Indian economy, in the systematic modernization of its armed forces, and in the deepening of its democracy so that it remains a resilient, cohesive, and united society.[hh] Those powers that wish to invest in India as a long-term balance should conceive of India as a balance in this sense rather than more narrowly as a dedicated ally willing to "sign up" to a formal alliance.

11. Engaging the Western Powers, Japan, and Russia

India has adopted a diplomatic style that is one of engagement with the major powers. For much of the Cold War, India found itself preoccupied with the Soviet Union and the communist bloc as well as the non-aligned movement. The end of the Cold War has freed it from all three actors. India now is

---

[gg]India's concerns are ably reflected in "India's Fear of China," *Economist.com*, June 24, 2003, downloaded from http://www.economist.com/agenda/displayStory.cfm?story_id=1871346. See also Aravind Adiga, "A Healthy Fear of China: India Needs its Powerful Neighbor to be a Challenger, Not a Partner," *Times Asia Magazine*, April 18, 2005, downloaded from http://www.time.com/time/asia/magazine/article/0,13673,501050418-1047545,00.html.\

[hh]This appears to be exactly what the US has in mind under the Bush Administration. It continues to be interested in India's economy. It has begun a dialogue on the resumption of an arms relationship with India. India and the US are discussing high-end platforms including AWACs and F-16s. The Defence Framework of June 2005 and the Joint Statement of July 2005 indicate that conventional weapons and civilian nuclear cooperation are on the table in India–US relations. And the Bush Administration has repeatedly lauded India's democratic, pluralistic society.

principally involved with the US, the Western European powers, Japan, and Russia.

India is determined to be pragmatic with the major powers. Pragmatism entails not allying with any one power but rather crafting relations to India's advantage with each of them. Economics is a major element of India's pragmatism. Engaging the major powers involves economic interactions on a scale that India had never contemplated in the past. India understands that there must be give-and-take in these relationships, that a "thick" relationship with them will be a mixed one in which differences will continue even as common goals are pursued, and that New Delhi must be patient in realizing the benefits of working with a range of powers. This engagement is pragmatic too in the sense that India usually avoids moralistic statements and judgments about international relations and the stances of the major powers. It is careful to make the point that all the major powers are committed to a rather similar policy and that this posture is sensible in a world in which there are several centers of power. New Delhi recognizes that the US is the primary power and will remain so for many years to come. But it is watchful of developments toward greater integration in Europe, the normalization of Japan, and the continuing arms relationship with Russia. In their regions and further afield, all these secondary powers are actors of influence and capacity. India has security dialogues, more or less formal, with each of these powers. It uses its relations with each of them to remind the US that is has other friends and potential partners. It uses the US to remind China that New Delhi has support in checking Beijing's Asian ambitions.

Part of India's motivation in putting so much into engaging the major powers is that it wants to position itself as a contending power. To be in the company of the major powers is to attract some of the awe and respect that attaches to those powers and to be thought of as part of the club. India is also pragmatic about these involvements. India's goals and objectives require it to deal with the Americans, Europeans, Chinese, Japanese, and Russians. There is no major issue of international politics in which the US does not have a decisive say. The US is also a vital source of diplomatic support, military technology, investment, and trade. The European powers are an attractive alternative to the US for diplomatic backing, military technology, investment, and trade. China is a rising superpower. The border conflict with China in any case must some day be resolved; the lost lands cannot be recovered through force and the contested areas presently under Indian control cannot be secured by military defence alone. Japan is important economically and technologically and in the long run is a potential ally against Chinese domination of Asia. Russia is still a strategic partner, helpful in the UN and India's most important source of arms. It also is part of a balance against China.

India's engagement with the major powers is at an unprecedented level. The number of bilateral visits, especially at the highest levels (Foreign Minister upwards), the range of contacts between Indian ministries and departments and counterparts in the major capitals, the proliferation of joint commissions, and the deepening links between the Indian armed forces and foreign militaries including joint exercises, training, port calls, and meetings, all these are of a degree that were unknown during the Cold War except with the Soviet Union.

12. Conclusion

How India adjusts to the international order in the next 10 years will depend on the extent to which some of India's hopes and ambitions can be realized at the international level, its regional ties improve, and its domestic politics remain open and inclusive.

Can India realize all of its ambitions internationally — nuclear respectability, a permanent Security Council seat, access to high technology, Asian security responsibilities, and recognized leadership of South Asia? This seems unlikely, at least in the exact measure that New Delhi wants, though there are developments that augur quite well for India. Two in particular are worth noting. First, the new relationship with the US as the most influential power, it is the US whose imprimatur will be required if the changes that India seeks to happen. The other big driver of India's success in getting the major powers to come round will be economics. If the economy grows at rates of between 6 and 10% and the buying power of Indians continues to rise, if the country remains open to foreign investment, if the economy continues to liberalize so that foreigners can do business more easily in India, the international community led by the major powers will gradually accommodate Indian ambitions, as it has accommodated China over the years. Accommodating India should be made easier by India's democratic political system which is a reassurance to the Western powers that there is a deeper convergence with India.

India's adjustment will be helped by improved regional ties, particularly with Pakistan. New Delhi is quite well aware of this, and at least part of its motivation in resuming the dialog with Islamabad over the past 2 years is based on the desire to be better regarded by the major powers and the international system at large. The possibility of a nuclear standoff with Pakistan is one that does concern the international community, and India's attempt to laugh this off only reinforces the worries of the major powers that see in such a stance a sign of irresponsible behavior. New Delhi's resumption of negotiations, especially on Kashmir, is a welcome step from the point of view of outsiders because it suggests that India is in a less confrontational mood which, in the presence of nuclear weapons, is a reassurance to the major powers. The major powers will be looking for more than just dialog though. India will have to achieve resolution of some major issues with Pakistan. Kashmir is a crucial area, and unless Pakistan simply gives up on the issue, which is most unlikely, New Delhi will have to show progress here that is more than just discursive.[ii]

The extent to which India's place in international order is normalized depends on its domestic politics as well. A pluralistic and democratic India, in which ethnic minorities are safe and in which the rule of law obtains, is an India with which the international community feels safe and can do business. Over the past decade and a half, India's record has been mixed, and there have been some very dark moments, particularly in the state of Gujarat in 2002. Right-wing extremism is still a threat. Violence in Kashmir and in the northeastern states is unabated, though it has declined.

An economically liberal India is crucial for India's image and for its ability to tie the major powers into a profitable relationship. Whether or not India remains economically liberal is dependent on its domestic politics as well. As

---

[ii] Under both the Vajpayee and Manmohan Singh governments, India has over the past 3 years tried to deepen its engagement with Pakistan. India and Pakistan have returned to the so-called six-plus-two formula worked out during Prime Minister Narasimha Rao's period. The two crucial issues here are Kashmir and security. The other six include a range of issues, from trade and people-to-people interactions to the lesser disputes. Pakistan has agreed in public to dismantle the terrorist camps, to crack down on the activities of militant groups, and to pursue a process of confidence building with India even as it negotiates on Kashmir. In return, India returned to the negotiating table on Kashmir and resumed air flights and other normal contacts that had been suspended after the 2002 crisis. A number of additional confidence-building measures have been negotiated or are in the process of being finalized including those relating to hotlines and the notification of missile tests. A more liberal regime of visas and travel has been instituted since 2003. The resumption of high-level meetings, at both the ministerial and prime ministerial level, has also been a feature of this period.

things stand, the prognosis is fairly good: all the major parties accept that liberalization is necessary and is politically and socially progressive. There are dangers ahead though. Regional inequities are growing: the big northern states are not attracting foreign investment and are stagnating economically. Political instability is compounding the problem. Caste wars and maoist insurgencies in northern India could lead to political collapse and a worsening of the economic situation. These states are politically influential and could become sources of opposition to liberalization. The states of Bihar and Uttar Pradesh are a drag on growth as well. The support for job reservations in the private sector is also potentially a drag on economic growth. The fiscal deficit is reaching severe proportions, and no government has shown much stomach in controlling it.

Internally, India may be beset by other problems. The HIV-AIDS epidemic in India is very worrisome and could, in a decade, set back the developmental gains of the preceding 15 years. India will soon have more HIV-AIDS victims than any other country in the world.[jj] Water shortages are becoming critical in some cities and regions. These could lead to large-scale civil unrest. There are water conflicts between states within India which could also turn violent.[kk]

India will certainly be an interesting country over the next decade. It has many of the ingredients of a great power, a power that will rise to prominence and will be accommodated reasonably stably. Its democracy and its economic openness and growth are the best hope that it will ascend peacefully.

[jj]For a recent review of India's HIV-AIDS, see Happymon Jacob, *HIV-AIDS as a Security Threat to India*, RCSS Policy Studies 28, Delhi: Manohar Publishers, 2005. One estimate is that HIV-AIDS will be "the single largest cause of death in India by 2033 with the disease accounting for 17% of all deaths and 40% of all infectious deaths" (pp. 17–18). The United States National Intelligence Council has estimated that by 2025 India will have 20–25 million HIV-AIDS infected people whereas China would have 10–15 million. The HIV–AIDS epidemic is affecting India's security forces. See Jacob, *HIV-AIDS as Security Threat*, pp. 35–41. The Indian government increasingly has had to acknowledge the fact that the disease has hit the security forces. See "Home Ministry to Set Up Task Force on AIDS," *The Hindu*, 23 June 2005.

[kk]The states of Tamil Nadu and Karnataka have been locked in a dispute over water for over a decade. More recently, Uttar Pradesh and Delhi are fighting over the Ganga river. See "Cauvery Basis States should Decide Distress Sharing Mutually: Karnataka," *The Hindu*, 24 June 2005 and "Water Politics," *The Asian Age*, 24 June 2005. On the general scarcity of water and what can be done about it, see Arun Firodia, "Failing to Harvest the Bounty: Inefficient Farming Methods Root Cause of Water Crisis," *The Times of India*, 24 June 2005.

CHAPTER 12

Globalization and India's Changing National Security Strategy

C. Raja Mohan

1. Introduction

The paper reviews the transformation of Indian national security strategy under the twin imperatives of the demise of the Cold War and the new wave of globalization and its impact on regional and international stability. During the 1990s India discarded many of the core beliefs of the past and generated political consensus behind a new set of propositions. These included the nature of national development strategy, its self-image in international relations, ties with the major powers, the re-conceptualization of ties with neighbors and regional adversaries, expanded engagement with the extended neighborhood, and the role of nuclear weapons. And if the 1990s saw India adapting to the changed international circumstances, the current decade is witnessing the regional and international impact of the relative rise of India, its changed national security strategy and altered approach to international affairs. This paper examines the conceptual shifts underlying India's foreign policy evolution since the end of the Cold War, and their impact on New Delhi's relations with the Subcontinent and extended neighbourhood. It also offers a brief analysis of the on-going attempt to integrate India into the global nuclear order which could mark the single most important consequence of India's changing national security strategy.

2. Conceptual Shifts in India's Policy

Most nations, and large ones especially, do not easily alter their international orientation. States tend to be conservative about foreign policy and national security strategy. Fundamental changes in the definition of national interest and the means to pursue them occur only when there is a revolutionary change either at home or in the external environment. The end of the Cold War, the collapse of the Soviet Union and the new wave of globalization, as well as a profound economic crisis at home at the turn of the 1990s forced India to rethink its national security premises. The old political and economic order at home had collapsed and externally, the end of the Cold War removed all the old benchmarks that guided India's security policy. Not only did many of the core beliefs of the old system have to be discarded and but a consensus had also to be generated on new ones. The collapse of the Soviet Union and the new wave of economic globalization left India scrambling to find new anchors for its conduct of external relations. Some of this change could be traced back to the mid-1980s, when India began to explore much needed adjustments to its national strategy. But after 1991, change became inevitable.[a]

One huge transformation in India's worldview was in relation to nuclear weapons. Since the late 1980s, India was dragged into an extended national debate on its nuclear policy. The nuclear tests at Pokhran in the summer of 1998 were about redefining India's approach to the question of power. They were part of the effort to resolve the long-standing tension between the idealism and realism in India's foreign policy. The end of the Cold War also put India's attachment to the idea of non-alignment into an unforgiving political spotlight. Non-alignment, for reasons right or wrong, has been widely seen as the singular feature of India's foreign policy since independence. The altered world forced India to examine the relevance of non-alignment in the conduct of external relations during the 1990s. As it rethought its commitment to non-alignment, India had also to reconsider its earlier rejection of formal alliances with great powers. Thus the decade also brought up the deeper question of where India stood in relation to the West, when the East and its economic model stood shattered. "Returning to the West" became a dominant imperative for India after the Cold War. India was the only liberal democracy in the world that stood apart, and a lot of the time against the West, throughout the Cold War.

---

[a] For a comprehensive discussion on the evolution of India's external relations after the Cold War, see Ref. 1. For views from outside, especially the US, see Ref. 2.

Beyond the specific moves India has made in different regions and on major global issues, the key feature of the 1990s has been the changing conceptual basis on which Indian diplomacy had been founded. If Nehru defined a unique foreign policy for independent India in search of a manifest destiny, the Indian leaders of the 1990s had to break out of the strait jacket that Nehru's foreign policy ideas had eventually put India into. Finding new ways of doing things and putting aside old ideas — rejecting them formally would have invited serious political trouble — while embarking on new approaches was central to the handling of the extremely challenging international environment that India found itself in 1991.

This has not been easy. The tension between the imperative of the new and the resistance of the old ideas on the conduct of security policy is real. The fear of the new and fondness for the old continue to be reflected in all aspects of Indian strategy from engaging the US to an optimal strategy toward the smallest of the neighbors. The "new" strategic policy of India is still a work in progress. Equally important is the flux in world affairs after September 11, 2001 that has left a large uncertainty on where the international system is headed in the coming decades. Yet it is not difficult to see that the direction of Indian strategy has changed radically since the end of the Cold War amidst internal and external impulses. Nor is it hard to glean the fact that India has begun to move toward a new set of assumptions about the nature of its interaction with the world. Not all of these were articulated self-consciously or clearly by the Indian political leadership. But its actions since the mid-1980s have slowly but surely transformed the ideas that have guided India's worldview. A few of those changes stand out and are unlikely to be reversed.

First was the transition from the collective national consensus on building a "socialist society" to building a "modern capitalist" one. The Socialist ideal had so dominated the Indian political discourse by the early 1970s that a Constitutional amendment was passed in 1976 to make the nation into a "Socialist republic." But 1991 saw the collapse of the Soviet Union, the veritable symbol of socialism, and the crumbling of the edifice of India's state-led socialist economy. Whatever the remaining pretensions of the political class, there was no question that building modern capitalism, in tune with the trends of globalization, was now the principal national objective. India's internal socialist orientation had its external complement in terms of India's closeness to the Soviet Union and the socialist bloc. But from the 1990s, the success of Indian national security strategy depended instead on the pace of India's globalization, its ability to deepen links with the US and the West, and capacity to bring its economy up to speed with China.

Implicit in this was the second transition, from the past emphasis on politics to a new stress on economics in the making of national security strategy. India began to realize in the 1990s how far behind it had fallen from the rest of Asia, including China, in economic development. Having got into the groove of the socialist rhetoric, Indian diplomats had little time for "commercial diplomacy" in the past. Now they were marketing the wares of India as a "big emerging market" and the new Information Technology power. With the socialist strait jacket gone, and the pressures to compete with other emerging markets, Indian strategy now entered new uncharted waters. In the past, the "begging bowl" for aid was symbolic of Indian diplomacy as it sought to meet the finance ministry's external financing requirements. India was now seeking foreign direct investment, and access to markets in the developed world. New Delhi also began to see that rapid economic growth is also the key to transforming its relations with its neighbors, including its long-standing adversaries, Pakistan and China.

A third transition in Indian foreign policy related to the first shift from "Third Worldism" to the promotion of its own self-interest. By the 1980s, for most Indians, striving for the collective good of the Third World and standing up against the Western world had become India's natural responsibility. Many of the international and regional security issues were viewed through the twin prisms of the Third World and "anti-imperialism." Any other approach was seen as a betrayal of the long-standing Indian consensus on foreign policy. The 1990s, however, brought home some painful truths. There was no real third world trade union that India believed it was leading. After a radical phase in the 1970s, most developing nations had begun to adopt pragmatic economic policies and sought to integrate with the international market. Much of the developing world had made considerable economic advances, leaving the South Asia way behind. If there was a "third world," it was largely within India and the Subcontinent. This meant that if India helped itself and developed faster, it would be uplifting much of the third world that was left. While the rhetoric on the third world remained popular, the policy orientation in India's external relations increasingly focused on India's own self interest. There was a growing perception, following from the Chinese example, that if India developed rapidly it had a chance to gain a place at the international high table. All this implied India would now be more interested in becoming a part of the "management" of the international system and not remain just a protesting leader of the third world trade union. As it began to shed the Third World shibboleths, India also began to discard the "anti-Western" political impulses that were so dominant in the world view that shaped Indian diplomacy right up to 1991. Rejecting the "anti-Western" mode of thinking was the fourth important transition of India's national security strategy. As the world's largest democracy, India was the most committed to Western political values outside the Euro–Atlantic world. Yet the Cold War saw India emerge as the most articulate opponent of the Western worldview. India joined the losing side of the civil war within the West — between the US and Western Europe on the one side and Soviet Russia on the other on both the economic and diplomatic choices that confronted it after independence. By the late 1980s, India was voting more often against the US and the West, than even the Soviet Union. And within the Indian political class, the rejection of the Western economic model as well as its foreign policy goals became second nature. At the root of this was the degeneration of anti-imperialism into a knee-jerk anti-Westernism.

The Cold War alignment of the Western powers with the military dictators in Pakistan and the Chinese communists reinforced the opposition to the West in the Indian security establishment. India's liberal intelligentsia — deeply influenced by the Labor left in Britain until the 1970s and American university radicalism after that — gave itself the role of critical opposition to the West — albeit within the framework of Western thought. In the process it ended up supporting the counter-productive India's anti-Western foreign policy. Further, there were the nativists, strongly represented in the BJP, who were deeply suspicious of the "corrupting" Western influences on traditional Hindu society. As a consequence, a strong anti-Western bias crept into Indian foreign policy supported by the left as well as the right and underwritten by the security establishment. The end of the Cold War also meant that the civil war within the Euro–Atlantic world was finally won by the US. That demanded India to break the decades old anti-Western approaches to foreign policy.

Finally, the fifth transition in Indian foreign policy in the 1990s was from idealism to pragmatism. Idealism came naturally to the Indian elite that won independence from the British by arguing with them against colonialism on the basis of first principles of enlightenment. Newly independent India believed mistakenly that it could conduct foreign policy on the same basis. India believed a new world order could be structured on the basis of the first principles of peaceful co-existence and international cooperation through multilateral endeavors. The new leaders of India had contempt for "power politics." They believed it was a negative but lingering legacy from 19th century Europe but had no relevance to the new times of the mid-20th century. India tended to see its role in world politics as the harbinger of a new set of principles, which if applied would transform the world. India had little time for the old melancholic approach of analyzing the world in terms of clash of interests and pursuit of power by individual states.

Although India's first prime minister and foreign minister Jawaharlal Nehru was a realist in his thinking about foreign policy and the importance of protecting national interest, the public articulation of India's foreign policy left the stamp of idealism all over. As India rediscovered statehood and the challenges of independent engagement with the world, the creation of domestic political support for foreign policy hinged on popularizing a simplistic set of principles. The moralism of India's foreign policy was so internalized by its elite that it had to unlearn a lot as it confronted a transformed world order at the turn of the 1990s. India has moved from its past emphasis on the power of the argument to a new stress on the argument of power. The conscious rediscovery of power as the crucial dynamic by Indian foreign policy makers does not mean India has become a cynical power unconcerned with the normative dimension of global politics. All that India has done is to reconfigure the mix between power and principle in the pursuit of its national interest.

3. Beyond the Territorial Imperative

The introduction of nuclear weapons in the Subcontinent, in a somewhat counter-intuitive manner has helped India reconstruct two of its core national security problems — the boundary dispute with China and the problem of Jammu and Kashmir with Pakistan. To be sure, the immediate aftermath of the nuclear tests had been a resurgence of tensions with both China and Pakistan. With the former they centered around India's naming of the "China threat" as a justification for its decision to acquire nuclear weapons and introduced a deep chill into the bilateral relations in 1998. With Pakistan the tensions were rooted in the attempts by Islamabad to change the territorial status quo through the use of terrorism. As a consequence there was a war over Pakistan's aggression in the Kargil sector of Jammu and Kashmir in 1999 and an intense military confrontation following the terrorist attacks on the Indian Parliament on December 13, 2001.

Nevertheless, by early 2004, the Atal Bihari Vajpayee government had initiated a new peace process with Pakistan and made a significant effort to transform bilateral relations with China. At the center of these two processes was an Indian commitment to address, in a purposeful manner, the long-standing conflicts with both its nuclear neighbors. For the first time in decades now, India is in the middle of serious political negotiations with Pakistan on the question of Jammu and Kashmir and with China on the boundary dispute.[b]

If there is one way to describe India's central strategic challenge after independence, it was the three-front problem. Flanked by the two wings of Pakistan on the east and the West, India also had to handle the Chinese on the north. The very construction of the Indian map was hobbled by this problem and further aggravated by adversarial relations with both China and Pakistan. Just as India became a free nation, China too, entered the modern world. A rising China and an emerging India, with their newfound nationalism and the imperatives of territorial consolidation inevitably clashed at the Himalayas. Meanwhile to the south of the Himalayas, the subcontinent was partitioned and India found itself in a prolonged confrontation with Pakistan. Kashmir turned out to be emblematic of the bitter legacy of Partition.

India's military, political and diplomatic energies were consumed for decades by this challenge. The break-up of Pakistan in the 1971 war reduced the three-front problem to a two-front one. But it did not in the end resolve the problem of coping with two adversaries who were themselves locked in an all-weather friendship. To make it worse, China and Pakistan also tied up with the US in the second phase of the Cold War. India then constructed a partnership with the Soviet Union. The collapse of the Soviet Union in 1991 left

---

[b] For the breakthrough in the negotiating framework on the boundary dispute with China, see "Declaration on Principles for Relations and Comprehensive Cooperation between the People's Republic of China and the Republic of India" issued in Beijing on June 26, 2003, during Vajpayee's visit to China. Available at the Indian Ministry of External Affairs website, <http://www.mea.gov.in/jdhome.htm>. For the new formulation on the peace process with Pakistan, see "India-Pakistan Joint Press Statement" issued in Islamabad, January 6, 2004, during Vajpayee's visit to Pakistan. Available at <http://www.mea.gov.in/sshome.htm>.

India exposed once again. But the steady improvement of Indo–US relations in the 1990s and the proclamation of a strategic partnership under the Bush administration eased the problem a little; however, it did not let India out of the box. Playing the great power game was fine, but it was not enough to transform India's two-front problem. India had to deal with this on its own and find an exit.

Should India try and solve the problem with Pakistan first or China? Vajpayee's answer was "let's attack on both fronts" — in a diplomatic sense. India's attempts to befriend China in the 1950s were interpreted by some Western analysts as a framework to avoid the three-front problem and as a means to neutralize Pakistan. When India reached out to the West for assistance in dealing with China after the 1962 debacle, the advice from the Anglo–American powers was to make up with Pakistan. This was the context in which India negotiated with Pakistan on the Kashmir dispute in the early 1960s. The most substantive discussions ever between India and Pakistan took place between their foreign ministers, Swaran Singh and Zulfikar Ali Bhutto, during 1963–1964. But these negotiations came to naught and the two countries drifted into a war in 1965.

Meanwhile, India's relations with China remained frozen amidst an enduring sense of bitterness in New Delhi. There was no way India could make a move to transform the relations with China despite the establishment of diplomatic ties in the late 1970s. Vajpayee, who was then the foreign minister, understood the problem and made a brave effort to change the dynamic with Pakistan in 1979. Indira Gandhi toward the end of her life began to see the no-win situation India had caught itself in. She opened border negotiations with China in the early 1980s, but there was a hard to swallow lump in the throat. A lot of credit goes to Rajiv Gandhi who for a moment appeared poised to attack the two-front problem. His 1988 visit to Beijing broke the mould of India's obdurate China policy. He opened the doors for a normalization of bilateral relations and initiated efforts to address the boundary dispute in a realistic manner. Rajiv Gandhi had also explored the brief opportunities that presented themselves in the late 1980s to embark on a journey of peace with Pakistan. His initiatives on the two-front problem came too late to be conclusive. Nor were they pursued vigorously by his successors until Vajpayee. By making the difficult mental leap on how to negotiate with China and Pakistan, Vajpayee reduced the political risk for his successors in handling the boundary dispute and the Kashmir question.

We need not be detained here by the debate on the nature of the settlements that India might eventually arrive at in its talks with China and Pakistan. They will be part of a very hard bargain. But the very decision to get there reflects a new political maturity and a determination to break out of the strategic trap that circumstances set for India at the time of Independence. The Kashmir dispute with Pakistan and the boundary problem with China formed a chain and a ball on India's feet. India is now ready to free itself. Success on either of the fronts or both would unleash India's military and diplomatic energies away from concerns of territorial defence to a greater emphasis on outward looking naval and special forces focused on peace and stability operations beyond Indian borders. Any doubts that the Congress Party, with its historic baggage over Kashmir and China boundary, might not pursue the agenda laid down by Vajpayee were quickly set at rest by the new Prime Minister Manmohan Singh.

4. Rethinking the Subcontinent: Discarding the Monroe Doctrine

The American War on terrorism has had its intended and unintended consequences for the Subcontinent. The Taliban was ousted, and the Army in Pakistan has become the instrument to clean up the jihadi mess that was nurtured by it in the 1980s and 1990s. Equally important, it has focused international attention on the subcontinent and its intra-state and inter-state wars. Never in the past has the international system paid so much attention to the problems of regional security in South Asia. During the Cold War, the external environment complicated the security politics of South Asia. Now external circumstances may have turned favorable to a reasonable resolution of South Asia's security challenges.

The accumulated impact of globalization on the politics and economics of the subcontinent over the last decade has begun to reveal a radical transformation. The Indo–Pak military confrontation since the attack on Parliament on December 13, 2001 has brought the Anglo–American powers into play in a manner that has not been seen since the early 1960s. The prospect, however remote, of a war between India and Pakistan escalating into a nuclear exchange has forced the international community to explore a final resolution of the underlying political conflict between the subcontinental rivals. The

Kashmir question is not the only one among the regional conflicts that is on the Anglo–American radar.

The expansive American war on terrorism has brought the US, with Britain in tow, and the European Union, into a political effort to deal with the other security challenges in South Asia — the tragic war in Sri Lanka and the Maoist insurgency in Nepal. The world has begun to impinge on the Subcontinent. Along with the global war on terror that is focused on Afghanistan, there have been Anglo–American efforts to defuse the Indo–Pak tensions, the Norwegian mediation between the Singhalese and Tamils in Sri Lanka, and the international initiative on Nepal led by Britain.

But external environment alone is not enough to resolve regional security problems. To some extent the pressures from below are already forcing states in the region to act more purposefully. After a series of military crises and real wars, India and Pakistan have finally recognized the importance of a sustained bilateral engagement that would involve both bilateral cooperation and conflict resolution. There is also recognition throughout South Asia that the time has come to deal with the civil wars within the region in a more innovative and political manner rather than trying to deal with them as law and order problems. The current efforts at peace within the region can at best be characterized as "work in progress" with no guaranteed prospect of success. But there is no denying the fact that the assumptions and premises on how to end conflict have begun to be questioned and revised in a fundamental manner. That is a reason for hope. More subtle, but even more significant, has been the consequences of economic globalization in the 1990s. Under pressure from the "Washington Consensus," all nations of the Subcontinent have adopted liberal economic policies. As they open up their markets to the world, the South Asian states are discovering that they cannot keep them closed to their own neighbor, India. While Islamabad continues to resist normal trade relations with New Delhi, some of the smaller countries of the region have begun to acknowledge that their economic future is now intertwined with that of India. There is no escape from the logic of globalization that demands deeper trade relations and economic integration with India. Meanwhile proposals for mega-projects for pipelines and transportation corridors, straddling across borders in South Asia, promise to further deepen economic integration in the Subcontinent.

Whatever might be its other negative consequences, the relentless pressures of globalization are helping to break down the economic walls within the Subcontinent. Trade volumes within South Asia have begun to surge, although entirely in India's favor at the moment. Bangladesh and Sri Lanka are among the top ten export destinations for Indian goods. Nothing less than a reversal of the economic partition of the Subcontinent is now on the cards. After British India was partitioned into separate states, insular economic policies and political differences had made borders into high-security barriers. Now globalization offers the prospect of transforming these borders into zones of economic cooperation and of reconnecting regions that were once part of the same economic and cultural space.

For all its own internal difficulties, the task of leading the region toward economic and political moderation and social development inevitably falls on New Delhi. One of the most significant developments in India since 1991 has been a radical rethinking about the relevance of a more effective region-alism in the Subcontinent and a sea change in the Indian policy toward its smaller neighbors. This was based on the recognition of the acute crisis that had enveloped India's relations with her neighbors at the turn of the 1990s.[c] At the heart of the changing Indian policy toward its neighbors is the so-called "Gujral doctrine," named after Inder Kumar Gujral who served as the external affairs minister during 1996–1997 and as prime minister during 1997–1998. The doctrine argued that if India's neighbors were willing to respect India's security concerns, New Delhi would not insist on reciprocity in resolving bilateral problems. Mr. Gujral's willingness to go more than half the distance in resolving the long-standing problems of the Subcontinent was followed by his successors. Although the doctrine was named after Mr. Gujral, given his enthusiastic articulation of it, the broad lines of it were followed by the preceding government led by P.V. Narasimha Rao (1991–1996) and that of Atal Bihari Vajpayee (1998–2004) who followed Gujral. The Manmohan Singh government too is following the same approach of emphasizing positive asymmetry in favor of the smaller neighbors, and has shown no desire to deviate from this direction.

No state bases its policy on altruism. India's new regional policy has been guided by three imperatives. First is the recognition that India cannot fulfill its aspirations for a larger international profile without addressing its problems in

---

[c]For a discussion of the Indian dilemmas on regional cooperation in South Asia, see Ref. 3.

the neighborhood. India cannot run away from its neighborhood. However frustrating it might be, there is no alternative available to Indian diplomacy other than a substantive and patient engagement of its neighbors. Second, as it copes with the emerging globalization of regional security, India has had to discard much of its traditional baggage about the role of other major powers in the Subcontinent.

That the Subcontinent is India's exclusive sphere of influence and New Delhi must strive to prevent the intervention of great powers in the affairs of the region are ideas that have long animated the nation's foreign policy. The notion of a Monroe Doctrine, similar to the one proclaimed for the Western Hemisphere by the US in the 19th century, was expounded by none other than Jawaharlal Nehru. India's first Prime Minister stressed the importance of keeping foreign powers out of Asia in the context of the attempts by the colonial powers to regain territories after the Second World War. Referring to the fact that America had secured itself from foreign aggression under the Monroe Doctrine, Nehru insisted that foreign armies have no business to stay on the soil of any Asian country. But the extended Cold War in Asia ensured that foreign armies stayed on. Even after the Cold War ended, there are no signs that they are about to leave. Nevertheless, the notion of the Monroe Doctrine took root in Indian foreign policy in relation to the Subcontinent. While India could not prevent Pakistan from bringing great power rivalries to the Subcontinent, it actively sought to insulate the rest of the region from intervention by external powers. The special relationships India had inherited from the British with regard to the security of some of the smaller neighbors reinforced the sense of South Asia as India's sphere of influence.

That approach has been neither credible nor effective. New Delhi does not have the luxury of pursuing a kind of Monroe doctrine for the region. Instead of trying to keep other powers out of the region, India has begun to recognize the importance of working with other powers to promote economic modernization, social harmony, and political moderation within the Subcontinent. India has begun to recognize that its primacy in the region cannot be sustained by mere fiat or by trying to keep the world out. In recent years, India has worked closely with the US and UK in finding ways to deal with the political crisis in Nepal. India has also worked with Norway in nudging forward the peace process in Sri Lanka. While cooperating with the Anglo–Americans on peace and stability in South Asia, India is also slowly coming to terms with the growing economic and political influence of China in the Subcontinent.

Third, India has begun to recognize that it has a huge stake in the rapid economic development of its neighborhood. India's economic performance has been the best in South Asia during the decade of 1990s. But that rapid development is no guarantor of stability in South Asia. Without all boats rising in South Asia at the same time, India can neither prosper nor be secure. While globalization is chipping away at the notion of South Asia as an exclusive sphere of influence of India, it is reinforcing the primacy of the Indian market in the long-term evolution of the South Asian economies. The integration of the markets of the Subcontinent over the coming decades is inevitable. This has opened the doors for unilateral Indian initiatives to promote economic integration and political stability in South Asia. Security multilateralism and positive economic unilateralism from India are the keys to a different future of the Subcontinent.

5. India and its Extended Neighborhood: Looking East and West

Although Asia was central to the conception of India's worldview at the time of independence, India steadily found itself marginalized from the dynamics of the mega-continent. The impact of the Cold War and the consequences of the Partition tended to rob the Indian Subcontinent of the centrality it had enjoyed in Asian politics under the British Raj. Its *de facto* alliance with the Soviet Union by the early 1970s put it at odds with much of Asia. And its inward-looking and insular economic policies resulted in declining trade and political contact with its neighboring regions. But the end of the Cold War liberated India from the past political constraints and the economic reforms initiated in 1991 allowed India to re-establish intensive commercial relations with different parts of Asia as well as to politically reposition itself in the region during the 1990s.

Toward South East Asia, India launched the Look East Policy in the early 1990s that helped it to join the multilateral institutions in the region.[d] In the second phase of the Look East policy initiated in this decade, India has focused

---

[d] For a discussion of India's Look East policy, see Ref. 4 and also Ref. 5.

on deepening its economic integration with the region, establishing physical connectivity, and developing defence and security ties. The geographic scope of India's Look East policy expanded to encompass South Korea, Japan, and Australasia. India has also been keen to join the APEC and ASEM but has been less successful. It had also campaigned actively to join the first founding meeting of the East Asia Summit which was held on December 14, 2005. The rising Chinese influence in South East Asia has been an important spur for India's greater activism in the region. India, however, has been careful not to present its competition with China for influence in the region as antagonistic rivalry and has instead focused on expanding its profile at this stage rather than engaging in an attempt to balance China.

India tried to replicate its success in South East Asia with similar efforts in other parts of Asia. India launched a forward policy to regain the influence it lost in Afghanistan during the Soviet Occupation and moved quickly to establish commercial and political relationships with the newly independent republics of Central Asia. The ouster of the Taliban provided an opportunity to expand India's economic and political exposure in Afghanistan. In Tajikistan, that borders the Subcontinent, India's ties have acquired a strategic dimension as New Delhi has been helping the military consolidation of the regime in Dushanbe. In pursuit of its regional security interests as well as its energy security considerations, India has intensified its cooperation with Iran as well as the GCC countries. In the Middle East, India moved away from its past imbalanced approach toward the region that included an ideological tilt towards the Arabs. While maintaining the traditional ties with Arab nations, India has managed to significantly upgrade relations with Israel, which has emerged as one of India's leading sources of defence technologies.

Even as India raises its level of interaction with Central Asia, the Persian Gulf and the Middle East, its traditional rivalries with China and Pakistan have remained enduring factors. India is now trying to find ways to mitigate them both. As two of the largest economies in the world and eagerly looking for long-term energy relationships in the Persian Gulf and the Middle East, India and China are bound to find themselves active players in the region. But there are also some political initiatives underway between India and China to limit their energy competition and find ways to cooperate in their quest for energy security. It is Pakistan, however, that has traditionally tended to limit India's quest for greater political influence in this region. There are signs that

India is trying to put its traditional approach to Pakistan on its head, when dealing with the Asian neighborhood to the West.

The Partition in 1947 removed India's physical access to the region. Pakistan, of course, is more than a geographic barrier between India and the Greater Middle East. It has effectively neutralized many of India's initiatives through its own special links to the Greater Middle East. As India unveils yet another effort at comprehensive bilateral engagement with Pakistan, it is trying to bring a different strategic perspective that seeks to put in place policies that will transform Pakistan from a barrier into a bridge to the West. At first cut, the thought that India and Pakistan could be partners in the Greater Middle East appears an outlandish idea. After all have not India and Pakistan contested each other's influence all over the Greater Middle East? Are not New Delhi and Islamabad deadly rivals in Afghanistan? But the past need not necessarily be a guide to the future.

The elements of a bold "Look West" policy are beginning to emerge in New Delhi. Such a policy begins by acknowledging the unique geopolitical significance of Pakistan and by turning it to India's advantage. Instead of viewing Pakistan as a perennial obstacle to the Greater Middle East, it could become a link connecting the Subcontinent to the energy-rich Persian Gulf and Central Asia. Pakistan could serve as the transit route for the movement of goods, people and energy between India and the Greater Middle East. If the idea fructifies, India will gain overland access to Afghanistan, Iran and Central Asia; Pakistan in turn will be able to trade along the Indian highways with Nepal, Bangladesh, and South East Asia. Today India is going to great lengths to develop access to Afghanistan and Central Asia through Iran. Pakistan similarly has to circumnavigate India to get to the East.

Pakistan's long-term economic interests coincide with India's "Look West policy." Gen. Musharraf, of course, insists that the resolution of the Kashmir question is the key to unleashing the geo-economic potential of the region. Pakistan itself has de-linked the construction of overland pipelines from Iran and Central Asia to India from its emphasis that Kashmir is the core issue. Overcoming its initial skepticism, India has now accepted Musharraf's offer on pipelines and has agreed to negotiate. The construction of these pipelines could effectively transform not just Indo–Pak relations but recast the geopolitics of the Subcontinent and the Greater Middle East.

Since the collapse of the Soviet Union, however, India began to engage the American and allied navies as well as those of South East Asia in bilateral exercises. Political and economic cooperation between India and the US has also rapidly expanded since the end of the Cold War. India and America now share the objective of peace and stability in South Asia. They have a joint interest in countering terrorism and extremism in the region. In Sri Lanka, where their navies will now work closely, New Delhi and Washington are both opposed to terrorism by the Tamil Tigers and seek to maintain the unity and territorial integrity of the island nation. India and the US also want to ensure the security of energy supplies from the Gulf region. They also seek to ensure the safety of sea-lanes that carry oil and a lot of other commerce in the Indian Ocean. While these broad common objectives were widely recognized in New Delhi and Washington, there had been no real occasion for the two countries to work together in managing security in the Indian Ocean. It arose in the wake of the tsunami strike.

The core group involving India, US, Japan, and Australia, was not directed against any other country; but it was inevitable that larger motives were read into its formation. The immediate motivation for the four-nation cooperation involving India and the US was one simple fact — that no one country could manage the consequences of the extraordinary disaster on its own. Amidst objections from Europe and China the core group was quickly disbanded. While the four-nation coalition was quickly folded into the larger relief operation conducted by the United Nations, the navies of the four nations continued to collaborate at the operational level. That India decided within 24 hours after the idea was floated in America to join the US and its traditional Asian allies in coordinating tsunami relief was in itself an important message about the likely future alignments in the Indian ocean region. The absence of China from this coalition and the fact that the Chinese navy stayed home when the India ships moved to alleviate the humanitarian crisis in the Indian Ocean tells a story of its own. This does not, however, mean India wants to align with the US against China. Even as New Delhi was taking the decision on the four-nation core group, the Indian Army chief was coincidentally winding up a successful visit to China that saw a decision to intensify bilateral defence contacts and put in place additional military confidence-building measures. Indian and Chinese navies have also held joint exercises.

Besides signaling a dramatic improvement in Indo–US military relations, India's Tsunami diplomacy also underlined the changing perceptions of the regional states about Indian naval activity in the Indian Ocean region. By mobilizing its navy to join the relief operations of its neighbors India has doubly transformed its strategy in the Indian Ocean. Nations do not easily accept foreign troops on their soil. Even amidst great tragedies, nations are acutely conscious of their territorial sovereignty. It is a testimony to the unprecedented circumstances generated by the tsunami strike and India's changing maritime strategy in the Indian Ocean that saw the Maldives, Sri Lanka, and Indonesia accept Indian naval presence without reservations. Colombo, which in the past was deeply suspicious of Indian hegemony, has allowed India to operate out of its ports and to conduct hydrographic surveys in its territorial waters. India now has active naval cooperation with a number of countries in the region and has signed important defence cooperation agreements with Sri Lanka and Singapore. It provides military assistance to many countries in the Indian Ocean from Vietnam to the Seychelles.

6. Towards Nuclear Accommodation

Until 1998, when India conducted five nuclear tests and formally declared itself a nuclear weapon power, its political objective was simple — to prevent the international system from capturing its un-exercised nuclear option. As a result, India was at the forefront of the international criticism of the global nuclear order, underlining its discriminatory character and emphasizing the centrality of global nuclear disarmament. After the nuclear tests, India's strategy changed fundamentally. It was aimed at consolidating its nuclear deterrent, reducing the costs of its defiance of the international system, acquiring international acceptance of its standing as a nuclear weapon state and removing the residual constraints on its acquisition of advanced technologies from outside. While this shift was neither fully appreciated at home nor understood abroad, India brought into affect a number of changes in its traditional nuclear policy.

These included support to such international arms control treaties as Comprehensive Test Ban Treaty (CTBT) and Fissile Materials Cut-off Treaty, and instituting stronger export controls. India, which traditionally rejected regional nuclear arms control, actively sought to engage Pakistan in building nuclear confidence-building measures. During the Nuclear Non-Proliferation Treaty

(NPT) Review Conference in 2000 and on the eve of the 2005 Review Conference, India has endorsed the broad objectives of the Nuclear Non-Proliferation Treaty and underlined its compliance with the obligations of nuclear weapons states under the treaty. Departing from its past opposition to regional nuclear weapon free zones, India began to endorse NWFZs in its neighborhood and offered negative security assurances to non-nuclear states. In the past, the burden of India's righteous but tiresome song was simple: it is opposed to the NPT, 1970, which decreed only five nations can legally possess nuclear weapons. India had little else to offer except a broad slogan on global nuclear disarmament. Demonstrating a new national confidence after 1998, New Delhi begun to declare that it is prepared for an accommodation with the global nuclear order. India is no longer carping at the world nuclear order; it wants to help manage it.

While India's effort to find nuclear reconciliation with the US did not succeed with the Clinton Administration, it found an unexpected level of convergence with the Bush Administration. Under Bush, Washington downgraded the importance of the CTBT and seemed reconciled to live with the nuclear weapons of India and Pakistan. Going beyond the old framework of the nuclear dialogue with New Delhi, the Bush Administration unveiled the Next Steps in Strategic Partnership (NSSP) with India that called for a series of reciprocal steps by both sides. Under the NSSP, India would address America's non-proliferation concerns and Washington, in turn, would loosen the controls over the transfer of advanced technologies to India.[e] At the beginning of its second term, the Bush Administration decided to go way beyond the NSSP. In a joint statement signed with the Indian Prime Minister Manmohan Singh on July 18, 2005, the US President George W. Bush made the bold commitment to make a nuclear exception for India.[f] Under this framework, the US agreed to modify its domestic non-proliferation law and change the global nuclear rules to facilitate full civilian atomic energy cooperation with India. New Delhi, in turn, agreed to separate its civilian and military

---

[e] For the text of the NSSP statement, see "Next Steps in Strategic Partnership with the USA" issued on January 13, 2004 in New Delhi and Washington. Available at <http://www.indianembassy.org/pm/vajpayee/2004/pm_jan_13_2004.htm>."

[f] For a text of the July 18 statement, see White House "India-U.S. Joint Statement," Washington, July 18, 2005; available at <http://www.indianembassy.org/press_release/2005/July/21.htm>. For a comprehensive discussion on making of the July 18 statement see Ref. 6.

nuclear facilities and place the former under international safeguards. It also undertook a full range of other non-proliferation obligations. The attempt to integrate India into the global nuclear order raised a storm of protests within the US, India and the international community. Washington and New Delhi, however, appear determined to complete the process of drawing India into the international non-proliferation system.

When completed, the accommodation of India into the global nuclear order might mark the single most visible consequence of the changes in India's national security strategy amidst the new wave of globalization. The Bush Administration's willingness to revise the three and a half decades old nuclear non-proliferation system is, in itself, a recognition of the shifting sands of international balance amidst a redistribution of global wealth and power, especially in favor of China and India. President Bush recognized that accepting India's nuclear exceptionalism was but a small price to pay for long-term cooperation with a rising power which could play a critical role in structuring a new balance of power in Asia and beyond. Fundamental changes in India's economic orientation at home under the pressure of globalization and its creative foreign policy since the early 1990s also allowed New Delhi to realize its long-standing aspirations for an international acceptance of its role on the world stage.[g] In that context, entry into the nuclear club house was perhaps more important for India than an immediate permanent membership of the United Nations Security Council. But the best of the potential consequences of India's changing national security strategy are yet to be seen. It is only when India succeeds in normalizing its relations with Pakistan and China, reintegrates the economies of the Subcontinent, and raises its economic and security profile in all parts of Asia and the Indian Ocean region, would the full range of implications from the rise of India, as part of the current transformative phase of globalization come into view.

References

1. Mohan, C.R. (2005). *Crossing the Rubicon: The Shaping of India's New Foreign Policy*, 2nd Edition. New Delhi: Penguin.
2. Ganguly, S. (ed.) (2003). *India as an Emerging Power*. Portland: Frank Cass.

---

[g]For a discussion of India's quest for great power status since independence, see Ref 7.

3. Muni, S.D. (2000). "India in SAARC: Reluctant Policy-Maker." In Hettne, B., Inotai, A. and Sunkel, O. (eds.) *National Perspectives on the New Regionalism in the Third World*. New York: Palgrave, pp. 95–99.
4. Sridharan, K. (1996). *The ASEAN Region in India's Foreign Policy*. Aldershot, UK: Dartmouth Publishing Company.
5. Grare, F. and Mattoo, A. (eds.) (2001). *India and ASEAN: The Politics of India's Look East Policy*. New Delhi: Manohar.
6. Mohan, C.R. (2006). *Impossible Allies: Nuclear India, United States and the Global Order*. New Delhi: India Research Press.
7. Nayar, B.R. and Paul, T.V. (2003). *India in the World Order: Searching for Major-Power Status*. Cambridge, UK: Cambridge University Press.

SECTION 4

Ethnicity and Identity in the New World

CHAPTER 13

India's Identity Politics: Then and Now

Vibha Pingle and Ashutosh Varshney

"I do not want my house to be walled in on all sides and my windows to be stuffed. I want the cultures of all lands to be blown about my house as freely as possible. But I refuse to be blown off my feet by any." — Mahatma Gandhi.[a]

The basic argument of this paper can be precisely stated: India's identity politics remains primarily internally crafted and driven. That globalization is having an impact is evident, but it is an influence secondary to the internal drivers of change. To paraphrase Mahatma Gandhi, one of India's most intuitive political theorisers of all times, the windows of the Indian house are now more and more open, and the winds are blowing about with ever greater force, but India's feet remain quite firmly internally planted. Whatever the consequences of globalization for India's *economy* and consumption patterns, the primary determinants of changes in India's *identity politics* remain domestic.

At one level, this is surprising. As Amartya Sen points out, "India's recent achievements in science and technology (including information technology), or in world literature, or in international business, have all involved a good deal of global interaction." And "these interactions are not unprecedented in Indian history."[b] Indeed ideas "as well as people have moved across India's borders over thousands of years, enriching India as well as the rest of the world."[c]

India's founding leaders were also remarkably globalized in their moorings and inspirations. Mahatma Gandhi's politics was formed by experiences in Britain, South Africa, and India, and some of his key concepts emerged from

---

[a]Mahatma Gandhi (1921). "English Learning." *Young India*, 3(6).
[b]Amartya Sen (1995). *The Argumentative Indian*. New York: Farrar, Straus and Giroux, p. 84.
[c]*Ibid.*, p. 86.

a dialog of Indian traditions with the ideas of Tolstoy and Thoreau. And Nehru's political life was defined by an encounter between his British and Indian experiences. Given how strongly these two figures shaped an entire generation, India's politics in the 20th century, including its identity politics, might be expected to have significant international influences.[b]

At another level, the persistence of a primarily internal cultural compass to navigate the uncertainties of transition is hardly surprising. Interaction and influence are two different categories. A certain cultural pride, if not cultural obduracy, goes with large countries like India (and China), heir to old civilizations and to long-lasting cultural traditions. Despite the opening of many windows, Mahatma Gandhi indeed remained culturally rooted in India, and Nehru, for all his British tastes so often commented upon, wanted his ashes scattered in the river Ganga after his death[d]:

> When I die, I should like my body to be cremated ... A small handful of (my) ashes should be thrown into the Ganga ... My desire to have a handful of my ashes thrown into the Ganga at Allahabad has no religious significance, so far as I am concerned. I have been attached to the Ganga and Jamuna rivers in Allahabad ever since my childhood and, as I have grown older, this attachment has grown ... The Ganga, especially, is the river of India, beloved of her people, round which are intertwined ... her hopes and fears, her songs of triumph, her victories and her defeats. She has been a symbol of India's age-long culture and civilization, ever-changing, ever-flowing, and yet ever the same Ganga ... Ganga has been to me a symbol and a memory of the past of India, running into the present and flowing on the great ocean of the future.

Before our narrative acquires too protean a character, as so many discussions of identity politics tend to become, we should indicate how we have constructed the analytical boundaries of this paper. With or without globalization, identity politics can cover a whole variety of issues, not all of which can be adequately analyzed at length here. To make the discussion tractable,

---

[d] "Will and Testament." In: Gopal, S. (ed.) (1980). *Jawaharlal Nehru: An Anthology*. Delhi: Oxford University Press, pp. 647–648.

let us first ask: what key questions emerge when we analyze the relationship between identity politics and globalization?

The first set of questions is conceptual. All of us may know the basic features of globalization — defined as trans-border crossings of capital, labor, services, technology and ideas — but how does one conceptualize identity politics? We need, first of all, to draw a distinction between identity and identity politics. In a recent account, Brubaker shows that in its latest phase, the concept of identity, born in the works of Erik Erikson, was psychological.[e] We are not psychologists and the changing Indian psyche, especially of the middle class, is not the area of our expertise. We will concentrate on identity politics, not on identity *per se*. Identity politics refers to politics driven by demands and concerns rooted in identities — religious, ethnic, linguistic, national, gender, etc.

This means that we shall not deal with how the nation's rising economic profile is instilling a new confidence among India's business and middles classes; or how for the first time in modern history, beyond the Western states of Gujarat and Maharashtra, successful businessmen, especially in information technology (IT), are becoming icons and role models for younger people, who were fascinated in the past primarily with politicians, film stars, cricketers and the Indian administrative service; or how the success of Indian diaspora in many professions and the rise to international prominence of Indian novelists in the English language have become a matter of pride for many in the middle class, indicating new ways of achieving creative excellence. These are important matters. Urban middle class conversations have quite dramatically changed in India. But we do not yet have evidence of mainstream politics being seriously altered by such developments.

With regard to identity *politics*, we suggest a distinction between two dimensions: macro and micro. The macro questions have to do with national, sub-national and group identities: how is India's national identity defined, and what kinds of group identities — religious, linguistic, tribal, caste-related — have been prominent in national politics? The micro questions have to do with how *families* and *individuals* adapt to, and counter, changes in environment, and what sorts of politics such adaptations and challenges spawn.

---

[e]Rogers Brubaker (2004). "Beyond Identity." in his *Ethnicity Without Groups*. Cambridge: Harvard University Press.

A second set of questions concerns the relationship of globalization and identity politics. There are two ways of thinking about it. One has to do with the consequences of globalization for identity politics, and the other with the consequences of identity politics for the globalization of a nation's economic life. Only the former is typically analyzed. We need to look at both sides.

In what follows, we begin with two larger and background discussions that will illuminate our specific arguments. We first discuss at some length (a) how to understand identity politics in a multicultural society, and (b) what the enduring features of India's identity politics in the 20th century have been. Subsequently, we ask how globalization has affected these relatively permanent features and also turn to the consequences of India's identity politics for the nation's march toward economic integration with the world economy. Compared to China, India's march is slow and steady, but it is unmistakable and, in our judgment, irreversible.

We make three arguments. First, we argue that at the macro level India's identity politics remains largely a conversation internal to India, though one global influence — the non-resident Indians (NRIs) community — has played a limited role in sustaining this identity politics. While the support of the NRI community did contribute to the strength of the Hindu nationalist movement and may do so again, there is little evidence to suggest that identity politics in India is moving along a course charted by identity politics elsewhere around the globe. Second, unlike the cases of Islamic fundamentalism in northern Nigeria and Christian fundamentalism in Latin America or the Philippines, the forces of religiously inspired politics in India (both Hindu and Muslim) have either not concentrated on micro issues — gender roles, abortion, marriage, divorce — or if they have, they have been unable to transform the basic contours of India's identity politics, which remains primarily focused on macro, not micro, issues. Third, the major preoccupation of India's popular politics has on the whole been with issues of *group identity*, not with questions of *economic development*. The latter has been a very important aspect of elite politics, not of popular politics. In what might constitute a little-noticed paradox, this gap between the major concerns of elite and popular politics provided in the 1990s the political space for an internationally oriented economic reform program to move forward. If India's popular politics in the 1990s had not been consumed by issues of national and group identities, economic reforms would have encountered much greater political difficulty than they actually did.

1. The Framework of Identity Politics

How should we understand the foundations of identity politics, in India or elsewhere?[f] After the Second World War, the expectation of statesmen like Nehru, or scholars, who later came to be known as modernization theorists, was that an onward march of modernity would before long obliterate people's attachments to religious, ethnic or caste groups.[g] In contrast, the passage to modernity all over the world — more in some places, less in others — has been accompanied by very different developments. As Charles Taylor has famously argued, two such developments — the demand for dignity and the urge to find one's authenticity — are critical for understanding the identity politics of individuals and groups.[h]

First, modernity has replaced the traditional discourse of *honor* with a conversation about *dignity*. Honor is reserved only for some and was characteristic of traditional social systems. In pre-modern times, human beings, even at the lower orders of society, customarily accepted pre-existing ascriptive hierarchies, or notions of birth-based superiority and inferiority. Living according to one's station in life, or leading one's life according to pre-assigned social roles, was the accepted norm. Modernity has transformed human life by giving precedence to dignity over longstanding hierarchies. Dignity is intrinsic to all human beings, and with modernity, more and more previously dominated groups and individuals have come to believe in the idea of equal dignity. Hierarchies can and do exist today, but they are increasingly achievement-based, not birth-based, and if the latter, are often challenged.

---

[f]The ideas in this section rely on two of our previous writings: Vibha Pingle (2005). "Faiths, Equity and Development." Background Paper, *World Development Report 2006*, Washington, DC: The World Bank; and Ashutosh Varshney (2003). "Nationalism, Ethnic Conflict and Rationality." *Perspectives on Politics*, 1(1), March, 84–99.

[g]For the older as well as the revised, newer versions of modernization theory, see Ronald Inglehart and Christine Welzel (2005). *Modernization, Cultural Change and Democracy*. Cambridge: Cambridge University Press; and Pippa Norris and Ronald Inglehart (2004). *Sacred and Secular: Religion and Politics Worldwide*. Cambridge: Cambridge University Press.

[h]Charles Taylor (1995). *Multiculturalism and the Politics of Recognition*. Princeton: Princeton University Press.

Second, modernity has also led to claims about recognition. Traditionally, an engagement with God was regarded as critical for discovering one's moral core. With modernity this conversation about morality is increasingly regarded as being with our inner self that is paradoxically understood not via meditation, but by means of dialogical contact with others. Dialogical contact, in other words, helps us answer "where we are coming from" and "who we are." With dialogical contact gaining prominence, misrecognition is regarded as causing injury; withholding recognition is seen as a form of oppression.[i]

Crude illiberal prejudice or hatred is, of course, an obvious source for such "confining, demeaning or contemptible" images. But the problem is much more complex. It is worth recalling that until this century, even well-meaning liberals believed in group-based notions of civility and barbarism. In one of the founding texts of liberalism, John Stuart Mill, for example, argued[j]:

> Nobody can suppose that it is not beneficial to a Breton, or a Basque of the French Navarre, to be brought into the current of ideas and feelings of a highly civilized and cultivated people — to be a member of the French nationality ... than to sulk on his own rocks, the half-savage relic of past times, revolving in his own little mental orbit, without participation or interest in the general movement of the world. The same remark applies to the Welshman or the Scottish Highlander, as members of the British nation.

In the modern world, thus, two different notions of worth have often been at odds: one stemming from the culturally inherited conceptions of groups as better or worse; and another arising out of a decline of social hierarchies and the rise of equality. By challenging the inherited structure or discourse of group hierarchy, the latter inevitably seeks to undermine the former.

Identity politics or what we might call the demand for recognition is thus, at its core, essentially the *politics of equal dignity* and the *politics of difference* (or authenticity). It has emerged both in the developing and developed world, and has roots in gender politics, sexual politics, ethnic politics, and religious interpretations, or some combination thereof. The founding arguments of many, if not all, of these movements combine tradition and modernity in

---

[i]Taylor, *Multiculturalism*, p. 25.
[j]John Stuart Mill (1990). *Three Essays*. New York: Oxford University Press, pp. 385–386.

unusual ways.[k] Many traditional ideas are revived or group traditions are fought for, but the language used is one of dignity and equal respect.

The resurgence of religious and ethnic identity movements has two related yet distinct implications for our concerns here. First, religious and ethnic movements have in various parts of the world also been accompanied by religious and ethnic nationalism, and *if such nationalism is majoritarian*, it has unequal, even threatening, implications for religious and ethnic minorities. Second, whether or not religious and ethnic minorities are threatened, such movements have tended to undermine the rights of vulnerable members of their own community. Nearly every religious and ethnic movement has, for instance, redefined the role and rights of women and insisted on a traditional conception of gender roles.

In short, the politics of dignity and the search for authenticity have some seemingly liberating features and some retrogressive ones. On the one hand, modernity tends to foster religious and ethnic movements which demand equality vis-à-vis other communities, and also tends to encourage the movements to define themselves in unique ways. On the other hand, these movements demand that their unique group identity (which defines the role of women or family lifestyles in a traditional manner) be recognized and respected by the state and other citizens. Thus, individuals and groups demand to be treated equally at the same time as they seek recognition for their uniqueness.

In what follows, we will not try to prove, or disprove, the arguments made above. This essay is not the place for a testing of grand theories. Our only claim is that this larger theoretical background will make much of what we say intelligible and put India's identity politics in a comparative and global perspective.

2. India's Identity Politics: the Patterns and the Playing Field[l]

In its nation-building effort since independence, India has primarily had to deal with four key group identities: language, religion, caste, and tribe. Nearly

---

[k]For example, gay rights movements demand the right to marry; women's rights groups in Egypt and Nigeria demand that the *Shariat* be imposed.

[l]This section relies heavily on Ashutosh Varshney (2002). *Ethnic Conflict and Civic Life: Hindus and Muslims in India*. New Haven: Yale University Press, and Delhi: Oxford University Press, and Ashutosh Varshney (1993). "Contested Meanings: India's National Identity, Hindu Nationalism and the Politics of Anxiety." *Daedalus*. summer.

Table 1.   India's principal languages.

Language	Spoken by percentage of India's population
Hindi	39.9
Bengali	8.2
Telugu	7.8
Marathi	7.4
Tamil	6.3
Urdu	5.1
Gujarati	4.8
Kannada	3.9
Malayalam	3.6
Oriya	3.3
Punjabi	2.8
Assamese	1.5

Source: Census of India.

Table 2.   India's religious profile.

Group	Percentage of population
Hindus	82.0
of whom a) Caste Hindus	67.2
b) Scheduled Castes	14.8
Muslims	12.1
Christians	2.3
Sikhs	2.0
Buddhists and Jains	1.2

Source: Census of India.

40% of the country speaks Hindi as its "mother tongue," but there are at least 15 other languages spoken as a "mother tongue" by at least ten million people each (Table 1). Although having a Hindu majority, India has several other religions (Table 2). There are three meta-categories of caste — upper, middle, and ex-untouchables (Table 3).[m] The last two, viewed as historically deprived, constitute a majority by a huge margin; the upper castes, not more than 18% of the country, have on the whole dominated the nation's political, social and economic landscape. Tribes, constituting 8.1% of the population (called the scheduled tribes, Table 3), are the least known but an important category, and

---

[m]Caste is essentially a local category, and there are thousands of castes in India. With some qualification, they can, however, be grouped together in larger, meta-categories.

Table 3. India's caste composition.

Group	Percentage of population
Upper castes	16.1
OBCs	43.7
Scheduled castes	14.9
Scheduled tribes	8.1
Non-Hindu minorities	17.2

Note: Since no caste census has been taken since 1931, the figures above can be seen as best guesses, not exact estimates. They are sufficient to show the overall magnitudes, however. Also, the upper castes in this calculation include the "dominant castes" that are no longer considered deprived, even though they were ritually not placed in the upper category (as explained in note w).
Source: Government of India (1980). *Report of the Backward Classes Commission* (The Mandal Commission Report), 1 (First Part), 56.

culturally quite distinct from the mainstream. They are mostly concentrated in the middle and north-eastern part of the nation. On the whole, language and tribe tend to be geographically concentrated, whereas religion and caste are more evenly spread throughout the country.

How did India's founding fathers seek to deal with these diverse group identities? Their strategy was twofold: (i) adoption of a "salad bowl," as opposed to a "melting pot" view of the national identity, a view that came to called "composite nationalism"[n]; and (ii) a reliance on democracy to resolve conflicts. A "salad bowl" view of national identity recognizes diversities as central to the nation. However, despite this principle, it is possible that some groups remain discontented, either because their distinctiveness is not recognized, or if recognized, not given equal treatment. If so, democratic mobilization of disaffection and making a point through the election process would be the way to show that the claim about the group's distinctiveness had popular support. Once popular support was demonstrated, it would allow Delhi to make adequate concessions.

Thus, the government would not accept all claims about cultural distinctiveness, only those which were demonstrably popularly backed. This gave a

---

[n] For a longer treatment, see Ashutosh Varshney (1993). "Contested Meanings." *Daedalus, op. cit.*, on which the discussion here heavily relies.

great incentive to political entrepreneurs to mobilize identity groups, making group conflict quite ubiquitous in India. But if diversity and democracy had to coexist together, there was no other way out. Groups were free to mobilize and make claims. The assumption also was that the greater the freedom to mobilize, the lesser would be the drive toward secession. The accommodation inherent in India's salad bowl strategy was expected to make insurgencies redundant. India's founding leaders were clear that if a violent insurgency nonetheless arose, it would not be tolerated and force would be used. Nehru, it is said, used to keep two statuettes on his desk: Gandhi's and Lincoln's. The former symbolized the willing embrace of diversities, the latter an unwavering opposition to violent insurgencies.[o]

An outgrowth of India's freedom movement, composite nationalism was legitimated by the country's constitution after independence. Fundamentally, this view of the nation evokes the image of nation as a family. In principle, all religions (as well as languages, castes, and tribes) have an equal place in the national family, and none will dominate the functioning of the state. In practice, this ideal has not been fully realized, nor is it easy to realize it, but the important point is that ideal was never given up formally. India's founding fathers never developed a notion of *bhumiputras* (sons of the soil). One's religious faith, linguistic, caste or social background would not determine citizenship in the country and the rights that go with it; birth in India, or naturalization, would be the sole legal criterion.

Although the Congress party, which led the freedom movement, has been the prime representative of this narrative in Indian politics, most political parties and currents have on the whole subscribed to this view of diversities and the nation. The main challenges to this ideology have come from two sources: religion and caste. They have clear implications for how the nation deals with group diversities.

2.1. *Hindu nationalism and its demand for recognition*

In the sphere where religion came to interact with politics, the "salad bowl" ideology came to be called "secular nationalism." A state governed by such an ideology would maintain "equal distance" from all religions, privileging

[o]Akbar, M.J. (1988). *Nehru: The Making of India*. Delhi: Penguin, p. 565.

none. The greatest challenge to this view has come from Hindu nationalism, a powerful force since 1989. The Hindu nationalist view of the nation is embedded in a "melting pot" model. Hinduism, according to this narrative, gives India its distinctive national identity, and other religions must *assimilate* to the Hindu center. India, according to this narrative, is originally the land of the Hindus. Most of India is, and has been, Hindu by religion[p] — anywhere between 65 and 70% in the early 20th century India and 82% today. India thus viewed is a Hindu nation.[q]

The term Hindu is further specified by Hindu nationalists. Savarkar, the ideological father of Hindu nationalism, gave a definition in *Hindutva*, the foundational text of Hindu nationalism: "A Hindu means a person who regards this land ... from the Indus to the Seas as his fatherland (*pitribhumi*) as well as his Holyland (*punyabhumi*)."[r] The definition is thus territorial (land between the Indus and the Seas), genealogical ("fatherland") and religious ("holyland"). Hindus, Sikhs, Jains, Buddhists can be part of this definition for they meet all three criteria. All of these religions were born in India. Christians, Jews, Parsis, and Muslims can meet only two, for India is not their holyland. "Their love is divided."[s]

For Hindu nationalists, Muslims and Christians are the principal enemies of the nation — especially the former, partly because of their numbers, and partly because a Muslim homeland in the form of Pakistan after all did partition India in 1947. The Muslims were 25% of the pre-1947 India, and even after the formation of Pakistan, they have been the largest minority, about 12.8% of the country's population at this point.

What should these communities, especially the Muslims, do to show that they are part of the Indian nation? In extreme versions of Hindu nationalism, a claim about the legal primacy of Hindus, which the Muslims must accept, is made. In other words, a differential bundle of *citizenship rights* is proposed.

---

[p]Some historians disagree. They argue that a Hindu identity is at best a creation of the last 200–300 years. Before that, there were different sects, but no Hindu identity as such. See Romila Thapar (1989). "Imagined Religious Communities? Ancient History and the Modern Search for Hindu Identity." *Modern Asian Studies* **23**(2).

[q]Sheshadri, H.V. (1989–1990). "Hindu Rashtra: What and Why." *Hindu Vishva* Silver Jubilee Special Issue, 25(12), p. 30. Nanaji Deshmukh (1989). *Rethinking Secularism*. Delhi: Suruchi Prakashan.

[r]Savarkar, V.D. (1989). *Hindutva*. Bombay: Veer Savarkar Prakashan (sixth edition), title page, elaborated further between pp. 110–113.

[s]Savarkar, V.D. *Hindutva, op. cit.*, p. 113.

Expressing his admiration for how Hitler dealt with the Jews, Golwalkar, one of the fathers of Hindu nationalism, wrote[t]:

> Race pride at its highest has been manifested (in) ... Germany ... The foreign races in Hindusthan [i.e., the Muslims] must adopt the Hindu culture and language, must learn to respect and hold in reverence the Hindu religion, must entertain no ideas but those of glorification of the Hindu race and culture [...and] may [only] stay in the country wholly subordinated to the Hindu nation, claiming nothing — not even citizen's rights.

Muslim acceptance of the cultural and political, not legal, primacy of Hindus for shaping India's future is, however, the generic Hindu nationalist argument, shared by moderates as well. That is, to become part of the Indian nation, Muslims must: accept the centrality of Hinduism to Indian civilization; accept key Hindu figures such as Ram as civilizational heroes, not disown them as mere religious figures of Hinduism; remorsefully accept that Muslim rulers of India between 1000 A.D. and 1757 A.D. destroyed pillars of Hindu civilization, especially Hindu Temples; not claim special privileges such as maintenance of religious personal laws; and not demand special state grants for their educational institutions. Via *Ekya* (assimilation), they will prove their loyalty to the nation. Maintaining distinctiveness would simply mean that "their love," as Savarkar put it, "is divided."

It is important to understand what is at stake here. Drawing a distinction between three terms — pluralism, syncretism, and assimilation — is perhaps the best way to illustrate the differences between the two views. Composite nationalism insists on pluralism and syncretism; Hindu nationalism on assimilation.

Pluralism would indicate co-existence of distinctive identities (*A respects, and lives peacefully, with B*). An example of pluralistic tolerance from Hinduism would be Mahatma Gandhi, while Maulana Azad, his colleague during the national movement, embodied pluralistic Islam. Syncretism would signify not a tolerant co-existence of distinctions, but a merging of cultures/religions, leading to a new form of culture/religion (*A interacts with B, and an amalgam C emerges as a result*). In its interaction with Hinduism, Islam, especially Sufism,

---

[t]Golwalkar, M.S. (1939). *We or Our Nationhood Defined*. Nagpur: Bharat Publications.

developed forms of piety and culture that represented Indian as opposed to Arab versions of Islam.[u] Syncretism should also be distinguished from assimilation. Assimilation means absorption into the dominant culture/religion (*A merges into B, losing its distinctive identity*); syncretism implies a give-and-take between cultures and religions (*C represents elements of A and B*). Sikhism is a syncretistic religion par excellence, combining elements of Islam and Hinduism, and becoming a faith in itself.

Pluralism in the secular nationalist view is embodied in laws and political institutions (such as personal laws of minorities about divorce, marriage and inheritance, and protection of minority educational institutions). The Hindu nationalists argue that emotions and loyalty make a nation, not politics, laws and institutions. Laws, they say, can always be politically manipulated.

In India, Islam has historically developed two broad forms: syncretistic, and exclusivist. Syncretistic Islam integrated into the pre-existing Indian culture, just as Indonesian Muslims retained their pre-Islamic heritage of Ramayana and Mahabharata. Exclusivist Islam can be a personal faith, or may also enter the political sphere, thus becoming an ideology, displaying sometimes what are known as fundamentalist qualities. Syncretistic Islam has produced some of the pillars of Indian culture, music, poetry, and literature.[v] Indian Muslims of various hues have, moreover, also fought wars against Pakistan. By not making these distinctions, the Hindu nationalists embitter even those Muslims who are syncretistic in their religiosity and culture, as also those for whom Islam is a faith, a way to sustain troubled private lives, but not a political ideology. In the Hindu nationalist discourse, these important distinctions blur. An anti-Muslim hysteria is often its natural outcome.

Since 1947, the Bharatiya Janata Party (BJP) has been the principal patron of religious nationalism in politics. The party was called the Bharatiya Jan Sangh (BJS) until 1977. The aim of Hindu nationalists, one should also note, is not only to emphasize the centrality of Hinduism to India, but also to build

---

[u] Worship at the graves of great Sufi saints resembles Hindu forms of piety in several ways: devotional music, deposition of flowers, and a priestly offering of the "sacred sweets" (*prasad*) bring the two together; idols (Hinduism) and graves (Islam) separate them.

[v] A very large number of Muslims have been exponents of Indian classical music. Muslim playwrights and poets, writing in Hindi, have also existed. Similarly, some of the leading Urdu poets have been Hindu (e.g., Firaq Gorakhpuri). The Taj Mahal, the most popular monument of India, has syncretistic Indo-Persian motifs. The tomb of Salim Chishti, a Sufi saint, is visited by millions of Hindus and Sikhs, not simply Muslims.

Hindu unity. The Hindus, after all, are a religious majority only in a manner of speaking. They are divided internally by multiple caste cleavages. As an ideology, Hindu nationalism is thus opposed to both composite nationalism as well as to the other principal caste-based ideology of the last 100 years, as discussed below.

2.2. *Caste politics and the demand for equal dignity*

The second big ideological challenge to composite nationalism has come from lower caste political parties and organizations.[w] Their ideology is not directly opposed to composite nationalism; rather, their notion of which diversities are important and should be central to nation making is different. The lower caste ideology speaks of the deeply hierarchical and unjust nature of the Hindu social order, in which the lower castes have historically had a lower bundle of rights and some have been most shabbily treated and oppressed by the upper castes. An egalitarian restructuring of Hindu society is the chief goal of the caste narrative: caste should not determine whether an individual is treated as an inferior or superior human being.[x]

This ideology, thus, concentrates on India's religious majority, the Hindus. When it speaks of non-Hindu groups, it does so by arguing that both religious minorities as well as the lower Hindu castes suffer from discrimination by the higher castes. An alliance of lower castes and religious minorities, therefore, is natural. Moreover, according to this narrative, to make up for centuries of caste oppression, affirmative action favoring the lower castes in government jobs and education should be the primary vehicle of achieving social justice.

The "lower caste narrative" has, by and large, risen to all-India prominence of late. It was a South Indian narrative to begin with, used as it was to mobilize the masses in the first half of this century in Southern India.[y] Capitalizing on their numbers in a democracy, the lower castes of South India

---

[w] For an account by one of the founders of the ideology, see Rammanohar Lohia (1964). *The Caste System.* Hyderabad: Lohia Samata Vidyalaya Nyas.

[x] For an overview of caste identities and caste politics, see Vibha Pingle (2003). "Caste: Continuity and Change." In: Sumit Ganguly and Neil deVota (eds.) *Understanding Contemporary India.* Boulder Colorado: Lynne Riener.

[y] Marguerite Ross Barnet (1967). *The Politics of Cultural Nationalism in South India.* Princeton, NJ: Princeton University Press, and Robert Hardgrave (1969). *The Nadars of Tamil Nadu.* Berkeley: University of California Press.

ended the political and social dominance of the Brahmins in the 1960s and 1970s. In the 1980s and 1990s, this ideology of politics finally spread to the North. The lower castes have come of political age in much of India, pressing the polity in new directions and achieving significant public policy successes. The changes in, and the enlargement of, India's affirmative action program, as it was originally conceived in the 1950s, has a great deal to do with the rise of lower castes in politics.[z]

3. Globalization and Macro Identity Politics

Have religious and caste identity politics been influenced by globalization? Has the cross-border movement of capital, labor, goods, services, technology and ideas, and India's greater integration into the international system, left a discernible impact on how India's language and religious groups, castes and tribes have formulated their politics and made claims on, or against, the polity? Globalization has no identifiable connection with language and caste politics, so we do not discuss them below. Globalization has had its greatest impact on how religion has come to be deployed as a group identity in Indian politics, especially in its Hindu nationalist version. Tribal politics has also become part of Hindu nationalist politics of late. At the heart of both reformulations is the role of India's diaspora in the Hindu nationalist imagination.

Following Benedict Anderson, diasporic attachments to the homeland are now called "long distance nationalism."[aa] When it first sought intervention in India's public sphere in the 1980s, India's diaspora — the so-called NRI community — was given a rather lukewarm treatment by the "homeland." In the 1990s, two things changed. Attracting enormous public attention, the diasporic success stories multiplied, especially in the Silicon Valley where Indians, mostly graduates of Indian Institutes of Technology, registered

---

[z]For a detailed treatment how lower castes have used democracy to advance their claims and power, see Ashutosh Varshney (2000). "Is India Becoming More Democratic?" *Journal of Asian Studies* March; Myron Weiner (2001). "The Struggle for Equality: Caste in Indian Politics." In: Atul Kohli (ed.) *The Success of Indian Democracy*. Cambridge: Cambridge University Press, and Lloyd Rudolph and Susanne Rudolph (1968). *The Modernity of Tradition*. Chicago: University of Chicago Press.
[aa]Benedict Anderson (1998). *The Specter of Comparisons*. London: Verso.

an extraordinary ascent, a phenomenon noted globally.[bb] Their entry into mainstream American society plausibly also introduced them to the claims made by minorities in America and tutored them in the language of identity politics. Second — and more important — the electoral fortunes of Hindu nationalism changed dramatically in the 1990s, bringing a BJP-dominated coalition to power in Delhi in 1998. The Hindu nationalist conception of India created space for diasporic intervention in Indian politics.

The basic issues in the debate over the political role of India's diaspora can be simply outlined . How does one define an Indian? Are millions of NRIs, ethnically Indian but citizens of other lands, really Indian? Is an Indian citizen, even if born outside India, someone like Sonia Gandhi, not Indian? Indeed, it was the intervention of Sonia Gandhi in India's electoral politics in 1998 that gave this debate an enormous intensity.

3.1. *Jus solis versus jus sanguinis*

On how a citizen is defined, there are two models available in the world. Some nations are based on what is called the principle of *jus solis* (soil); others on *jus sanguinis* (blood). These ideal types are not perfectly realized anywhere. The best real-world examples of the first model are France and the US; and the typical illustrations of the second would be Germany and Japan.[cc]

Nationhood in the first model is defined in terms of a set of principles: liberty, equality and fraternity in France, and the five principles of the Declaration of Independence — liberty, equality, individualism, democracy, and the rule of law — in the US.[dd] *Anyone* can be "French" or "American", including ethnic Indians, so long as they subscribe to these principles. Naturalization is relatively easy in these countries. In the Olympic teams of France and USA, naturalized citizens, migrants until recently or children of migrants, belonging to all sorts of races, are present by the dozen. They hold American and French flags with transparent pride and emotion.

[bb] See for example the special issue of *Businessweek* on "China and India: What You Need to Know." August 22/29, 2005.

[cc] Rogers Brubaker (1992). *Citizenship and Nationhood in France and Germany*. Cambridge: Harvard University Press.

[dd] Samuel Huntington (1983). *American Politics: The Promise of Disharmony*. Cambridge: Harvard University Press. Huntington's view has changed by now. For the argument that American is not defined by political ideas, but by cultural inheritance, see his *Who Are We?* New York: 2004.

The second model does not allow easy naturalization, but lets ethnicity be the decisive, often the only factor, in citizenship. Those born to ethnically German parents anywhere in the world can become German citizens without any difficulty, even if they have lost German as their language. After the disintegration of the Soviet Union, many ethnic Germans, who had lived in the Soviet Union and come to speak Russian as their first language, migrated to Germany and became German citizens. In contrast, several million Turks, living in Germany since the 1960s, including a large proportion, who were born in Germany, are still "guest workers." Only a small fraction of "guest workers" have been allowed German citizenship. Japan has a roughly similar idea driving its nationhood and citizenship.

By celebrating and courting overseas Indians, who are mostly citizens of other countries, and unleashing political venom on Sonia Gandhi, who has been an Indian citizen since 1984–1985 and has lived in the country longer, the Hindu nationalists sought to take Indian nationhood in the *jus sanguinis*, or the German and Japanese, direction. The leaders of Indian freedom struggle, Gandhi and Nehru, had never defined the nation ethnically. Rather, they gave Indianness a cultural definition: those who accepted Indian culture, including foreigners, were welcome to be Indians. Mahatma Gandhi famously argued that even Englishmen could be Indians so long as they accepted Indian culture as their own. "It is not necessary for us," said the Mahatma, "to have as our goal the expulsion of the English. If the English become Indianized, we can accommodate them."[ee] Since the term "ethnic Indian" for Hindu nationalists for all practical purposes means "Hindu Indian," Gandhi's argument about Hinduism and India also worth noting: "If the Hindus believe that India should be peopled only by Hindus, they are living in a dreamland. The Hindus, the Muslims, the Parsis and the Christians who have made India their country are fellow countrymen."[ff]

After a vigorous debate marked by some dissent, India's Constituent Assembly (1946–1950) accepted the Gandhian idea of citizenship. Indians in Southeast Asia and in South and East Africa, the Assembly argued, had to be citizens of their adopted countries, not of India. There was a demand that they be given Indian citizenship.

[ee] Mahatma Gandhi (1938). *Hind Swaraj*. Ahmedabad: Navjivan Press, pp. 45–46.
[ff] *Ibid.*

By Mahatma Gandhi's definition, which India's constitution adopted, Sonia Gandhi is only *ethnically* Italian, but *culturally* Indian. Even though "constructed" in the long run, ethnicity is typically inherited in the short run. In contrast, cultures and nations can be adopted. By accepting Indian ethos, making a family in India and living in the country, and finally engaging in political campaigns, Sonia Gandhi had made her ethnicity, as in the Franco–American model, irrelevant to her citizenship. A debate on whether a foreign-born citizen could be the head of government would not have been in defiance of the spirit of the constitution. But the Hindu nationalists focused on something analytically and politically very different: can a foreign born and ethnically un-Indian person be Indian? India's constitution has no doubts on this matter. The answer is yes.

None of what we have said above should be construed to argue that contemporary India should become indifferent to the NRIs. Thanks to globalization and advances in communication technology, the first decade of the 21st century is not the same as the 1950s. Frequent contact with the ancestral homeland is possible, and diasporas in contemporary world have become an asset to many countries. If the NRIs are willing to contribute to the lands they came from, there is every reason to embrace their goodwill, ideas, resources and energy. It will not only be unpragmatic, but an utter folly, to do otherwise.

But defensible pragmatism is not the same as an overarching principle. The BJP-led government turned the debate into the latter. In a highly symbolic gesture, it also appointed two Indian ambassadors for Washington, one officially acceptable to the US government, another bearing the same title but managing the affairs of NRIs. The community ambassador also had special access to, and special claims on, the visiting BJP dignitaries.

It is this new definition of India *as a community of blood* that opened the space for the intense participation of overseas Hindu nationalist organizations in tribal education and proselytization. Overseas groups for long have been involved in "development" activities. Making India's tribal communities Hindu, however, was not one of their main goals. In central and Western India, tribal religiosity has on the whole historically been ambiguous. Large-scale attempts at tribal conversion to Hinduism and tribal participation in anti-Muslim violence, as was true in Gujarat 2002, are new developments.^{gg} It is hard to prove rigorously the exact connections between the tribal anti-Muslim violence and Hindu nationalist campaigns. All the same, without the Hindu nationalist campaigns, jointly undertaken by domestic and NRI organizations, it is not easy to explain why such developments took place at all.^{hh}

4. Globalization and Micro Identity Politics

Entering politics in a big way in many parts of the world, questions of micropolitics — family, marriage, gender relations, and sexuality — have, however, remained relatively unimportant in Indian politics. The transmission of global ideas on India's micropolitics has been minimal.

It is by now unmistakably clear that with the prominent exception of Christian religiosity in Western Europe, in both developing and developed world and among the believers of the world's most popular faiths — Islam, Christianity, and Hinduism — there has been a remarkable rise in religiosity.[ii] Much of the politics in these countries has acquired a religious tinge.

In a widely noted argument, Olivier Roy has recently suggested that in the Muslim world, political Islam and its calls to establish an Islamic *state* have been replaced by a "globalized Islam" that is concerned with establishing an Islamic *identity* that transcends cultural boundaries, as engagement with modernity and globalization continues.[jj] The leaders of "globalized Islam," and to a greater degree the leaders of political Islam in Europe, Southeast Asia, and the Middle East, have been increasingly concerned with defining the boundaries of their community and of the Islamic *Umma* (community). They have attempted to do this by redefining the role of women in society, specifying what may be considered acceptable individual behavior. While there are some variations from country to country, Islamists in most countries have chosen to restrict

---

^{gg}Ganesh Devy (2002). "Tribal Voice and Violence." In: Siddharth Vardarajan (ed.) *Gujarat: The Making of a Tragedy*. Delhi: Penguin India.

^{hh}There is another side to the tribal question, confined primarily to Northeastern India. The best arguments available on India's Northeast show a link between the neglect of the region by Delhi and the rise of tribal discontent, sometimes violently expressed. The northeastern India seeks an equal inclusion in the nation and polity, and will not settle for a politics of central neglect. Sanjib Baruah (2005). *Durable Disorder?* Delhi: Oxford University Press.

ⁱⁱPippa Norris and Ronald Inglehart (2004). *Sacred and Secular, op. cit.*

^{jj}Olivier Roy (2004). *Globalised Islam: The Search for a New Ummah*. London: Hurst and Company; and New York: Columbia University Press.

the role of women in the public space, define the attire women may wear, and specify the "right" contours of the relationship between men and women.

Christian movements, like Islamic movements, have also been on the rise. The Catholic Church and Evangelical Protestant churches have all gained in popularity on the coat-tails of identity politics. Membership in churches, especially evangelical churches, is growing in all regions except Western Europe, and the competition between churches is triggering all manner of religious extremism and fundamentalism.

Evangelical Protestant churches as well as the Catholic Church have been increasingly concerned with micro politics — with redefining gender relations, women's rights, gay rights, and marital relations. Many of them have sought to restrict the rights of women formally protected by national constitutions, international law and by international declarations. In Chile and the Philippines, the Catholic Church has not only promoted the hard-line position on birth control that has been adopted by the Vatican, but it has also engaged in *real* politics seeking to better control the political and social agenda. In the United States, the radical rhetoric and activities of evangelical groups have sought to undermine, among other things, birth control policies and HIV/AIDS prevention programs adopted by the United States as part of its aid activities in the developing world.

Intriguingly, Hindu nationalism and Muslim politics in India have both baulked at this trend. At the present time, the Hindu nationalist movement consisting of three prominent organizations are: the BJP, the Rashtriya Swayamsevak Sangh (RSS), and the Vishva Hindu Parishad (VHP). Of the three, the BJP is viewed as political (in the narrow electoral sense), the second as cultural, and the third as religious. The VHP consists of priests as advisors as well as office holders. Despite VHP's importance in the movement, Hindu nationalism has been less concerned with religious or social reform, more with political and nationalist mobilization.

This is not to say that micro political issues have been entirely absent. Arguments about a common civil code — identical laws on marriage, divorce, and inheritance for all of Indians regardless of what the different religious codes say — have repeatedly appeared in Hindu nationalist discourse. But these arguments have been presented in the context of discussions about secularism and national identity, not as arguments about micro identity politics or as having implications for them.

In the last decade, some Hindu nationalist groups have every year staged protests on Valentine's Day, threatening those "deracinated," "modern" young Indians who seek to emulate the West in the matters of heart. A few others have also been concerned with "sanskritising" lower castes, seeking to give them a status closer to the upper castes.[kk] But these issues have not ignited passions in Hindu nationalist politics. No major Hindu nationalist leaders have staked their careers on a common civil code, or on reforms in the Hindu caste system. All social or religious reform ideas have been sacrificed at the altar of an anti-Muslim, anti-Christian political program. Nothing moves and drives Hindu nationalism more than an anti-Muslim campaign.

Muslim leaders in India appear to be similarly concerned with influencing national identity debates. Their efforts have been directed at thwarting the Hindu right's agenda and at interpreting secularism in the Indian context. Unlike their counterparts in the Middle East or North Africa, they have not sought to transform Muslim micro-politics by redefining gender rights or the role of women in society.[ll]

Why has the Hindu right paid little attention to micro-politics, especially gender-based micro-politics? Why have India's Muslim leaders tended ignore it as well?

4.1. *Hindu micro politics: religious interpreters or religious interlocutors?*

Religious leaders who seek to redefine micro-politics especially with regard to gender issues generally present themselves as interpreters of religion all over the world. In India, however, this has not been the case. Despite the fact that many leaders of the VHP are priests, they are not regarded as, nor do they appear to regard themselves as, *interpreters* of Hindu texts. They are seen instead as mere *interlocutors* between the Hindu religious world and the political world. Is this peculiar to Hinduism?

[kk] A well-known RSS leader, Govindacharya, sought to take Hindu nationalism in this direction. But his ideological status and power in the RSS hierarchy remain unclear. He has not been able to turn caste reform into a principal project of Hindu nationalism.

[ll] The Shah Bano case, we argue later, had less to do with gender based micro-politics and more to do with the politics of redefining India's secular identity.

The multiplicity of Hindu religious texts arguably means that priests who are politically powerful or prominent do not necessarily take on, or are bestowed with, the mantle of "interpreters." Leaders of Islamic politico-religious movements in Nigeria or Egypt have, by contrast, positioned themselves as serious interpreters of Islam, not simply as interlocutors between the religious Islamic world and politics. The route for becoming a "legitimate 'interpreter' of Hinduism, who not only is a 'representative' of Hindu society but who also refashions the core elements of Hinduism, is not as clear as it is in Islam, or Christianity."[mm]

These days the RSS (the cultural wing of the Hindu nationalist movement) does present its ideology as an interpretation of Hindu culture (though not of Hinduism) and does concern itself with gender-based micro politics. However, none of the various elements of its interpretation seriously challenge existing beliefs about gender relations held by most in the Hindu community. The RSS's definitions, in other words, as not significantly at odds with the definitions widely accepted by the Hindu community.

The RSS glorifies mothers and sisters at the expense of wives — much as the popular Indian cinema in Hindi does, or for that matter cinema in Tamil, Telugu, Marathi, etc., do. While *purdah* (veiling) is critiqued by the RSS and the VHP because it is seen as what "Muslims do," overexposing Hindu women's "bodies more and more to the public gaze"[nn] is frowned upon. Hindu nationalist leaders think that the ideal mother is one who teaches her sons "true" Hindu culture, brings out their virile qualities, and encourages them to battle India's enemies.[oo] Again, this is not significantly different from the message traditionally delivered by India's popular films.

Thus, both the religious wing of the Hindu nationalist movement (VHP) as well as its cultural wing (RSS) have little to say about gender micro politics in India that is controversial or that is seemingly out of sync with the beliefs and interpretations of the Hindu community more generally. Both are more

---

[mm]This was not always true of Hindu religious leaders. Buddha and Mahavira in ancient times, and to a lesser extent the leaders of Brahmo Samaj (Rammohan Roy) and Arya Samaj (Dayanand Saraswati) in modern times both headed religious reform movements and attained the status of interpreters of Hinduism, leading in some cases to the formation of new religions like Buddhism.
[nn]Golwalkar (1980). *Thoughts*, pp. 491–493.
[oo]Bacchetta, Gender in the Hindu Nation: RSS women as ideologues, p. 34.

importantly only minimally concerned with influencing debates about micro politics and are primarily focused on macro political issues. The BJP, the electoral wing of Hindu nationalism, not surprisingly, is also concerned with macro identity politics as it engages with other political parties at the national, state and local levels.

4.2. *Muslim micro politics: ignoring global trends and thwarting the Hindu right*

As noted earlier Muslim leaders in India also do not appear to be particularly interested in micro political issues. There are no visible social and religious movements from within the Islamic community striving strenuously to limit the space for women in the public space, or to make women's rights a political and social issue. There are comments here and there by the Muslim clergy about whether Sania Mirza, an Indian Muslim teenage tennis star, was appropriately attired, when she played at the US open, but such comments die out before long, and no systematic political thrust ever appears. Even the landmark Shah Bano Case in 1985 and the adoption of the Muslim Women's (Protection of Right of Divorce) Law by parliament in 1986, a seemingly critical event for gender relations in the Muslim community, does not appear to have redefined gender micro-politics within the Indian Muslim community. It appears, to the contrary, to have provoked debate and discussion about the nature of India's secularism.

Shan Bano, a Muslim woman, was divorced by her husband of 43 years who refused to give her alimony. To justify his actions, he cited the *Shariat*, which requires that the children of the divorced women provide maintenance to the mother; or if the children are not capable of doing so, the community institutions, the Waqf Boards, do so. The Supreme Court ruled that Muslims divorce, especially the issue of alimony, could be covered by some of the secular laws of the country. The court ruling led to protests by many of India's Muslim leaders and organizations. In an attempt to keep the electoral and political affections of Muslims, the leaders of Congress party, ruling the country at that time, sought to overturn the court's verdict. Under India's constitution, courts can be overruled by the legislature, if more than two-thirds of parliament members agree to do so. In 1986, Congress Members of Parliaments (MPs) constituted nearly three-fourths of India's directly elected lower house. A whip to enforce party discipline in parliamentary vote was issued by the Congress party. As a result, India's parliament, by a huge majority, in effect outlawed the Supreme Court's verdict that divorced Muslim women were entitled to alimony.

Generating much momentary passion, the Shah Bano case was a key event in the nation's politics in 1985–1986. It was also potentially an opportunity for political leaders to make a decisive shift in Indian politics toward issues concerning family, marriage, and gender rights, but that was not to be. Women's organizations, some including Muslims, did protest the governmental decision, but they had no capacity to mobilize the masses. Muslim organizations on the whole supported community identity over claims of gender justice. The Hindu nationalists were the greatest political adversaries of the government and they did mobilize large numbers of people against the government's moves. But it soon became clear that the Hindu nationalists were less concerned about debating gender rights, of Muslims or Hindus, and more interested in using the Shah Bano debate as an instrument in debates about macro identity politics. The Shah Bano case, according to them, showed that (a) the Muslim community did not wish to enter the national mainstream, maintaining separatist traditions; and (b) India's "pseudo-secular" Congress government pandered to the Muslims for the sake of votes, and was not interested in reforming "backward" Muslim religious laws. Thus, the Shah Bano case, instead of initiating a new era of gender politics, became an element in the anti-Muslim Hindu nationalist politics, which came eventually to be dominated by other issues such as contested shrines and perceived historical wrongs. Gender relations simply became an inconsequential footnote in this politics.[PP]

4.3. *The middle eastern migration*

Another issue is of relevance here. The Hindu nationalists have often claimed that ever since the large-scale migration of India's Muslims to the Middle East began in the 1970s, international Muslim organizations, especially those from the Middle East, have penetrated the educational and religious life of Indian

---

[PP] For a fascinating discussion of the Shah Bano Case framed in terms of community identity versus gender justice, see Niraja Gopal Jayal (1999). *Democracy and the State.* Delhi: Oxford University Press, Chapter 3.

Muslims, strengthening their religious "fundamentalism" and deepening sepa-ratist attitudes. A survey conducted in six Indian cities in the mid-1990s raises serious doubts about the veracity of such claims.[qq] While six cities are hardly sufficient for robust all-India generalizations, the fact that they are located in very different parts of India — two in the north (Aligarh and Lucknow), two in the west (Ahmedabad and Surat) and two in the south (Hyderabad and Calicut) — makes them highly suggestive.

Three survey results, contradicting Hindu nationalist arguments, stand out. First, the religious organization that reached all cities was not Middle Eastern, but Indian — namely, the Tablighi Jamaat. It is a quietistic orga-nization, interested in the expansion of Muslim piety, and is not associated with politics or separatism at all.[rr] Second, a substantial proportion of the Muslim community respected this organization, but did not necessarily agree with its views about what the authentic forms of religious piety were. Third, an overwhelming proportion of Muslim respondents argued that *taalim, sehat aur rozgaar* (education, health, and employment) were more pressing issues for Muslims than *mazhab aur zubaan* (religion and language). By education, these respondents meant modern, not religious, education.

Even communities whose members have migrated to the Middle East seek-ing employment in large numbers do not appear to be significantly influenced by the global trend within Islam toward redefining gender micro-politics. The state of Kerala has witnessed the most voluminous migration to the Middle East. Nearly a fourth of Kerala's population has family members in the Middle East, and migrant remittances are customarily estimated to constitute up to a half of the state's gross domestic product.[ss] And Muslims are the largest participants in Kerala's labor outflows to the Middle East.

A recent study argues that compared to the families of Hindu and Christian migrants, those of Muslim migrants have undergone considerable

---

[qq]The survey, conducted under the joint auspices of Harvard University and Delhi's Center for the Study of Developing Societies, was for a study of Hindu-Muslim violence. See the questionnaire in Varshney, *Ethnic Conflict and Civic Life, op. cit.*, Appendix A, especially p. 304 and 307. Findings for this part of the survey are being reported here for the first time.
[rr]For details of this organization, see Yoginder Sikand (2002). *Origins and Development of Tablighi Jammat (1920–2000)*, Leiden: Brill.
[ss]Banerjee, S.K., Jayachandran, V. and Roy, T.K. (1997). "Has Emigration Influenced Kerala's Living Stan-dards?" paper presented at the T.N. Krishnan Memorial Conference, Trivandrum: Center for Development Studies, September 7–9.

changes.[tt] It shows that the latter spend a substantial proportion of the rising incomes on Muslim religious institutions, including mosques and Waqf Boards. This has become a standard way to announce a family's upward mobility among Kerala's Muslims. These religious institutions have not produced fundamentalist politico-religious organizations or leaders concerned with micro identity politics. They appear to have merely strengthened the existing religious institutions.

The Muslim League, a moderate Muslim party, continues to be the leading Muslim political organization in Kerala. It has been a great beneficiary of rising Muslim incomes as a result of migration, but it is primarily interested in the customary gamut of modern politics — cabinet positions, jobs, business, and education — not in religious issues. Religious fundamentalism, represented by a right wing Muslim party, remains a small part of Kerala politics. Thus, the heartland of Muslim migration to the Middle East continues to combine politics and religious belief without fostering the radicalization of either macro or micro identity politics.

Even when the odd Islamist group rears its head in India and intervenes in micro identity politics, it is quickly shot down by other religious and/or political Muslim groups in India. Consider the recent case of the *fatwa* against women's participation in electoral politics. The Islamic seminary of Deoband, Darul Uloom, appears to have issued the *fatwa* in response to a journalist's question about Muslim women running for public office and campaigning during elections. The *fatwa* was strongly critiqued by both Muslim clerics and Muslim politicians and its legitimacy was challenged as well.

Two factors appear to move Muslim leaders in India away from the global trend: first, the challenge posed by Hindu nationalists also forces India's Muslim groups to focus on macro identity concerns rather than on micro identity questions. Second, the multiplicity of Islamic religious and/or political organizations within the context of democratic institutions works against the rise of any group that promotes extremist positions. India's democracy undermines Islamic extremism, as it does Hindu extremism.

In short, Hindu nationalism as well as Muslim confessional politics has not been concerned with policing and monitoring the boundaries of their

---

[tt]Prema A. Kurien (2002). *Kaleidoscopic Ethnicity: International Migration and Reconstruction of Community Identities in India*. New Brunswick, NJ: Rutgers University Press, especially Chapter 8.

community. They have arguably not sought to redefine the " 'core' identity" of Hinduism or Islam. They have instead been primarily focused on how the idea of India incorporates members of their community. This is in sharp contrast to how right-wing religious politics have behaved in other parts of the world. As recently argued, Islamists and Islamic religious leaders are increasingly unconcerned with controlling state politics; rather, they want to tighten their grip on their community of followers, concentrating on redefining and reinforcing the boundaries of their community.[uu] Not so in India.

5. Economic Reforms and Identity Politics

In the economic circles, it is often argued that India's economic reforms of the 1990s were made necessary by the macroeconomic crisis of mid-1991, when India ran into a serious balance of payments problem and had foreign exchange reserves worth only 2 weeks of imports. This economic view, though necessary, is not sufficient. It has two analytic faults. First, a macroeconomic crisis requires stabilization, not structural adjustment. Stabilization programs are short-run and macro; they can, in principle, solve a balance of payments crisis. In contrast, structural adjustment, besides being long-run, also covers policies that change the microenvironment of firms: how and where to borrow capital, how to price products, where to buy inputs and where to sell outputs, which technology to use, etc. In 1991, India went for both macro stabilization as well as structural reforms. A purely economic explanation cannot account for why India *continued* on the path of economic reforms *after* the short-run balance of payments problem was resolved. India's foreign exchange crisis was over within 2 years — in 1993.

Second, and more important, a basic restructuring of economic policies has to go through a well-defined political process in India. Specifically, the annual government budget becomes the key indicator of changes in economic policies, but it is an instrument over which the executive does not have final authority. The government can only present a budget, but cannot approve it. In a parliamentary system like India's, the legislature must approve the budget. In many countries, the budget simply sums up the health of government finances. In India, given the historically entrenched and highly interventionist

---

[uu] Olivier Roy (2004). *Globalised Islam: The Search for a New Ummah.* London: Hurst and Company.

role of the state in the economy, all big changes in economic policy, especially those that reduce the role of government and, therefore, alter taxes, public expenditures, and economic laws, show up prominently in the budgetary instrument. If a budget is not approved by parliament, the government can neither economically function nor introduce market-oriented economic policies. We must, therefore, not only ask why the government introduced reforms, but why India's parliaments repeatedly endorsed them by approving the budget.

From the viewpoint of the political process, the answer is clear. Economic reforms were a big concern in India's elite politics, but a secondary or tertiary concern in the nation's popular politics. Ethnic conflict and identity politics drove India's mass politics. A political space like this is essentially two-dimensional, with ethnic politics playing itself out on one axis and reform politics on the other. Scholars of economic reforms have generally assumed that reforms are, or tend to become, central to politics. That is a one-dimensional view. Depending on what else is making demands on the energies of the electorate and the politicians — ethnic and religious strife, political order and stability — the assumption of reform centrality may not be right. The main battle lines in politics may be drawn on issues such as how to avoid (or promote) a further escalation of ethnic conflict, whether to support (or oppose) the political leaders if there has been an attempted coup, whether to forgive (or punish) the "crimes" of high state officials. *Paradoxically, it may be easier to push through reforms in a context like this, for politicians and the electorate are occupied by matters they consider more critical.*[vv] That is what happened between 1991 and 1996 in India. It is the nation's preoccupation with identity politics during the 1990s that gave economic reformer the political room to bring in many market-oriented reforms.[ww]

Elite politics is typically expressed in the institutionalized realms of the polity: debates within bureaucracies and cabinets, interactions between business associations and government, dealings between labor aristocracy and

---

[vv] This argument, of course, does not mean that an ethnic civil war is the best context for reforms. A distinction between ethnic conflict and ethnic breakdowns is required. It is the latter, which is being highlighted above. National anxieties about increasing ethnic violence or declining ethnic relations may provide a niche for reformers to push measures that might otherwise generate considerable political resistance.

[ww] For a fuller development of this argument, see Ashutosh Varshney (1999). "Mass Politics or Elite Politics?" In: Sachs, J., Varshney, A. and Bajpai, N. (eds.) *India in the Era of Economic Reforms*. Oxford: Oxford University Press.

political parties, etc. In contrast, street is the primary theater of popular politics. Issues that unleash citizen passions trigger mass politics. Its characteristic forms are agitations, demonstrations, civil disobedience, riots, and assassinations. Elite concerns — investment tax breaks, stock market regulations, tariffs on imported cars — rarely filter down to popular politics. In contrast, ethnic conflict is almost always in popular politics.

But what, analytically speaking, would allow a policy or issue — economic, cultural, or political — to enter popular politics? Three factors are typically critical: (a) how many people are affected by the policy, (b) how organized they are, and (c) whether the effect is direct and short-run, or indirect and long-run. The more direct the effect of a policy, the more people are affected by it and the more organized they are, the greater the potential for mass politics. This reasoning would apply to economic policy as well as to non-economic matters, such as ethnic disputes.

Within economic policy, following this reasoning, some issues are more likely to arouse mass contestation than others. For example, inflation, by affecting more or less everybody except those whose salaries are inflation-indexed, quickly gets inserted into mass politics. A financial meltdown has a similar effect, for a large number of banks and firms collapse and millions of people lose their jobs. Short of a financial collapse, stock market disputes or fluctuations rarely, if ever, enter popular politics in less developed countries.

What of trade liberalization and currency devaluation? They are often integral parts of neoliberal economic reforms. Are they part of popular politics or elite politics? In countries like Mexico, they are known seriously to have affected popular politics. In Venezuela, they were followed by a military coup, and a link between the reforms and the coup was explicitly made.[xx]

If a country's economy is heavily dependent on foreign trade, a lowering of tariff walls, a reduction in quantitative trade restrictions and a devaluation of the currency will indeed be of great concern to the masses, for it will directly affect mass welfare. In 2001, trade constituted more than 50% of the GDP of Singapore, Malaysia, Thailand, the Philippines, Mexico, Hungary, South Korea, Poland, and Venezuela, and between 40 and 50% of the GDP of Israel, Chile, China, and Indonesia. Changes, especially dramatic changes, in the

---

[xx]Moses Naim (1993). *Paper Tigers and Minotaurs: The Politics of Venezuela's Economic Reforms.* Washington DC: Carnegie Endowment.

trade and exchange rate regimes of these countries have a clear potential for popular politics. However, if trade is a small part of the economy, as has been true of India and Brazil historically, changes in trade and exchange rate regimes will be of peripheral, short-run importance to the large sections of the population.[yy] In 1991, India's trade/GDP ration was a mere 15%. Even after a decade and a half of reforms, it has only reached 25%. If it continues to grow like this, trade may well enter popular politics before long. But that has not been true thus far.

Compared to economic policy, consider now the role of ethnic conflict in politics. Ethnic disputes tend quickly to enter popular politics because they isolate a whole group, or several groups, on an ascriptive basis. They also directly hit political parties — both ethnically based parties (which may defend, or repel attacks on, their ethnic group) and multiethnic parties (which may fiercely fight attempts to pull some ethnic groups away from their rainbow coalitions). Because they invoke ascriptive, not voluntary, considerations, the effects of ethnic cleavages and ethnically based policies are obvious to most people and, more often than not, ethnic groups are either organized, or tend to organize quickly.

In a survey of mass political attitudes in India conducted in 1996,[zz] only 19% of the electorate reported any knowledge of economic reforms, even though reforms had been in existence since July 1991. In the countryside, where two-thirds of India still lives, only about 14% had heard of reforms, whereas the comparable proportion in the cities was 32%. Further, nearly 66% of the graduates were aware of the dramatic changes in economic policy, compared to only 7% of the poor, who are mostly illiterate. In contrast, close to three-fourths of the electorate, urban and rural, literate and illiterate, rich and poor, were aware of the 1992 mosque demolition in Ayodhya; 80% expressed

---

[yy] The overall size of the economy complicates the meaning of low trade/GDP ratios. Smaller economies tend generally to have a high trade/GDP ratio, making trade very important to their political economies. With the striking exception of China, however, the largest economies of the world — the U.S., Japan, Germany — are less trade dependent. Still, trade politics, as we know, has aroused a great deal of passion in the U.S. and Japan. The meaning of the same ratios can change, if the leading sectors (autos, computers) or "culturally significant" sectors (rice for Japan, agriculture in France) of the economy are heavily affected by trade.

[zz] The survey was conducted by the Center for the Study of Developing Societies (CSDS), India's premier research institution for election studies, under the leadership of Yogendra Yadav and V.B. Singh. For the larger audiences, the findings are summarized in *India Today*, August 15, 1996. All figures cited below are from the CSDS survey.

clear opinions of whether the country should have a uniform civil code or religiously prescribed and separate laws for marriage, divorce and property inheritance; and 87% took a stand on the caste-based affirmative action.

Further, economic reforms were a non-issue in the 1996 and 1998 elections. In the 1999 elections, the biggest reformers of the land either lost or did not campaign on reforms. Economic reforms turned out to be an issue in the 2004 elections, but not a critical determinant of the outcome.[aaa]

This insight also makes it easier to understand the pattern of India's economic reforms. India's decision-makers had greater success introducing and executing reforms that directly affected the welfare of elites, and less or no success touching areas that directly affected mass welfare. Policy arenas such as trade and exchange rate regimes, capital markets, industrial investment regimes were examples of the former; and matters such as food and fertilizer subsidies, agricultural policy, privatization, labor laws and rules about small-scale industries were instances of the latter. Counterfactually speaking, if India's policy makers had attacked the economic irrationalities of the latter set of policies in the early years of reform, the politics could well have become impossible to manage. An important reason for the success of economic reforms is that using the distractions provided by communal and caste politics, which determined the political coalitions in the 1990s, the less politically difficult reforms were embraced first.

6. Conclusion

The various arguments made in this paper can be reduced to two basic propositions. India's identity politics, only partially influenced by globalization, remains primarily internally driven; and it is the prominence of identity issues in the nation's popular politics that provided political room for India's integration with the world economy. Ethno-communal conflict may seem ubiquitous in the country, but that is entirely to be expected in a highly ethnically and religiously diverse democracy, which has stood firmly on the principle that groups are free to mobilize support and make claims on the state. Democracy, therefore, becomes both the channel through which conflict is waged, as

---

[aaa] Ashutosh Varshney (2004). "Towards a Gentler India." *India Today*, June 5.

well as the channel through which conflict is solved or managed.[bbb] With the prominent exception of Kashmir, whose peculiarities are well-known,[ccc] this larger theoretical understanding of democracy holds good for India as well.

It is worth speculating under what circumstances the self-limiting nature of conflict in India would cease to exist. Can the multi-stranded group conflict really explode out of control, making the policy unstable and its relationship with the outside world unpredictable?

A takeover of Indian politics by the right-wing of Hindu nationalism is the most plausible *speculative* scenario, which can trigger such a dark future. The extreme versions of Hindu nationalism are against the idea of India developed during the freedom struggle, and also against the self-correcting equilibrium Indian politics has come to represent: an equilibrium provided by groups fighting for their rights and dignity, making vociferous claims and advancing through politics, but always stopping short of mutual annihilation and settling for some widely accepted principles of victory and defeat, namely the vote, elections and democracy. The ideologically pure Hindu nationalism has no commitment to democracy, only to an aggressive, muscular and orderly Hindu nation where minorities, especially the Muslims, would "behave" or be forced to "behave."

Political predictions can be hazardous, especially because "exogenous shocks" like that of September 11, entirely unanticipated but quite possible, can transform politics in wholly unexpected ways. But that is not what one can bet on, while thinking about the future. One goes by the normal logic of a political system, and if we follow that route, we can safely say that the extreme versions of Hindu nationalism have virtually no chance of coming to power through the mechanism of vote. Even moderate Hindu nationalism had to, and will have to, make all kinds of political compromises to come to power, which it lost last year.

To conclude, while extreme Hindu nationalism can undermine India as a nation and will almost certainly be intensely inward-looking, it is most difficult to conceive of a political situation arising out of the usual course of democratic politics, which will allow it to control the Indian state. India's diversities and

---

[bbb]Robert Dahl (1991). *Democracy and its Critics*. New Haven: Yale University Press.
[ccc]Ashutosh Varshney (1991). "India, Pakistan and Kashmir: Antinomies of Nationalism." *Asian Survey*, November.

its democratic institutions, however imperfect, make that nearly impossible. Diversity and democracy have become the institutionalized and deeply rooted common sense of Indian politics by now.

Acknowledgments

This paper was subjected to a spirited criticism by Professor Cheng Beng Huat at the conference on "Managing Globalization: Lessons from China and India," Lee Kuan Yew School of Public Policy, Singapore, 4–6 April 2005. We have certainly been able to revise some details of our own argument in light of his remarks, and are grateful to Professor Cheng for that.

CHAPTER 14

Identity Politics in an Era
of Globalization

Pratap Bhanu Mehta

1. Introduction

This paper will examine facets of India's identity dilemmas. It is divided into six sections. Section 2 argues that in India identities have been and are created through a process of politicization, not on the basis of shared attributes. This gives Indian identity an indeterminate character, but nevertheless I argue that the range of interconnected differences make Indian identity strong. Section 3 delineates the four principal mechanisms by which these connections are weaved into a political whole. Section 4 offers some general reflections on identity dilemmas and the form they take in the modern world. Section 5 looks at one particular attempt to benchmark Indian identity — Hindutva, and argues that the difficulty is not only with Hindutva, but with any attempts to benchmark an identity. Section 7 looks at the prospects of Hindutva gaining political ascendancy. Section 8 looks at the way in which Indian identity is now differently configured in relation to the rest of the world.

2. Identity and Politicization

The idea of India is the repository of an immense range of contending hopes and fears. For all its antiquity and depth, its sense of geography and territoriality, and its intricate cultural linkages, modern India had to fashion a new identity for itself. The distinctness of new identity was that politics was going to be at the center of this process in more than one sense. Although Indians frequently appealed to its traditions and cultures, its civilizational values, these had to be interpreted in light of aspects of modernity that were shaping India in equal measure: the presence of the modern state, the rise of democratic politics, the aspirations of egalitarianism and the ambitions of industrialization. But India's identity came to be politicized in a deeper sense. The invention of republican citizenship in India was indeed a momentuous event, and a rupture with the past. While many had hoped that the new constitution would simply be encased within the supposed historical identity of India, its diverse and complex cultural sympathies, few imagined that the opportunities afforded by republican citizenship would intensely politicize all areas of organized collective existence in India. The resources of history and culture, rather than providing comfort and continuity, would themselves be the first categories to be subject to intense political scrutiny. Whatever anyone may claim about the identity of India, what its historical essence consisted of, what the sources of its unity were, the simple fact was this: Whether or not republics had existed in ancient India, whether or not democracy had cultural roots, in 1951, for the first time in Indian history all Indians were declared to be citizens. Henceforth they would themselves, within the arenas and opportunities for struggle provided for them by the constitution, define their own collective identities, negotiate and renegotiate the terms of social cooperation, and as republican citizens take charge of their own destiny.

Universal adult suffrage was going to have social implications far beyond its immediate political significance. As one of the most thoughtful commentators of the time K.M. Pannikar put it, "many social groups previously unaware of their strength, and barely touched by the political changes that had taken place, suddenly realized that they were in a position to wield power." The right to participate in choosing one's electors was the most dramatic way of affirming the equality of all citizens. Although the right to vote is seen by many as a meagre right, whose exercise is a periodic ritual that does little to enhance the well being of those who exercise it, that right itself transforms the meaning of social existence. It is an assertion that all authorities are a conditional grant, that, suffrage establishes the sufferance, as George Kateb so eloquently put it. Democracy, as its earliest observers were quick to note, represents the dissolution of inherited modes of authority, indeed of the whole concept of authority itself. Democracy, once instituted, is an incitement to politicize all areas of social life; it introduces, over time, a process of critique that questions and subverts all certainties of social life.

The process of democratization will thus always produce radical uncertainty about authority and identity alike. As the legitimacy of old ways of instituting authority and recognizing identities dissolve, without being replaced by new norms and conventions, the experience of democracy will be profoundly confusing. As Tocqueville put it incomparably: "Obedience, then loses moral basis in the eyes of him who obeys; he no longer considers it as a divinely appointed duty; and he does not yet see its purely human aspect; in his eyes it is neither sacred nor just and he submits to it as a degrading though useful fact. There is an unspoken intestinal power between permanently suspicious rival powers. The lines between authority and tyranny, liberty and license, right and might seem so jumbled and confused that no one knows exactly what he is, what he can do and what he should do."

The experience of democracy has opened up numerous points of dissent, new conflicts of values and identities and a permanent antagonism of meaning and interest that often leaves Indians with a sense that society is flying off in many different directions at once, and the unity of reference points seems to vanish. But it could be argued that new bonds have been created through this politicization of all aspects of life, it is through the process of intense argument that a new shared public is being created. The important thing about the experience of modern India is not that Indians always necessarily have a shared conception of identity but they have agreed to argue about the question. The story of modern India is the story of Indians constantly struggling to articulate, discover and debate what it means to be Indian.

The point of this possibly banal truism is that it always has been and will be very difficult to give an interpretation of Indian identity in what might be called substantialist terms. This is a conception of identity that privileges some substantial trait — religion, race, culture, ethnicity, shared history, and common memory — that can be objectively identified and then configures an identity around it. Indeed as I shall argue below, threats to India often arise from trying to give its identity some substantial meaning in this sense. There is an old joke about India's identity: it does not occur to most Indian's to doubt it until someone begins to give arguments to prove its existence. This joke captures something profound about the way in which Indian identity has been constituted, and also the circumstances under which this identity is put under stress, as I will show below. But the thorough politicization of identity suggests that Indian identity will not be constituted necessarily through shared attributes or aspirations but through what Khilnani once called "*interconnected differences.*" Does this mean that India does not have an identity? If this demand implies that there is something we all unequivocally share, the answer is no. But it does not preclude the thought that we all have lots of different reasons and ways in which we define our relationships to each other. *There is no "unity" in diversity, rather we are diverse in our unities*, and we might identify with connections to India, each in our own way.

It is for this reason that there are grounds to be suspicious of any authoritative narrative of Indian identity, including one that emphasizes its pluralism. I think pluralism is the defacto reality of India, and Indian politics has a remarkable capacity to negotiate difference and plurality. Faced with exclusivist cultural nationalism or nationalisms, we often try and imagine other more complex identities. We try to imagine an India where, instead of singularity we emphasize plurality, instead of purity we emphasize the essentially hybrid character of all identity, instead of exclusivism we emphasize the syncretistic and so on. We thus prefer a different range of adjectives to describe cultural states of being: syncretistic, pluralism, hybrid, liminal, incomplete, interdependent, composite, become terms in vogue. The point of these categories is both political and conceptual. Conceptually we try and show that the binary oppositions on which exclusivist identities thrive (say Hindu–Muslim) are subverted by the complex experience of history. It often becomes meaningless to describe some cultural artifact, say a particular form of music, as exclusively Hindu or Muslim; elements of both converge to produce a new musical form altogether. Some identities are described as liminal, inhabiting that zone, where they cannot be described as either/or. We try and construct a shared history around these moments: hybrid cultural forms become more politically respectable than pure ones and so forth.

Politically the hope is that subverting the binary oppositions that exist between categories that demarcate people into separate groups will somehow lead people to acknowledge the webs of interdependence that bind people together. It will lead them to recognize that the cultural forms that they inhabit owe a good deal to cultures they are about to stigmatize as inferior, foreign or impure. Once it is shown that different cultures have commingled to produce new cultural forms, we will be relieved of the allure of singular identities. To recognize the many layers that constitute our own selves and our history, is to find space for acknowledging all the complex contributions that have made us what we are. This acknowledgment then allows us to open up to difference: it allows us to see that those whom we stimigatize as foreign are also themselves part of our identity. Thus a good deal of weight is placed upon describing India as "composite" or "syncretistic" for these are the only terms that can accommodate the true complexity of Indian identity, and can resist the violent abridgment of identities that takes place in the name of more singular conceptions. The locus classicus of such sentiment is Jawaharlal Nehru's, which celebrated a cultural miscegenation, describing India as:

> "An ancient palimpsest on which layer upon layer of thought and reverie had been inscribed, and yet no succeeding layer had completely hidden or erased what had been written previously."

This is, in so many ways, an attractive conception of Indian identity. It allows for the possibility that the garb of modernity will continue to coexist with the many layers already inscribed on Indian civilization. It allows Indians to transcend tradition without making it despicable. And it accurately reflects the de facto reality of modern India.

But this conception should not be taken as an authoritatively settled account of Indian identity, nor as a widely accepted political conception for a number of reasons. First, *de facto* pluralism is not the same thing as *de jure* identification with that pluralism. Whether the reality is accepted as the norm depends upon concrete political choices. While most Indian cultural practice conforms to this Nehruvian vision, this claim can be and is often politically challenged by forces such as Hindu nationalism that regard this pluralism as a source of weakness and regret. I will discuss the political potential of this critique below, but it is worth emphasizing that this critique of Indian identity will remain a powerful force in Indian politics. It is also part of the million mutinies, the numerous acts attempts to redefine India's identity, that still dot the public space.

Second, even an acceptance of pluralism can be made quite incompatible with high degrees of violence and intolerance. The constitution of India into plural groups opens up the possibility of political competition between them that can often result in violence. Indeed, one of the paradoxes of the modern Indian experience is that cultural acceptance of difference is quite compatible with the political conflict between groups. Third, this pluralism is also an "objectifying" bird's eye view of India. It does not pay adequate attention to the fact that a society can look pluralistic, while its various constituents are not. It would be too premature to see India's conception of its own identity as settled in any way. *But the process of churning itself is producing a myriad of interconnections on the basis of which it could be argued that the Indian Union is stronger even if the identity remains contested.* The strength of the Union depends upon four key mechanisms. And there is every reason to think that these mechanisms have only grown stronger rather than weaker.

3. The Sinews of Union

India is one of the most astonishing political experiments in recorded human history. A billion people, a significant proportion of which remain unlettered and unpropertied, constituting themselves into a republic; a bewildering variety of languages and religions weaving themselves into the tapestry of a single nation; a society in which political equality and universal suffrage has preceded the introduction of social equality. For the most part India has managed its diversity very well. This diversity has been facilitated by four mechanisms. The first is, simply democracy. It can be confidently asserted that India has stayed together as a nation because of democracy. The threat of secessionism or regional conflict is invariably more a product of the authoritarian moments of the state, rather than its democratic tendencies. The threat of secessionism arises usually when the Center tries to impose a single version of Indian national identity or actively subverts democracy. Challenges of regionalism have proven more tractable whenever the Indian State has gone in for democratic incorporation or accommodation. Indeed, secessionist movements have proved to be more intractable in precisely those states — Kashmir and the North East, where the Indian Government has found it difficult to break the cycle of authoritarianism and excessive intervention. Even the brutal insurgency in Punjab was brought to an end because the possibility of democratic incorporation always existed. Kashmir is a special case because of its peculiar history. But even here, it could be argued that it is authoritarianism from the Indian State that gave the secessionist movement its political lease of life and provided an opening for internationally backed militants. Now, when for the first time in more than 15 years, there is semblance of peace in Kashmir and a real political process underway, it is because the Indian Government finally managed to conduct free and fair elections, not just for state assemblies but for civic bodies as well. The political conflicts in Kashmir are far from over, but democratic incorporation affords the best chance of peace.

The second mechanism is simply the size and power of the Indian State. There is some truth to the proposition that it is very difficult to mount collective action against the Indian State. It makes the costs of contemplating taking on the state immensely high. India is large enough to sit on any problem long enough without a real threat of the central state itself imploding. Most nations collapse, not because of social forces, but because of the implosion of central authority. That has never been a serious possibility on India's horizon. The potential internal power of the state has given solidity to Indian identity.

The third mechanism is an imaginative construal and negotiations over rights. The manner in which linguistic differences were accommodated became a benchmark for a more imaginative conception of the nation. After independence, Hindi speakers, the single largest language group in the country began to press for the adoption of Hindi as a national language, a demand that elicited fierce opposition from states of the South. Nehru engineered a pluralist compromise where a dozen or so languages were given official status with the possibility of adding others to the list; states were demarcated on linguistic lines to give political recognition to the status of some languages, schools were asked to introduce a three language formula, and English was retained as the language of the state, to be phased out over a long period. The important thing about this compromise was that it refused to anchor Indian identity to any single privileged trait. Indeed, the source of resistance to an Indian identity came from attempts to tie it to a single privileged trait; as soon as the threat of that vanished, so did the resistance. Indeed, it is arguable that by granting political recognition to competing demands the Indian state defused the force of vernacular nationalism in two ways. First, it accommodated them in a spirit of democracy. Second, over time the linguistic orientation in these states began to be determined by the imperatives of the economy rather than by the requirements of cultural identity. To take an example, two states, West Bengal and Tamil Nadu, which had postponed the teaching of English till grade five on grounds of cultural nationalism, recently reintroduced English at the primary level to make their students more competitive. India's linguistic arrangements gave expression to the idea of a layered Indian identity, an accretion of different elements. If one element was politically privileged, or others sought to be abridged, the potential for resistance was great. If the threat of privileging one element was removed, the possibilities for accommodation were profound. Indeed, the way in which actual linguistic practices are now evolving in many parts of India, with languages and vocabularies bleeding into each other, at least at the level of mass culture, is both a sign of the possibilities of cultural fusion. Salman Rushdie once described Mumbai street language as HUG ME (Hindi, Urdu, Gujarati, Marathi, and English), making the point that if culture is left free of political superintendence, if it the anxieties of identity are not placed upon it, it will evolve in its own merry, impure and messy way.

The fourth mechanism is the actual practices of politics that allow for a good deal of power sharing between the provinces and the Center. While India's federalism privileges the Center and the formal powers of the Central government have, in a vast majority of areas, been growing, informal practices of politics allow for considerable power sharing. This is done through two mechanisms. First, the state has very rigidly adhered to an impartially applied mechanical formula in the transfer of resources from the Center to the states. The fact that an independent commission recommends these allocations has probably reduced the bargaining burden on politics between the Center and the States considerably. There is some worry that the palpably growing inequality between clusters of states might put pressure on the Indian union. Over the last decade and a half the states of Southern and Western India have done considerably better on most measures of economic and social performance than the states of the Hindi Belt and Eastern India. While growing regional inequality is a matter of some concern there is reason to suppose that this will not politically weaken the Indian Union for a number of reasons. The sheer economic interdependence of these states, the actuality of significant and large scale internal migration (a great leveler) and India's slow but steady moves towards creating an integrated national market are more than likely to offset the pressures generated by this inequality. India has also made a political compromise to defuse the issue. The inequality between these states is also reflected in demographic trends within these states with population in South India growing more slowly than in the North. Under the India constitution, this should have occasioned a shift in political power as well, since representation is tied to demography. North India would have gained up to 20 more seats in parliament if the correlation between demography and representation had been followed as mandated by the constitution. But all political parties have agreed to freeze regional apportionment for a further period of 20 years, defusing any anxieties the better performing states might have had.

Second, there is considerable evidence that regional political parties in many of the states have acquired a major stake in power at the Center and arguably the central government has itself become more representative of the nation as a whole. Politics has allowed those interconnected differences to be articulated in ways that do justice to both the connections and the differences. A taste for politics transcends differences.

4. Identity Games

What is the quest for an identity about? There is a dizzying variety of ideas that is often condensed into the term identity: identity can operate on a political, cultural, social, psychological, or even psychoanalytic plane. At one level the identity of a nation is a question about the relationship between the individual and the larger collectivity. How are the emotional and affective bonds that form the basis of national identification composed? How do they motivate people to form a larger social connection in which individuality is renounced or attenuated into a larger group called the nation? How does this identification induce manifest acts of sacrifice, altruism and even violence? Without such emotional identification, the concept of identity remains an abstract idea; it does not structure or motivate political action. The production of such emotional identification is an extremely complex and ill understood matter, but it is fair to say that the modern Indian nation has produced its fair share of identification with the idea of India. Probably the most central element in this emotional imagination is the idea of territoriality that transcends different nationalist imaginations.

The second aspect of identity is a sense of specificity. Identity is bound to something that makes you different, makes you the being that you are and not someone else. A good deal of the challenges of identity that modern nations face is in terms of defining their specificity. As many observers have noted, identities are no longer connected to participating in distinct cultural practices. In fact, cultures and nations have, for good or for ill, ceded so much space to the modern economy, the modern state, and often the egalitarian aspirations of modernity, that it is more difficult to hold on to a sense of difference that is embodied in a concrete way of life. Or to put it slightly more precisely, much of the realm of public collective action, especially the polity and the economy, is not the site for expressing such differences in ways that become the cornerstone of identities. Rather the differences are expressed more in private spaces or social spaces. It is precisely because substantive values and horizons of meaning are shrinking that greater and inordinate weight is placed on markers of difference. As Valentine Daniel put it "nationalism is the horripilation of culture in insecurity and fright." Finally, in the realm of culture, it is often argued that culture is to be valued because it is constitutive of someone's identity. This alignment of culture with identity can be misleading in a couple of ways. First, the minute we are talking of identity we are talking of difference rather than diversity. It is possible for individuals or groups who are more alike each other in most respects to have a profound sense of having a different identity, a different sense of who they are. Indeed, as many have argued, we see more and more identity conflicts not because of the objective diversity between people, but because of their increasing likeness. Stress on difference becomes a way of defining identity in the face of narrowing differences in other spheres of life. It is a commonplace experience of the modern world that, contrary to what Arjun Appadurai argues, culture, politics and economy get disembedded from each other. After all it is not an accident that when defending cultural diversity very few are defending the right of a society to be governed by a Hindu view of the division of labor, or for Central Banks to run on Islamic principles of usury or power to be allocated by Confucian conceptions of elite. While it is true that culture is not simply an add-on to material resources, it is palpably misleading to argue that the culture, economy and politics cannot to some degree be disembedded from each other. This is a greater functional differentiation that modern societies produce.[a] In this context, it is quite possible that individuals and groups are sharing more and more, they are embedded in similar matrices of political and economic institutions, yet want to assert their sense of difference. In fact, as Michael Ignatieff has argued, following Freud's insight that conflicts born of the "narcissism of small differences

---

[a] Niklas Luhmann, *Observations on Modernity* (Stanford: Stanford University Press, 1998); Pratap Mehta, *Cosmopolitanism and the Circle of Reason, Political Theory, October 2000.*

are most acute," identity differences do not by themselves signal greater diversity. Rather invocation of identity may be a sign that diversity is decreasing.

This is an old anxiety about modernity. Bhudev Mukhopadhyaya, the 19th century Bengali poet who enjoined Indians to strenuously hold onto their toilet habits because in the long run this would be the only site at which they could assert a real sense of cultural difference was a bit indelicate, but not far off the mark. If the economy and politics are governed by their own logic and imperatives, where in concrete ways of acting will a way of life be embodied? This is a pressure that most religiously based conceptions of identity are facing under conditions of globalization and modernity. It is not an accident that almost all religions of the world — Christianity, Islam, Hinduism, Judaism, and Buddhism — have constructed a narrative for themselves, in which they appear beleaguered, as ways of life get more disembedded from their dictates. There is an old saying that "We put ourselves under God's Yoke most when we feel His presence the least." And there is something to this thought that effective secularisation of society will increase religiously based assertions. In a world where it is no longer clear how ones convictions can be embodied as a way of life in large spheres of social action, people look toward willful acts of assertion to embody their convictions. That is why so much weight is placed on markers of difference. Arguably, the United States is undergoing, such a political phenomenon, even though its full strength is mitigated by the enduring power of American institutions. I mention this only to signal the fact that the politics of religious assertion is likely to remain a feature of organized political life in many countries and India is no exception.

The third aspect of forming an identity is the maintenance of boundaries in the process of creating the perilous pronoun "we." What are the patterns of exclusion and inclusion that the process of identity formation entails? Who is the outsider and who is the insider? What are the terms on which citizenship and political standing are defined? This is both a question of legal and political status. Legally at any rate, India has adopted a republican conception of citizenship, where citizenship rights are not tied to any substantial benchmarks of ethnicity or religion. But politically there have been attempts to define the boundaries of exclusion and inclusion based on some substantial notion of what it means to be an "authentic" Indian. The question of inclusion and exclusion is not just a question of political rights, but of representation as well.

In a society composed of different communities there is the obvious question: what counts as fair terms of representation? The paradox is that this question cannot be settled by representation itself. Arguably, India's identity, both before and after partition, has been marked by the difficulties of resolving this question, as in the case of the Hindu Muslim divide.

Very crudely put, the dilemma was this. Once it was admitted that deviation from one person one vote was warranted for the protection of the interests of minorities, the question became: what counts as adequate protection? One-third or one-fourth guaranteed representation at the Center? Veto power for minorities at the Center? The truth is there never was any real stable answer. Any position was liable to create a political backlash. One-third reservation and some Hindus would argue that too much had been given away. One-fourth and some Muslims would argue that too little had been secured. The backlash to any position would in turn generate a further backlash. The Hindu Mahasabha's reaction to Jinnah's proposals seems gradually to have radicalized him, in turn unleashing another round of reactions. This vicious circle found its ultimate denouement in Partition, an outcome nobody apparently wanted, but no one could prevent.

Partition did not resolve this issue. The result was a colossal anomaly whose ramifications are still with us. The Indian state had a Janus face toward Muslims. On the one hand they presented their own solicitousness toward Muslims by selectively directing benefits toward them: funding madarsas, arranging Haj pilgrimages, protecting personal laws from judicial scrutiny. It is certainly not the case that only Muslims were beneficiaries of this politics. The state selectively doled out resources that had no justification on any conceivable interpretation of our constitutional principles to a variety of groups, and it is part of the grave misinformation campaign of our times to suggest that the state and religion are illegitimately entangled only when it comes to Muslims. Hindu places of worship receive enormous maintenance grants from the state, so called secularized laws of Hindus are as much about the consolidation of a Hindu communal identity as they are about modernizing Hinduism. On the other hand the state was doing its best to make sure that Muslims were more and more effectively alienated from the political process itself. Muslim representation in all spheres of public life: parliament, press, police, civil service, big business was and still remains on average far below what their numbers would warrant. One does not have to believe in strict proportional representation to acknowledge that public life and public institutions of this country are thoroughly unrepresentative as far as Muslims are concerned (one amazing example of this is the refusal of the state to fund Urdu medium secular education, but its willingness to subsidise madarsas). This alienation could not but have a deleterious affect both on Muslim politics and the politics of the nation as a whole. The alienation from public life produced its own vicious cycle. The less Muslims could acknowledge public life as being, in some important sense, their own, the more they turned inward to tradition; the more inward they turned, the more handle their opponents got to accuse them of being anti-national or anti-modern. The fact is that Indian politics acknowledged Muslims, in so far as it did, only as a supplicant minority, not as full citizens. In most cases the state gives selective benefits to groups to integrate them into a wider process and co-opt them. In the case of Muslims, the resources of the state directed toward them, were meant to reinforce their status as minority, not to integrate them more fully into the political process. Muslims remained locked in a dilemma not of their own making. The more their leadership and the state emphasized their status as minority requiring a distinct ensemble of rights and privileges, the more they set Muslims up for a majoritarian backlash. On the other hand, the wider political culture was doing its best to prevent Muslim integration into the wider process in the same breath as it was demanding it. The result: Muslim politics became impossible in any genuine sense of the term.

After the violence in Gujarat, this dilemma became even more pronounced. But there are hopeful signs. The most significant one is that there are enormous amounts of social churning amongst Muslims themselves. While there was a good deal of opposition to the Supreme Court judgment in the case of Shah Bano, a recent Supreme Court ruling (*Daniel Latifi vs Union of India*) which effectively restored a Muslim women's right to alimony, met with no opposition; there is immense pressure to democratize the Muslim Personal Law Board; new initiatives have been taken in the field of personal law including the modification of the marriage contract, and a rival all women's personal law board has also been set up. Such initiatives make break the cycle of alienation from mainstream politics, but the struggle over full membership in a cultural sense is still likely to continue for some time to come. The failure represented by partition is still a recurring motif in Indian politics, and casts a shadow on who is excluded and included.

5. Hindutva and the Identity Trap

Although many would argue that Hindu moral theory furnishes arguments that strengthen a particular kind of tolerance, Hindus have generated their own brand of intolerance. While the processes of reform within Hinduism led it inexorably toward democracy, many see in Hindu nationalism a threat to democracy. Given the history just recounted, the heterogeneity of Hinduism itself, and the sense in which Hinduism has made modernity its own, it is unlikely that any Hindu mass movement will be able to set up anything close to a theocracy in the usual Western sense of the word. It is not insignificant that even Hindu nationalism seems to feel an imperative to legitimise itself as a secular ideology: Movement apologists typically claim that they are not against secular principles as such, but declare themselves discontented that Hindus, India's majority, are asked to accept secular limits while minorities receive numerous exemptions based on their various religious identities.

This line of rhetoric, with its narrative of complaint against perceived subjugation, indicates a crisis within Hinduism. While there is much that is still religiously vital about Hindu piety and the remarkable account of life and creation that Hindu teachings provide, being a Hindu is increasingly coming to mean being identified with participation in the invention of a communal identity that can now fully, and often furiously, discharge its role in history. It is an identity constituted by a sense of injury, a sense of always having been on the losing side, of being a victimized innocent. This narrative strings together Mughal rule with the loss of territorial integrity during partition. It draws sustenance from the all too real threat posed by international Islamist jihadism and plays upon the sentiment that modern secularism itself is a contrivance biased in favor of minorities. Much of the understanding of history that sustains this sense of injury is false or oversimplified. But of greater import is that Hindu identity is coming in many ways to rest upon a sense of resentment that puts minorities at risk and threatens liberal democracy.[b]

---

[b]Other religions besides Hinduism are tempted by their own versions of such a narrative, of course. Alarmingly prominent versions of Islam tout feelings of resentment against the West, while more marginal yet by no means invisible Christian elements in the United States traffic in the idea that Christianity is under siege. (Interestingly, both Muslim and Christian extremists tend to place Jews high on their lists of enemies.) These narratives of victimization and resentment bespeak a wider failure of these religions to endow everyday life under the complex conditions of modernity with a sense of meaning or purpose, and also a refusal by significant currents within each religion to accept the facts of difference.

It has often been observed that religious or ideological extremism betrays a covert lack of faith and confidence. One wonders if this is not the case in India today: Do too many of the subcontinent's Hindus (the Hindus of the diaspora are another matter) fear that their religion can no longer prove its worth through its achievements, its intellectual vitality, or its aspirational creativity, and so must hug its resentments that much harder? Does anger and extremism, in other words, weave a kind of security blanket for those who are wondering about the meaning and relevance under complex modern conditions of their own religious tradition (and the questions this raises about their own commitment to it), but who for various reasons prefer what may well be the easier course of seeking enemies without rather than answers within?

In practice, the most immediate threats to democracy from Hindu nationalism have taken the form of efforts by nationalist intellectuals and activists to set benchmarks for national identity. The book that has most influentially stated the nationalist case, V.D. Savarkar's *Hindutva*,[c] begins by asking: "What is India?" The author, who is an intellectual godfather to India's ruling Bharatiya Janata Party (BJP), rehearses various answers that have been proffered (India is a civilization; India is a community of shared history; and the like). In each case, he shows that the answer either raises more questions than it settles or avoids the issue. Appeals to "common history," for instance, ignore the reality that "history" in the relevant sense is not a set of brute facts about the past, but rather a chosen human interpretation of the past: Only people who already think of themselves as having something in common, argues Savarkar, will see themselves as possessors of a common history. Much the same could be said of political institutions: They do not constitute unity so much as reflect it. We also learn that neither language nor (perhaps surprisingly) religion can supply the answer: India is home to a profusion of tongues and religions, and the Hinduism of the majority is internally quite diverse.

Calling all the bluffs behind these alternative accounts of India, Savarkar argues that only the concept of nationhood can command the necessary respect at home and abroad and summon the collective endeavor that history demands of all aspirants to national status. But what makes a nation? In Savarkar's logic, whatever the people share in a nation worthy of the name has to be something that is beyond beliefs, social practices, culture, political institutions,

[c]Vinayak Damodar Savarkar (1999). *Hindutva: Who Is a Hindu?* Bombay: RSS Publications Division.

or history. It must be something that exists over and above all the divisions that cleave us along these lines, something that is more enduring than our political vicissitudes and religiocultural differences.

What could that be? Here Savarkar invokes the trope of blood, of common kinship. Surely a sort of common racial descent unites Indians; whatever their differences, they are united by a common blood. Savarkar is looking for a way of giving India an identity that can encompass all other differences. His answer is that being Indian means essentially possessing a common ethnicity, which he names Hindutva or "Hindu-ness." This is what all Indians have in common, including Muslims, Christians, Sikhs, Jains, and Buddhists. For Savarkar and the many to whom he appeals, the call of race or blood, or even common values that overshadow all our differences is that it answers the question of what it is to be an Indian. If this vision meets with opposition, he adds, it is because many communities such as the Muslims do not acknowledge who they really are. Rather than giving moral priority and their highest allegiance to their true identity, they direct their devotion beyond India. Rather than acknowledging their common descent, they seek to differentiate themselves. But a benchmark of Indian identity is refusing to follow foreign gods.

6. The Blind Alley of Identity Politics

What to make of all these? The first thing to note is that Savarkar's opening question is a trap. It does not admit of a natural answer. It only exposes the fragility of any conception of identity. It will lead inevitably to a contest over an authoritative definition, and the strong will bear it away. Moreover, any process of creating an identity will lead to the creation of that identity's "other." Indeed, the difficulty for most minorities in India now is that their "otherness" is overdetermined. If Indian identity is about fidelity to a religion, they are excluded. If it is about belonging to the single race envisaged by Savarkar, those who do not acknowledge such a race are excluded. If we say Indian identity is constituted by some values, say tolerance, then some may be accused of failing to exemplify those values. In short, every attempt to come up with a benchmark or a litmus test for Indian identity will cause mischief. I suspect that simply counterposing some other and more liberal conception of Indian identity will not be enough to match the BJP and the other forces of Hindutva that are now entrenched in politics and society. But the root of the problem is not Hindutva. The root of the problem is the obsession with identity that makes the ideology of Hindutva seem possible and even sensible. The wisest course is to go to first principles in order to reject the fatal allure of the identity question altogether.

Politically, what the 900 million Hindus, 130 million Muslims, and all the other groups in India need to do if democracy is to be sustained is not so much to invent a new conception of Indian identity — even one that emphasises pluralism and tolerance — as to frame a social contract within which they can peacefully manage their fundamental differences. Hindus, in other words, do not need to ask "What do we share?" but rather "How can we live together when we disagree about what we share or even share nothing at all?" The challenge, contra Savarkar, is not to find or invent a basis of unity; the challenge is to live on the basis of difference. Liberal democracy, since it is very much about managing differences, and not mythically or violently willing them away, can be of enormous help with this project, indeed must lie very near its heart if the project is to have good prospects for long-term success.

And succeed it must, for any attempt to produce an authoritative conception of India, whether informed by Hindutva or any other ideology, will be fraught with exclusion and violence. So long as Indian political discourse is driven by a need to benchmark collective identity, some subset of citizens will always be at risk. The threat posed to minorities comes not only from this or that conception of nationalism, but from the inherently dangerous and ill-advised character of the quest to benchmark identities.

7. Political Prospects for Hindutva

What are the conditions under which the Hindutva quest for benchmarking are likely to be potent?

Hindutva works as an explicit plank of mobilization when the following conditions are obtained. First, Hindu nationalism is, as Ashutosh Varshney pointed out, a politics of anxiety. There has to be a framing context or a specific event that generates anxiety that the politics of Hindutva can tap. Such an anxiety can be generated by terrorism, a narrative that stitches together events attributed to terrorists like Godhara and Akshardham, or during the 1980s the fall out from Shah Bano or secessionist movements. The BJP then taps into this anxiety, and gives it an ominous form. Arguably there is no such framing context, no immediate event to fuel a politics of anxiety and resentment. It is thus becoming intrinsically difficult to unleash the energies of Hindutva. This is not to say that such a framing context cannot reappear in the near future: the present government could act ineptly and imprudently; India — Pakistan tensions could again flare up because of lack of progress in Kashmir, providing a trigger for "terrorism." But in the absence of such events the BJP will find it difficult to capitalize on nationalist mobilization.

Second, the openings to the politics of Hindutva were provided by Congress itself, which encouraged competitive religious mobilization to wrest concessions from the state. After 1985 and the politics that emerged in the aftermath of the Shah Bano decision, Congress found it very hard to make credible the claim that it was being even handed with all communities. It tried, by first caving into Muslim orthodoxy and then by courting the Hindu right, but it could not effectively combat the charge of "pseudo-secularism" from either end. The Shah Bano affair gave grist to the mill of those who thought Congress was excessively partial toward minorities; the demolition of the Babari Masjid and the riots against Muslims that followed in the states like Maharashtra made its claims to protect minorities appear hollow. The charge of pseudo-secularism was an indictment of Congress politics. It meant two different things, though in practice they would often run together. One was the claim that Congress really was succumbing to "minorityism," an unfair privileging of minorities. Again the "truth" of this charge is beside the point; what is important is that fact that the groundswell of ideological, cultural, organizational propaganda that the Sangh Parivar produced made this charge seem credible to many. The second claim was that Congress was really not interested in the transformative agenda of secularism at all, because, rather than extricating politics from religion, it went on implicating them even more. On either reading, the authority of Congress' secular credentials was suspect. Instead of befriending all religions it had ended up giving all of them reason to suspect its motives; instead of a balancing act, it had produced a politics of perpetual concessions that made all religious groups active and none entirely happy.

Historically this balancing act entailed by the parity model can be dubbed as "Congress secularism." After all, during the independence movement the Congress could make room within itself for both the Hindu right, and orthodox ulema, at the same time as it championed the cause of modern secularism.

Rajiv Gandhi was not averse to allowing the Ayodhya issue to be politically reopened in the aftermath of Shah Bano; Mrs Gandhi gave Sikh fundamentalism an opening in organized politics and then tried to capitalize on a Hindu backlash; anti-conversion legislations and bans on cow slaughter were crafted first in states ruled by Congress at the same time as it was trying to position itself as a protector of minorities. In principle this was a win–win strategy all around. Each religious group could wrest concessions from the Congress without anyone of them becoming a target. And this politics of placating one group after the other as the political need arose was ideologically legitimized in the name of a distinctive brand of India secularism. Indian secularism was not to be defined by strict separation between Church and state; the state could patronize all manner of religious ambitions so long as it did so even handedly, and without advocating the establishment or dominance of one religion. Congress secularism was both pro-Hindu and protector of the minorities at the same time. What the BJP managed to do successfully is to argue that you could no longer be both at the same time: minorities came to be defined against Hindus.

It is too early to be confident that the Congress itself will not engage in the politics of competitive group mobilization. But there are reasons for thinking that political parties might now become a little more principled on the issue of secularism and defuse the anxieties created by a politics of opportunism. This is in part because, as I shall discuss below, minority politicians have become a lot more aware of the costs of this kind of politics.

Third, what would be an issue around which Hindutva politics would mobilize? In some ways it has already become the dominant sentiment: on all the issues, be it cow slaughter, conversion, cultural transformation, expansion of its base amongst tribals, the acceptance of religion in politics, changes in the self-perception of Indians, political marginalization of minorities, Hindutva is already mainstream. It has already redefined the public sphere in ways that cries of "Hinduism in danger" no longer have quite the same appeal. The BJP has already managed to redefine the public sphere in ways that cries of "Hinduism in danger" no longer have quite the same appeal. Here the BJP may be a victim of its own success.

The one major issue on which Hindutva politics could mobilize would be building a temple Ayodhya. But this is a tricky one to use. For one thing, any mobilization on this issue runs the risk of inviting the question: what has the BJP been up to on this issue for five years? It can now mobilize on this issue only when one of two conditions are obtained. Either it is utterly desperate, or there is a reasonable chance that this mobilization will result in the construction of the temple. Given current institutional and legal constraints, the BJP cannot launch another movement, because a movement without an end result will simply yield diminishing returns. It will take this issue up only when it is now in a position to deliver on it. It is easier to organize movements for the sake of it when you are in opposition, they are harder to justify when a party holds the reins of power. And the temple issue also gets sustenance from a larger framing context that was unavailable this time.

Third, the political forces that represent Hindutva are themselves in a good deal of internal disarray and may not able to mobilize. The moral authority of the BJP leadership has been considerably eroded by their performance in power and now in opposition. Fourth, India as, is familiar, has too many cross cutting cleavages for a single conception of identity politics to become thoroughly dominant politically. Finally, there is an inbuilt limitation to the politics of identity. This politics centres on key symbolic objectives and has to reinvent itself once those objectives are met. An identity can set some parameters on governance, it is not itself a substitute for governance. Political parties cannot, in the long run, be sustained by single point agendas that a politics of identity usually entails.

All of this is by way of suggesting that the political conditions for making Hindutva dominant in Indian politics are not going to be easy to create. This does not entail that Hindutva will not remain a significant and formidable political force; and it certainly does not entail that it will not be culturally dominant. Hindutva movements still have considerable grassroots presence, and cultural support. But they are most likely to remain the potential source of a violent undertow to Indian politics, not its main center.

8. Identity and the World

Identity is also about the way in which a nation faces the world. And it is here that arguably India has seen the most profound changes. There has been a quiet revolution underway in India's approach to the world. The central elements of this revolution were simply but pointedly articulated by Manmohan Singh in a little noticed addressed recently delivered to the India Today Conclave. The speech very craftily takes its cue from a statement of Nehru's: "Talking of foreign policies, the House must remember that these are not just empty struggles on a chess Board. Ultimately foreign policy is the outcome of economic policy." Dr. Singh's speech was one of the fullest elaborations of what this claim might mean for the 21st century.

Simply put, Manmohan Singh called for as intense an engagement with the global economy as we can possibly muster. Behind this call lies a very sophisticated understanding of the currency of power in the modern world. India's approach to the world had for decades been hostage to some fundamental misconceptions. We confused autonomy with autarky, sovereignty with power, and interdependence with a lack of independence. Our own insecurities and inhibitions had created a conceptual fog around how power operates in international society. That fog has now been decisively lifted. Dr. Singh's speech was recognition of the fact that the more we engage with the global economy, the more our power will grow. This is not just because of the obvious fact that an increasing share of world trade and investment will make India important. It is also because the only sure path to peace is to create powerful constituencies in other countries who have a vested interest in supporting your cause. Trade and investment create the lobbies that transform relations between states.

Indeed, if the actions of this and the previous government are any guide, India is arguably proceeding with globalization more rapidly than with liberalization. We may still go slowly on disinvestment, labor reform and reform of the state. But for all the pressures of the left, the one area where India is forging ahead without inhibitions is integration with the world economy. Duties are on downward trend, we are pursuing free trade agreements and pipelines galore, and the momentum towards liberalizing foreign investment is inexorable. This is all being made possible not just by new economic thinking, but by a re-articulation of our foreign policy. The NDA had taken the initiative in terms of intensely integrating India with the rest of Asia. There were two imperatives behind this move. The first was clearly economic. But the second was a way of saying to our neighbors, that India not going to be tied down by the security complexes in its neighborhood. It was forging ahead with its plan of integrating with the rest of Asia. It was up to our neighbors to join the party or be left behind. Indeed, the thinking was that it might be politically easier for our neighbors to create economic links with us, if these were seen as part of an Asia wide trend.

On this score, Manmohan Singh has continued to be assertive and clear eyed. Despite opposition from within the Congress party, India honored its Free Trade Agreement with Thailand. But what was remarkable about Singh's speech was its willingness to call South Asia as a whole to face up to its historical potential. Singh argued that "we can jointly create reciprocal dependencies for mutual benefit. So far this potentially benign process has been hobbled by narrow political calculations."

But Manmohan Singh's speech was remarkable for its grasp not just of the relationship between economic and foreign policy. It also linked foreign policy with pluralism and a new kind of multilateralism. Ask the question: what kinds of societies are, over the long haul, going to be best able to take advantage of globalization? One element of the answer is going to be pluralism and openness. Japan's economy is suffering because it has in some senses remained a closed society incapable of accepting immigration as a solution to its demographic woes. Europe is struggling to acknowledge that it has become multicultural, and the sense of identity of some of its nations is so fragile that a headscarf can put it at risk. Even, China's capacity to negotiate pluralism is still an open question. For all its warts, India has the capability of positioning itself as a negotiator between different civilizations and ways of life. Although, as Singh acknowledged, we can be hostage to intolerance and extremism, India is one of the few societies in the world that is capable of negotiating a deep pluralism. The NDA's foreign policy, sound as it was in some respects, was premised on frittering away India's crucial historical inheritance. But this inheritance is also an asset in a globalizing world; it ought to be the cornerstone of our foreign policy. Manmohan Singh's speech was riposte to both the left for its resistance to openness, and to the right for its resistance to pluralism.

Finally, both economic globalization and pluralism have to be linked to what can be described as a multicentric multilateralism. This is not the multilateralism centered on a moribund institution like the UN. It is a multilateralism that enduringly binds nations in webs of interdependence through a series of overlapping institutions. India is now seeking to join almost any multilateral arrangement that will admit it as a member, from APEC to G-8. These arrangements involve sovereignty trade-offs. But the underlying vision is that these sovereignty trade-offs are more than compensated by the real power that accrues from participation in these institutions.

The three elements of this foreign policy: uninhibited economic openness, pluralism and membership of multilateral institutions reinforce each other. Genuine economic openness is not sustainable without an open society and a willingness to participate in regional arrangements signals a commitment to openness and dialogue.

It is abundantly clear that, as articulated in Dr. Singh's speech, India now has a clearer conception of its role in the world. We used to blame outside powers for all our ills. Now Indian Prime Ministers chide India for its own inhibitions and reluctance to take advantage of the world. This is a sea change in India's foreign policy, facilitated by growing economic confidence. And it could be argued that whether or not conducting nuclear tests was wise security policy, the way in which they were handled, helped India overcome a crisis of confidence that had besotted its foreign policy. The NDA broke the wood, now Dr. Singh seems to be going for the carving.

Translating this vision into reality will require immense effort. While economic policy can drive foreign policy, economic policy itself is a product of artful political manoeuvring. But it opens up two intriguing possibilities for Indian identity.

First, by seeking to open up its borders with the rest of Asia, India is once again striving for connections in its own natural neighborhood. It has signaled its willingness to economically integrate with the rest of Asia and it is possible that over time this will revolutionize the way in which India conceives of the region. In utopian moments it is possible to imagine India's border regions culturally and economically relinking with their traditional trading zones: Tamil Nadu with Sri Lanka, Indian Punjab with Pakistan Punjab, the North East with South East Asia. It is now feasible that these regions can establish economic linkages, yet remain firmly wedded politically to India. The idea is that India will need a strong center, but not necessarily a well defined circumference. What is striking is the degree to which this vision is being talked about and is likely to be the cornerstone of Indian policy. There is some consensus that by letting Indian integrate with the rest of Asia (a free trade zone from Kabul to Manila!) India will make it easy for its neighbors to open links with it, in the context of wider regional cooperation. Second, the economic successes of the last decade and half have made India a little more confident that it can become a dominant regional player. But the implications for Indian identity are this: India may no longer tie itself down to thinking in the confined terms that it had become used to after 1962, but a much wider regional imagination will once again begin to shape it. A distant prospect still, but more plausible than a few years ago.

The second intriguing possibility it opens up for Indian identity is this. There is no doubt that greater integration into the world economy, or even the aspiration, transforms an understanding of national identity. Think of two scenarios. In the first instance there is an emerging nationalist party, with significant anti-minority sentiment. But this party has none of the following aspirations. It does not feel obliged to send signals that can attract foreign investors and depositors, its routine engagements with the outside world are episodic rather than spread across a wide range of domains, it sees international rivalries as a zero sum game, has little potential for learning from the rest of the world and thumbs its nose at international institutions and norms.

In the second scenario, the same nationalist party, with similar anti-minority sentiment, comes to power in a context where it has to recognize that the health of the economy and, by implication, national power, depend upon a certain level of international credibility. It recognizes the need to attract investment and have a plausible face to carry in forum after forum. It learns quickly that mutual interdependence is a surer path to national power than autarky, that power is not a zero sum game and that the international system can be engaged with only in terms of reciprocity. It learns that a mere declaration of sovereignty cannot be confused with real power, and that there might be something to be learnt from how other nations got to be influential. It does not take much to figure out in which scenario the nationalist party will be forced to tame its belligerence.

It would be complacent and false to believe that integration into the world economy will tame fanatical nationalism by some over determined logic. Nationalism and anti-minority sentiment are products of political choices and these choices can be exercised often against the national interest. There is no guarantee against political fanaticism. But it could be argued that globalization is a contributing factor to that moderation.

India always cared a good deal about what the rest of the world thought of it but it now cares for a more tangible measure of its success: its ability to attract investment and jobs from overseas. It is difficult to think of this as mattering unless India had greater aspirations to integrate into the global economy. In subtle ways, the desire to present India in a certain light has forced the Government to confront questions about India's credibility; it has nudged it to make sure that India gets the headlines for the right reasons.

Belligerent nationalism feeds on a politics of anxiety. Compared to the early 1980s, the politics of anxiety seems to have diminished in intensity. This is, in no small measure, due to two factors. India has become more confident of its ability to deal with the rest of the world, and it is difficult to imagine this confidence in the absence of the process of globalization. Rather than producing an identity crisis, globalization has given an opportunity to India to feel less insecure. In an autarkic world, we had no sense of how we might prove our possibilities. Globalization, by providing opportunities for international success, has made that anxiety less pressing. If Indians feel that they are ready to take on the world, they might feel less compelled to take it out on each other. Glory is a glorious identity to have, and if Indians are more confident that this sort of recognition is in their grasp, it might ease their anxieties. It is still only a hope. But freedom and openness suit India's character more. That is the only identity that can sustain it in the long run.

CHAPTER 15

Politics of Identity in Post-reform China

David A. Kelly

The idea that political and economic communities are profoundly shaped by fundamental processes of subject formation ("identities") of the sub-groups and individuals that make them up may seem all too obvious in the post-Cold War era. Identities may be based on primordial attributes like blood descent, gender, or ethnicity, or the attribution of religion, sexuality, or culture and the such. For contemporary social science, regardless of whether such traits are achieved or ascribed, primordial or constructed, subjectively accepted, rejected or ignored, they touch on the political through acts of recognition, acts which are likely to have dimensions that are strategic for the state as well as ethical for the individual.[1,2] Thus while membership of a given blood group may be more primordial, more universally verifiable than any of the supposed markers of "race," insofar as recognition of the trait is confined to the medical profession, it does not come within the ambit of identity politics. By the same token, many forms of persecution in history, including campaigns against heresy, unorthodox opinion, thought crimes and the like from medieval witch-hunts to ethnic cleansing, may be based on no empirical criteria whatsoever; yet the political and ethical issues of recognition apply exactly as if they were. Identity does not require that markers objectively exist — only that they be deemed to do so.

In all the above senses, "identity" has been having a heyday. The terrorist attacks on New Yorks' World Trade Center of September 11, 2001 have fundamentally altered the attitudes of many observers, social scientists included. Liberal and neoliberal notions of convergence and modernization, together with Marxist or other leftist notions of class struggle leading to the ultimate formation of a higher human solidarity, held sway in post-War social discourse, if only in the imagination of their proponents. Neither seems to be holding up well. Fukuyama's end of history quickly yielded to Huntington's clash of civilizations, and the latter is often felt, whatever its faults of conception and detail, to provide a better fit with contemporary political reality.

India and China represent widely divergent models of multi-ethnic states: in the simplest terms, in building their states from heterogeneous component regions and peoples, India is a union — not a federation — of states, China a unitary political entity. Identity-related social theories and policies generated in response to their experiences are equally divergent. As the two move ever closer to the status of quasi-superpowers, at least in their immediate regions, attention inevitably turns to the role of primordial identity relations in their recent histories and immediate futures. As the Indian case is dealt with elsewhere in this volume, we confine ourselves for the most part to the People's Republic of China (PRC). There, the new administration of Hu Jintao and Wen Jiabao has called for "building a harmonious society."[3] Behind this, as commentators on all sides have been quick to point out, lies the reality of a China which contains sizeable reservoirs of mistrust, injustice, and conflict. This chapter attempts to map the terrain of identity politics in China in a way that relates a tension-ridden political and cultural history to official images of economic success, "peaceful rise" and social harmony. The implications for Chinese as a player on the global stage will lead to our conclusion.

As sketched in above, identity takes in political, sociological, and psychological variables. A whole flank of theory, often labeled postmodernist, is devoted to the proposition that identities — notably those of class, gender, and ethnicity — are "socially constructed." Inasmuch as globalization tends to place all primordial relations under a microscope, providing plenty of cases of the reconstruction of identity in the wake of ever-freer flows of material and intellectual assets,[a] it would be unwise to treat such viewpoints as irrelevant. Nonetheless this is not the main front to be pursued here.

---

[a]Note, for example, the self-congratulatory invocation of "Asian values" in the early 1990s, and their subsequent discrediting in the wake of the Asian financial crisis.

The more modest framework used by Pingle and Varshney in Chapter 13 seems useful here:

> With regard to identity politics, we suggest a distinction between two dimensions: macro and micro. The macro questions have to do with national, sub-national, and group identities: How is [the] national identity defined, and what kinds of group identities — religious, linguistic, tribal, caste-related — have been prominent in national politics?
>
> The micro questions have to do with how families and individuals adapt to, and counter, changes in environment, and what sorts of politics such adaptations and challenges spawn (Chapter 13 in this volume).

In China, identity at the "macro" level, while heterogeneous and strongly demarcated, is relatively inert in political terms. Differences of religion and ethnicity are largely overwhelmed by the demographic fact of the supremacy of one ethnic group, the Han[b] (some 95% of the population). In many instances non-Han groups who have the option of assimilating into Han society tend to be more differentiated by identity issues which divide the Han. This has the effect of transferring political interest from ethnicity to those other issues.

Variations of ethnic and religious identity in the PRC tend to play a secondary role to variations in citizenship. For the purposes of this paper we shall not treat citizenship in the abstract terms of constitutional law and political theory — where the citizenry is usually a theoretically uniform population of agents endowed with identical rights and status — but as bearers of superimposed status and class attributes that are complex and variable. Gaps between urban and rural citizens, between the skilled and the unskilled, between people with reliable elite connections and those without, between the advantaged and the disadvantaged, form the politically volatile divisions of identity in contemporary China.

---

[b]The word Han is potentially troublesome, denoting, in different contexts, the historical Han dynasty (206 BCE–220 CE); the dominant ethnic group on the Chinese mainland; and their language. Context is relied on here to keep these meanings distinct.

1. China's Identity Structure: Macro-Dimensions

China's national identity has been powerfully shaped by both ethnic/racial and cultural frames of reference. The notion of a distinctive Chinese civilization founded 5000 years ago continues to play a shaping role[4] the PRC has even been described as a "civilization masquerading as a nation."[5,6] Without going to such extremes, it can be agreed that the traditional state was dynastic, its writ unconstrained by fixed territorial boundaries, its supreme political norms implicitly universal, and its primary channels of loyalty phrased in particularistic terms. "Peasants used to pay loyalty to the ruler of 'all under heaven'" (Shih 2002b). The view that this places classical China outside the general comparative framework of states is open to serious challenge, notably in the light of political formations in the pre-dynastic era of the Warring States (656–221 BCE) which closely resemble the early modern European state; indeed "it is of critical importance that China was once a system of sovereign territorial states in the classical era."[7] Nonetheless, it is the dynastic era which more concretely constrains and shapes contemporary state-formation. Here we must speak of a "movement between the pole of ethnicity, stressing the importance of common descent, and the pole of culturalism, emphasizing cultural qualities that can be acquired."[8] By the time of the Western incursions of the 19th century, the "system of sovereign territorial states" had long been overlaid by a very different order, and a series of reconstructions of political identity, including an acceptance in principle of the Westphalian model of the sovereign nation state, could be undertaken only against great internal resistance. This process of reinvention is incomplete, with serious discontinuities in the narrative arising in the wake of the civil war between Nationalists and Communists, as seen today in the contested status of Taiwan. Many ostensibly national institutions are weak or compromised. The People's Liberation Army (PLA), for example, which might be expected to provide a pillar of nation building as have other military institutions in the developing world, remains a Party army and is unlikely to be converted to a citizen army soon. The partisan origins of the division between the PRC and the Republic of China surviving on Taiwan help differentiate it from comparable cases elsewhere in the world such as India and Pakistan, an analogous sundering of a once unified cultural history, or Israel and Palestine, an analogous pattern of incompatible bases of legitimacy.

Putting Taiwan to one side, the PRC inherited the geographical outlines of the Qing dynasty to a great extent, having recovered wide territories that had become all but lost to the Republican and Nationalist regimes. The China plain, the heartland region, is mainly occupied by Han Chinese, speakers of the Chinese language (*Hanyu*) in its many dialects; the surrounding border areas are occupied by the larger non-Han ethnic groups and Han who have settled among them. The ruling Communist Party was intimately shaped by several aspects of this ethnic geography. In the first place the Soviet Union to which they looked as a blueprint in their early years had evolved very fixed views about the "national question," a key exponent of which was Stalin himself.[9] Secondly, the Chinese Communist Party (CPC) spent its formative years wandering in the Western minority regions, where over time its own quite different approach to the national question emerged. The early CPC made considerable efforts to establish a new era in ethnic relations, condemning the "greater Han chauvinism" of the past, particularly of the Guomindang (Kuomintang or Nationalist Party), which began life as a movement to overthrow the Manchu dynasty, and only somewhat belatedly drew up a framework in which the non-Han peoples could participate as members of one nation. We shall return to the issue of ethnic identity below.

At no time has it been easy to describe China in terms of religious allegiances like those found in other major centers of civilization such as the Middle East, Europe or India. Han Chinese were once of the same largely Mahayana Buddhist allegiance as the Japanese, Koreans, and Vietnamese, but revolution and other modern forces have today reduced this ancient faith to simply one option among several. The fusion of Confucianism and Legalism in the early Han Dynasty shaped the core values of a political elite who for the next two millennia sought to align the cosmic sources of spirituality with the state, symbolized by the Emperor and his deputed officials, in what is termed "family-state holism." Buddhism had its high moments in the Wei-Jin (AD 220–588) and Sui-Tang (AD 581–907) eras, and aspects of its philosophy were gradually worked into the Confucian-Legalist mix, but the Empire's suspicion of clerical orders was endemic, and led to many rounds of suppression of Buddhism, which often revived but never prevailed. China is for the first time "conceived in terms of excluding the foreign" in the Tang scholar Han Yu's famous poem "Memorial on the Buddha's Bone," in which the poet writes to the Emperor, "Your servant submits that Buddhism is but one of the practices of barbarians which has filtered into China since the Later Han."[10,11] Even harsher was the judgment on more authentic Chinese spiritual movements, deriving from Daoism and recurrently mutating into millenarian cults capable of bringing dynasties to a violent end. The present official suppression of Falun Gong owes much to this heritage.[12,13]

The long-lasting Yuan (Mongol) and Qing (Manchu) dynasties which displaced ethnic Han rulers in the latter half of the imperial era were often more accepting of outside religions and their domestic adherents. Islam spread through the Northwest and Southwest largely in track with Mongol incursions to produce the largest populations of monotheists in China. Muslims are broadly divided into the Uyghurs of Xinjiang, and the Hui living in dispersed settlements, also in the Northwest but closer to the Han heartland, often scattered among Han majority populations, and often indiscernible from them in attributes other than religious belief and practice.[14] It may be noted that the Ming, which intervened between the Yuan and Qing dynasties, "was in fact an ethnically mixed administration with many central Asians playing a leading role."[15] But helping shape China's identity politics is the fact that monotheism has never held the reins at the top of society; nor has it ever held spiritual authority under a formula like the division of Church and State found in the West. Conflict between religions was until modern times of less significance in Chinese history than it was elsewhere. With warfare and suppression rarely fuelled by the passions of monotheism, and hence little required as tools of state, accommodation was accepted and indeed cultivated. The classical state could generally rely on assimilation to work in the end.

In the 20th century the Guomindang and the Communists, both Leninist parties, created (for a time) successful regimes which exalted the head of state to quasi-divine status, but were in formal terms atheistic, denying any claims of formal religion to political relevance. Under the CPC, the Chinese government recognizes five "legitimate" religions: Buddhism, Daoism, Islam, Catholicism, and Protestantism. It monitors their activities rigorously and makes every effort to suppress variant or upstart subgroups which might come to pose a threat to the secular order. In the reform period challengers to this order have indeed emerged, and the number of religious affiliates is likely to be several times greater than that acknowledged in official statistics (the total number of adherents of the five recognized religions official was estimated at 136 million, some 11% of the population, in 1999). The challenge posed to the established order means that religion is by no means a negligible factor in Chinese politics, but should not be exaggerated. Despite the Falun Gong scare, there is little evidence of political groups based on religious identity aspiring to, let alone capable of taking over the state (as in Iran for instance) or even claiming a pivotal role within it (as with Islamic groups who demand state backing for Shari'a law; or as with the religious Right in America). Compared to Islam in Indonesia, Catholicism in the Philippines, or Hinduism in India — all cases in which religious identity is far from politically inert — faith-based politics in China belongs in the minor leagues. An upshot of this is that when one meets a citizen of the PRC one can make few assumptions as to his or her spiritual allegiance or religious identity — unlike in the case of an American (who will in many cases bear the traces, positive or negative, more or less pronounced, of Judaeo–Christian values); of an Indian (who is likely to bear cultural values rooted in Hinduism, Islam, or one of the set of recognized religions). The point is not that Han Chinese lack spirituality — an easily refuted claim — but that there is no "default" spiritual identity.[c] We shall return to this notion shortly.

Ethnicity is another matter. Modern scholarship must contend with the pressure of a powerful mythology which since the late 19th century has insisted on the conflation of ethnicity, culture, and territorial sovereignty. This is summed up in invocations of Chinese people of today as "sons of the dragon," or of the Yellow Emperor. These totemic figures derive from Han history and have little basis in the non-Han cultures; nevertheless the latter are, willy-nilly, named as stakeholders in the cultural capital of the Han.[16] As noted, modern Chinese nationalism, seeking resolution of long and bitter conflict between Han and Mongol, Han and Manchu, Han and Western powers and, not least, Han and Japanese, established the category of "national minorities" as stakeholders within the nation state, endowed with notionally equal citizen rights. Under the Constitution, Autonomous Regions (*zizhiqu*) are territorial units distinct from the provinces (*sheng*) where the Han majority reside, and

---

[c] In information technology, a *default* refers to a "setting or value automatically assigned to a program or device." http://en.wikipedia.org/wiki/Default_%28computer_science%29. By *default identity* is meant one which is assigned to a subject in the absence of efforts (either by the subject or by others) to assert anything to the contrary. In a classic parallel, the term "British" labels the default identity of people of English, Scots, Irish, and Welsh extraction. Note that many attributes of this identity, like language, are in fact English. Likewise the default identity of Australians is labeled "Anglo–Celtic."

nominally the preserve of non-Han Chinese — Mongolians, Uyghurs (in Xinjiang), and Tibetans. While variously defined ethnic minorities number in the hundreds, the PRC recognizes 55 "national minorities," most with linguistic and cultural traditions quite separate from the Han, in communities scattered through the length and breadth of China.[17] Whereas the empire generally regarded non-Han peoples as aliens awaiting assimilation to Han culture, the establishment of the PRC in effect cemented in place a Chinese ethnic "salad bowl" which gains symbolic recognition in the official political sphere through the operation of quotas for minority delegates to legislative and advisory assemblies like the National Peoples Congress (NPC) and the Chinese Peoples Political Consultative Commission (CPPCC). Membership of a national minority must be supported by a birth certificate. Standard identification documents specify, along with ethnicity, one's date of birth, gender and place of origin. All of such minorities are recipients of the abstract category of citizenship within the PRC Constitution, and allowed notional political autonomy which, while stringently forbidding secession and opposition, does afford a wide range of compensatory privileges. Members of minorities enjoy freedom from mandatory population planning applying to the Han. In many regions their languages and scripts enjoy official recognition and are widely visible in official texts. These and other special extensions of citizenship, referred to by Shih Chih-yu as "citizenship projects," have undoubtedly contributed to building separate ethnic identities,[17,18] indeed to the point that minority identities such as the Yi, Miao and Qiang "involve more artificial construction than authenticity."[19]

In only a few cases, notably the Tibetans, the Mongols and the Uyghurs of Xinjiang (mainly Sunni Muslims whose language is closely related to Turkish), do these minorities occupy territorial bases and maintain cultural identities on a scale large enough to offer hopes of secession or even organized resistance. Furthermore, the state's citizenship projects and the identities they induce are increasingly subject to forces of globalization whose overall impact is on the whole favorable to maintaining Han dominance. In 2005 Mr Raidi, a senior state official of the Tibetan minority, traveled to Perth, Western Australia, to open a Confucius Institute.[20] Confucianism has virtually no affinities with Tibetan culture, but it is unproblematic to associate it with the *Zhonghua* (supra-Han) Chinese national identity, which Raidi assumed by default on this occasion. The *Hindutva* [Hindu-ness] described in Pratap Bhanu Mehta's

Chapter (14) in this volume seems by comparison a virtual rather than actual category.

Globalization supports tendencies other than the spread of characteristically Han values and commitments within China. International, particularly American media are simultaneously influencing the Han identity by a process of osmosis which, while frequently ringing nationalistic alarm-bells, is extremely difficult to control.[21] A current example is the TV show "Supergirl," which stormed up the ratings in mid 2005. This program, essentially a karaoke singing competition for young women, was viewed as subverting traditional cultural values associated with the coastal cities: the winners were all from western Chinese cities like Chengdu and Changsha. Their spiky hair and androgynous body language sounded a death-knell for the bland (not to say saccharine) femininity that had been well established in the mainland media, largely under the sway of Taiwanese and Hong Kong (*gangtai*) models. Even more significantly, the fact that winners were determined by majority vote, using SMS messages received from the live audience, counted as a notable departure from Han and Communist norms, in both of which political and cultural role-models are subject to scrupulous elite selection and screening.[22] Of particular interest in this context is the impact of Korean media culture. A fad for the "Korean Wave" of pop music, movies and TV soap operas has been growing for over a decade, clearly signifying the premium in the marketplace enjoyed by this "modernization with an East Asian face." This amounts to "soft power" carrying with it Christian evangelism and democratic values that might be more readily rejected if presented in American or other Western formats.[23]

Whatever the outcomes of these impacts, the general point holds that to the extent that non-Han assimilate the dominant Chinese cultural identity, they become subject by default to these transforming influences as well. Of course, "Supergirls" or Korean soap-opera scenarios are no more likely to entirely colonize Chinese culture than are the "gangsta" rappers, who have dominated popular music in recent years, to colonize that of the USA or countries that consume large amounts of its cultural products. The processes of cultural change are combinatorial and contingent, with novel influences rarely appearing in isolation and traditional elements never completely disappearing. Thus the regional identities deriving from China's traditional division into provinces — like the challenge to the established value hierarchy from

Hunan and Sichuan noticeable in the "Supergirl" phenomenon — may be accentuated by globalization, and transferred into the default identity. Regional identity operates on a series of scales, with the traditional provinces and certain major cities — Beijing, Shanghai, Tianjin, Chongqing, Guangzhou, and Shenzhen — dominating the public mind. North, South, East, West, and Central are also of importance, but are less susceptible to political activation than the provinces and cities.[24]

China's unitary constitutional structure seems decisive here. The established political culture of most of China's modern elites has rejected federalism, so that the "autonomy" extended to regional units is accompanied by few formal jurisdictional separations. China's territorial units lack a constitutionally validated forum (like the Senate in many constitutional democracies, or the Soviet of Nationalities in the former Soviet Union) where their interests may be voiced and negotiated. Leaders of the party and state agencies at provincial level owe their positions to Central delegations. They may be and frequently are transferred to other provinces or to positions in the vertically organized bureaucracy under the Ministries and Commissions of the State Council. This severely limits the development of regional political identities among members of the Central elite.

As will be shown at greater length below, while the PRC has its own version of the "salad-bowl" of ethnic and regional identities found in other large multi-ethnic societies, for a nation of 1.3 billion there is a conspicuous lack of diversity due to forces of homogenization. One of the operative factors here is the de-resourcing of regional China. Whereas local elites in the classical era upheld a thriving social ecosystem in which temples, private schools, guilds and local philanthropic institutions were to be found in abundance, contemporary regional and rural China is in chronic financial deficit, its viable enterprises transferred upwards to the provincial level or higher, and only its social welfare obligations transferred down. With few rewards offered to people of ability, families who do produce high-performing children will encourage them to transfer to the cities to advance their prospects. For the rest there is little opportunity for personal development.

The era of collectivization must be given a good deal of the blame for today's colorless uniformity. The rise of the market has done a great deal to alleviate it, but the preference of immense numbers of people for holding their moments of greatest family festivity in a MacDonald's rather than in a traditional restaurant should warn us that this is no one-way street. The market for its part operates under severe restrictions, among which the homogenizing tendency is again prominent. There are so far more incentives to duplicate than to diversify.

2. Micro-Dimensions of Identity Politics: Citizen Identities

The concept of the citizen is, as noted, a cornerstone of nation building in multi-ethnic societies. We may think of citizenship as a social contract in which particularistic modes of identity are traded for abstract equality and recognition in the framework of the nation state. The measure of its success is the extent to which the sources of communal conflict are drained, and the human resources so liberated contribute to stability and development. Citizenship thus receives major inputs from political and cultural history, and has equally major outputs in social and economic policy.

China, while coming to modernity with a rich mix of ethnicities, languages and traditions, has an overriding theme of Han domination and assimilation. To "create" citizenship for non-Han groups was a project initiated by the Nationalist regime and inherited with important changes by the Communists, largely motivated by the need to mobilize resistance to Western and Japanese interlopers. China's many constitutions reflect this in their formal declarations of equality of all citizens in the unitary *Zhonghua* (Chinese, including non-Han) state in which Han identity is notionally subsumed.[25] In reality, however, not only does Han identity operate as the "default" mode of citizenship, but even the Han have undergone successive waves of "citizenization," "de-," and "re-citizenization." Re-citizenization refers to the early reform period between 1978 and 1992, described by Yao, an economist at Beijing University's China Economic Research Center, as a "Pareto process" in which all sectors of society gained. In this framework, economic growth since the late 1990s has ceased to be Pareto positive, as gaps between "advantaged" (*qiangshi*) and "disadvantaged" (*ruoshi*) groups have lead to increasingly volatile cleavages of social identity.[26]

The rural majority were, it has been suggested, "de-citizenized" by Mao's collectivization policies.[27] Even now their second class status is constantly referred to in the Chinese media, in academia and, strikingly, in official publications. Yet Qin Hui also emphasizes that contrary to popular prejudice, the urban residents were equally de-citizenized, being confined to productive enterprise work units (*danwei*) which enforced equivalent levels of dependency on their employees. Furthermore, the economic reforms given official sanction by Deng Xiaoping in 1978 coincided with a *re*-citizenization of the peasantry in advance of urban residents, the effects of which are still being felt: in their confrontations with rent-seeking local officials, peasants are far more likely seek legal remedies than displaced workers, who continue to rely on appeals to socialist morality and their lingering mythological status in Marxism-Leninism as "masters of the nation."[28]

It is necessary to place the social impact of the planned economy in wider perspective.[29] Property is officially segregated in various ways: central versus regional, state- versus collectively owned, urban versus rural, but the main categories reflected in the 1982 *Constitution of the PRC* are state, collective and private ownership. Prior to the reforms officially ushered in by Deng Xiaopeng in 1978, collective ownership, never clearly defined, was prevalent. An "all-but-state-owned" sector, it arose out of the Communist Party's inability to create a system of state ownership as complete as that of the USSR. The collectives were allowed nominal ownership of major assets, but did not in reality have final disposal rights. There was clear discrimination according to differences of rank. At the apex of the pyramid sat centrally managed State-owned Enterprises (SOEs), below which were regional ones, then the urban collective economy. Lowest of all was rural collective agriculture. Before the reforms, the state, as Great Provider to the state-owned economy, dispensed free medical care, education, very low-cost housing, and other public goods. Members of the collective economy missed out.

Given this ranking of productive units by their mode of ownership, those working in them also were implicitly endowed with different social status, more pronounced than parallel cases in Eastern Europe and the Soviet Union. Prior to the Mao's disastrous experiments in the Great Leap Forward (1958–1960), historically unprecedented migration controls were put in place in order to preserve this hierarchy. Fundamental here was the *hukou,* or residential registration document — an internal passport which strictly limited freedom of movement or occupation. Its meaning was as much economic (without it the citizen had no rights to rations of food and other basic consumption items) as political (the police system depended on the *hukou* to classify and manage "good" and "bad" social identities). A quasi-caste system arose. Marriage between people in units of higher and lower strata was discouraged; movement from a higher to a lower stratum was used as a form of political punishment, while political advancement was spelled out by movement the other way.

The peasants on the collective farms and later People's Communes were situated at the base of the pyramid. Lacking physical freedom, they resembled medieval serfs. The logic of the reforms called for an extension in the first place of economic freedom to this lowest stratum. But the resulting "marketization" was to develop only on condition that it did not threaten the status hierarchy. Despite the reforms, the pyramid and its stability mechanisms have remained surprisingly resilient. While maintaining the pyramid structure, economic growth at later stages was realized by steadily expanding the economic freedom of the peasants, and successfully creating income opportunities for the vast rural labor force.

The first major breakthrough in reform was the household responsibility system (HRS) of the late 1970s. Decollectivization greatly raised the efficiency of agriculture, but success of the HRS lay also in the fact that it was not as threatening to the entire pyramid as certain leadership factions had feared. This was largely because land was not privatized: the peasantry had only acquired usage rights over their plots. The term and rules of transfer of these rights were neither defined nor safeguarded. Thus "collective ownership of land" perpetuated the center's control over the peasantry. Local cadres could make use of their power over land allocation and transfers to obtain personal advantage.

The HRS eliminated material bottlenecks to the country's economic growth, and set rural labor power free. Between 1978 and 1982, it allowed 900 million peasants to allocate their time without interference, and become a prime force driving the market economy. This was because the facts of pre-HRS surplus of labor had been concealed by the low efficiency of collectivized agriculture; post HRS, the bulk of this surplus emerged. Making use of this rural labor surplus became an unavoidable issue for the policymakers of the time. Quite clearly, this surplus could not be used without adopting market methods. And the reformist leadership made conscious use of this in pushing for market reforms.

A second growth wave was fuelled by the rapid expansion of rural industry. This was the result of combining cheap rural labor with industrial capital in the countryside. The countryside rather than the cities was imperative: if the peasants came into the cities it would destabilize the pyramid. A slogan of the time was "leaving the land, not the county": letting peasants start industries where they were, even though in terms of economic location and environmental protection it was far from rational, even though China's degree of urbanization was far lower than that other countries at the same income level.

"Leaving the land but not the county" was limited in the successful coastal regions by local labor supplies and in the hinterland by local economic backwardness. Hence, in order to expand the employment of the rural labor force, peasants had to be allowed to move in search of work. While state-owned industrial capital was swelling in the midst of high-speed growth, due to the need to protect the stability of the pyramid it refrained from employing peasants, even though the latter were willing to accept lower wages than urban residents. Peasants going to other places to find work was mainly realized through the expansion of private capital.

The combination of private capital and cheap rural labor in the developed coastal regions and cities came about through two circumstances. First, foreign capital expanded the processing industries on China's coastal regions. In the early 21st century, processing industries (including local and foreign-invested) directly employed a total of some 20 million agricultural migrant workers (*nongmingong*, generally abbreviated to *mingong*), and indirectly an even greater number. In Guangdong alone, where export processing became most developed, *mingong* from outside the province numbered some 12–14 million. Second, China's urban service industries developed rapidly. Prior to reform, this sector was seriously retarded; as urban residents' incomes rose and the operating environment for privately owned business improved, more urban jobs opened up for migrants. In the major cities there are now some 100 million workers from the countryside, of whom over half work in the service sector, and without whom the economy would come to a standstill. As a prominent newspaper editorialized during the SARS epidemic of early 2003.[30]

> In rural regions, after the reforms in division of financial functions, the profit motive was strengthened at every level of government; many regions had a situation in which state functions were devolved downward, while ownership of assets was transferred up. This led to serious shortfalls in the local governments' public funding allocations

(particularly for education and public health). This was another reason for the Center to promote village self-government. Meanwhile in the cities, due the existence of a large surplus labor force, cheap migrant labor became the engine of economic growth of the developed regions, though improvements in their level of social security were relatively slow. The tension between the advantages of cheap labor and safeguarding the rights of the migrant workers became daily more obvious with swiftly rising economic standards. Without safeguards, stability is problematic; bottlenecks in the household registration system and social security create problems in the administration of a highly mobile group of migrant workers.

As the editorial went on to say,

The *mingong* are "suspended in mid-air," unable to settle securely in the cities, moving between village and town year after year, not seasonally, but year-round. A body suspended in mid-air is not stable: this is a law applicable not only in physics but in human society as well. When a society of over one billion people is unstable, their social actions may have a direct impact on the stability of the society as a whole. During SARS, the danger this group brings to rural society when it returns home is only the beginning. In fact, anything which impinges on the livelihood of this group, even if its onset is less sudden, even if their actions are quite unorganized, will nonetheless not only trigger unrest within this group, but also bring about wider social instability.

Even without a SARS emergency, the rural migrant workers are an intractable problem for the social order based on the hierarchy of ownership forms. They have played a key role in economic growth, particularly in the processing industries along the coast and the southeast. Often giving up their *cunmin* [village citizen] status due to long residence in the cities, they fail also to qualify as *shimin* [city folk; urban citizens], forming a third level below both.[31] While political and economic segregation has been somewhat softened by relaxation of the *hukou* system, they remain critically disadvantaged in social terms due to inadequate human and social capital. Discussing identity-related themes in the novel *Gaobie Weilian* [Farewelling Vivian], a Shanghai critic writes:

> The mentality of Shanghai's residents is stubbornly dualistic: city-folk (Shanghai people) versus country-folk (non-Shanghai people); those from south of the river (rich people from the Ningbo–Shaoxing area) versus those from north of the river (people from the Yangzhou area), etc. These ideas of status and hierarchy, being the products of oppression, are also the instruments of new oppression, indeed are the handed-down legacy of feudal society. In today's society, they express themselves in two forms: first, cultural status (what is discussed, how it is discussed), and second, consumption status (what is worn and how, what is eaten and where).[32]

Differences of social status are of course found in virtually all societies, but the depth and rigor of the division reflected here is difficult to exaggerate. In 2003, showing a photograph of a woman of Beijing origin to another woman from rural Anhui province, the present writer was struck by the response of the Anhui woman, who when asked how she knew the regional identity of the woman in the photograph, immediately listed a series of attributes, including hairstyle, clothing, posture, and "attitude." The occupational status that they shared (housekeeper) meant little in comparison to the consumption-related markers of regional identity.

These status divisions have direct economic expression in the distribution of income and social security benefits, as noted in the contributions of Pei and Oi to this volume. Despite official rhetoric in which Marxism is often invoked as a repository of the ideal of social justice, the divisions in their present form are clearly artefacts of the socialist era and its attempts to set up a planned collectivist economy. An important further consequence flows from this, namely that policies intended to ameliorate these economic discrepancies and perceived social injustices are placed in considerable difficulty. The advantaged members of society are unlikely to support redistributive polices which transfer resources to people with whom they feel little or no identity.[26]

The division between advantaged and disadvantaged (*qiangshi* and *ruoshi* in Chinese) is a good case in point of our earlier argument that divisions within the Han tend to outrank those between the Han and other ethnicities. This is not to deny, for example, that proportionally more Uyghurs than Han are disadvantaged, or to argue that disadvantaged Han feel strong bonds of solidarity with disadvantaged Uyghurs. But the population of 200 million disadvantaged migrant workers are a more real and present danger to the state than all of Xinjiang put together (even though it is in the state's interest to claim the opposite). It is also more difficult to advance policies of positive discrimination in favor of minorities like the Uyghur without arousing resentment among the Han.

3. Identity and the Outside World

How do these dimensions of identity affect China's emergence as a global influence? As noted, China's identity politics is marked by a bias toward unity. Diversity and pluralism, often praised and indeed idealized in other political cultures, require special argument in everyday discourse in the PRC. Unity and unification are trump cards in political rhetoric. This basic value setting is part of a cultural system, a mutually reinforcing relation between the political and normative orders: a single Party asserting a single culture. Nonetheless, the reality of China is a society which, if not as diversified as Europe or India, is nonetheless far from the monolithic entity celebrated in cultural rhetoric, and whose diversity may be expected to expand with economic growth.

In relations with the external world, this is reflected in a relative inability to give outsiders, minorities or hybrids a voice within China. It is as yet inconceivable for a Sonia Gandhi — the foreign-born wife of an elite politician who becomes a citizen and wins a leading political position in her adopted nation — to emerge in China. Equally credulity-stretching is the thought of Condoleeza Rice — female and African American, yet rising to the exalted post of Secretary of State — having a Chinese equivalent (an Uyghur, say, or Tibetan woman holding a position of power in the Politburo). It may be argued that, not long ago, the elevation of Madam Gandhi and of Ms Rice seemed equally improbable — India and the USA have come a long way. But this is the point: those judgments were correct for the USA and India in their time, and are by the same token correct for today's China, which has yet to come that long way.

A contemporary offshoot of the traditional imperative of unity is a heavy stress on sovereignty, one of whose corollaries is a general defensiveness regarding the operation of external agencies. Mehta in his contribution to this volume (Chapter 14) writes that India has become

> more confident of its ability to deal with the rest of the world, and it is difficult to imagine this confidence in the absence of the process of globalization. Rather than producing an identity crisis, globalization has given an opportunity to India to feel less insecure. In an autarkic world, we had no sense of how we might prove our possibilities.

Taking this insight as a conceptual transparency and superimposing it on China, it is evident that China too has moved away considerably from the blinkered assumptions of cultural essentialism, assumed victimhood and volunteered isolation of the past. These were all brought to a pitch in the Cultural Revolution, and the same process of exhaustion with, indeed revulsion from, the extremes of that era that led to the overthrow of Maoist fundamentalism and to "reform and opening up" has propelled China back into the world, to an acceptance of global norms. But the abandonment of the Mao jacket in favor of the business suit (at which even well-educated visitors to the country perpetually express surprise) may at the same time be misleading. Is the man or woman beneath the global accoutrements quite as confident in his or her ability to deal with the rest of the world as the Indian? What differences should one attend to?

One simple, relatively mechanical difference can never be overlooked: language.[33] Indian writers have not merely gained proficiency in English — at least two generations of them have taken the international world of letters by storm. On a more mundane level, the status of English as a *lingua franca* in India is difficult to imagine ever being achieved in China, albeit this signal attribute of globalization is inevitably making inroads there. Government officials at all levels nowadays tend to have what is called "excellent English"; the ability to communicate in it is very important for one's career prospects, and ambitious people do everything possible to raise their level of proficiency. Yet the range of this competency often remains severely circumscribed. The abstractions of politics, economics and other disciplinary discourses are troublesome and need years of tertiary study to master, but in both Chinese and English the level required is easily exaggerated. The terminology used in these fields is stereotyped and spelt out in reference books of all kinds. Not so the language of the novel, the cinema or even the TV soap opera. As anyone who deeply studies a foreign language in maturity is aware, among the hardest things to learn are those which the native speaker absorbs in early infancy: the wording and connotations of nursery rhymes, stories, games, and so on. Special problems attend the interface between Chinese and most other languages. No major modern languages use a pictographic script with the exception of Korean and Japanese (and these two have phonetic scripts which are known to all and in which most expressions can be rendered if necessary). A language dependent on a pictographic script has a definite conservative bias: where phonetic scripts can both recombine old words and coin totally new expressions, it is difficult in a pictographic script like Chinese to go beyond the first of these, i.e., combining ancient pictograms (characters) in new combinations. Apart from *avant garde* artistic experiments, vanishingly few attempts are made to introduce new meanings by recourse to coining new characters. Given that new meanings can be and often are grafted onto ancient signifiers, this is not an insuperable difficulty; but the upshot is that combined with several other linguistic factors in Chinese culture, the proficiency in foreign languages of Chinese native speakers, even those of high intellectual attainment, tends to remain passive rather than active. Because making the transition to English requires a great deal of the intellectual capital bound up in the sacrificed handling of their mother tongue, it is difficult for Chinese writers in English to achieve recognition. To the extent that language plays a strategic role, this applies in greater or lesser measure to other callings. Finally, while the study of Chinese is clearly on the increase worldwide, the inherent difficulties of a tonal language using a pictographic script make it very unlikely to function as a world *lingua franca* on the same level of functionality as English.

Language is for the most part merely a vehicle of cultural interaction. There are other traits which people with modern Chinese identity carry from their specific socialization which may reduce confidence in their "ability to deal with the rest of the world." Amitav Ghosh coined the term "ladder of development" to describe an intellectual construct he found operating in a developing country (Egypt): only cultures belonging to societies on the same or higher rung of the ladder are worthy of serious consideration. There is an imperative need to reduce cognitive dissonance by classifying all aspects of culture according to the position on the ladder of the society bearing them. Thus the Imam, a native of the village near Cairo where Ghosh did his fieldwork, demands of Ghosh an explanation of how India, placed high on the ladder in virtue of possessing nuclear weapons, can at the same time burn the dead, to the Imam an unacceptable and implicitly uncivilized practice.[34] The Mao era and the Cultural Revolution may be fading memories, but among the cultural shibboleths propagated by the education system — one of the more conservative institutions in the PRC — is a particularly powerful version of the ladder of development, leading to a rigid dualism of "China" and "the West." People can and do detach themselves from the powerful inertia of this essentializing framework on an individual level, but not always consistently or without considerable difficulty. Among its effects is a low level of interest in discriminating between variations within "Western" cultures.

Most distressing for Westerners who encounter this framework is the pre-conceived idea that, as in China, there is a default or exemplary cultural model in the West, namely the American. The exalted status accorded to the USA goes hand in hand with a deep-rooted belief that America is a "dangerous anti-China force." The US, particularly following the policies triggered by the Tiananmen incident of June 4, 1989, was "reimagined as on the side of forces and policies, the democratic movement and economic sanctions, which threatened to desta-bilize China by subverting control by the ruling... CCP."[35] A bleak picture may be painted of the chauvinism instilled by a range of state institutions, but it need not be thought of as a major source of Chinese foreign policy, for

> there is no public opinion in China, only public sentiment. The kind of ill-informed [Chauvinistic] feelings ... are highly volatile. They have no solid formation in informed debate. They can change overnight. One day, the Cultural Revolution will save the world; the next day, it is a disaster. The same holds with the character of Lin Biao. Sentiment lacks substance. The chauvinistic passion in no way captures some Chinese essence, not even the essence of Chinese nationalism (*ibid.*, 5).

Indeed, given a political opening up,

> The Maoist framing of Chinese consciousness in which the Chinese people are singular innocent victims of evil foreigners could implode (loc. cit.).

Other constructs however, like the ladder of development, that interact with the fervent nationalism cultivated by state policies, may be more stable. While China has produced one of the most successful and influential diasporas in the world,[d] their potential influence has been diluted by the inertia of the cultural system and the stereotype-driven mentality it propagates. Deep suspicion of cultural and ethnic hybrids attaches to them as well. Many thousands of ordinary PRC citizens have traveled overseas, some as students immersing themselves in other societies for years at a time before returning home. Over time they may be expected to overcome such insecurity-driven mental constructs, which are of course merely variations on the "us versus them" framework which is a human universal. Clearly as the national identity diversifies under the impact of the market and diversity of possibilities of consumption and ownership and so on, one may anticipate a reciprocal diversification of what can be discriminated. As China moves up the ladder of development, Chinese people may become more aware of the plurality of ladders.

4. Conclusion

We spoke at the outset of China's tension-ridden political history and of the contemporary slogan of "building a harmonious society." The fear of many intellectuals in China is that "harmony" may be interpreted to reflect the evergreen desire of the political elite for political unity and cultural uniformity. Noted liberal historian Zhu Xueqin writes,

> Harmony doesn't mean having uniform interests, but knowing how to deal with different interests in a democratic way to avoid a zero-sum game. People should recognize that "all the people of one mind" [as promoted in slogans] at the beginning of China's opening period has ended, replaced by a more diverse society with various interests. The

---

[d]This expression is used in the loose sense of a body of nationals of a country who live more or less permanently outside its boundaries, while continuing (partially) to identify with it. Wang Gungwu has argued vigorously against a stronger, politically loaded sense of "diaspora," used originally in reference to the Jews, which implies a coherent social organization and, maximally, a potentially or actually claimed right of return.[36]

key issue is not who demands equality or who does not, but rather to understand why the society is so unfair and how to change it.[37]

Understanding why society is so unfair is, as we have pointed out, intimately linked with identity politics, with deep-seated constructions of "us and them." Unfairness is structured by official policies affecting resource distribution, but these in turn rest on the basis of how the specific identities of social actors are themselves defined and allocated. It may not be enough, for example, to abolish the household registration system that helped create the third-class citizenship of migrant workers, because once such a role is taken as given, there may be more than one mechanism to allocate it to the actors. China is empirically a more diverse society, but this diversity is poorly recognized in official discourse. Dressing a roomful of people up in stylized "ethnic costumes" for the National Peoples Congress is far from convincing as a mode of recognition and overlooks other key lines of division in society. Victoria Tinbor Hui's notion of pre-Qin China as a "system of sovereign territorial states" has been alluded to: the recurrent efforts of the political elite China to limit the re-emergence of a buried cosmopolitan heritage amounts to a repression of the collective imagination. Re-legitimating diversity — recognizing more identities within the scope of citizenship — may prove to be a *sine qua non* of a harmonious society and a peaceful rise for the nation.

Acknowledgments

The author thanks Wang Gungwu and Edward Friedman for helpful comments to earlier versions of this chapter. Normal caveats apply.

References

1. Gutmann, A. (ed.) (1994). *Multiculturalism: Examining the Politics of Recognition*. Princeton: Princeton University Press.
2. Fukuyama, F. (1992). *The End of History and the Last Man*. New York: Free Press.
3. China Daily (2005). "Wen: China to build a harmonious society." China Daily 7 February 2005 http://www.chinadaily.com.cn/english/doc/2005-02/07/content_415880.htm.
4. Wang, G. (1991). *The Chineseness of China: Selected Essays*. Hong Kong: Oxford University Press.

5. Terrill, R. (2003). *The New Chinese Empire: And What it Means for the United States.* New York: Basic Books.

6. Pye, L. (1990). "China: Erratic State, Frustrated Society." *Foreign Affairs* 69(4), 56–74.

7. Hui, Victoria Tin-bor (2005). *War and State Formation in Ancient China and Early Modern Europe.* Cambridge: Cambridge University Press.

8. Loden, T. (1996). "Nationalism Transcending the State: Changing Chinese Conceptions of the Chinese Identity." In: Tønesson, S. and Antlöv, H. (eds.), *Asian Forms of the Nation.* Richmond: Curzon Press, pp. 270–296.

9. Liu, X. (2004). *Frontier Passage: Ethnopolitics and the Rise of Chinese Communism, 1921–1945.* Stanford: Stanford University Press.

10. Owen, S. (1996). *The End of the Chinese Middle Ages: Essays in Mid-Tang Literary Culture.* Stanford: Stanford University Press.

11. Halsall, P. (1999). (Website containing complete text of Han Yu's critique of Buddhism) http://acc6.its.brooklyn.cuny.edu/%7Ephalsall/texts/hanyu.html.

12. Sciwert, H. (2002). *Popular Religious Movements and Heterodox Sects in Chinese History.* Leiden: Brill.

13. Ownby, D. (2003). "A History for Falun Gong: Popular Religion and the Chinese State since the Ming Dynasty." *Nova Religio* 6(2), 223–243.

14. Gladney, D. (2006). Chapter on "Islam in China" for *The Cambridge History of Islam*, vol. 2 (forthcoming).

15. Dillon, M. (2004). *Xinjiang — China's Muslim Far Northwest.* London and New York: RoutledgeCurzon.

16. Sautman, B. (1997). "Myths of Descent, Racial Nationalism and Ethnic Minorities." In: Dikötter, F. (ed.) *The Construction of Racial Identities in China and Japan: Historical and Contemporary Perspectives.* Honolulu: Hawaii University Press, pp. 75–95.

17. Mackerras, C. (2003). *China's Ethnic Minorities and Globalisation.* London: RoutledgeCurzon.

18. Shih, C.-Y. (2002a). *Negotiating Ethnicity in China: Citizenship as a Response to the State.* London, New York: Routledge.

19. Shih, C.-Y. (2002b). "Ethnic Economy of Citizenship in China: Four Approaches to Identity Formation." In: Goldman, M. and Perry, E. J. (eds.) *Changing Meaning of Citizenship in Modern China.* Cambridge, MA: Harvard University Press, pp. 232–254.

20. UWA (2005). "Australia's first Confucius Institute at UWA." http://www.uwa.edu.au/media/statements/2005/May/australias_first_confucius_institute_at_uwa.

21. Donald, Stephanie Hemelryk and Yin Hong (eds.) (2002). *Media in China: Consumption, Content and Crisis.* London: RoutledgeCurzon.

22. Bakken, B. (1999). *The Exemplary Society: Human Improvement, Social Control and the Dangers of Modernity in China.* Oxford: Oxford University Press.

23. Onishi, N. (2006). "A rising Korean wave: If Seoul sells it, China craves it." *New York Times.* http://www.iht.com/articles/2006/01/02/news/korea.php.

24. Fitzgerald, J. (2002). *Rethinking China's Provinces.* New York: Routledge.

25. Fitzgerald, J. (1998). *Awakening China: Politics, Culture, and Class in the Nationalist Revolution.* Stanford: Stanford University Press.

26. Yao, Y. (2004). "Jianli yige Zhongguode shehui gongzheng lilun" [Establishing a Chinese theory of social justice]. Available online at http://philo.ruc.edu.cn/pol04/Article/ethics/e_politics/200409/1144.html.

27. Qin, H. (1999). "Lun xiandai sixiang the gongtong dixian"[The Common Baseline of Modern Thought], preface to the Korean edition of Qin Hui, *Tianyuanshi yu kuangxiangqu* [Pastorals and Rhapsodies]. In: David K. (ed.) *The Mystery of the Chinese Economy*, Part 1, special issue of *The Chinese Economy* **38**(4), 12–22.

28. Yu, J. (2004). "Dangqian nongmin weiquan hudong de yige jieshi kuangjia" [An explanatory framework for current peasant rights defence activities]. *Shehuixue yanjiu* [Research in Sociology] no. 2, available online at http://www.sachina.edu.cn/Htmldata/article/2005/12/739.html.

29. Kelly, D. and Luo, X. (2006). "SARS and China's Rural Migrant Labour: Roots of a Governance Crisis" (with Luo Xiaopeng). In: Phua Kai Hong *et al.* (eds.) *Population Dynamics and Infectious Diseases in Asia.* Singapore: World Scientific Publishers.

30. *Economic Herald* (2003). "Nurture Citizen Awareness, Promote a Transformation of Governance," *21 Century Economic Herald*, 15 May 2003, p. 1. http://www.nanfangdaily.com.cn/jj/20030515. Translation by David Kelly available at http://newton.uor.edu/Departments&Programs/AsianStudiesDept/kelley.pdf.

31. Kelly, D. (2006). "Public Intellectuals and Citizen Movements in China in the Hu-Wen Era." *Pacific Affairs* **79**(2), (forthcoming) pp. 183–204.

32. Zhang, N. (2001). "Shimin shenfen de jiaolü" [The anxieties of townsman status]. *Nanfang Zhoumo*, **29**, 19.

33. Hodge, B. and Louie, K. (1998). *The Politics of Chinese Language and Culture.* London: Routledge.

34. Ghosh, A. (1994). *In an Antique Land History in the Guise of a Traveler's Tale.* New York: Vintage Books.

35. Friedman, E. (2003). "Chinese Nationalism: Challenge to US interests." In: Stephen, J.F. and Michael, E.M. (eds.) *The People's Liberation Army and China in Transition.* China: Center for the Study of Chinese Military Affairs. Online at http://www.globalsecurity.org/military/library/report/2003/pla-china_transition_09_ch05.htm.

36. Wang, G. (2001). "Diaspora, a Much Abused Word" (Interview by Editor). *Asian Affairs*, vol. 14. Hong Kong: Winter, pp. 17–29. http://www.asian-affairs. com/Diasporas/wanggungwu.html.

37. Zhu, X. (2005). "Harmony stems from democracy," *China Daily*, 28 December 2005 http://www.chinadaily.com.cn/english/doc/2005-12/02/content_499872. htm.

38. Bulag, Uradyn, E. (1999). "Ethnic Resistance with Socialist Characteristics." In: Perry, E.J. and Mark, S. (eds.) (2003). *Chinese Society: Change, Conflict and Resistance.* New York: Routledge Curzon, pp. 178–197.

39. Chow, Kai-wing (1997). "Imagining Boundaries of Blood: Zhang Binglin and the Invention of the Han 'Race' in Modern China." In: Dikötter, Frank (ed.) (1997). *The Construction of Racial Identities in China and Japan: Historical and Contemporary Perspectives.* Honolulu: Hawaii University Press, pp. 34–52.

40. Harbsmeier, C. (1998). *Science and Civilisation in China.* Volume 7, Part 1: *Language and Logic.* New York: Cambridge University Press.

CHAPTER 16

International Relations, Ethnic Identity, and Minority Rights in the New Global Economy: The Chinese Diaspora in the United States

L. Ling-chi Wang

1. Ethnicity and International Relations

Relations between China and the US are continually being shaped by the emergence of China as a new global power and by the fluctuating, and indeed, frequently volatile relations between China and the US. For world peace and prosperity, there can be few more important relations in the world today than those between these two countries. How they manage their relations will have significant consequences on the world and on issues of ethnicity and identity for the Chinese minority in the US and the Chinese diaspora worldwide. As important as this is, it is also an area of research least understood by politicians and mass media alike and given little scholarly attention in universities and colleges and critical scrutiny in the media, especially in media-saturated society of the US. What little is in the US media is frequently fragmented and sensational at best and misinformation and disinformation at worst.

In the management of globalization today, ethnicity and identity form some of most complex and troublesome issues. The end of the Cold War saw not just the acceleration of globalization and the rise of new powers, like China and India, but also the emergence of world disorder, driven by unforeseen forces of racism, identity politics, xenophobia, ethnonationalism, religious fanaticism, and ethnic conflict and cleansing on both sides of the former Iron Curtain and by the repudiation of multilateralism and the undermining of international laws and institutions by the world's sole superpower, the US. The conference offers us an opportunity to probe more deeply into this murky and emotionally charged area, to understand the new and uncharted world order in which we find ourselves, and to begin to find ways to extricate ourselves from the current conundrum or worse, morass.

I shall begin this working paper with an overview on the relations between the rise of China and the Chinese diaspora about which quite a few exaggerated, and sometimes, dangerously provocative claims have been made in recent years, notably by some neoconservative intellectuals and politicians in both Japan and the US and in the US-dominated international mass media and book publishing. These claims invariably influence public opinions and shape policy formations with domestic racial and political consequences and international repercussions, as we shall see later. In the second and third sections of this paper, I shall look at two related areas, central to my analysis: the centrality of race and race relations in US–China relations and the persistence of race in the changing US–China relations. Here I discuss how the presence of the Chinese minority in the US shaped not just the race relations between the Chinese minority and the Euro–American majority but also the diplomatic relations between the rising imperialist power, the US, and the declining and deteriorating China in the second half of the 19th and the first half of the 20th centuries. The next section I shall discuss the discourse on the rise of China in partisan politics in the US and how the discourse affects the bipartisan consensus on China since President Nixon and on the rights and welfare of Chinese America in the context of highly partisan, acrimonious quadrennial presidential contests. I shall conclude this paper with suggestions on how to read and understand US–China relations against the backdrop of emerging China and an increasingly assertive Chinese America, determined not to be treated as a second-class citizen on the one hand nor as a colonial outpost for either Taiwan or Mainland China on the other hand.

1.1. *China's rise and the Chinese diaspora*

The rise of China as a new global power in the post-Cold War world is frequently and sweepingly attributed and connected to the Chinese diaspora in books and articles by scholars, columnists, and journalists since 1990s. Since Chinese in the US are routinely swept into this essentializing, homogeneous, amorphous group called variously *huaqiao* or *huaren* in Chinese and

"Overseas Chinese" or "Chinese diaspora," it is necessary to begin this paper with some clarifications and some background information on how the discourse of rising China influences the political debate on US–China relations and the well-being of Chinese America.

Among the most frequently raised questions on the connection between China's rise and the Chinese diaspora are: what is the nature and content of this association or connection? What is the connection, network or *guanxi* among the Chinese entrepreneurs in various countries, especially the Chinese entrepreneurs in Southeast Asian countries and Chinese–Americans in science and technology in the US? Is there a network or *guanxi* between China's emerging businesses and industries and the Chinese entrepreneurs in the diaspora? When a Chinese entrepreneur from another country invests in a project in China, is he driven by a desire to help modernize China, a sense of racial and cultural solidarity, political loyalty to his ancestral homeland, or is he simply motivated by the bottomline imperative, say, the productivity and profitability China has to offer him? And, most important and even alarming, what are the political and economic implications for these connections for the countries in which these Chinese diasporas are located?

These are legitimate, but also emotionally and politically charged questions. In fact, similar questions were raised in studies done on the Chinese in Southeast Asia and North America during the first two decades of the Cold War, the heyday of "red scare," and in North America and Australia toward the end of the 19th century, the era of "yellow peril." For the time being, they are also questions on which not much research has been done and no simple answers can be obtained, as can be seen from more nuanced studies collected in a recent book, *Chinese Entrepreneurship and Asian Business Networks*, edited by Thomas Menkhoff and Solvay Gerke (2002). The first order of business, therefore, is to clarify the terms and data used in these studies and to determine the validity of the central claims that China owes its rapid economic ascendancy in the past two decades to the Chinese diaspora and that the Chinese minority, as in the past, continues to pose serious political, economic, diplomatic, and security problems for countries in which they settled. The paper uses the Chinese diaspora in the US as a case study.

Historically, there always existed a tension between the Chinese diaspora and its ancestral homeland in China. This tension manifested itself in many forms. The point of contention can be personal, cultural, legal, economic, or political, depending on the time and place of occurrence and the magnitude and complexity of various tensions. For example, driven by necessity, Chinese merchants and peasants in coastal provinces, most notably, Fujian and Guangdong, sought business and employment opportunity abroad, even though the Chinese government at times banned such emigration and at other times, Chinese immigrants encountered racial discrimination and violence in host countries where they visited temporarily or settled permanently. Wherever they went, they had to manage their relations with homeland and with the host society, both of which could be either friendly or hostile, or, in many cases, ambivalent and ambiguous. In other words, life in the diaspora was quite precarious and perilous and Chinese abroad, both individually and collectively, had to undergo constant negotiations between the opposing pull and push and make difficult choices, depending of the ever fluid and dynamic circumstances. There were also conflicting desires between returning and abandoning China and between retaining Chinese culture, identity, and life-style and desinicising and assimilating into the mainstreams of the host societies. In short, Chinese in the diaspora learned to live and survive among these tensions, to navigate between these and other conflicting desires and interests, and negotiate for what was practical and achievable.

Before World War II, these mixed, and at times ambiguous patterns, sentiments, and desires provoked controversies, generated both positive and negative racial stereotypes, and aroused considerable suspicion and racial antagonism between China and the diaspora, and between the Chinese minority and the dominant societies. But, after World War II, especially with the advent of the Cold War, the pre-war tension abruptly and traumatically ended with a decisive break between the homeland and the diaspora, between the diaspora in the East and in the West, and between the two sides of the Chinese civil war, the Mainland and Taiwan in the next 40 years. China was contained, isolated, and ostracized behind the "Iron Curtain" or "Bamboo Curtain." Walls of separation were built and institutionalized, and suspicion and hostility ensued. The great division was reinforced and enforced by antagonistic politics and mutually exclusive ideologies on both sides. Yet, the prewar racial stereotypes, prejudice, and hostility persisted, making the experience of the Chinese diaspora during the Cold War difficult and oftentimes, painful. Cut off totally from their homeland and segregated, distrusted, and discriminated against by race and national origin in the countries in which they settled, the Chinese diaspora on both sides of the East–West divide had to initiate the long process of finding their ways to plant their roots permanently and to survive and thrive under diverse and frequently, hostile conditions with varying degree of success and failure.

It was not until President Richard Nixon's historic trip to China in 1972, during which he reversed the US policy of containment, that the Chinese diaspora in various countries slowly emerged from racial isolation and political repression and found breathing spaces and relaxed climates. The US–China détente quickly paved the way for the opening and international engagement of China, including, but not limited to China's entry into the United Nations, Deng Xiao-ping's historic economic reform in 1978, the normalization of US–China relations in 1979, the end of the Cold War in 1989, and China's entry into the World Trade Organization (WTO) in 2001. In many ways, Deng's own characterization of his reform initiative, the New Long March, can be described as China's own march into globalization, a march that has taken China from being a secluded, underdeveloped country during the Great Proletariat Cultural Revolution to being a major global power, whose GDP, according to CIA's National Intelligence Council, is expected to equal the UK this year, Germany in 2009, Japan in 2017, and the US in 2042. It is this phenomenal rise that brings me now to the first major question of my paper: the correlations between China's rise and the Chinese diaspora .

It is not clear exactly when and who started making the link between or attributing the rise of China as a global economic power and the direct foreign investments in China by the so-called "Overseas Chinese." Unfortunately, the term "Overseas Chinese," a politically and emotionally charged translation of *huaqiao*, has been loosely and erroneously used to include all persons of Chinese ancestry, regardless of their nativity and nationality, outside of China in the media and in scholarly books. It is a conflation or catch-all term for China's citizens sojourning abroad, Chinese in Hong Kong, Macau, and Tai-wan, which China affectionately calls *tongbao* (compatriots), and Chinese who have permanently settled in and integrated into some 140 countries around the world, or what China calls *huaren* or *huayi* (ethnic Chinese or foreign persons of Chinese ancestry). In Chinese, these various designations have distinctive legal and political connotations. But, conflation of these terms under "Over-seas Chinese" poses serious problems. As a racial or national signifier, it makes no distinction among Chinese *tongbao* in Taiwan, Hong Kong, and Macau,

Chinese born abroad, *huayi*, Chinese who have either become or awaiting to become naturalized citizens of another country, *huaren*, and Chinese holding passports of China and traveling abroad as tourists, business persons, or students, *huaqiao*. Most publications make no attempt to distinguish Chinese investors from Hong Kong and Taiwan, the *tongbao*, from the ethnic Chinese investors from Southeast Asian countries and the rest of the Chinese diaspora when they obviously have very different legal and political statuses. Likewise, most multinational corporations doing business in Asia also treat them as basically the same and lump them routinely together by a geographic designation, the Greater China or Greater China Economic Zone, a convenient regional designation for the corporate management of business in China, Taiwan, and Hong Kong.

Needless to say, such a conflation is wrong and has consequences that can be divisive at the very least and racist and explosive when misunderstood and abused. It is a disservice to the Chinese in the diaspora outside the Greater China designation, especially ethnic Chinese from Southeast Asia and North America.

Both Hong Kong and Taiwan are historically parts of China and China's treatment of compatriot investors from these two areas, the *tongbao*, are quite different. They are courted and given more favorable business terms than the Overseas Chinese who are citizens of various countries, therefore, subject to different investment laws and regulations in China. From the point of view of the magnitude and chronological order of Chinese foreign direct investment in China, there is also a sharp difference between the *tongbao* and the Chinese from the diaspora. Chinese investors from Hong Kong and Taiwan were the biggest and earliest. Not only were they among the first to respond positively to Deng's reform, their investment in China represented a lion's share of the cross-border investment. In the first two decades of the reform, investment by Chinese from Hong Kong and Taiwan constituted about 80 percent of total foreign investment in China. Hong Kong, in fact, led the way since the early 1980s in the cross-border investment in Guangdong, contributing on the one hand to the breakneck growth and industrialization of Guangdong province and on the other hand, to the rapid de-industrialization and restructuring of Hong Kong's economy from manufacturing to a financial service base by 1990s. This was followed by investors from Taiwan who went to both Guangdong and Fujian and later, went in a mad rush to the greater Shanghai area in 1990s. Quite differently, Overseas Chinese began investing cautiously and slowly in the 1980s and increased gradually in the 1990s, driven largely by the imperatives of globalization. In this respect, the massive *tongbao* investment in China was considerably 10–15 years ahead of their Western and Japanese counterparts, including those from the Chinese diaspora .

The Economist certainly played an early role in identifying the overseas links between China's rise and the Chinese investors from Hong Kong and Taiwan. As early as 1992 and 1993, it reported their heavy investment in China and the profound impact it was having on China. That these "compatriots" together injected a disproportional amount of capital, manufacturing and marketing know-how, and management skills in the 1980s and 1990s is beyond dispute. As *The Economist* correctly pointed out, the lion's share had come first and foremost from Hong Kong and Taiwan. In fact, China's early rise can almost be attributed to China's own investment and the investment of the *tongbao*. Together, they made up about 80% of foreign direct investment in the first two decades of the reform. It is simply wrong to indiscriminately attribute the rapid rise of China to Overseas Chinese investments.

Other questions deserving of more in-depth probe are: what prompted the Chinese investors from Hong Kong and Taiwan initially and later from Southeast Asia to take the lead in the foreign direct investment in China ahead of Western and Japanese investors? What finally convinced Western European, American, and Japanese corporations to massively invest in China beginning in late 1990s? Without going off the focus of this paper, let me briefly make the following points relevant to my subject matter. First, Deng Xiao-ping must be given credit for his vision, foresight, and determination in initiating the bold economic reform and opening of China to foreign investors in 1978. He made it politically possible for his protégé, Zhao Zi-yang, to proceed with bold reform programs in 1980s. Deng was also the one who decided to stay the course after the suppression of the Tiananmen protest in 1989 and the summary removal of Zhao. Against strong domestic opposition to his reform programs and American and European condemnation, he pressed forward the reform, which he succinctly called "gaige" and "kaifang," and created the favorable climate for foreign investment when Western and Japanese investors were told to stay away from China.

Second, it would be wrong to deny the fact that having a shared racial, linguistic, and cultural origin gives Chinese investors outside of China a distinct ease and advantage and sense of shared identity and interest in conducting business with their counterparts in China. Besides, there is a lingering legacy of Overseas Chinese desire or what William Overholt called, "sense of exhilaration," to invest in their home villages and counties, from building a school to a factory, a paved road to a power generator, dating back to the 19th century. Nevertheless, we should keep in mind that these investors are motivated by profit, not charity or good feelings.

Third, the Chinese government made a deliberate decision to attract and welcome Chinese investors from Hong Kong, Taiwan, and throughout the world to invest in China by providing favorable terms and conditions for them. Fourth, the economic sanction and arms trade ban imposed by the US, European Union (EU), and Japan in the wake of the Tiananmen suppression offered a rare and largely non-competitive opportunity for Chinese investors from Hong Kong and Taiwan to take full advantage of China's low production cost and huge market. It was the bottomline that was the decisive factor in their decision to pour money and move their production facilities into China. It was this rare window of opportunity they seized and exploited successfully ahead of the Western investors. Lastly, the accelerated process of globalization after the end of the Cold War and the anticipation of China's entry into the WTO made China in late 1990s not only the most compelling destination for foreign investors, but also the necessary place for manufacturing companies to stay competitive in the global market and to capture a share of China's huge market. This was the same driving force that prompted Taiwan investors to look and move westward by circumventing trade and investment restrictions imposed by their anti-Mainland, pro-independent government. It was risky investment, but it was risk worth taking.

It was against this background that William H. Overholt wrote his prophetic book, *The Rise of China: How Economic Reform Is Creating a New Superpower* in 1993, a book based on a series of articles he had published between 1990 and 1993 in various periodicals, anthologies, and US congressional hearings. In it, he correctly placed the successful connection between China rise and the Chinese investment in the context of Deng Xiaopeng's reform and policy of openness. He even contrasted the orderly economic reform undertaken by China with the chaotic *Sudongbo* (Russian/East European) approach or the shocked therapy advocated by Western scholars and politicians and blindly adopted by former Eastern Bloc regimes after 1989. He wrote (p. 348),

> China's economic success has had a more subtle effect on the morale, sense of identity, and direction of the overseas Chinese communities in Singapore, Malaysia, Indonesia, Thailand, and elsewhere. There is a widespread sense of exhilaration here, a feeling that after centuries of weakness China is once again on the path to greatness. This unwritten pleasure is seldom expressed to non-Chinese, but it exists, and it is having a palpable impact as the business leaders of the overseas Chinese communities visit their ancient home villages, invest there, build schools and temples and hospitals, provide advice to local authorities and, in the case of the more influential, to planners in Beijing.

Unlike many writers after him, Overholt's optimistic assessment of China's rise was not colored and driven by ideological, political or racial bias, but guided, instead, by facts and his background in strategic planning and future forecasting, as Ezra Vogel correctly pointed out. His analyses and projections were further enriched by his understanding of Chinese history and culture, the dynamics of change occurring in China under Deng's aggressive economic reform programs. Unfortunately, many subsequent writers and commentators chose to ignore history and culture and selectively exaggerate certain events, trends, figures, and target groups favorable or fitting to their desired analyses and political agendas. Two most noteworthy examples of such selective analyses and exaggerations are studies on the *guanxi* between the Overseas Chinese and China and China's rise and the insistence that China could not possibly make meaning progress without making democratic reform demanded by the June 4 Tiananmen protesters. Both analyses are based more on ideological and political bias than the realities on the ground. The former, as mentioned above, is based on the deliberate conflation of several types of Chinese investors for the purposes of assigning an exaggerated role to the Chinese Overseas and the latter, especially the frozen visual image of the lone man in front of a tank, has become both the beginning and the end of many a study on China since 1989.

No book is more sensational on the subject than the 1995 book, *Lords of the Rim: The Invisible Empire of the Overseas Chinese*, by freelance journalist Sterling Seagrave. According to Seagrave, the Overseas Chinese are made up of a highly interconnected and subversive transnational network of 55 million who control up to $2 trillion in assets (p. 285). "The existence of this invisible offshore empire with dynamic underground linkages and vast financial reserves may explain why the Earth wobbles on its axis (p. 285)," he concludes. Explaining the secret of Overseas Chinese power and success, he writes, "No group has been more effective in applying Sun Tsu's ideas to daily life, to commercial strategy and business operations, and to survival itself, than the Chinese Overseas... After repeatedly being persecuted in their adopted countries, they became particularly expert at invisibility (pp. 32–33)." They are so well schooled in Sun Zu's *Art of War*, that they already dominate the Pacific Rim and are poised to take over the world, ominously including the US (p. 277), as Sun long ago advised, "Be so subtle that you are invisible. Be so mysterious that you are intangible. Then you will control your rivals' fate (p. 31)." The key to their success is invisibility, mystification, and deception. As Seagrave concludes, "We can easily see how a grasp of Sun Zu helps Asian politicians and CEOs confuse and manipulate their Western counterparts in the international marketplace" (p. 31). The book ends with this prediction: "Of one thing we can be certain: the age of Sun Zu has returned. It is sunrise on the Rim. The year 2000 is the Chinese Year of the Dragon — an auspicious beginning for what may also be the Century of the Dragon (p. 308)." In fact, the book is full of sweeping generalizations and racist stereotypes about the success of Overseas Chinese that can only inspire fear and suspicion and provoke tension and hostility toward Chinese abroad by race.

Discriminate readers in the West may question Seagrave's language and conclusions. However, the main theme of China's rise and economic hegemony on the strength on Overseas Chinese business network did capture the imagination and arouse considerable interest of many a Western journalist and researcher. Several books and feature articles by prominent writers, economists, and social scientists appeared in rapid succession in late 1990s to reinforce the theme, though without the sensational and provocative language of Seagrave. Among these are the works of three prominent economists, Jim Rohwer, former executive editor of *The Economist*, Murray Weidenbaum, former chair of President Reagan's chairman of the Council of Economic Advisers, and John Naisbitt, a leading megatrends forecaster, who published, respectively, *Asia Rising: Why America Will Prosper as Asia's Economies Boom* in 1995, *The Bamboo Network: How Expatriate Chinese Entrepreneurs Are Creating a New Economic Superpower in Asia* and *Megatrends Asia: Eight Asian Megatrends That Are Reshaping Our World* by John Naisbitt in 1996. Such optimistic assessments of China's rise generated mixed responses. Many small businesses saw a rare opportunity to expand their businesses to China while multinational corporations realized the potentials for lowering the cost of production and expanding their global market into China. For others, China's rise meant a threat to their jobs and businesses. Still others, such as some in the US and Japan, China's rise meant the erosion of their hegemony in the region and across the world.

These and other books and newspaper columnists and editorials helped legitimize and advance the networking, racial and kinship *guanxi*, between China's rapid rise and the Overseas Chinese business network. Based largely on casual observations, journalistic reports, anecdotes, and at times, impressions and hearsays, rather than rigorous research, they cemented and raised the visibility of the *guanxi* connections between China's rise and the role played by the investment of Overseas Chinese. Disregarding history, the deliberate conflation of the Chinese from Hong Kong and Taiwan with the Chinese from countries in Southeast Asia and North America easily aroused racial resentment and tension for the Chinese minority living in these countries. The May 1998 anti-Chinese riot in Indonesia was an inevitable result of spread racial tension and hatred and the failure of taking aggressive measures to educate the public and address legitimate issues of inequality and injustice. The 1997 Asian monetary crisis only added fuel to the fire and inflamed the ill-informed public against Seagrave's "invisible empire of the Overseas Chinese."

As we shall see later, it did not take much to transform this theme of China's economic rise into the rise of "China Threat" in second-half of 1990s and early 21st century among ethno-nationalists in countries in Asia, the right-wing groups in Japan, and the political and ideological neoconservatives in the US. This transformation, as we shall also see later, changed significantly the political perceptions of China and the diplomatic relation between China and the US, and China's relations with its neighboring countries. It also directly affected the public images, treatment, and civil rights of the Chinese diaspora in various countries, including the Chinese in the US. It is to the latter we now turn.

2. Chinese in the US and US–China Relations

As strange and ironic as it may sound, no country is more alarmed by China's rise than the most powerful nation of the world today, the US (Since the US invasion and occupation of Iraq 2 years ago, the US sense of vulnerability can hardly be considered an extreme case of paranoia). Yet, no relation between two countries in the world is more important (both to each other and to the world at large) than that between China and the US. Since the demise of the Soviet Union in 1989, the rise of China has been the focus of heated political debate between the Democratic and Republican parties and among the leaders within each party. The debate centers around whether the rising China poses a threat to the global hegemony and the national security of the US, what the diplomatic policy toward China should be, and how to deal with the Chinese–American population which is presumed to have direct and close ties with China. The debate around these three major questions reflects not only serious inter-party and intra-party disagreements based on conflicting interests but also the inherent partisanship in the American political system. In this and the next sections, I shall argue that the perception and treatment of the Chinese in the US is a decisive factor in shaping US relations with China just like US–China relation exerts profound impact on the well beings of the Chinese in the US. In other words, race and race relations play a critical role in determining domestic racial policies toward the Chinese minority and foreign policies toward China and the treatment of Chinese–Americans lies at the intersection of domestic and foreign policies.

Let me begin by suggesting the uniqueness and centrality of race in determining domestic race relations and foreign policy formations in the US. The close connection between the treatment of the Chinese in the US and US–China relations is based on race and ethnicity and in spite of democracy and the rule of law in the US, race remains one of the most decisive factors in determining the treatment of the Chinese minority in the US and in the conduct of US policies toward China. Let me make four points that will help make clear the importance of this connection.

First, China has occupies a special place in the American imagination since the US was founded in 1776. Indeed, diplomatic historian Michael Hunt called the relationship "special" in his 1983 book, *The Making of Special Relationship*. What makes the relationship special is the role of special interests in the conduct of US policies toward China. To most American diplomatic historians, the history of US–China relations is dominated by two primary interests: trade with and mission to China. China trade, or more accurately, "The Old China Trade," played an indispensable role in the economic development in the first few decades of the founding of the republic. But, just as important was the self-image of the US: a Christian nation poised to play a leading role in elevating and civilizing the backward countries of the world, especially heathen and backward China. The Manifest Destiny motivated and drove the superior race to help uplift the degraded interior race through trade and mission.

In fact, the American desire to convert the heathen Chinese was a national obsession. Rev. William Speer, one of the early American missionary to China and later, the first Presbyterian missionary to Chinatown, San Francisco during the Gold Rush, wrote in 1870 a 700-page book, *The Oldest and the Newest Empire: China and the US*, which successfully captured the essence of these two interests. The book also put him in an untenable position of having to defend his missionary work among the Chinese immigrants in California against the mounting violent movement to exclude the Chinese from the US. That movement eventually succeeded in pushing the US Congress to enact a series of 15 Chinese exclusion laws, beginning in 1882, which ironically closed the door to Chinese immigration in a period when the US and its Western allies were doing their utmost, including the use of force and unequal treaties, to keep China's door open to Western trade and missionary penetration and exploitation.

I refer to this early account of US–China relations not only to suggest the contradictory themes of amity and enmity between "the oldest and the newest empires" but also to locate the two dominant sources of tension between the two countries, trade and mission, which continue to shape their relations to this day. In addition, I also want to introduce the main point of my paper: the role of race in the interaction between the two countries throughout history or how the Chinese diaspora in the US was shaped and reshaped by the ups and downs of relationship between these two countries. If we are to learn anything from history, including the management of globalization, then managing race relations is one lesson we can ill afford to miss or ignore.

Second, the significance of race was immediately felt when Chinese immigrants first arrived in the US. When gold was discovered in California in mid-19th century, "the world rushed in," to borrow J.S. Holliday's (1971) book title. Chinese immigrants joined hundreds of thousand that went to California, some to seek fortunes, others, employment opportunities, and still others, adventures. But, the experience of Chinese immigrants was quite different. The unique Chinese experience is succinctly captured by the titles of two books on the early Chinese immigrants in California: *The Unwelcome*

Immigrant: The American Image of the Chinese, 1785–1882 by Stuart C. Miller (1969), and *The Indispensable Enemy: Labor and the Anti-Chinese Movement in California*, by Alexander Saxton (1971). Chinese immigrant labor was considered indispensable, yet at the same time, as an unwelcome enemy. For pre-Gold Rush geographer/explorer, Aaron Palmer, and historians like Mary R. Coolidge, Ping Chiu, and Saxton, Chinese labor was indispensable for the economic development of the western states of the US and it is a challenge to explain why a nation founded on principles of freedom, democracy, equality and rule of law greeted Chinese immigrants with hatred and hostility. Miller blames the hostile reception on the largely negative, racist, and derogatory depictions of the Chinese by in books and articles written in the 18th and 19th centuries by American businessmen, missionaries, and travelers who had gone to China. Such negative depictions, while necessary to arouse the urgency of saving millions of souls in China and thus, increase the financial support for Christian missions, deeply inscribed racist images and stereotypes into the American public consciousness. In other words, sending missionaries to convert heathen Chinese on the other side of the Pacific was good for the American soul and conscience, but allowing an unassimilable, inferior race to reach American shores was unthinkable and intolerable. To the anti-Chinese forces, the only policy choice was the immediate enactment of laws to exclude and if possible, expel them. But for missionaries like Rev. William Speer, Chinese immigrants were god-sent: he could now convert them to Christianity in the US and send them back to do the work of God in China.

Third, caught between those who wanted their labor and souls and the angry majority that demanded their exclusion and expulsion, the Chinese diaspora in the US became the unsuspecting and unwilling victims of divisive political debates at all levels of the US government and the unending US–China diplomatic wrangles over the treatment of the Chinese in the US. For men like the builders of the western frontier, such as the founders of the Union Pacific Railroad Co. and California's agribusiness, diplomats like William Seward and Anson Burlingame, and missionaries to San Francisco's Chinatown, like Revs. William Speer, Otis Gibson, and Augustus Loomis, and southern plantation owners in the post-Civil War era, Chinese immigrants were both critical and necessary. The Burlingame Treaty of 1868, dubbed "a cheap labor treaty," in fact, helped obligate China to lift the ban on Chinese going to the US, thus enabling the railroad builders and southern plantations to massively recruit Chinese to the US. However, the Democrats were able to repeatedly use popular anti-Chinese sentiment to defeat Republicans in several western states, rehabilitate the party after the Civil War, successfully pushed several anti-Chinese legislations in western states and in the US Congress throughout 1870s, and force the US government to renegotiate the Burlingame Treaty, thus, paving the way for passage of the first Chinese exclusion law in 1882. "Chinese must go!" was the dominant political slogan and the objective was to stop "the yellow hordes," later "yellow peril," from overrunning the superior white race (to put the exclusionist demand in perspective, there were 105,000 Chinese out of a US total of 50.2 million in 1880). The law effectively terminated Chinese immigration based solely on race, and denied the Chinese already in the US the right of naturalization on the same basis, rendering them perpetual aliens and in the wake of the US Supreme Court decision in *Fong Yu Ting versus the US* in 1893, denying them the rights guaranteed by the Bill of Rights in the US Constitution. By democratic legislative means, race trumped American commitment to principles of democracy, equality, and the rule of law. Chinese became the first race to be singled out for exclusion and Chinese immigrants in the US became perpetual aliens, disenfranchised in a democratic country.

The last point I wish to make is how during first two decades of the Cold War, the McCarthy era, race took on added meanings for the Chinese in the US. As we know, China became Enemy No. 1 of the US and the policy of the US toward the newly founded People's Republic of China was the containment of China by political, economic, and military means. The domestic consequence of this policy was: every Chinese–American became a suspected internal enemy and a national security risk. A new meaning was piled on top of the old problem of racism. The "yellow peril" of the past was reinforced by a "red scare." Being Chinese–American became synonymous with treason and espionage. Even though there was no evidence of Chinese espionage and subversion, Chinese–Americans, by virtue of their racial and national origin, became a threat to the national security of the US and in the process, the target of suspicion and political repression. I shall elaborate this point in the next section.

The above four points clearly demonstrate the centrality of race and ethnicity in defining the treatment of the Chinese in the US and in formulating and conducting US diplomatic policies toward China. Just as important is how domestic racial policy toward the Chinese in the US is connected directly with the formulation of foreign policies toward China, a point driven home by Robert McClellan's 1971 book, *The Heathen Chinee: A Study of American Attitudes Toward China*, 1890–1905. The two constantly interact with and dynamically influence each other. It is to this last point we now turn.

3. The Persistence of Race in Changing US–China Relations

If the treatment of Chinese–Americans depends on the fluctuating relations between China and the US, improvement in their relations should bring predictable relief to the Chinese in the US. It did. But the improvement of treatment did not in any way result in the elimination of racism, much less undermine the centrality of race in structuring and representing the social realities of the US. Herein lies the dynamic and persistent character of race in American democracy. Let me elaborate.

The first and one of the most significant easing of racial prejudice and discriminatory treatment occurred during World War II when China became an ally of the US in the war against Japanese imperialism and militarism. Led by Henry Luce, the publisher of several influential national magazines, the mass media gave sustained and favorable coverage on the heroic Chinese resisting the Japanese aggressor and young Chinese–Americans enthusiastically joining the US armed forces in the war. Public images of and attitudes toward Chinese changed drastically from largely negative to positive depictions. The US unilaterally renounced the unequal treaties between China and the US, provided economic and military aid to the Nationalist regime in its fight against the Japanese occupation of China's coastal provinces, and rewarded President Chiang Kai-shek the status of being one of the Big Four. As a friendly gesture to China and a strategy to counter Japan's anti-US propaganda in China, President Franklin Roosevelt persuaded the US Congress to repeal the 15 Chinese exclusion laws in 1943 to help boost Chinese military morale. The repeal law further granted Chinese immigrants in the US the right of naturalization and after heated congressional debates, set an annual quota of 105 for Chinese admissible into the US as immigrants for the first time since the 1882 Chinese exclusion law. Even though Roosevelt hailed the historic repeal, there was no celebration in Chinatowns across the US.

For Chinese–Americans, these wartime gestures were largely symbolic: they did little to grant them full and equal status as citizens of the US. The 105 quota, in fact, ensured the continuation of Chinese exclusion until 1965. As Chinese–Americans soon discovered, these gestures were superficial and temporary at best. Returning Chinese–American veterans and their wives found racial discrimination in the job market had remained intact and restrictive housing covenant severely denied them equal and fair housing. The spectacular collapse of the US-backed corrupt regime of Chiang Kai-shek in the Chinese Civil War immediately after the end of World War II abruptly ended the brief period of good will and friendship toward China during the war. The US military intervention in the Taiwan Strait to protect Chiang and his followers angered the victorious Chinese Communist Party in the Mainland. The eruption of war on the Korean Peninsula, 1950–1953, soon turned China into Enemy No. 1 of the US, and Chinese–Americans, no longer just a despised and discriminated against race, became an internal enemy, a threat to the national security of the US.

Partisan political power struggle also played a critical role in shaping American attitudes toward China and Chinese–Americans. As Republicans held the Truman administration responsible for "the loss of China" in a protracted acrimonious national debate and McCarthyism stepped up the campaign against both internal subversion and ideological and political dissidents at home, racial prejudice and suspicion against Chinese–Americans mounted and internal national security racialized. Anti-communism became synonymous with anti-sinicism. Containment of China by political, economic, and military means quickly became the bipartisan policy of the US, the policy that justified direct US military interventions from Korea in north Asia to Vietnam in Southeast Asia.

Until his death in 1972, J. Edgar Hoover, the FBI director, routinely declared all Chinese–Americans to be potential spies for China when he made annual requests for special appropriations at the US Congress to keep all Chinese–Americans under surveillance. National security was thus ethnicized and being Chinese in the US became synonymous with espionage and treason.

Throughout the first two decades of the Cold War, the image of Chinese–Americans as perpetual foreigners was revived and took on added meanings: by virtue of their race, they were presumed to be a national security risk. Until his death in 1972, J. Edgar Hoover, director of the FBI, routinely appeared

before the Appropriations Committee of the US Congress to declare Chinese–
Americans as the potential enemy within and he used the declaration to seek
special appropriation to keep Chinese–Americans under surveillance. I consider Hoover the inventor of the racial profiling of Chinese–Americans as an
internal security threat. His contention was reinforced by American consul-
general in Hong Kong, Everett Drumwright, who issued a sensational report
in which he alleged that China was infiltrating the US with illegal immigrants
and that the vast majority of Chinese in the US were illegal immigrants. Law
enforcement agencies, such as, the FBI, CIA, Immigration and Naturalisation
Service (INS), Federal Grand Juries, Internal Revenue Service (IRS), and the
Office of the Foreign Assets Control in the US Treasury Department were
used to intimidate, harassed and prosecute individuals and organizations suspected of being sympathetic to China. In some extreme cases, some were
driven to suicide, others denaturalized, and still others, deported or threatened with deportation with a status of "suspension of deportation," a legal
limbo that denied them freedom to travel abroad and which marked them
for surveillance at home. Sending monthly remittance home to support their
parents, wives, and children — a legacy of exclusion laws — became a federal
crime. When their loved ones pleaded them to send the remittance, such pleas
were branded as "communist extortions" by both the US government and the
mass media.

To counter such massive political repression, traditional Chinese–
American organizations, the *huiguan* (district associations) and *gongsuo* (family
associations), were mobilized with the help of Taiwan's Nationalist agents to
take part not just in high-profile anti-communist and anti-China demonstrations and propaganda, but also in identifying and suppressing any Chinese–
American known to be critical or disloyal to the Nationalist regime in Taiwan.
In effect, the Nationalist regime succeeded in extending extraterritorial rule and
repressive long arms into Chinese America by taking advantage of the hostile
US relationship with China, to tighten its grip and transform it into a colony
within the US and to use it to undertake anti-China lobbying in Washington,
DC throughout the Cold War. The Nationalist repression would not have been
as effective had it not been for the consent of the US law enforcement agencies.
Their shared interests in stamping out communist infiltration and subversion,
however, resulted in the suppression of the Chinese–American constitutional
rights of free speech and association.

Fear, intimidation and harassment hovered over and permeated the community as Chinese–Americans were forced to seek refuge in silence and anonymity, rather than in asserting their legitimate rights as equal and free citizens of the US.

Over the next 20 years, Chinese–American rights and freedom were effectively suspended even though no Chinese–Americans were convicted of espionage or treason. The Nationalist agents were given a free reign over Chinese America. The first relief from this period of great fear and repression arrived in 1972 when President Richard Nixon abandoned the policy of containment of China and initiated what we now know as a new bipartisan consensus policy of strategic cooperation with China in a global struggle against the USSR for the remaining years of the Cold War. Even though China was in the middle of an unprecedented and brutal Cultural Revolution and the Vietnam war was still raging, American media, intellectuals, and political leaders welcomed China as a new partner of convenience and chose, instead, to see China, once again, as a huge market for American goods and services and an opportunity to revive American missionary zeal, this time, bringing a secular gospel of freedom, democracy, and American cultural values to the billion Chinese. A steady stream of curious journalists, scholars, business leaders, and politicians toured the new China and published glowing reports and books about their encounters in what was frequently and romantically portrayed as a socialist paradise or an egalitarian utopia. The new romance with China conveniently overlooked some of the worst abuses and atrocities perpetrated by the young Red Guards and their older patrons in the Chinese Communist Party.

After the reform faction of the Chinese Communist Party finally put the destructive Cultural Revolution to rest, restored law and order throughout China, and purged the extreme leftists from power, Deng Xiao-ping reemerged from internal exile as the paramount leader. Deng wasted no time in launching China's new Long March to modernization. His reform and openess policies rapidly transformed China into an outward and forward looking market economy and put China on the road to a sustained accelerated economic growth. In January 1979, he led a delegation to President Jimmy Carter's White House to inaugurate the normalization of relation between the two countries. A Republican president initiated the US–China détente in 1972 and now, a Democratic president was embracing China as a partner in the search for peace, stability, and prosperity. The White House ceremony was a symbol of bipartisanship consensus over US relation with China: the US was ready to engage China in a bilateral relation that would be beneficial to both countries and to the rest of the world. Deng's bold domestic initiatives won him praises and admiration throughout his tour of the US. In fact, twice he was named *Time* magazine's "Man of the Year," a clear indication of how China was seen by the American public and political class. In spite of occasional bumps on the road, especially during election times, the bipartisan consensus persisted until the administration of President George W. Bush, as we shall see.

For Chinese–Americans, the new friendly US–China relation was a liberating and invigorating experience. For the first time since 1949, they were allowed to reestablish contact with their parents, wives, children and relatives severed since 1949, visit their ancestral villages, and best of all, talk about their views on China openly, and purchase imported food and products from China with the fear of violating US laws. Under the heavy influence of the African–American civil rights movement, Chinese–Americans began to understand and appreciate the meaning of being free and equal as Chinese–Americans and to demand and exercise their civil and political rights as citizens of the US. In spite of deeply entrenched public and institutional racism, Chinese–Americans made a significant and steady inroad into the mainstream American society. For the first time in the US history, Chinese–Americans took pride in their racial and cultural identity without a feeling of inferiority complex and asserted their rights without inhibition or apology. The normalization of US–China relations further paved the way for Chinese–Americans to gradually liberate themselves from the extraterritorial domination and repressive long arms of the Nationalist regime in Taiwan. Taiwan, as noted earlier, had taken advantage of the hostile relationship between the US and China by tightening its grip on Chinese America and transforming it into an anti-China lobbying force in Washington, DC throughout the Cold War.

4. Rise of China: Its Impact on the Bipartisan Consensus and Chinese America

When the Cold War finally ended in 1989 with the rapid collapse of the Soviet Union and its Eastern European satellite countries, the US, just like at the end of World War II, emerged as the unchallenged superpower militarily, economically, and politically. President George Bush pronounced the dawn of a New World Order. Many pundits rushed to predict the inevitable and imminent demise of the communist Chinese state. Francis Fukuyama, in his widely read book, *The End of History*, declared that the ideological battle between totalitarianism and liberal democracy was over and the future of the world belonged to free-market capitalism. In the ensuing years, however, the world did not quite follow the confident script laid out by exuberant politicians and commentators in the early 1990s. Ethnonationalism rose and ethnic conflict broke out everywhere. The economy of "democratic" Russia turned sour, poor, and chaotic while China, defying widespread Western dire predictions, has been enjoying more than two decades of uninterrupted and enviable rapid economic growth. In the process, it successfully lifted hundreds of million of its poverty-stricken people out of abject poverty, unprecedented in human history. The stark contrast between the two former communist giants attracted inevitable attention. Before long, the success of the Chinese model turned into a discourse on the rise of China and the decline of Russia. With it also surfaced a return of the China threat thesis of bygone years.

The catalyst for the return appears to be the imminent return of Hong Kong, the "Pearl of the Orient" and the symbol of free-wheeling capitalism, to "communist" China in 1997. Will the "Chinese communists" crush the free people of Hong Kong just like it put down the Tiananmen protesters? Suddenly, the political and intellectual discourse on the rise of China by the mid-1990s turned into the threat of China to US interests in Hong Kong, Asia, and indeed, to the US itself. Leading the charge were conservative national magazines, such as the *Weekly Standard*, *American Spectator*, *National Review*, and the *New Republic*, and newspaper, like the *Washington Times*. Behind these publications was a neoconservative group, Project for a New American Century, made up of prominent Republican conservative intellectuals and politicians who believed strongly that the US must take advantage of its military superiority by adopting a more expansive vision of the world, meaning, taking unilateral steps toward empire, more specifically, implanting "freedom and democracy" on foreign soil and taking more belligerent and preemptive stands toward the former Yogoslavia, Iraq, Libya, Iran, North Korea, and the rising China. Their view was also reflected in non-fictional study in Richard Bernstein and Ross Munro's *The Coming Conflict with China* and fictional work in Humphrey Hawkesley and Simon Holberton's *Dragon Strike: The*

Millennium War. These perspectives and ideas quickly found their way into policy debates between the ruling and opposition parties.

Unfortunately for Chinese–Americans, the bipartisan consensus over the US policy toward China began to disintegrate when both the Democratic and Republican parties discovered how American public opinion toward China can be conveniently and productively manipulated and exploited for partisan political gains without necessarily inflicting irreparable damage to US–China relations around presidential election years. The *modus operandi* works this way: one party orchestrates attacks on the opponent's perceived weakness toward a demonized China and makes extravagant promises to voters on what it will do upon getting elected. Once elected, the winner would try to repair whatever diplomatic damages done to the US–China relations by returning to the bipartisan consensus. The assumption is that all will be or can be forgiven and forgotten by the voters whose memories are consistently short-term.

The willingness of both parties to use China as a political bogeyman or scapegoat for a wide range of problems in the struggle for political control of the White House and the US Congress can be traced to the development of several global trends in the past 20 years, the most important of which is the rise of China as a global economic and political power. That makes China an easy target. Because of the close connection between China and Chinese–Americans as perpetual foreigners and national security risk, both parties find demonizing China and inciting public fear and hysteria to be one sure way of winning popularity and votes at the expense of their opponent. What neither party knows or cares is how their exploitation and scapegoating invariably turns Chinese–Americans into collateral casualties. Let me briefly summarize how this development came about.

The success of Deng Xiao-ping's economic reform and opening of China since 1978, as pointed out earlier, is one major factor in the rise of China. If China's rise threatens American global domination or national security, the logical political question, like the earlier debate on "the loss of China," then, who is responsible for its rise? Over the past two decades, several simplistic answers have surfaced: the secretive and subversive Overseas Chinese with their *guanxi* among themselves and with China; the failure of the executive branch to take decisive actions against "the butchers of Beijing" and to aggressively push for democracy in China; the unfair competition and systematic appropriation of

American intellectual property; and the stealing of American military secrets. The beauty of these simplistic, politically inspired answers is that none of them requires China to take specific actions to prompt a torrent of groundless allegations and neither do they requires factual substantiation to prove their validity. In fact, in the context of partisan power struggles and winning elections, the simpler the answers the better because American voters demand instant and simplistic answers, especially answers that can be reduced to sound bites and used to help win elections. Complex analyses and nuanced answers turn off voters. Professional campaign strategists, poll takers, P.R. handlers, and spin masters understand the importance of simplicity in a life-and-death political struggle or the need to dumb down in order to reach the gullible public at the lowest common denominator. When it comes to dealing with China and the Chinese question in the US, politicians of both parties understand what it takes to discredit the opposition in order to win. In fact, it is a tradition that dates back to the very first anti-Chinese campaign in 1852 when California Gov. John Bigler ran for reelection. Democrats deployed the same strategy in 1870s and early 1880s by blaming Chinese immigrants for high unemployment rates and economic recession. In 1950s, Republicans accused the Democrats for the "the loss of China" when China was never American's to lose. Thus, the rise of China is a fact that can be established by analysis based on evidence, but to transform that fact into political allegation, or more accurately, fiction or construction, such as, the threat of China to either American global economic interests or national security, requires no proof in the context of American quadrennial presidential contest.

When Bill Clinton was the Democratic presidential candidate, he sharply criticized President George Bush's policy toward China. He bluntly accused the Republican president for "cuddling to the butchers of Beijing," referring specifically to the violent suppression of the Tiananmen protest in 1989. After Clinton won the election, it was his turn to be attacked by the Republicans who had control of the US Congress. In the 1996 presidential campaign, Republicans accused President Bill Clinton and his party for accepting illegally laundered political contributions from China in return for more friendly relations with China, including more lenient policies for exporting highly sensitive technologies capable of military applications and compromising the national security of the US. According to the Republicans, Clinton and his fellow Democrats used several Chinese–Americans, including John Huang, Charlie

Yah-lin Trie, Johnny Chung, and several others to launder money for the reelection of Clinton. Before long, the highly corrupt system of campaign contribution was racialized and both China and Chinese–Americans were accused of trying to corrupt American democracy. As a result, the Republicans came close to defeating Clinton by tapping into the reservoir of historic racism and by demonizing both China and Chinese–Americans through politically charged Congressional investigations and strategic leaks of sensational misinformation to the media.

During his second term, the Republican controlled Congress continued its barrage of attacks on Clinton on two fronts: his extramarital affairs with several women and his policy toward China. The former resulted in a failed impeachment and the latter in the weakening of the bipartisan consensus and a disaster for Chinese–American civil rights. During the second term, the Republicans concentrated their attacks on Clinton's security management of highly secretive national weapon laboratories, especially in the Los Alamos National Laboratory where the US carried out its advanced research and development of nuclear weapons. They accused the Clinton administration of security laxity, thus, compromising American national security. Specifically, with great political fanfare, the Republicans established in 1998 a special committee headed by Congressman Christopher Cox to investigate the Clinton administration's laxity in both the export control of militarily sensitive technologies and the security management of the labs. The Cox Committee completed the work in December 1998 in a three-volume report, *The Cox Report*, in which it made several serious allegations against Clinton. Of particular interest to this paper are three: (1) that China has made significant advances in its nuclear arsenals by stealing the most advanced designs of American nuclear weapons; (2) that China has been able to do so because of the laxity in the security of America's most advanced weapon laboratories, especially, the Los Alamos National Laboratory (LANL); and (3) That China has been successful in using Chinese–American scientists working in these laboratories to steal these secrets. It further suggested that Chinese–Americans with relatives in China and Chinese owned businesses with China connections were all potential spies, recalling the sweeping allegations of the late J. Edgar Hoover.

Through leaks to the national media, by early 1999, these sensational findings of the Cox Committee were flooding the national media and more than a dozen Republican-controlled Congressional committees were determined to uncover the Democratic failures and betrayal of national interests on the one hand and to hunt for the Chinese–American scientists responsible for selling out the US on the other hand. Overnight, Chinese–American scientists and engineers across the nation became suspects in the nuclear theft. Democrats were forced to defend themselves against the Republican and media assaults as they worried about the political fall-outs in the looming 2000 presidential contest. Fear and collective guilt descended upon the entire Chinese–American community because what allegedly had been stolen, as the public came to know later, was "the crown jewel of American nuclear arsenals" that had the potential of causing the death of hundreds of millions of people.

It was against the background that Chinese–American scientist, Dr. Wen Ho Lee at the LANL, was identified in the national media as the No. 1 suspect in March 1999. In the next 9 months, the media was flooded with sensational stories about him based mostly on leaks from various sources within the government while Lee, his relatives, friends, and colleagues throughout the US were subjected to intense investigation by hundreds of government investigators. After 9 months of investigation and media barrage, during which Lee was effectively lynched in the court of public opinion, the FBI and federal prosecutors found not a shred of evidence against him. Nevertheless, the Clinton administration decided to indict him in December 1999 on grounds that he had mishandled voluminous classified information in this secured lab in the LANL. He was promptly arrested and placed in solitary confinement without a trial and conviction for 9 months. Throughout these 9 months, the public continued to be told of the crimes he had committed and Republicans stepped up their attacks on Clinton and his Vice President Al Gore who was the anointed Democratic presidential candidate. To make the long story short, in September 2000, 2 months before the presidential contest between Gore and George W. Bush, the presiding judge James Parker freed Lee with a profound apology to him from the bench and denounced government officials at "the highest level" for misleading him in the prosecution and mistreatment of Lee. To date, there was no evidence produced by the government that Lee was a spy for China.

The incarceration and prosecution of Dr. Wen Ho Lee by the Clinton administration prevented Republicans from raising issues of lab security and the alleged theft of US nuclear secrets by China through Chinese–Americans in the 2000 presidential campaign. In fact, throughout the presidential campaign, George Bush did not raise these two issues against Democrat Gore because the prosecution and detention of Lee by the Clinton administration turned a political liability into an asset: the administration can claim effective management of lab security and law enforcement because the central figure was already in solitary confinement awaiting trial. Besides, commenting on a pending criminal prosecution is widely considered prejudicial and therefore inappropriate. Instead, Bush decided to criticize Clinton's "strategic partnership and cooperation" with China and promote his alternative policy of "strategic competition" with China. His position represented a significant departure from the bipartisan consensus in place since President Nixon. It was also a position developed by the Project for a New American Century, whose objective was to take advantage of the power of the US and to change its relations with the world, including taking a confrontational approach toward China that would abort China's rise as a global power, capable of challenging the US global domination. Prominent figures in the group were Dick Cheney, Richard Perle, Donald Rumsfeld, Paul Wolfowitz, and Richard Pipes, all of whom played important roles in influencing Bush's policy toward China, that is, before September 11, 2001. What saved China from being one of his targets for confrontation was the need to enlist the support of China in his war on terror. In fact, China quickly assured Bush of its support of his war on terror and its willingness to pressure North Korea into disarming its nuclear weapons. In the process, China even managed to secure some significant concessions from Bush over Taiwan's movement toward independence.

It was in this sense we can say that President Bush reneged on his campaign promise on China and returned to the bipartisan consensus as all presidents did since President Nixon, Democrat or Republican alike. For the same reason, Chinese–Americans averted a potential disaster on their rights and welfare in the US.

Finally, will Bush continue the engagement and partnership with China in his second term? It is too early to tell. However, there are signs and moves made at home and abroad since the beginning of his second term that seem to suggest that his administration is returning to the pre-September 11 position. For example, the team President Bush has been assembling suggests that the neoconservatives are moving from the second and third level to top positions in his cabinet, such as Rice, Negroponte, Bolton, Wolfowitz, and Goss. On the foreign policy front, the statements made by Secretary Rice during her recent trips to Europe and Asia reflect a hard-line approach to China, from arms ban to Taiwan's defence, from trade to the six-party approach to North Korea. At home, FBI appears to be singling out Chinese and Chinese–Americans for high-profile investigations for espionage and subversion, most of which seem flimsy and groundless, especially the highly publicized Boston "dirty bomb" case which linked several Chinese "illegal immigrants" to terrorism a day before President Bush's inauguration. The Boston case turned out to be a hoax and the FBI and Homeland Security had to quietly and embarrassingly admit their error in judgment. It is still too early to make a call on whether these developments in the last three months signal a shift in Bush's policy toward China and Chinese America. They certainly deserve to be monitored closely.

5. Conclusions

In this paper, I tried to use the experience of the Chinese diaspora in the US to examine the complicated and dynamic relations between the Chinese minority and the American society and how these relations affect US–China relations. Throughout the paper, I maintain the centrality and persistence of race in shaping their experience, citizenship, and rights on the one hand and in influencing the changing US–China relations throughout history on the other hand. Race, domestic economic problems, and partisan power struggles in the US, rather than what China actually did or did not do, are the key driving forces in the fluctuating diplomatic relations between China and the US. In saying this, I am not suggesting that China has not precipitated conflicts with the US through its policies and actions. It did and on numerous occasions. What I am suggesting is that many diplomatic crises in the relations between the two countries were created from sources within the US and since the normalization of US–China relations in 1979, several crises were the result of partisan power struggles in election times, having no direct bearing on what China did. These were crises originating in the unique political system of the US. The most glaring recent examples are the fabrication of the Cox Report accusing the Clinton administration for allowing China to steal American nuclear secrets, the prosecution and persecution of Chinese–American scientist, Dr. Wen Ho Lee, solely on the basis of his race without a shred of evidence, and the invention of the China threat thesis by the neoconservative faction within the Republican party, which has as much validity as the claims of weapons of mass destruction before the invasion of Iraq.

I also tried to show that Chinese entrepreneurs and investors outside of China did play a significant part in the economic rise of China after Deng Xiao-ping inaugurated his policies of reform and openness in 1978, but their role ought not to be exaggerated and above all, erroneously conflated with the earlier and more significant contributions of Chinese from Hong Kong and Taiwan. The distinction between the Chinese from Hong Kong and Taiwan and the Chinese from the diaspora is critical. It is simply wrong to suggest that Chinese overseas, rather than Chinese from Hong Kong and Taiwan, were instrumental in the rapid ascendancy of China in 1980s and 1990s and that their investments in China were driven primarily by racial solidarity and loyalty, rather than the conjunction of globalization, attraction of high profitability and productivity in China, and a rare historic window of opportunity occasioned by the economic sanction imposed by the US, Japan, and the EU in the wake of the Tiananmen incident in 1989. Failure to make these distinctions can cause racial tension and even violence for the Chinese minority in various countries, especially those in Southeast Asia.

Finally, I hope this study helps call attention to the importance of race in the study of Chinese diaspora in various countries throughout the world and of the intersection between domestic race relations and diplomatic relations in any given country. Globalization has brought about unprecedented international capital and labor migration and also opportunities and miseries to untold numbers of people and countries. It has also created interracial and intraracial tensions in virtually every country throughout the globe and frequent international conflicts. These problems require sober and critical examination. Only through such examinations will we know how to effectively address the problems.

Authors' Biographies

Asher, Mukul G.
is currently a Professor at the Lee Kuan Yew School of Public Policy. Specializing in public sector economics and social security issues in Asia, he has published extensively in international journals, and has authored and edited several books. He has been a consultant to the World Bank, International Monetary Fund, World Health Organization, Asian Development Bank, Organization for Economic Cooperation and Development, and other institutions. He has interacted with policymakers as a resource person in several Asian countries such as India, Indonesia, Vietnam, People's Republic of China, and Sri Lanka. He is on the Editorial Board of International Social Security Review, a leading journal in the field. He teaches applied public sector economics and economic reasoning for public policy.

Bajpai, Kanti Prasad
is the Headmaster of the Doon School, Dehra Dun, India. He is a specialist on India's national security and foreign policy. His most recent books are *Roots of Terrorism* (2002) and *International Relations in India* (2 volumes, 2005).

Basu, Kaushik
is the C. Marks Professor of International Studies and Professor of Economics, and the Director of the Program on Comparative Economic Development, Department of Economics, Cornell University. His published works include *Collected Theoretical Papers in Economics, Volume 1: Development, Markets and Institutions, and Volume 2: Rationality, Games and Strategic Behavior,* Oxford University Press, 2005.

Goswami, Omkar   is the Chairman of CERG Advisory, which provides corporate consulting and economic advisory services within and outside India. With a doctorate from Oxford, Goswami taught for 18 years in India and abroad. From 1998 to March 2004, he was the Chief Economist of the Confederation of Indian Industry, India's apex industry organization. He has served in several government committees, and has been a regular consultant to the World Bank, IMF, ADB and OECD. He is an independent director of companies such as Infosys Technologies, Dr. Reddy's Laboratories, Infrastructure Development Finance Company and Crompton Greaves. Apart from his regular columns, Goswami has authored three books and over 75 research papers.

Jia Qingguo   is a Professor and Associate Dean of the School of International Studies of Peking University. He received his PhD from Cornell University in 1988. He is a member of the Academic Degree Review Board of the State Council of China, Vice President of the China Association for Asia-Pacific Studies, and a board member of the China Association of American Studies and the National Taiwan Studies Association. He is also a member of the editorial board of several international academic journals. He has published extensively on US–China relations, relations between the Chinese mainland and Taiwan, Chinese foreign policy and Chinese politics.

MacFarquhar, Roderick   is the Leroy B. Williams Professor of History and Political Science, Harvard University, and the once and current Director of the John King Fairbank Center for East Asian Research. His publications include *The Hundred Flowers Campaign and the Chinese Intellectuals, The Sino-Soviet Dispute, China under Mao; Sino-American Relations, 1949–1971; The Secret Speeches of Chairman Mao;* the final two volumes of the *Cambridge History of China* (edited with the late John Fairbank); *The Politics of* China: *The Eras of*

Mao and Deng (2nd Edition) and a trilogy, *The Origins of the Cultural Revolution*. The founding editor of *The China Quarterly*, he has been a fellow at Columbia University, the Woodrow Wilson International Center for Scholars, and the Royal Institute for International Affairs. In previous personae, he has been a journalist, a TV commentator, and a Member of Parliament. His jointly authored book on the Cultural Revolution will be published by Harvard University Press (2006).

Mahbubani, Kishore

is the Dean of the Lee Kuan Yew School of Public Policy, National University of Singapore. Prof. Mahbubani was Permanent Secretary at the Foreign Ministry of Singapore from 1993 to 1998. He also served two stints as Singapore Ambassador to the UN, and was President of the UN Security Council in January 2001 and May 2002. He was conferred The Public Administration Medal (Gold) by the Singapore Government in 1998 and the Foreign Policy Association Medal in New York in June 2004. He is the author of *Can Asians Think?* and *Beyond the Age of Innocence: Rebuilding Trust between America and the World*. Prof. Mahbubani has been named one of the Top 100 Public Intellectuals by Foreign Policy and Prospect magazines.

Mehta, Pratap Bhanu

is the President of the Center for Policy Research, Delhi. He is also Member Convenor of the Knowledge Commission appointed by the Prime Minister of India. He has previously taught at Harvard and at the Jawaharlal Nehru University, New Delhi. He has published widely in political philosophy, law, intellectual history and politics in India. His most recent books are *The Burden of Democracy* and an edited volume, *India's Public Institutions*. He has also engaged prolifically with public debates in major national and international publications including *The Financial Times*, *Indian Express* and *Telegraph*. He obtained his BA from Oxford and has a PhD in Politics from Princeton.

Mohan, C. Raja	is a Professor of South Asian Studies at the Jawaharlal Nehru University and the Strategic Affairs Editor of *The Hindu*, a leading English language daily published from New Delhi, Chennai and eight other cities in India. Earlier he was the Washington Correspondent of the paper. Prior to that he was a Senior Fellow at the Institute for Defense Studies and Analyses in New Delhi. At IDSA, Dr Mohan's work related to arms control and international and regional security issues. He has a Masters degree in Nuclear Physics and a PhD in International Relations from Jawaharlal Nehru University in New Delhi. Dr Mohan served on India's National Security Advisory Board during 1998–2000. He was a Jennings Randolph Peace Fellow at the United States Institute of Peace in Washington DC during 1992–1993. His book *Crossing the Rubicon: The Shaping of India's New Foreign Policy* has been published by Penguin India (April 2003).
Oi, Jean C.	is the William Haas Professor in Chinese Politics and Professor of Political Science at Stanford University. On leave from Stanford during 2005–2006 she is currently the MBA Class of 1962 Visiting Professor of Business Administration at the Harvard Business School. A comparativist specializing on China, her research focuses on questions of political economy and the process of reform in transitional systems. Her current research is on corporate re-structuring and corporate governance in China. Her latest books are *Rural China Takes Off: Institutional Foundations of Economic Reform* (University of California Press), and *Property Rights and Economic Reform in China* (Stanford, 1999), co-edited with Andrew Walder.
Pei, Minxin	is a Senior Associate and Director of the China Program at the Carnegie Endowment for International Peace in Washington DC. He received his PhD in Political Science from Harvard University in 1991 and taught politics at Princeton University from 1992 to 1998. His main interest is US–China relations, the development of democratic political systems,

and Chinese politics. He is the author of *From Reform to Revolution: The Demise of Communism in China and the Soviet Union* (Harvard University Press, 1994) and *China's Trapped Transition: The Limits of Developmental Autocracy* (Harvard University Press, 2006).

Pingle, Vibha   is a Fellow at the Institute of Development Studies, University of Sussex, UK. She previously taught at Brown, Harvard, Rutgers and Notre Dame, all in the United States. She received her PhD in Sociology from Brown University, USA.

Shah, Ajay   studied at IIT, Bombay and USC, Los Angeles. He has held positions at the Center for Monitoring Indian Economy (Bombay), Indira Gandhi Institute for Development Research (Bombay) and the Ministry of Finance (New Delhi). His research interests include policy issues on Indian economic growth, open economy macroeconomics, public finance, financial economics and pensions. In the past decade, he was extensively involved in the policy process in the reforms of the equity market and the New Pension System.

Varshney, Ashutosh   is a Professor of Political Science at the University of Michigan, having previously taught at Harvard. His recent works include *Ethnic Conflict and Civic Life: Hindus and Muslims in India* (Yale University Press, 2002) and *Democracy, Development and the Countryside: Urban-Rural Struggles in India* (Cambridge University Press, 1995).

Vasudevan, Deepa   is a Research Assistant at the Lee Kuan Yew School of Public Policy, National University of Singapore.

Wang, L. Ling-chi   is an Associate Professor of Asian American Studies at the Department of Ethnic Studies, University of California, Berkeley. His publications include the *Concise Bibliography of Overseas Chinese* (Berkeley: Asian American Studies, 1992) and *The Chinese Diaspora: Selected Essays* (edited with

Wang Gungwu: 2 volumes, Times Academic Press, Singapore, 1998). His research interests are on Asian American history, Asian American civil rights issues, Overseas Chinese, US foreign policies in Asia, bilingual education and Asian Americans in higher education.

Xu Xin   is the National Security Fellow at the John M. Olin Institute for Strategic Studies at Harvard University and he also holds the post of Associate Professor of International Relations, School of Asia Pacific Studies, Ritsumeikan Asia Pacific University, Japan. His specialty is Chinese foreign policy and East Asian international relations. His current areas of interest include the new Taiwan issue, East Asian security politics, multilateralism and Asian regionalism. He is currently working on a book manuscript entitled "China and East Asia: Reshaping Power and Identity in the Post-Cold War Era."

Zhang Xiaoji   is a Senior Research Fellow and Director-General of the Foreign Economic Relations Research Department, Development Research Center (DRC) of the State Council, People's Republic of China. Holding an MA and PhD from the Economics Department, Beijing Normal University, Dr. Zhang joined the DRC in 1984 and has engaged in research on macro-economic policies since then. He held a research appointment at the School of Oriental and African Studies, University of London from 1990 to 1991. He is a standing member of the China Association of International Trade.

Editors' Biographies

Goh,
Gillian H.L.
    is a Postdoctoral Fellow at the Lee Kuan Yew School of Public Policy. She completed her doctorate at the University of Western Australia in 2001 and later spent some time at the Department of War Studies, King's College London, as a visiting Research Fellow. She has published in the areas of North Korean nuclear security and the ASEAN method of conflict management, and her current research focus is on the scope for potential cooperation between India and China.

Kelly,
David A.
    took a PhD in East Asian Studies at Sydney University, later holding a Fulbright Fellowship at the University of Chicago (1984). He worked in the Contemporary China Centre, Australian National University, and School of Politics, Australian Defence Force Academy, and lived in Beijing from 2000 to 2004. Among his works are *Chinese Marxism in the Post Mao Era* (1991) and *Asian Freedoms: Journeys of an Idea in the Cultural Contexts of East and Southeast Asia* (1998). He is a member of the editorial board of *Contemporary Chinese Thought*.

Rajan,
Ramkishen S.
    is currently an Associate Professor at the School of Public Policy, George Mason University in Virginia, USA. He was previously a Visiting Associate Professor at the Lee Kuan Yew School of Public Policy, National University of Singapore, and prior to that he was on the faculty at the School of Economics, University of Adelaide for five years. He has been a frequent consultant to the Asian Development Bank in

Manila and the UN-ESCAP in Bangkok and a number of regional think tanks. Professor Rajan specializes in International Economic Policy with particular reference to developing Asia-Pacific. His current specific topics of interest include international capital flows, foreign exchange reserve management, exchange rate regimes and economic regionalism, and he has published extensively in these areas.

Index